PUBLIC AND SITUATED DISPLAYS

The Kluwer International series on Computer Supported Cooperative Work

Volume 2

Public and Situated Displays

Social and Interactional Aspects of Shared Display Technologies

Edited by

Kenton O'Hara
The Appliance Studio,
Bristol, U.K.

Mark Perry
Brunel University,
Uxbridge, U.K.

Elizabeth Churchill
Fuji-Xerox Palo Alto Laboratory,
Palo Alto, California, U.S.A.

and

Daniel Russell
IBM Almaden Research Center,
San Jose, California, U.S.A.

SPRINGER-SCIENCE+BUSINESS MEDIA, B.V.

A C.I.P. Catalogue record for this book is available from the Library of Congress.

ISBN 978-90-481-6449-3 ISBN 978-94-017-2813-3 (eBook)
DOI 10.1007/978-94-017-2813-3

Printed on acid-free paper

Contents

Contributing Authors

Stefan Agamanolis is a principal research scientist and the director of the Human Connectedness research group at Media Lab Europe, the European research partner of the MIT Media Laboratory. In addition to investigating ways technology can support and enhance human relationships, his research interests include object-based representations for media, interactive storytelling, responsive environments, and automated video editing. He holds MS and PhD degrees in Media Arts and Sciences from Massachusetts Institute of Technology.

Daniel van Alphen works in the field of Product- and Interface Design. In 2002, he graduated in Industrial Design from the University of Arts in Berlin [UdK Berlin]. He earned his degree with a first version of the GossipWall and ViewPort Artefacts in collaboration with the Research Division "AMBIENTE – Workspaces of the Future" at the Fraunhofer institute IPSI in Darmstadt, Germany. Recently, he teaches at the UdK Berlin and works in close cooperation with the AMBIENTE-Team.

Julie Black is currently a computer science student at Stanford University where here interests include theoretical computer science and human computer interaction. She has worked at the Palo Alto Research Center and the Massachusetts Institute of Technology's Media Lab. Her past research projects have included designing and developing a prototype for an extensible public display system atop the Speakeasy framework for recombinant computing and the analysis of different holographic imaging techniques.

Keith Cheverst is a Lecturer of Computing at Lancaster University. He obtained a PhD in 1999 in the area of Mobile Computing. His current research focuses on exploring the issues that arise from the development, deployment and evaluation of context-aware applications within the fields of ubiquitous and mobile computing. His experience within these evolving fields is reflected by his membership in the program committees of numerous international conferences.

Elizabeth Churchill is a Senior Research Scientist at FX Palo Alto Laboratory, Inc. (FXPAL) working on the design and use of computer-based tools for communication, collaboration and coordination. She has published within the areas of artificial intelligence, cognitive science, cognitive psychology, human computer interaction and computer supported cooperative work. She co-started the ACM's conference series on Collaborative Virtual Environments, and was the co-chair for the ACM's 2002 Conference on Computer Supported Cooperative Work.

Karen Clarke is a Research Associate in the Computing Department at Lancaster University where she conducts ethnomethodologically informed studies of Computer Supported Co-operative Work (CSCW). Her research interests include healthcare informatics, studies of IT use in work and in the 'home', human factors in system design and methods in social enquiry. My PhD is a critique of claims to a feminist methodology. Previously she worked on the 'Virtual Ethnography' project at the University of Leeds which examined the use of technology in sixteen homes using video recording techniques and conventional ethnographic methods.

Andy Crabtree is a Senior Research Fellow in the School of Computer Science at the University of Nottingham with an interest in collaborative systems design. He is a sociologist who has conducted ethnographic studies in wide range of settings for purposes of IT research. His recent work includes Designing Collaborative Systems: A Practical Guide to Ethnography.

Laurent Denoue is a research scientist at FX Palo Alto Laboratories in the Social Computing Group and Immersive Technology Group. His work has looked at annotation systems for electronic books and real-time note sharing applications. He has a PhD from the University of Savoie.

Anind Dey is a Senior Researcher for Intel Research Berkeley. He performs research in the area of ubiquitous computing, focusing on sensor-based interactions, ambient displays and application prototyping. He received a B.ApSc (Computer Engineering) from Simon Fraser University, and two M.S. degrees (Aerospace Engineering and Computer Science) and his PhD in Computer Science at the Georgia Institute of Technology.

Alan Dix is Professor of Computing at Lancaster University. Since 1985 he has worked in many areas of human-computer interaction research starting off with formal methods based on his early training in mathematics, but more recently in issues ranging from architectures for mobile applications to user experience and the relationship of interface design to the literary arts. He is the author of *Human-Computer Interaction* the most widely used textbook in the field.

Keith Edwards is a Senior Member of Research Staff at the Palo Alto Research Center (PARC), where he leads the Speakeasy project on evolvable interoperation in *ad hoc* networks. Keith's research interests sit at the intersection of distributed systems and human computer interaction--how systems concerns "show through" to the user experience and, in turn, how the requirements of the user experience manifest themselves in the system. Recently, he has been working to understand how to apply user-centered design and evaluation techniques to the creation of infrastructure technologies.

Daniel Fitton is presently a research student at Lancaster University in the second year of his PhD. Having found the area of ubiquitous computing fascinating as an undergraduate at Lancaster he decided to continue his studies and explore this area further. His present interests lie in situated interactive displays and this is reflected in his recent work on both the Equator and CASCO (Investigating Context Aware Support for Cooperative Applications in Ubiquitous Computing Environments) projects.

Rich Gossweiler is a principle research scientist at CSC working for NASA Ames Research Center. His background is in 3D graphics, systems and user interface research. He has worked at SGI, Xerox PARC and IBM Almaden Research Center. His recent work includes co-developing the BlueBoard project at IBM and working on the MERBoard project at NASA Ames.

Antonietta Grasso is a researcher at Xerox Research Centre Europe in the Contextual Computing Group. Her work has focused on wide area inter-organizational process support systems and on usage of ubiquitous user interfaces in support of communities of practice and knowledge sharing. Prior to joining Xerox she worked at the Cooperation Technologies Laboratory at the University of Milano where she worked on open architectures for process support.

Jonathan Helfman is a Senior Researcher at FX Palo Alto Laboratories. His research interests include the technical and social aspects of combining visualization, user interface design, and software engineering to create multimedia experiences to access, communicate, manipulate, and discover patterns in large amounts of data. Before joining FXPAL he studied film animation, electrical engineering, video processing, and computer science. Previously he has worked at Bell Labs and AT&T Labs. He has a PhD in Computer Science from the University of New Mexico.

Terry Hemmings is a Research Fellow in the School of Computer Science at the University of Nottingham. He has conducted long-term studies of the domestic environment that has provided valuable insights into the social impact of new technologies in the home. His recent work is sponsored by the EU's Disappearing Computer Initiative *ACCORD* project and focuses on the impact of ubiquitous computing in the home.

Elaine Huang is a PhD student in the College of Computing at the Georgia Institute of Technology in Atlanta, Georgia. Her research focuses on understanding the interactions between members of small workgroups and how technology can support their needs, specifically as pertains to their awareness of each other. Her recent work on Semi-Public Displays addresses this issue through the use of large peripheral displays for calm information dissemination.

John Hughes is a Professor in the Sociology Department at Lancaster University. In a long, interminable career, John Hughes has published in the fields of political socialization, political sociology, and research methods. His current interests, however, are in the field of Computer Supported Cooperative Work which involves ethnographic studies of work activities to inform system design and working with computer scientists at Lancaster. His other interests include Ethnomethodology and Wittgenstein.

Michael Kozuch is a Senior Researcher with Intel Corporation. His interests lie in mobile computing systems, at the intersection of file systems, machine virtualization, and networking. In his current work on Seamless Mobility, he is developing a set of technologies that enable mobile users to move effortlessly between different computing environments. As part of this effort, Dr. Kozuch has built Internet Suspend/Resume, a system that allows users to suspend a complete computing session at one Internet-connected site and resume the session at another site.

Simon Lewis is Technical Director at the Appliance Studio leading the engineering, design and innovation teams. He is currently developing lightweight ubiquitous display technologies and technologies for supporting local and remote collaboration. Formerly he was at Hewlett-Packard Laboratories and British Telecom Laboratories where he worked on of network management, expert systems, medical information systems, order-configuration, mobile communications, telecommunication services, and information appliances. He has a degree in Electronic Engineering and Computer Science from University College London is also the author of The Art and Science of Smalltalk.

Blair MacIntyre is an Assistant Professor in the College of Computing and the GVU Center at the Georgia Institute of Technology. He has a BMath and MMath from the University of Waterloo, and a MPhil and PhD from Columbia University. His research interests focus on supporting the creation and evaluation of augmented reality systems. He has been involved in augmented reality research for 12 years, and currently directs the Augmented Environments Lab.

Carsten Magerkurth is a scientific staff member of the research division "AMBIENTE – Workspaces of the Future" at the Fraunhofer institute IPSI in Darmstadt, Germany. He has a hybrid background of Psychology and Software Engineering that intersects in research work for ubiquitous computing environments and computer supported cooperative work. He is currently involved in user interface design for hybrid worlds to augment the physical properties of smart artefacts in virtual spaces. Before joining AMBIENTE, he studied Psychology and Mathematics at the University of Mainz, Germany, from 1996 to 2001. In his spare time, Carsten Magerkurth develops entertainment software for multiple computing platforms.

Jennifer Mankoff is an Assistant Professor of Electrical Engineering and Computer Science (EECS) at the University of California at Berkeley. Her research focuses on evaluation techniques appropriate for the application domains of accessible technology and ubiquitous computing. Her research has been supported by the Intel Corporation, Hewlett-Packard, Microsoft Corporation, and the National Science Foundation. She earned her B.A. at Oberlin College and her Ph.D. in Computer Science at the Georgia Institute of Technology.

Joe McCarthy is a researcher at Intel Research Labs in Seattle. His research explores how technology can help to create, maintain and enhance relationships in the real world – in particular how physically co-located groups can be supported by a physical space that can sense and respond to people and activities within it. He has a PhD. in computer science from the University of Massachusetts. He co-chaired the ACM 2002 Conference on Computer Supported Cooperative Work (CSCW 2002), and the Fifth International Conference on Ubiquitous Computing (UbiComp2003).

Martin Muehlenbrock is a Researcher at Xerox Research Centre Europe. His research interests include Contextual computing and devices & intermediation; Action-based collaboration analysis for group learning; Computer-supported collaborative learning, shared workspace environments; and Artificial intelligence in education. He has a Ph.D. in Computer Science from the University of Duisburg in Germany.

Paul Murphy is a Senior Software Engineer at FX Palo Alto Laboratory, Inc. (FXPAL) working in the Social Computing Group. Trained as a computer scientist, he has worked over the past ten years at a number of technology research and development companies, including Informix, UUNET and Hewlett-Packard. He has designed and implemented both custom and shrink-wrapped software for key systems and markets. In addition to his technical expertise, he has a keen interest in social/industrial psychology and human-computer interaction.

Elizabeth Mynatt is an Associate Professor in the College of Computing at the Georgia Institute of Technology. There she directs the research program in "Everyday Computing" - examining the implications of having computation continuously present in many aspects of everyday life. Prior to her current position, she worked for three years at Xerox PARC — the birthplace of ubiquitous computing. Dr. Mynatt is the Associate Director of the Georgia Tech GVU Center, and is responsible for research and educational objectives in human-computer interaction.

Les Nelson is a Senior Research Scientist at FXPAL. His research has centred on social computing, where information is distributed from online activities for public interactions; conversational interfaces, including interfaces for public uses of personal technologies such as a cell phone, and interfaces for embedding communication technologies into workplace objects; tangible computing: where physical objects represent computational objects and where our physical manipulation of these invokes the appropriate computational operations. He has worked at Lockheed Research & Development. IBM Federal Systems Division (long since merged and renamed) as a software engineer on mission critical real-time systems.

Mark Newman is a research scientist at the Palo Alto Research Center. His areas of research include end-user programming and tools and frameworks for designing and prototyping interactive systems. Recently he has been working to connect these areas of research to the field of ubiquitous computing through his work with the Speakeasy recombinant computing project. Earlier he was the co-designer of the DENIM informal web design tool.

Kenton O'Hara is a Senior Researcher at the Appliance Studio. His research looks the social and behavioural impacts of information artifacts in areas such as large displays for individual and collaborative work; mobility and communication in domestic and knowledge work contexts; remote conferencing; intelligent environments, signs and situated displays and wearable and ubiquitous computing in work and consumer domains. Formerly, he has worked at Rank Xerox EuroPARC, HP Laboratories and BT Laboratories. He has a degree in Psychology, and a PhD in Cognitive Psychology and HCI.

Trevor Pering is a Senior Researcher with Intel Corporation in Santa Clara. Throughout his career, he has focused on many different aspects of mobile and ubiquitous computing, including hardware platforms, system software, and the user experience. His most recent project, the Personal Server, focuses on a very personal version of mobile computing that treats a user's mobile device as the center of their digital world. He graduated from UC Berkeley with a Ph.D. in the area of low-power operating system support for mobile platforms.

Mark Perry is a lecturer at Brunel University and has been working in the area of human-computer interaction and computer supported co-operative work for the last 10 years. The focus of his work lies in the investigation of artefactual, social and organisational behaviour from an information-processing perspective. Mark's research interests cover the investigation of mobile work, the design and use of mobile technology, and the development of distributed cognition as a framework for researching user behaviour.

Daniela Alina Plewe studied Philosophy, Literature, and Anthropology at the Free University, Berlin, Videos at the Université Paris VIII, and Experimental Media Design at the UDK Berlin. Since 1991, she is active as an artist participating at international exhibitions and festivals, e.g., Ars Electronica, Canon Art Lab, Tokyo and at the UCLA. Since 2002, she cooperates with the AMBIENTE-Team at the Fraunhofer institute IPSI in Darmstadt, Germany. Her focus of interest is in cognitive science and economic theories of social interaction.

Thorsten Prante is a scientific staff member of the research division "AMBIENTE – Workspaces of the Future" at the Fraunhofer institute IPSI in Darmstadt, Germany. He studied Computer Science, Software Ergonomics, and Architecture at the Darmstadt University of Technology, where he earned his diploma degree in 1999. He works and publishes in the field of User Interfaces/Interaction Design for Ubiquitous Computing and Computer Supported Cooperative Work. He teaches at the Darmstadt University of Technology, both at the Department of Computer Science and at the Department of Architecture.

Carsten Röcker is a scientific staff member of the research division "AMBIENTE – Workspaces of the Future" at the Fraunhofer institute IPSI in Darmstadt, Germany. He studied Electronic Engineering at the Darmstadt University of Technology with the main emphasis on Communication Networks and Multimedia Systems. Carsten earned his degree in 2000 with a thesis on the generation of metadata for learning environments while working for the DaimlerChrysler Research Center in Ulm, Germany.

Tom Rodden is Professor of Computer Science at the University of Nottingham. He has pioneered research into the social aspects of computing and has a keen interest in the development of CSCW and Ubiquitous Computing. Tom Rodden is Director of the groundbreaking Equator Interdisciplinary Research Collaboration, which brings social scientists, artists and systems designers together to explore foundational challenges in IT research as the computer moves into the 21st Century.

Yvonne Rogers Previously Yvonne was a Professor in the School of Cognitive Sciences at Sussex University where she was director of the Interact Lab. She is interested in new paradigms for computing, especially ubiquitous, pervasive and tangible interfaces. Her research focuses on augmenting everyday learning and work activities with interactive technologies. In particular she designs external representations, especially dynamic visualizations, to support more effectively "external cognition".

Mark Rouncefield is a Senior Research Fellow in the Computing Department, Lancaster University, concerned with carrying out a number of ethnomethodologically informed ethnographic studies of Computer Supported Cooperative Work (CSCW). His research interests involve various aspects of the empirical study of work, organisation, human factors and interactive computer systems design, with a recent focus on Healthcare Informatics. He is particularly associated with the development of ethnography as a method for informing and evaluating systems design. Previous research projects include 'Software Engineering and Business Process Change' the ESRC 'Virtual Society' Programme; and the SYCOMT Project (Systems Development and Cooperative Work: Methods & Techniques).

Daniel Russell is Senior Manager of the User Sciences & Experience Research (USER) lab at the IBM Almaden Research Center. The USER lab includes a number of interaction and collaborative technologies including real-time video analysis for interaction, human factors analysis of input devices, and the development of working spaces for collaboration. Dan has been working in HCI and leading groups in user experience design at Xerox PARC, Apple Computer and IBM for over 15 years.

Jana Sedivy is a researcher at the Palo Alto Research Center and has been exploring usability issues around *ad hoc*, serendipitous use of resources in networked environments. Previously, she has done work in 3D information visualization and natural language interpretation.

Trevor Smith is a researcher in the computer science laboratory of the Palo Alto Research Center. His research interests include recombinant networks and OS design. Before coming to PARC, he was an application engineer at Be, Incorporated.

Norbert Streitz is the head of the research division "AMBIENTE - Workspaces of the Future" of the Fraunhofer Integrated Publication and Information Systems Institute in Darmstadt, Germany. His work has developed shared interaction and cooperation technologies for multiple Roomware components, embedding displays in walls, tables, chairs, etc. He taught in the Dept. of Computer Science of Darmstadt University and at the Institute of Psychology of Aachen University. He chairs the Steering Group of the EU-funded initiative "The Disappearing Computer". He has degrees in physics and cognitive psychology, and more than 15 years experience in the areas of HCI, Hypertext, CSCW, and recently Ubiquitous Computing.

Alison Sue has been a member of the USER Group at IBM Almaden Research Center since January 2000. She is currently studying how people interact with large information displays and their use of productivity tools in that environment. Her professional interests also include accessibility and information management. Outside of work, Alison enjoys baking desserts, playing piano and rock climbing. Alison received her B.S. degree in Electrical Engineering/Computer Science from the University of California at Davis.

Jay Trimble is a computer scientist at NASA's Ames Research Center where he is the Project Manager for the Mars Exploration Rover Human Centered Computing Project, and the group lead for the Ubiquitous Computing and User Centered Design Group. His research interests are in the development and application of human centered design methods for software to support collaboration in space mission systems. He has an M.S. degree in Computer Science from the University of Southern California, and a B.A. in Geology from U.C. Berkeley.

Stephen Voida is a PhD student in the College of Computing at the Georgia Institute of Technology. His research interests include augmented environments, ubiquitous computing, and technology in the workplace. He has an MS in HCI from Georgia Tech and a BS in computer science from Arizona State University. He is currently a member of both the Augmented Environments and Everyday Computing labs and is affiliated with the GVU Center.

Roxana Wales, PhD, is a human-centered computing Research Scientist with SAIC at the NASA Ames Research Center. She uses ethnographic methods to understand the interactions of technology, work flow, work practice, communications, information needs and decision processes within a work system, with a particular interest in understanding the larger implications for those interactions on the total system. She has worked on projects for the Space Shuttle and the International Space Station as well as done a study of airline and airport operations to support the design of NASA technology.

INTRODUCTION TO PUBLIC AND SITUATED DISPLAYS

Kenton O'Hara, Mark Perry, Elizabeth Churchill and Daniel Russell

1. Introduction

Public, situated displays are a ubiquitous part of our environment and visual culture. Prehistoric cave drawings, framed photographs, blackboards in classrooms, posters, billboards, flip charts, road-signs and point-of-purchase displays are all visual forms of communication that play a vital role in the way we understand, navigate and behave in our environment. They inform us about places, amenities, and events of interest and reflect the activities of others. They offer a rich resource around which conversations and group activities are structured, complementing verbal communications and shaping group dynamics. They act as important cultural reference points in the construction of shared meanings, beliefs, desires and the memories of groups and communities.

Changes in the design of displays over the years reflect important changes in environmental, cultural, political, economic and architectural circumstances. Technological shifts have had a particularly noteworthy impact, in terms of the materials and media from which displays are constructed and in terms of the broader technological context within which they are situated. Roadside signs are a particularly good example of this: their form and function has shifted with the emergence of materials such as neon and modern plastics, with the evolution of transportation technologies and with the influence of mass media communication technologies such as television (Mahar, 2002).

Perhaps one of the most significant technological shifts in recent decades has been the development of networked computer technologies. While non-digital displays continue to be prevalent, increasingly information is presented on dedicated, digital, display technologies situated in public places. For example, airport displays show departure and arrival times, digital advertisements line the roadside, signs outside conference rooms show meeting schedules, 'ticker tape' displays offer share price information, office lobbies are adorned with company listings and maps, and parking lot displays tell us the number of empty spaces that are available on each floor. This trend will continue. Technical advances in display technologies will offer new form factors, reduced costs, and further opportunities for authoring, distributing, displaying and interacting with information in the environment.

These developments represent design opportunities for novel forms of communication, coordination and collaboration, and raise questions about the emergence of social behaviours around situated displays. The purpose of this volume is to chart and address these questions. A collection of invited chapters from key researchers in the area offer examples and reflections on the social, technical and interactional considerations in the design of such display technologies. In the remainder of this chapter we offer some background, context and observations before offering an overview of the chapters in this volume and some speculative comments on future research.

2. Issues in the Design and Use of Public, Situated Displays

Within the field of Computer Supported Cooperative Work (CSCW) there has been a long history of exploration into the design, placement and use of public, situated displays. Early media space experiments at PARC and EuroPARC began a continuing tradition of research in the area, providing important insights about privacy, awareness, coordination and information persistence (Bellotti and Sellen, 1993, Dourish, 1993; Bly, Harrison and Irwin, 1993; Gaver *et al.*, 1992; Kantarjiev and Harper, 1994).

Shared interactive display surfaces represent another important research theme that runs through the literature from early work with shared drawing surfaces (e.g. Bly and Minneman, 1990, Pedersen, *et al.*, 1993) to richer more recent examples such as Streitz *et al.*'s i-Land (1999) and Johanson *et al.*'s (2002) Interactive Workspaces Project. These examples provide an understanding of the role of such displays in conversation and their influence on the dynamics of group interaction.

Research in this area has more recently begun to expand into new areas such as community notice boards (e.g. Houde *et al.*, 1998; Snowdon and Grasso, 2002; Churchill, *et al.*, 2003), digital photo frames (e.g. Mynatt *et al.*, 2001), signage (e.g. O'Hara *et al.*, 2003) and ambient, informative, aesthetic displays (e.g. Ishii *et al.* 1998).

The displays that have been designed and studied differ in their form factor (from small monitors to wall displays) and in the form of content that is displayed (e.g. video, text, images). They also differ in terms of whether content is authored (e.g. advertisements), evolving (e.g. meeting notes and sketches), or *ad hoc* (e.g. video tunnels). They further differ in terms of the kinds of content interaction supported. Designs also vary depending on whether displays are intended primarily for single users or multiple users, and on whether focused collaboration around content is anticipated or not. Within these broad spectra, research has looked at the social, physical and cognitive consequences of design and placement including how to make displays attractive, their role in awareness of others' activities, how to maximise visibility and/or legibility for different viewers using the display simultaneously, how to establish 'floor control' on shared display content, and how to mount displays to maximise their effectiveness.

Complementing this focus on technology design and development, work practice studies have contributed much to our understanding of the use and function of public displays, both digital and non-digital (e.g. Heath *et al.*, 2000; Harper and Hughes, 1993; Bellotti and Rogers, 1997). The studies have revealed much about the interaction between technology and its location of placement, or 'situatedness'. Studies have also highlighted the importance of understanding how negotiations around the design and use of public artifacts such as situated displays take place, but also of recognizing and honoring people's views on what information is displayed. This is particularly the case regarding (culturally variant) notions such as *personal*, *private* and *public*. In the sections that follow we will outline observations from this research regarding these issues.

2.1 Public and Publicity

As the central theme of this edited volume is the design and use of *public displays,* it is important to unpack what we mean by the term. Let us first consider the notions of *public* and, from that, *publicity*. As an adjective, *public* is used to mean anything that: concerns or affects the people or community; is maintained for or used by the people or community; is participated in or attended by the people or community; is connected with or acting on behalf of the people, community, or government; and/or is open to the knowledge or judgment of all the people. *Publicity* is "information that concerns a person, group, event, or product that is disseminated through various media to *attract public notice*". It refers to the "public interest, notice, or notoriety achieved by the spreading of such information", to the "act, process, or occupation of disseminating information to gain public interest", and is simply defined as "the condition of being public" (see www.dictionary.com).

Work in CSCW, and more generally, research into social practices and protocols around the use of networked information and communication technologies has led to interesting observations regarding how we determine and negotiate the private and the public in our own lives. It has been amply demonstrated that people cannot rely on the same social and spatial mechanisms for managing issues of publicity and privacy that they use in face-to-face situations when in the presence of networked information technologies (e.g. Bellotti and Sellen, 1993; Dourish, 1993; Harper, 1992; Bly, Harrison and Irwin, 1993; Bly *et al.*; 1998; Palen, 1999; O'Hara *et al.*, 2003). Reflecting on this work and drawing on the work of Altman (1975), Palen and Dourish (2003) characterize publicity as diametrically opposed to *privacy* along a continuous spectrum. For these authors, publicity and privacy are aspects of the "selective control of access to the self"; the execution of that control is a dynamic process where the "boundary" between publicity and privacy is constantly negotiated, according to context and circumstance. Context and circumstance include physical environment, audience, social status goals, motivations and the artefacts (e.g. networked information technologies) that are being used. Networked information and communication technologies "disrupt or destabilize the regulation of boundaries". Such negotiations are intimately related to how we wish to present ourselves within our social groups. This can be seen in the use of shared displays in support of meetings; here, the concept of *evaluation apprehension* has been discussed whereby people experience inhibitions in disclosing particular content publicly for fear that they will be judged negatively by others using the display (Nunamaker, 1991)

In this discussion of publicity, the concern has been very much with self (including self as affiliated to particular social groupings and organizations). But there are other aspects to publicity that need to be articulated here. These refer more to the display as an object both in terms of the physical hardware and in terms of the information contents of the display.

As physical objects, displays are subject to *ownership* or *access*, by individuals, groups and organizations. Ownership and access are complex and multi-layered concepts that are subject to ongoing processes of negotiation. Consider ATM machine displays. ATMs are owned by specific banks, but are made available as public resources via their public displays – both to customers of that bank and to customers of affiliated banks, subject to particular conditions (e.g. sufficient credit). Although used by one person at a time, they are nevertheless public displays in terms of their *potential* to be used by a broader population; the ATM is a *timeshared* public resource. As a timeshared resource, they are subject to competitive rules as to when they can be used. Timeshared ownership has many different levels of granularity. To illustrate, consider shared electronic whiteboards in meeting rooms. These are again owned by a larger organization but for the particular period of a meeting they become the resource of the meeting members. A further contrast to the ATM example is that electronic whiteboards are used by multiple people simultaneously whether through direct interaction or as a passive member of the audience. Certain members of the group using the whiteboard display have at any one time a greater degree of ownership. A person leading a presentation has a greater degree of ownership over, or at least access to, the resource than a passive audience member; they may change the contents of the display while an audience member is still referring to it for the purpose of making a note. As with other aspects of publicity, these levels are open to negotiation among the members of the group using the display, leading to ongoing shifts in ownership. Thus the particular audience member in this instance may make an explicit request for the previous content to be revisited and thereby negotiating a temporary shift in ownership.

Timesharing is also important in terms of information persistence and competition for screen real estate. This can be seen in a number of public displays discussed in the literature such as community notice boards. Because all the information to be made public cannot be shown simultaneously at any particular time, models are adopted where content is cycled through on a periodic basis (e.g. Houde *et al.*, 1998; O'Hara and Brown, 2001; Churchill *et al.*, 2003; Churchill *et al.* Chapter 10 this volume; Snowdon *et al.*, 2002; Grasso *et al.* Chapter 11 this volume). Likewise, with certain types of office door display there is competition for screen real estate between messages left by the owner and those left by other people (e.g. see Cheverst, Chapter 6 this volume) – who owns this display, then, is something that is mediated both through the technology and social protocol. Thus, different models of information persistence affect the way in which publicity is achieved. In txTboard (http://www.appliancestudio.com), a device that receives and displays SMS messages from mobile phones, a new incoming message "displaces" what was previously being displayed. Therefore the ability to persistently display a piece of information for a particular public effect is constrained by the arrival of a new message from another person.

Another important dimension of publicity to consider and one that is intimately related to ownership, is the notion of *control.* Public displays vary according to the level of control that particular group members are given over the information that can be placed, manipulated or taken away from these displays. This has an impact on the way the display comes to be incorporated into the every day activities of the population using them. Road signs are an example of public display where the people using the information are given no control over the information contents of the display (with the exception of vandalism). Rather, the information is at the control of a centralised agency. Such control models also occur in digital systems such as the departure displays in airport lounges or railway stations. Other public displays are dependent upon a more open control model in which members of a particular group have the ability to determine what appears on the display. The selection and placement of community notice board contents are often open to wider group of people. Yet even within the genre of community notice boards different levels of public control may operate. As Churchill *et al.* (2003 and Chapter 10 this volume), certain community notice boards have stricter content control models, whereby content is moderated by a gatekeeper. Churchill *et al.* also note that ownership also has implications for the identity boundary between those who place content and those who read content: controlled displays often have a "brand" identity. Increasing levels of ownership often also imply some responsibility for content that appears.

To summarize, issues to consider in designing for public information artifacts organize around the politics and ownership of information, that is how it is represented, distributed and read. In addition, we need to consider the politics of display ownership, access and control. Next we turn to considerations of where displays are located.

2.2 Situated Displays

All activities and artefacts are located within particular environmental and social contexts. In addition to *physical* ergonomic issues that are perennially relevant in the design of artefacts, perspectives such as Situated Action, Distributed Cognition, and Activity Theory have demonstrated the importance of understanding the social and environmental situation in which artefacts are immersed (e.g. Suchman, 1986; Hutchins, 1995; Engeström, Miettinen, Punamäki, 1999). Our intention in this section is to outline some of our observations regarding the impact of the behavioural contexts within which displays are immersed by virtue of their spatial location, the relationship between space and meaning of information, zones of influence and activity around these displays and the way that spatial arrangement of displayed information can structure collaborative computation. We hope this discussion will offer a framework of design issues through which subsequent chapters can be read.

Some aspects of display situatedness relate to issues already discussed, namely privacy, ownership, identity, control, and relevance. For example, the spatial positioning of a display has important implications with respect to ownership. An important determinant of displayed content is assumed audience. We can see this illustrated in some of the studies of community notice board displays. Churchill *et al.* (Chapter 10 this volume) note how notice boards in different areas of San Francisco have different content that reflects topics of relevance to the different communities. Likewise, Snowdon *et al.* (2002) demonstrated shifts in content according to changes in location. This had to do, in part, with the different size and diversity of the potential audience associated with thee different places. When placed in the refectory, which has a large and diverse audience potential, the content was much more generic than that seen on the notice board when placed in a group space. In this respect judgments of relevance were easier to determine for the smaller group size associated with the group space than it was for the larger potential audience associated with the refectory. Further, spaces may have shifting populations, resulting in shifts in potential audiences for the displayed information (e.g. a space could be a café catering to parents and children in the daytime and performance space catering to musicians in the evening). Much of this also has to do with the management of publicity and privacy; the same factors that influence judgements about relevance also impact on what people think appropriate to reflect about themselves or the organisation to the, spatially defined, potential audience.

As well as the nature and size of the audience, the behavioural characteristics associated with places will affect how displays are perceived and used. This is illustrated nicely in some of the literature on community notice boards. Corridors are transitional places whereby people are passing through to get from one place to another. Engagement with electronic notice boards in these places tends to be less interactive than when the same notice board is placed in a communal kitchen area. The behavioral context the kitchen space, for example is one where people might be waiting round for the kettle to boil or taking time to have a drink, offering greater opportunities for prolonged engagement with the contents of the notice board (Houde *et al.*, 1998; Churchill *et al.*, 2003; Chapter 10 this volume).

Spatial positioning can also determine the interpretation of information. How signs are interpreted is inextricably linked with where they are situated; a road sign indicating the next junction is for London would not make sense positioned in a different location. Likewise an electronic office door sign (e.g. Cheverst *et al.*, Chapter 6 this volume) which displays a message "gone to lunch" can only be fully interpreted by virtue of its adjacency to a particular individual's office. Moving the display to a different location would change the interpretation of this information.

The interpretation of displays may be defined by spatial location, but displays can, in turn, be part of the creating the way in which people use a space. For example, an electronic whiteboard in within a space demarks that area as a place where group collaboration can take place. If displays of this kind are *suggestive* of behaviours, signage is *directive*. Signage in railway stations and airports, for example, explicitly direct people through space. Signage is a good illustration that situating information displays at particular points in the environment can have significant consequence for the ordering of the activity of individuals and groups. For example, the placement of a paper document on a keyboard or a Post-It note on a document can signify prioritisation of intended action (e.g. O'Hara *et al.* 2003). As Crabtree *et al.* argue in this volume (Chapter 8 this volume), the positioning of paper mail within a home can embody meaning regarding what action needs to been taken and by whom. Such spatial positioning of information has been demonstrated to be important in the structuring of collaborative computations (cf Kirsh, 1995; Perry, O'Hara, Spinelli and Sharpe, 2003). An example of this can be seen in fieldwork observations of a design team doing concept development work in a team room (Perry, O'Hara, Spinelli and Sharpe, 2003; Spinelli, 2003). Here, the design team arranged foam board displays around the room. Each foam board display corresponded to a single design concept and contained all the paper-based artefacts related to that particular concept. Prior to beginning a meeting the design leader spent time moving the displays around the room arranging them in a particular order. The ordering of these displays around the room embodied a particular narrative structure that was used to evaluate the concepts under consideration, and order the activities of the meeting and subsequent client presentation.

A further feature of a display's situatcdncss concerns the zones of influence that radiate from around the display and the extent to which social, behavioural and interactional properties are influenced at different distances from displays. An interesting historical example of this effect can be seen with the development of road signage and its relationship to progress in transportation technologies. As transport moved from pedestrian forms through to the automobile, the speed at which signs were approached became much quicker. As such, road signage and advertisements needed to be perceived by people from a greater distance that influenced things such as the form factor of these road side displays (e.g. increase in size), materials used (e.g. neon lighting) and the nature of information on them. In terms of the computer based displays within the scope of this book, a number of authors highlight the different properties of displays according to where people are situated with respect to them (e.g. Streitz *et al.*, Chapter 16 this volume; Rogers and Rodden, Chapter 3 this volume; Churchill, *et al.*, chapter 10 this volume; O'Hara *et al.*, Chapter 5 this volume). Displays can passively inform or attract attention from a distance but provide progressively more details and interactional capabilities as people move closer.

Spatial positioning of information is also important in the structuring of collaborative computations (cf Kirsh, 1995; Perry, O'Hara, Spinelli and Sharpe, 2003). Ongoing spatial arrangements of displayed information, the way it is positioned, stacked and ordered, can be used to constrain the order of actions. An example of this can be seen in some fieldwork observations of a design team doing concept development work in a team room (see Perry, O'Hara, Spinelli and Sharpe, 2003; Spinelli, 2003 for further details). The design team arranged foam board displays around the room. Each foam board display corresponded to a single design concept and contained all the paper-based artefacts related to that particular concept. Prior to beginning a meeting the design leader spent time moving the displays around the room arranging them in a particular order. The ordering of these displays embodied a particular narrative structure that was used to order the activities of the meeting and subsequent client presentation.

Spatial arrangements of displayed information also map onto conceptual organization – space being used to carry symbolic meaning. Again in Perry *et al.* (2003), the design team used spatial display as a means of embodying the categorization of ideas. Ideas categorized as weak were displayed in a distant corner of the room while those that were considered to have potential were displayed on the foam boards closer to where the team was working. This kind of spatial clustering in support of conceptual organisation is also seen in many whiteboard type applications. Flatland is a case in point (Mynatt *et al.*, 1999). This electronic whiteboard allows spatial clusters of displayed information to be moved round, scaled and annotated in support of individual and collaborative cognition.

3. Overview of the Book

This book brings together chapters that examine public and situated displays from social, technical and interactional perspectives. The book is divided into four sections that reflect key aspects of work that the technologies are designed to support. In the first section, the key theme is *Knowledge Work and Collaboration*, detailing the role displays play in supporting knowledge based tasks for individuals and groups. The second section focuses on *Awareness and Coordination* exploring how peripheral display of information in the environment provides an understanding of ongoing group activity and events and the management individual activities within the context of these. The third section looks at *Community and Social Connectedness*. In this section displays are used as a means to foster the development of social relationships by providing resources for conversation and for understanding community activities. Many also offer new forms of social interaction. In the final section on *Mobility*, authors explore displays as situated access points to people's personal information, supporting movement around the environment whilst retaining access to remote information. Although the sections provide a useful organising framework for thinking about the key foci of the various research contributions, the boundaries between themes are not clear-cut, and many of the chapters in the book will occasionally cut across the section themes.

3.1 Knowledge Work and Collaboration

The first section discusses displays as a resource for supporting synchronous group work. In Chapter 1, Russell and Sue present BlueBoard, a large interactive plasma display appliance for showing content such as documents or whiteboard sketches around which small and large group discussion can be scaffolded. One of the key aims of their design is how to support quick access to this information to encourage lightweight and spontaneous interactions between groups of people. Through their fieldwork observation they highlight important properties of up-close side-by-side interaction around the BlueBoard and the way that groups spatially organize themselves around the display. Increases in group size are shown to have large effects on spatial organisation of the group, meeting dynamics and the management of turn-turn taking. Importantly these collaborations are located within the broader context of people's work that extends beyond the boundaries of these *in situ* collaborations - information being brought from and sent back to individual workspaces.

In Chapter 2, Trimble, Wales and Gossweiler describe the use of their MERBoard system, a collection of several distributed, large touch enabled plasma displays for sharing, annotating, distributing and saving information. The system is designed to support the activities of a large team of over 200 scientists and engineers comprising several subgroups within and across which information needs to be shared. They are able to show how situating displays is an ongoing process with displays being held up and moved around according to the ongoing information needs of the evolving group/subgroup structures. Importantly, they locate this system within a broader ecology of display artefacts such as paper documents, flip charts and large printed images. Exploring this larger ecology of displays highlights the range of affordances of different display form factors, sizes and media types. Understanding these different properties has provided much of the motivation for a key design feature of the MERBoard system namely its ability to be accessed across personal computers, smaller boards and larger boards.

The 3rd chapter, by Rogers and Rodden, explores a variety of different display systems in a range of different collaborative settings and examines how particular display configurations afford certain socio-cognitive properties of the interaction. In the Opinionizer system, for example, a large vertically oriented interactive display is used to support the exchange of opinions on a particular topic among informal gatherings of people. They note how activities occur at different spaces relative to the display location. This suggests to them the importance of designing to encourage movement across the thresholds these activity spaces. With the eSpace concept, they leverage some of the socio-cognitive properties of horizontal surfaces in dyadic consultation situations such as between a travel agent and customer. In contrast to the asymmetrical access to information afforded by a PC screen, the horizontal display configuration affords much more equitable access to the information across both parties allowing the interaction to be less one-sided in favour of one or other party. The horizontal orientation is also discussed as a means by which the public/private aspects of the information can be managed. In a further concept, the Dynamo system, they address the particular problem of sharing personal information from devices such as laptops, PDAs, cameras, and PCs with other members of a meeting group. In contrast to interactive whiteboards or shared editing surfaces, they use a large shared display as a communal interactive resource for fluidly sharing this information from these diverse sources in the context of an ongoing meeting.

In chapter 4 Mynatt *et al.* look at how large interactive surfaces for knowledge work and how they support spatial organisation of information, task management, background awareness and coordination and the fluid transition from individual to collaborative knowledge work. Flatland is a whiteboard designed for use in a personal workspace. The work highlights the importance of spatial layout and clustering as a means by which information is quickly perceived, processed, and organised into meaningful chunks. Building on these foundations of spatial layout, Kimura is another system of peripheral projected displays connected to an individuals PC. While the PC displays information for the primary user activity, the peripheral displays show background activity context projected as visual montages. These allow background activities to be monitored and organised again using affordances of spatial arrangement. The abstract representation of the montages gives the displays an ambient quality that can only be interpreted by the initiated thereby providing a socially mediated means by which privacy and relevance can be managed with other group members. The privacy and relevance theme is continued in the same chapter through discussion of the semi-public displays project, a situated ambient display for providing work and social awareness of other group members.

3.2 Awareness and Coordination

The second section focuses on how peripheral displays in the environment help people monitor and understand the status of ongoing activities and events. By supporting our awareness of what is going on beyond the boundaries of our current task focus, these displays provide resources that can facilitate our ability to manage tasks and coordinate then with those of others. In Chapter 5, O'Hara, Perry and Lewis discuss a networked room reservation display positioned outside meeting rooms to show status information about room use. Using fieldwork observations they explore how the displayed information comes to be appropriated for the socially negotiated aspects of shared room use. While the information displayed is minimal it becomes embellished with social context that supports judgements about appropriateness of interruption or overriding the booking information. The information also becomes a useful resource for picking up snippets about the activities of others as well as a resource for informing people about your activities. One of the key characteristics of the device is the way it extends control of the display's contents to the community of users. O'Hara *et al.* explore this with respect to trust and security as well as how display behaviour and content are artfully modified to manage aspects of publicity and privacy, and information relevance.

In a similar vein Cheverst, Fitton and Dix in Chapter 6 present their experiences with Hermes an office door display allowing messages to be left by owner and visitor. Of significance is their choice of location in which they explore situated displays: offices having properties that are both private and public, and potentially of value to both owner and visitor. The authors explore various ways in which this tension between the public and private and between visitor and owner can be explored. These include authentication methods for access to certain levels of content, using situatedness to determine content control levels for particular individuals (e.g. only the owner can send messages from remote locations), shifts between low and high fidelity information; and different levels of information persistence between temporary and default messages. The system is contrasted with other context aware systems through its emphasis on the social mediation of the information provides.

Chapter 7 turns its attention to the social construction of displays emphasizing the act of display. In this chapter Crabtree, Hemmings and Rodden show how paper mail within the domestic setting is actively displayed in certain locations to provide for the communication and coordination of everyday practical action and imbue meaning about the temporal flow of work within a domestic setting. Relevance to household members is organized through particular assemblages of displays, in particular using location as a means to orient particular household members to the information. Items make up a distributed network of interrelated situated displays throughout the home. Items do not reside in single locations but are moved around the environment from display to display according to particular communication and coordination needs. These spatial and temporal constructions of displays are argued to be ignored by certain technologies such as email thereby missing the significance in coordinating action among household members.

Non-digital displays are also the focus of Chapter 8 Clarke *et al.* present some ethnographic observations of shared information displays within the healthcare domain looking at their role in the coordination of patient care. Using the example of bed management, they discuss the role of the beds board in this process – a situated representation of bed occupancy. Rather than providing some objective representation of bed occupancy the authors describe how a great deal of managerial work is devoted to the interpreting and recalculating of the statistics meshing the information with more local changeable and situated information. It is this broader context within which calculability and accountability are managed and made visible that is important to consider when designing digital replacements for these coordination artefacts.

Finally in the section, chapter 9 by Dey and Mankoff explores the theme of peripheral displays for monitoring activities without being the centre of the users attention. In particular, they focus on a particular subset of peripheral displays, namely ambient displays (in contrast to notification displays) the domain of which they argue lacks guidance in terms of good design and evaluation. Using their experiences developing two peripheral ambient display concepts, the Bus Mobile and the Light Display, they present a heuristic evaluation technique adapted for the peculiar properties of peripheral ambient displays.

3.3 Community and Social Connectedness

The third section of the book turns to the issue of community and social connectedness and the roles which public displays in nurturing community activities and social bonding for collocated and distributed groups. In Chapter 10, Churchill, *et al.*, describe a network of Plasma Posters, large screen digital displays to which a community of people can post content about local services, events and activities of potential interest to the rest of the community. Drawing on observations of how people use physical bulleting boards and other existing information sharing practices, the plasma posters were designed to provide a community generated resource that encouraged offline face-to-face conversation and social interaction. Their plasma poster network is shown to be a new communication channel for people with particular types of content being posted. An important thread in the work is the impact of location on both posting, peripheral noticing and active reading behaviour. In terms of posting behaviour this is not simply in terms of type of content posted but also the fact that location as a definer of audience is inherently fuzzy. These uncertainties affect judgements about content relevance and audience interest and can even create apprehension among certain community members about posting certain content. Location is also seen to make a big difference in the types of reading that took place there in part due to the different rhythm of the places.

Chapter 11 by Grasso *et al.* examines how to support the sharing of information to promote informal communication within and between different work communities. After highlighting some of the key communication needs of these communities, they identify how these are addressed through particular characteristics of large public display technologies. Their Community Wall technology again adopts a notice board model for displaying information of relevance to a group of people. Relevance is explored both in terms of the parameters that impact on it, such as type of public space and group size operating within that space as well as systems for enhancing relevance, such as using automatic recommender systems, displaying user ratings of relevance and explicit system rules for prioritizing content. Context aware sensing technologies are also discussed as a means by which the behaviour of the system might be modified according to who is there and why.

In Chapter 12 McCarthy explores several peripheral display concepts designed to enrich *casual* interactions of people in the same environment. Using appropriate sensing mechanisms the displays respond to the activities and interests of coproximate people and create a greater visibility of their activities and interests. This provides conversation keys that facilitate informal interaction in the workplace and enhance the sense of community. The first of these is GroupCast; a large personal display situated in casual groups settings. An infrared personnel badge system is used to detect people within the vicinity of the display. By exploring the overlapping interests profiles of the people detected by the display, the display presents content about which one or all of the people will be able to initiate conversation. The system design is cognisant of potential privacy problems here and balances plausible ignorability with expressions of mutual interest A second concept, UniCast, is deployed for use by an individual within their personal workspace presenting content specified as interesting by that individual. While an essentially "individual" display, the persistence of the information can also provide cues for interpersonal interaction. Perhaps more importantly, though, the system is useful in providing a low effort way of deriving an individual interest profile that can be used by GroupCast –

thereby overcoming what would otherwise be the pragmatic difficulty of content acquisition for profile creation. Finally a third concept, OutCast, is a public display situated outside an individual workspace. The content on this is used to inform visitors to that space about whereabouts and schedule of the owner (when they are detected as being away from the office) as well as represent the public persona of the occupant. Again the intention here is to provide a resource for greater understanding of other members within the workplace that can facilitate the sense of community important to knowledge work.

The book then turns to the work of Agamanolis and his colleagues at the Media Lab. In chapter 13 they argue that public and situated displays have the potential to offer new forms of human connectedness. They present a range of situated display based concepts that demonstrate these new forms of human relationships and which create an enhanced sense of presence, intimacy and togetherness between family and group members. The concepts explore relationships between people that are copresent in the same space, that are distributed across space and also that that are distributed across time. The work also turns attention towards different facets of human relationships that go beyond information exchange and communication resources. An example of this can be seen in the Breakout for Two concept, which looks at the sense of togetherness fostered through a physically competitive activity across networked displays.

3.4 Mobility

The final section takes a brief tour into how public and situated displays in the environment can be used for as an access point for information. In this respect they can be seen as a resource for mobile activities offering certain affordances that liberate people from the need to carry round bulky pieces of equipment. In chapter 14 Pering and Kozuch describe this notion as *situated mobility* in which the limitations of small mobile devices are augmented with Internet connected situated displays. They thus combine device and web-based mobility as a more attractive mobile solution that allows particular information and even whole desktop environment to be migrated across locations. As well as augmenting personal devices with situated displays they also discuss how situated displays can be augmented by the personal identification capabilities of personal mobile devices with the display proactively adapting to the specific needs of the individual. Throughout the chapter they also takes a more abstract look at the particular design challenges of situated mobility in terms user experience: for example, how to manage the situated display as a competitive resource in a pubic space viewed and shared by multiple people simultaneously or a different points in time.

The ability to support the much envisioned *walk-up* and access anything from anywhere functionality of public displays in a variety of environmental settings is further considered by Black *et al.* in chapter 15. The perspective of their work is on the platform infrastructure necessary to achieve this as embodied in their Speakeasy architecture. For them interacting public displays cannot require complicated login, configuration and software installation procedures. Rather the platform infrastructure needs to be interoperate with a range of existing services, devices and media types of it is to support a range of individual and collaborative activities in a variety of public and private environmental settings. Furthermore with the need to adapt over time, they discuss the importance of *forward compatibility* for these walk up and use displays – the need to cope with emerging devices services and media types that might not have been hard-coded into the display system at the time of creation.

The discussion of informal communication, gossip and organisational atmosphere are continued in chapter 16 by Streitz *et al.* who combine static ambient displays integrated into the architectural environment with mobile devices to create what they call "social architectural spaces". The conveyance of atmosphere, they argue is not really supported by direct means of communication currently provided by PCs. Rather they look to exploit the ability of humans to interpret information via many different codes by relying on the ambiguities and implicit information of ambient displays. The Hello.Wall concept they describe operates according to 3 different zones of interaction. The ambient zone represents the atmosphere through light patterns presenting information independent of a particular person. When a person enters the notification zone, person specific information is conveyed through "secret" patterns of information augmented by a personal mobile device called ViewPort. A final zone is the cell interaction zone in which users can interact with individual cells on the display. The authors explore a number of different scenarios that could be realized through this particular social architectural space.

From the brief overview of the book, the importance of consolidating the range of research and perspectives in this area can be seen. The themes in the book, while central within CSCW research for many years, until now have remained disparate making lessons from one display domain difficult to apply to another. Arranging them as unified text allows parallels to be drawn between the factors (social, the technical and design) across all of these domains. The framework presented provides a way for researchers to navigate around these factors and domains and thus, we hope, facilitate a more integrated approach to research in the future.

References

Altman, I. *The Environment and Social Behavior: Privacy Personal Space, Territory and Crowding*. Monterey, CA: Brooks/Cole Pub Co., 1975.

Bellotti, V. and Rogers, Y. From Web Press to Web Pressure: Multimedia Representations and Multimedia Publishing. In Proceedings of CHI'97 Conference on Human factors in Computing Systems; 1997; Atlanta. GA, USA: 279-286.

Bellotti, V. and Sellen, A. Design for Privacy in Ubiquitous Computing Environments. In Proceedings of ECSCW '93, European Conference on Computer Supported Cooperative Work; 1993; Milan, Italy: 77-92.

Bly, S. and Minneman, S. Commune: A Shared Drawing Surface. In Proceedings of Conference on Office Systems; 1990; Boston, MA, USA: 184-192.

Bly, S. Cook, L., Bickmore, T., Churchill, E. and Sullivan, J.W. The Rise of Personal Web Pages at Work. In Summary Proceedings of CHI '98 Conference on Human factors in Computing Systems; 1998; Los Angeles, CA, USA: 313- 314.

Bly, S., Harrison, S. R., & Irwin, S. Media spaces: bringing people together in a video, audio, and computing environment. In Communications of the ACM, 1993; 36(1): 28-47.

Brown, B. and O'Hara, K. Place as a Practical Concern for Mobile Workers. To appear in Environment and Planning A.

Churchill, E. F., Nelson, L., Denoue, L. and Girgensohn, A. The Plasma Poster Network: Posting Multimedia Content in Public Places. To appear in Proceedings of INTERACT '03; 2003; Zürich, Switzerland.

Dourish, P. Culture and Control in a Media Space In, Proceedings of ECSCW '93, European Conference on Computer Supported Cooperative Work; 1993; Milan, Italy Milano, Italy: 125-138.

Engeström, Y., Miettinen, R. and Punamäki, R. *Perspectives on Activity Theory*. Cambridge: Cambridge University Press, 1999.

Gaver, W., Moran, T., MacLean, A. Lovstrand, L., Dourish, P. Carter, K. and Buxton, W. Realising a video environment: EuroPARC's RAVE system. Proceedings of the CHI '92 Conference on Human Factors in Computing Systems; 1992; Monterey, CA USA: 27-35.

Harper, R. and Hughes, J.A. " "What a f-ing system! Send 'em all to the same place and then expect us to stop 'em hitting": Making Technology Work in Air Traffic Control". In *Technology in Working Order: Studies of Work, Interaction, and Technology*, Button, G., ed. London: Routledge, 1993.

Harper, R. H. R. Looking at Ourselves: An Examination of the Social Organisation of Two Research Laboratories. In Proceedings of CSCW '92 Conference on Computer Supported Cooperative; 1992, Toronto, Canada: 330-337.

Heath, C. C., Knoblauch, H. and Luff, P.. Technology and social interaction: the emergence of 'workplace studies', British Journal of Sociology, 2000; 51(2): 299-320.

Houde, S., Bellamy, R., Leahy, L. In search of design principles for tools and practices to support communication within a learning community. SIGCHI Bulletin, 1998; 30(2): 113-118.

Hutchins, E. *Cognition in the Wild*. Bradford: MIT Press, 1995.

Ishii, H. Wisneski, C.Brave, S. and Dahley, A., Gorbet, M. Ullmer, B. and Yarin, P. ambientROOM: Integrating Ambient Media with Architectural Space. In Summary Proceedings of CHI '98 Conference on Human factors in Computing Systems; 1998; Los Angeles, CA, USA: 173-174.

Johanson, B., Fox, A. and Winograd, T. The Interactive Workspaces Project: Experiences with Ubiquitous Computing Rooms, IEEE Pervasive Computing Magazine, 2002; 1(2).

Kantarjiev, C.K. and Harper R. Portable Porthole Pads: An Investigation into the Use of a Ubicomp Device to Support the Sociality of Work. Rank Xerox EuroPARC Technical Report, 1994, EPC-1994-110.

Kirsh, D. The Intelligent Use of Space. In Artificial Intelligence, 1995; 73: 31-68.

Mahar, L. *American Signs Form and Meaning on Route 66.* New York: Monacelli Press, 2002.

Mynatt, E.D., Igrashi, T., Edwards, W.K., & LaMarca, A. Flatland: New dimensions in office whiteboards. Proceedings of CHI '99 Conference on Human Factors in Computing Systems; 1999; Pittsburgh, PA, USA: 346–353.

Mynatt, E.D., Rowan, J., Craighill, S. and Jacobs, A. Digital family portraits: Providing peace of mind for extended family members. In Proceedings of CHI '01 Conference on Human Factors in Computing Systems; 2001; Seattle, Washington, USA: 333-340.

Nunamaker, J. F., Dennis, A. R., Valacich, J. S., Vogel, D., George, J. F. Electronic Meeting Systems to Support Group Work. Communications of. ACM, 1991; 34(7): 40-61

O'Hara, K. and Brown, B. Designing CSCW Technologies to Support Tacit Knowledge Sharing Through Conversation Initiation Workshop on Managing Tacit Knowledge at ECSCW '01 Conference on Computer Supported Cooperative Work; 2001; Bonn, Germany

O'Hara, K. Perry, M. and Lewis, S. Social Coordination Around a Situated Display Appliance. In Proceedings of CHI '03 Conference on Human factors in Computing Systems; 2003; Ft. Lauderdale, FL, USA: 65-72

Palen, L. and Dourish, P. Unpacking Privacy for a Networked World. In Proceedings of CHI '03 Conference on Human factors in Computing Systems; 2003; Ft. Lauderdale, Florida, USA: 129-136.

Palen, L. Social, Individual and Technological Issues for Groupware Calendar Systems. In Proceedings of CHI '99 Conference on Human factors in Computing Systems; 1999; Pittsburgh, Pennsylvania, USA:17-24.

Pedersen, E. McCall, K., Moran, T., Halasz, F., Tivoli: An Electronic Whiteboard for Informal Workgroup Meetings. Proceedings of InterCHI '93 Conference on Human Factors in Computing Systems; 1993 Amsterdam, The Netherlands: 391-398.

Perry, M., O'Hara, K., Spinelli, G. and Sharpe, B. The role of space in socially distributed cognition: some issues for cognitive engineering, 2003 (in preparation)

Snowden, D. and Grasso, A. Diffusing Information in Organisational Settings: Learning from Experience. In Proceedings of CHI'02 Conference on Human Factors in Computing Systems; 2002; Minneapolis, MA, USA: 331-338

Spinelli, G. *Socially Distributed Cognition: Computational Space And Collaborative Artefacts For The Workspace.* PhD Thesis, DISC, Brunel University, 2003

Streitz, N., J. Geißler, T. Holmer, S. Konomi, C. Müller-Tomfelde, W. Reischl, P. Rexroth, P. Seitz, R. Steinmetz i-LAND: An interactive Landscape for Creativity and Innovation. In: Proceedings of CHI '99 Conference on Human Factors in Computing Systems; 1999 Pittsburgh, PA USA: 120-127.

Suchman, L. (1987) *Plans and Situated Actions.* Cambridge: Cambridge University Press.

TxTboard http://www.appliancestudio.com/sectors/smartsigns/txtboard.htm

PART I:

KNOWLEDGE WORK AND COLLABORATION

Chapter 1

LARGE INTERACTIVE PUBLIC DISPLAYS: USE PATTERNS, SUPPORT PATTERNS, COMMUNITY PATTERNS

Daniel M. Russell and Alison Sue
IBM Almaden Research Center

Abstract: Large displays have several natural affordances that should make it simple to support collaborative work. They are large enough to hold multiple work areas and are easy for a small group to see collectively. The BlueBoard is a large plasma display with touch sensing and a badge reader to identify individuals using the board. The onboard software acts as a thin client giving access to each participant's content (e.g., home pages, project pages). The client also has a set of tools and mechanisms that support rapid exchange of content between those present. The overall design of the BlueBoard is one that is easily learnable (under 5 minutes), very simple to use, and permits novel uses for collaboration. Our initial field study revealed a number of social issues about the use of a large interactive display surface, yet indicated that a shared public display space truly has distinct properties that lends itself to sharing content. Extreme learnability & overall simplicity of design makes BlueBoard a tool for collaboration that supports intermittent, but effective use for side-by-side collaboration between colleagues.

Key words: Large displays; ease-of-use; collaboration; CSCW; side-by-side exchange.

1. Introduction

Large displays are rapidly growing more affordable and offer new opportunities for ubiquitous placement in work environments (Buxton *et al.*, 2000; Fox *et al.*, 2000; Houde *et al.*, 1998; Pedersen, 1993; http://www.SMARTTech.com; http://graphics.stanford.edu/projects/iwork/; Streitz *et al.* 1999; Elrod *et al.*, 1992). A trip through any airport or transportation center will, today, show many large displays in use. Most are non-interactive, but this is changing as network capability becomes more

K. O'Hara et al. (eds.), Public and Situated Displays: Social and Interactional Aspects of Shared Display Technologies, 3–17.

ubiquitous and interaction methods become more robust and commonplace (e.g., touch screens, hardened keyboards, voice).

While kiosks have been popular items as information displays for some time, they lack the ability to act as general purpose access devices. Generally speaking, kiosks are placed in a space to sell a product or to push a particular set of information.

But when a kiosk has a personal authentication device (e.g., biometric device or badge reader), is placed on a high-speed network, and uses a large display, the nature of the device changes in a fundamental way. No longer is it just a dispenser of canned information, but it becomes something new – a Large Information Appliance (LIA).

Placed into a work setting, LIAs are shared, communal information appliances that operate under a substantially different set of assumptions than the kinds of information tools normally used by individuals.

Working practices are especially subject to social effects when the devices are large and communal. In our initial tests, we have found a number of somewhat unanticipated interactions between the device as a thing to use, and the device as a place.

1.1 An example: BlueBoard

The BlueBoard is a LIA device based on a large 1.3 meter plasma display (XGA) with a resistive touch screen (from SMART Technologies - http://www.SMARTTech.com) and a badge reader for personal identification (an HID brand RFID reader connected to the serial port (http://www.HIDCorp.com)), with a laptop PC secured in a lockbox bolted to the rear of the display, running the BlueBoard thin client software. The BlueBoard thin client application fills the entire display (i.e. no "desktop" is viewable) (see figure 1-1).

In ordinary use, the BlueBoard is intended for both very fast personal use (walk up, check your calendar, walk away – all within a few seconds), and for small group collaborative use (a small number of people stand around the BlueBoard to sketch ideas, pull up information from their personal space, compare notes, share content, create something new).

In our design, a BlueBoard has no keyboard or mouse. While this seems restrictive, our goal is not to have BlueBoards become just another personal computer – it is consciously designed to support lightweight, fast encounters and simple spontaneous collaborative meetings. We do not believe that providing full keyboard capability (and corresponding security control problems) works to the BlueBoard's advantage when in a public space.

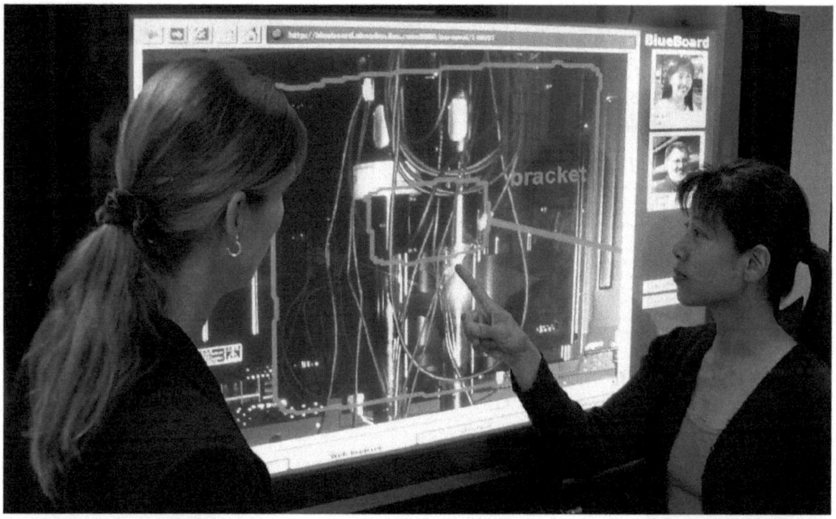

Figure 1-1. The BlueBoard is a Large Information Appliance offering fast access to personal information with tools for collaboration and small groups of people working side-by-side. The display has a touch screen overlay and a badge reader on the right corner for person identification. Network access is assumed.

In the BlueBoard, the badge's unique identifier is sent to a Badge ID database that authenticates the user, handing back a URL to that person's personal content residing on a Content server.

The act of swiping your badge by the reader brings up a representation, called a "personal icon" or p-con, of the badge owner in a column on the right hand side of the display (see Figure 1-2).

1.2 Appliance Design for Personal vs. Communal Uses

There's an inherent design tension in LIAs. They are good for group work with peers standing shoulder-to-shoulder, working together, but they are also very handy for rapid, personal, one-person information access. Unlike other information appliances, a LIA must support both single and multiple users. It needs to work for a single person walking up to the BlueBoard to check their calendar, and it needs to work for small groups of people working together. Consequently, there are two very different sets of overall goals: design the LIA for individual information access, and design the LIA for multiple people using the display at the same time.

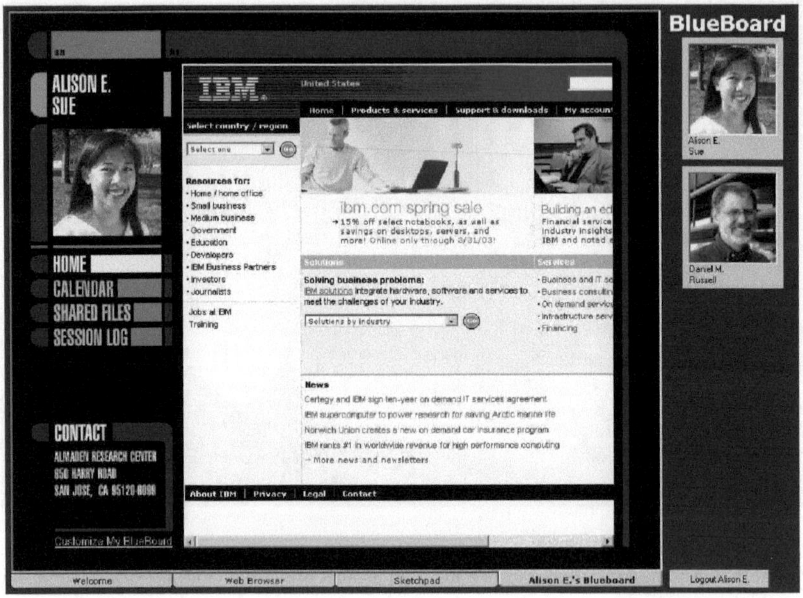

Figure 1-2. A typical BlueBoard personal display. This kind of content is set up by each user as their "home page." Content can be shared with another person by dragging the content (window, image, URL) to their p-con. Here, Alison is showing her home page to Daniel.

We have come to recognize that several design issues must be addressed to achieve both sets of goals: (1) representing people who are participating in a session at the BlueBoard, (2) providing adequate tools for use at the board (e.g., a whiteboard function, a browser, etc.) and (3) keeping personal information private while making public information available.

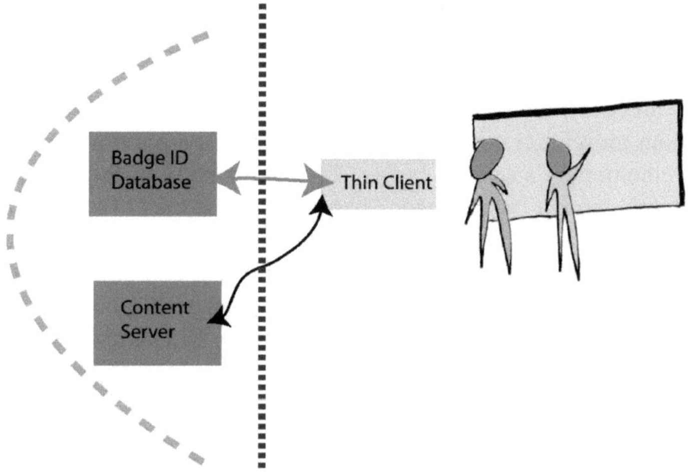

Figure 1-3. A BlueBoard links backend content (on a webserver) with presentation on the large plasma display with a touchscreen and badge reader. The badge ID is sent off for authentication, returning either an "unknown user" error, or an authenticated set of URLs in the Content Server. The effect is that a user "logs in" by simply swiping their badge at the display, getting rapid access to their content.

1.3 Representing a Person: p-cons for Access and Sharing

When more than one person is using the device, the device needs to know whose content is being viewed. There also needs to be a way to easily share content among the users who are all using the board at the same time.

The *p-con* is just an image of the person representing that person's content. When a badge is swiped, a person's p-con appears in the p-con dock on the right side of the display (see Figure 1-2). When more than one person is logged in, all of their p-cons show up on the display (currently up to six).

The p-con becomes the rapid access point for personal content. A user sets up their BlueBoard content ahead of time, linking items such as calendars, presentations, continually updated information (stock quotes, project status, etc.) to their home page. Then, once badged-in to the BlueBoard, a finger touch on the p-con brings up their home page (see figure 1-3).

The p-con is also used to share information between simultaneous users. If one user is showing a slide from their content or an especially interesting web page, a drag-and-drop movement from the page to a p-con will deposit a copy of that content in the session buffer for that p-con. When the p-con's person badges out (leaves the BlueBoard session), the contents of the session buffer are emailed to them. In this way, sharing information is extremely simple – when you see something you like, just drag it to the p-con and the content is shared.

Since all content shown on the BlueBoard is some variant of a web page, dragging an individual item (e.g., a block of text or a picture) just copies that item into the person's session buffer. To make a copy of the entire page, the user will drag from a "whole page" handle (the title bar) to the p-con.

In essence, the p-con is a mechanism for storing content until the user badges out. At badge out time, the contents of the p-con buffer are packed up into an email message and sent off to the p-con owner's email space.

We have consciously avoided overly complex mechanisms such as group management or automatically trying to move the p-con buffer contents into their personal content web. An important goal is that the BlueBoard be usable with a tiny amount of training. Currently, to simplify things, only people present can share content, and sharing is done by logically moving shared material into their email. In a similar vein, we've attempted complex window management schemes for doing split screens, but have not yet been able to devise a way that allows the split screen to be simple to explain and use. It's too easy to become confused between foreground and background. Since an overriding goal is simplicity, we continually return to those roots in making design choices.

1.4 Tools for Rapid Use in Place

Public, shared, communal devices all need to be extremely simple to use and must be intrinsically useful even without special registration. We want people to be able to simply walk up to a BlueBoard and do useful work.

To date we have built a simple toolbar that allows a passerby to gain immediate access to several functions: a whiteboard sketching tool, a calendar that shows the current day / week / month, and a web browser.

These functions continue to be accessible after badging in as well. As with all other content shown on the BlueBoard, this content can be dragged to a p-con for sharing via an email connection.

1.5 Keeping Personal Information Private

Because BlueBoard is so easily viewable, implemented on a large screen, keeping private information safe from unintended viewers becomes important. When a person first sets up their BlueBoard content they can specify a homepage, which will be the first page to appear upon badging in. This could be a newsfeed, public web page, or public version of an individual's calendar, for example. If no homepage is specified, BlueBoard will show a newsfeed web page by default. Private content, such as a private calendar, sensitive files, or personal links, is accessible but requires an additional click to view. This way, private information isn't viewable until the person wants to view it or share it with others.

1.6 BlueBoard Knows its Place

A BlueBoard is a relatively static device. Weighing in at somewhat more than 68 kilograms (150 pounds), it is not an easily portable pocket-sized gadget.

When the BlueBoard is not in use, we have found it useful to loop through a set of content pages that are relevant to the location. In our meeting room setting, the BlueBoard shows project web pages and other web sites of local interest (such as the IBM home page, the IBM Research home page, news sites, etc.). The "attract loop" of displayed pages is set in a local file and tailored to the site and time. Each page is shown for a few seconds before the next page appears. When these pages are shown, the touch screen is still active. If a passerby finds the page of particular interest, just touch the screen, and the looping stops, giving full web browser capability. (We discovered that people often couldn't get to the board in time to stop the display. So we added a "back" button in the upper left corner, which works in the way you'd expect.)

We are working towards giving the BlueBoard a better sense of where it's located. Ideally, location information would be determined by a locator beacon (e.g., a in-room BlueTooth device) and then used to determine what pages would be of local interest. (Say, lab project pages would be shown on the lab BlueBoard, while corporate wide interest pages would be shown on a BlueBoard placed in the foyer.)

Similarly, we have done initial tests allowing people in a workgroup to email messages to the BlueBoard Attract Loop, much as was done in the Lens shared public display at Apple's research lab (Houde *et al.*, 1998).

2. Social Effects of LIAs: A Field Study

BlueBoard is designed to be a place where a small number of people can quickly and easily work together. But what actually happens in small group use?

We ran a field study of the BlueBoard in use by small groups at a workshop held at the IBM Almaden site. Badges were given to 163 participants, 90% from outside of IBM, and with no advance knowledge of the test. The database was initialized with their email addresses and pointers to their home pages.

At the beginning of the workshop, a brief four-minute demonstration of the BlueBoard was given to all participants simultaneously, and the BlueBoard was made available in the hallway immediately outside the auditorium for non-directed use during the breaks and an extended lunch. (The BlueBoard was one of many demonstrations in the hallway.) The instruction covered badging-in, access to one's home page through the p-con, exchanging URLs, use of the whiteboard tool, sharing whiteboard content between badged-in people, and badging-out to cause shared content to be automatically emailed away.

People were videotaped using the BlueBoard, and six were given a post-use informal interview that asked questions about their goal in using the board, particular problems they had, and possible future extensions.

During the 110 minutes of BlueBoard availability, it was nearly constantly in use as participants would walk up, badge-in and begin exploring its capabilities. Although no task was set, we saw several apparently authentic work uses of the board during the time we observed. These included demonstrations of participant website development ("let me show you this great thing I did..."), explicit sharing of web pages, and uses of the whiteboard for non-trivial diagrams.

After the workshop, we collected our field notes and analyzed the video. As would be expected, we learned a number of pragmatic user interface lessons from our observations: inconsistencies in the UI widgets and idioms, the particular difficulty of using a touch screen with long fingernails (they generate an uncertain touchdown point on the resistive touch sensor), how high we can place elements on the screen to be used by short people, and so on.

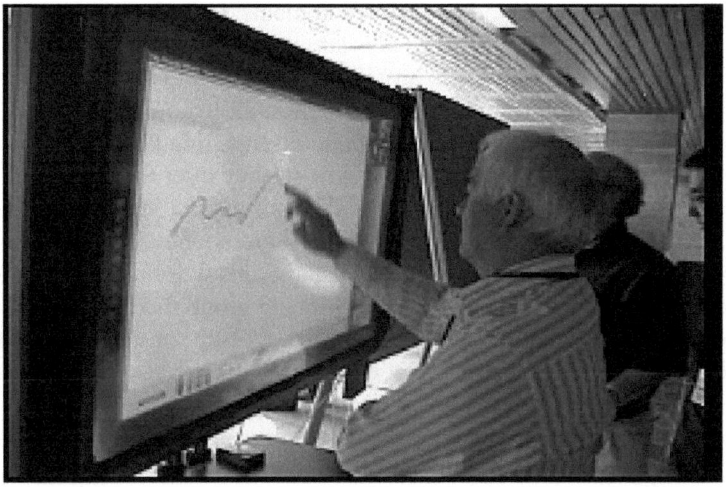

Figure 1-4. BlueBoard setup in the field study. The whiteboard tool is always one touch away from instant use. The image can be dragged onto the artist's p-con or onto another p-con to be emailed when that person badges-out. In this instance, the user controls the use of the board while three other users watch, waiting their turn.

2.1 Observations on Group Use

Although we were initially simply looking for instances of authentic work-like uses of the BlueBoard, and the degree to which all the BlueBoard features could be used after such short instruction, we were struck by the number (and importance) of social interaction effects that took place. Here are the six most evident effects we noted in our analysis:

1. *Social learning through exposed interaction*: The interface style of the BlueBoard is evident – a user can only touch parts of the display to make things happen. Consequently, the entire interaction process is visible to everyone; there are no hidden keystrokes or sudden mouse movements that are difficult to understand. Participants who are unsure of how to use a particular function of the BlueBoard were able to very easily see how someone else could do the thing they wanted. In the course of study, we saw many examples of someone picking up a behavior by seeing someone else use it in the course of their interaction.
2. *Etiquette of multiple person use is unclear:* When a group was using the BlueBoard, other participants were often uncertain about what kind of behaviors would be acceptable. Should one badge-out while another person was engaged in making a point? Was it permissible to badge-in

without making any kind of verbal comment? Time and again we saw hesitations as new BlueBoard users struggled with these momentary crises. Similar issues arise in any kind of workgroup that is focused on a shared information resource (including non-electronic) – what are appropriate behaviors for engaging and disengaging (Bellotti and Rogers, 1997)? We believe these questions will subside over time as board use becomes more commonplace and practices evolve. (See Figure 1-4.)

3. *Who drives?* Groups using the BlueBoard often tended to have one person dominating the interaction. Usually, this was the person doing work at any one moment, either by showing group members their content, navigating to a web page to show a result, or working on the whiteboard. Less frequently, but encouragingly, we also saw several instances of small groups (2 – 4 people) where there was NOT an obvious group leader. These more cooperative discussions were almost exclusively whiteboard drawing sessions where turn-taking was rapid and fluid.
4. *Learning to work together – evolution of turn-taking:* It happens that the BlueBoard touchscreen cannot handle more than one touch point at a moment. If two people touch the screen simultaneously, the cursor jumps to the midpoint between them. When two people are using the whiteboard tool together, it is immediately obvious to the drawers that this is true, and a turn-taking practice rapidly comes into place. We note with some satisfaction that complex floor controls were never asked for nor needed. Instead, because the people drawing could immediately see the consequences of their actions, and because they were physically adjacent, they could easily tell when their partner was about to draw and coordinate their joint actions.
5. *Reaching across*: The size of the BlueBoard is an important determiner in the way groups of people work with it. In the small dynamic workgroups, 2, 3 or 4 people would stand effectively shoulder-to-shoulder, each person reaching in to touch and operate the BlueBoard. By contrast, when a single person was leading the discussion, they would tend to stand in front of the board with other members (from 1 to 5 others) making an arc in front of the board. We noticed many instances of hesitation when controlling the board required reaching across another person standing in a controlling position. That is, like reaching for a plate at the dinner table, participants considered the reaching maneuver to be perhaps slightly rude – and an assertion of control over the proceedings.
6. *Group sharing of information*: As others have pointed out, shared information artifacts need not be electronically based, but simply available to many people simultaneously (Bellotti and Rogers, 1997). When such shared displays are being created and edited in real-time,

there is a distinctly opportunistic use of the information being used in the meeting. Even when a single person is controlling the flow of events, being able to share the experience of editing *in situ* provides additional important side-channels of information exchange. In our study we noted several instances of side-comments being incorporated into the flow of the discussion, comments that might have never been a part of a virtual discussion.

7.

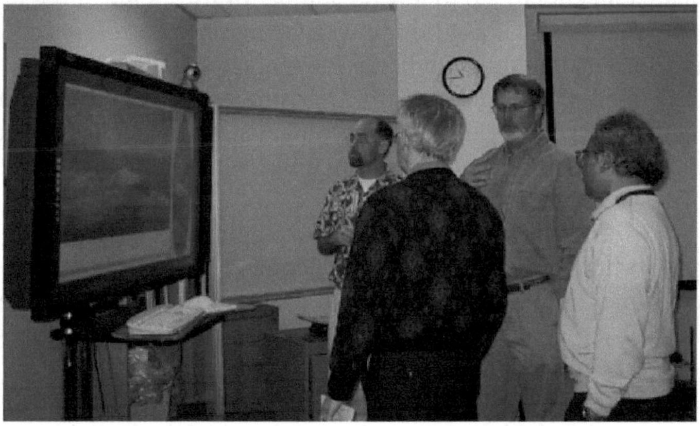

Figure 1-5. An example of BlueBoard being used by a small group. Here, people are standing for a short-term discussion session.

2.2 Observations on Individual Use

In addition, we had several observations about individual uses of the BlueBoard:

1. *Text input:* Although participant home pages were not optimized (or even minimally set up to take advantage of the BlueBoard), it didn't seem to matter except in cases when text input was required for search or login. Since search strings tend to be short, a virtual keyboard of some kind will suffice. But login authentication requires typing in a password, and as noted above, interactions on a BlueBoard / LIA class device are easily observable for co-participants in a group setting. The ability to type in a URL to a web page would have been useful. Instead, participants were limited to selecting only links within an existing web page. In the field study, no keyboard was available, so participants simply did without, but it is a problem that will have to be resolved.

2. *Drawing is important:* The whiteboard tool was put into the BlueBoard initially as a small drawing capture area. Over time, though, we have been consistently surprised at the utility of the whiteboard tool and the novel uses people have found for it. While the whiteboard tool is currently very simple (simple vectors drawn point-to-point by finger-dragging), the simplicity of the tool, its attractive similarity to finger-painting, and most importantly, its automatic capture via being emailed as an attachment, all led to a wide number of uses. One of the unexpected uses noted during the field study was the number of times people would write their email address and drag it to an acquaintance's p-con. This would effectively send the recipient an image with an email address in it – quickly and simply, all without typing. (Similar instances of people scheduling appointments by writing times, dates and places were also seen.)
3. *Easy to use*: Of the six behaviors shown in the introductory four-minute demonstration, we saw all of them in competent use by first-time users. Some of the skill users demonstrated was clearly due to social learning through observation, but we were pleased to find that the affordances of the interface were fairly apparent.
4. *Few badge-outs*: On the other hand, the one behavior that was problematic was badging-out when leaving the BlueBoard area. Nearly everyone who had done some work (e.g., created a whiteboard image or saved a URL to their p-con) successfully badged-out. But around 50% of those who did not capture an image or other content failed to badge themselves out of the BlueBoard. (The number is approximate, plus-or-minus 10%, because we did not accurately track badge-out events.)

3. Subsequent Experience

After this field study was conducted, we placed a BlueBoard into our ordinary working environment. In particular, the BlueBoard shown here (in Figs 1-1, 1-4 & 1-5) was put into daily use as the main display surface within our lab commons area.

While our initial expectation was for BlueBoard to be used by small groups (as in Fig 1-5), we rather quickly learned that real meetings in our environment tend to be somewhat longer, more leisurely events with many people sitting around or near a conference table. Often, most participants have a wireless laptop. While short, impromptu, lightweight small group discussions do take place, the dominant use has grown to be support for larger, sit-down meetings (see figure 1-6).

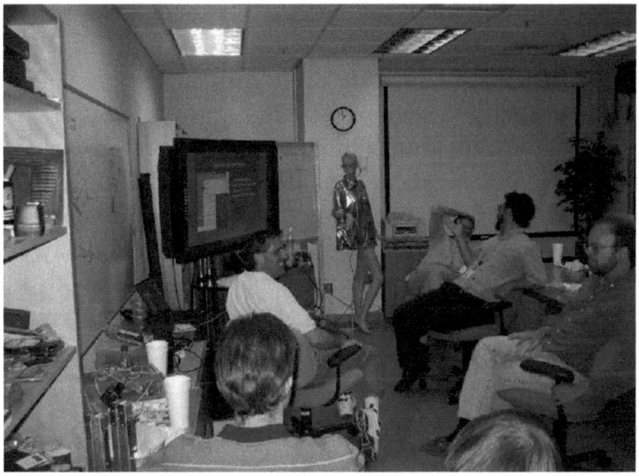

Figure 1-6. An example of BlueBoard being used by a larger group, where people tend to sit in chairs with a designated presenter driving the system.

4. Other Work

There are many large display projects in the research world, but few that combine personalization with simple shoulder-to-shoulder collaboration tools. Nevertheless, several projects are sufficiently similar to merit attention.

The DynaWall from GMD is a very large wall display with a touch surface (Streitz *et al.*, 1999) that supports people working together on a merged set of SoftBoard displays (http://graphics.stanford.edu/projects/iwork). The DynaWall explores interesting issues in group work and very large-scale interactions, but does not yet afford lightweight walk-up interactions, personal identification, or easy sharing of content. One extremely useful feature of the DynaWall is the ability for multiple people to work simultaneously on different panes of the large, tiled multiple display surface.

Similarly, the Interactive Workspaces Project at Stanford (Fox *et al.*, 2000; http://graphics.stanford.edu/projects/iwork) also emphasizes large, sophisticated display areas for information rich display manipulations. While they've been developing new interaction techniques for large displays, they too do not support simple walk-up, rapid use.

For lightweight information access, there are many professional providers of kiosk systems, relatively few of which offer network service access for general information (as opposed to specialized networks, such as banking networks for ATMs). Other kiosk systems (Christian and Avery, 1998; Grize *et al.*, 1997) provide web services or vision-based person-tracking schemes, but none seem to actually know what users are present, or what their personal information content might be.

One interesting development has been the work of our colleagues at NASA Ames who have been creating MERBoard (Russell *et al.*, 2002), a variation on the BlueBoard theme. Their system shares many characteristics of the original BlueBoard design, but has been extended with additional tool and design features to more neatly fit into their work requirements.

5. Summary

Large displays, kiosks, and information appliances are all common. Yet few have tried to be all three at once. The trend towards increasing use of large displays in public spaces creates the opportunity for a new kind of ubiquitous/pervasive device: the *large information appliance, or LIA*; a device that delivers personal information to authenticated, identified users in a kiosk-like environment.

Designing large information appliances requires balancing the need to work across a wide variety of user populations, work for a number of simultaneous users, while operating in a variety of locations and uses.

The social effects of a communal working space are subtle and varied: people have distinct styles when working in public, yet the value of a shared work surface seems unquestionable.

Our goal in the BlueBoard project has been to provide very rapid access to personal content while providing the easy-to-use functions of an information appliance supporting both communal and personal use. The important difference between BlueBoard and other kiosk systems is the design of the use experience for a kiosk that knows who is using it while supporting fast access and simple sharing of content.

Acknowledgements

This work would not have been possible without the extraordinary talents of Rich Gossweiler, who implemented nearly the entire BlueBoard thin client, and Sydney Gould, who conducted the field study reported here. In addition, we would like to thank Cal Swart and Michael C. Greenwood of IBM's Watson Lab; Alan Peterson and Dan Walkowski of Reactivity, Inc., and Tania Choi of ThinkVisually.com. We are also indebted to our NASA colleagues at the Ames Research Center, Jay Trimble, Roxana Wales, Ted Schaub and Alonso Vera.

References

Buxton, W., Fitzmaurice, G. Balakrishnan, R. & Kurtenbach, G. Large Displays in Automotive Design. IEEE Computer Graphics and applications, 2000; 20(4): 68-75.

Christian, A. D., Avery, B. Digital Smart Kiosk Project: About Faces. Proceedings of CHI '98 Conference on Human factors in Computing Systems; 1998 Los Angeles, CA USA: 155-162.

Fox A., Johanson B., Hanrahan P., and Winograd T., Integrating Information Appliances into an Interactive Workspace, IEEE Computer Graphics and Applications, 2000; 20 (3): 54-65.

Grize, F., Aminian, M. Cybcerone: A Kiosk System Based on the WWW and Java. Interactions, 1997 4(6): 62-69.

HID Corporation, http://www.HIDCorp.com

Houde, S., Bellamy, R., Leahy, L. In Search of Design Principles for Tools and Practices to Support Communication within a Learning Community. ACM SIGCHI Bulletin, 1998; 30(2): 113-118.

Pedersen, E. McCall, K., Moran, T., Halasz, F., Tivoli: An Electronic Whiteboard for Informal Workgroup Meetings. Proceedings of InterCHI '93 Conference on Human Factors in Computing Systems; 1993 Amsterdam, The Netherlands: 391-398.

SMARTBoard. http://www.SMARTTech.com

Stanford Interactive Workspaces Project http://graphics.stanford.edu/projects/iwork/

Streitz, N., J. Geißler, T. Holmer, S. Konomi, C. Müller-Tomfelde, W. Reischl, P. Rexroth, P. Seitz, R. Steinmetz i-LAND: An interactive Landscape for Creativity and Innovation. In Proceedings of CHI '99 Conference on Human Factors in Computing Systems; 1999; Pittsburgh, Pennsylvania, USA: 120-127.

Bellotti, V., Rogers, Y. From Web press to Web pressure: multimedia representations and multimedia publishing. In Proceedings of CHI '97 Conference on Human factors in Computing Systems; 1997; Atlanta, GA, USA: 279-286.

Elrod, S., Bruce, R., Gold, R., Goldberg, D., Halasz, F., Janssen, W., Lee, D., McCall, K., Pedersen, E., Pier, K., Tang, J., Welch, B. Liveboard: A Large Interactive Display Supporting Group Meetings, Presentations and Remote Collaboration Desks, Video, and Screens. In Proceedings of CHI '92 Conference on Human Factors in Computing Systems; 1992; Monterey, CA, USA: 599-607.

Russell, D. M., Trimble, J., Wales, R. Two paths from the same place: Task driven and human-centered evolution of a group information surface. Make IT Easy Conference; 2002; San Jose, CA, USA.

Chapter 2

NASA'S MERBOARD

An Interactive Collaborative Workspace Platform

Jay Trimble, Roxana Wales, Rich Gossweiler
NASA Ames Research Center

Science Applications International Corporation, Computer Sciences Corporation

Abstract: This chapter describes the ongoing process by which a multidisciplinary group at NASA's Ames Research Center is designing and implementing a large interactive work surface called the MERBoard Collaborative Workspace. A MERBoard system involves several distributed, large, touch-enabled, plasma display systems with custom MERBoard software. A centralized server and database back the system. We are continually tuning MERBoard to support over two hundred scientists and engineers during the surface operations of the Mars Exploration Rover Missions. These scientists and engineers come from various disciplines and are working both in small and large groups over a span of space and time. We describe the multidisciplinary, human-centered process by which this MERBoard system is being designed, the usage patterns and social interactions that we have observed, and issues we are currently facing.

Keywords: Pervasive computing, ubiquitous computing, human-centered computing, collaboration, computer supported cooperative work, user-interface, common information space

1. Introduction

In 2003, NASA will send two robot rovers to explore the surface of Mars. Dubbed Mars Exploration Rovers (MER), they will operate as mobile science platforms and be the most capable systems ever sent to explore the surface of the Red Planet (see figure 2-1). With a planned mission lifetime of 90 days per rover, every day on the Martian surface represents a significant amount of time to gather important science data.

K. O'Hara et al. (eds.), Public and Situated Displays: Social and Interactional Aspects of Shared Display Technologies, 18–44.

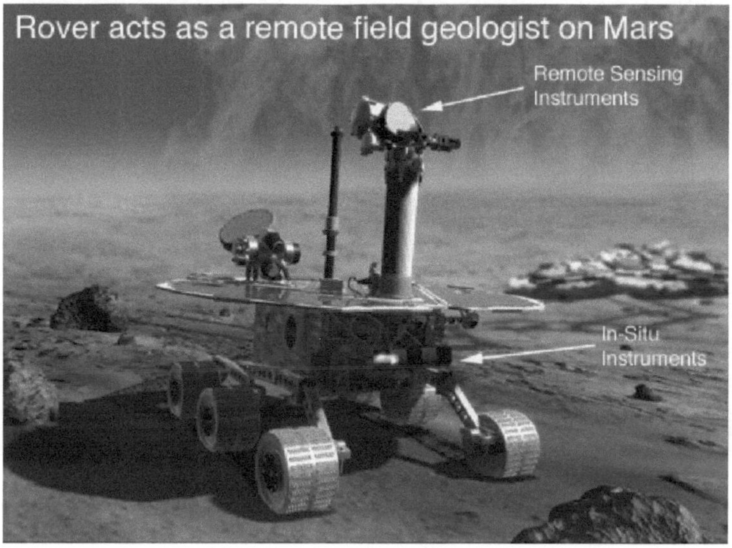

Figure 2-1. Mars Exploration Rover has remote sensing instruments, and in-situ instruments.

To maximize the productivity of the MER Rovers, the Mission Operations Team at the Jet Propulsion Laboratory (JPL) will communicate with the rovers every day. The science and engineering teams will receive data from the rovers, analyze the data, determine a strategy for operations for the next day, and develop daily command sequences. These command sequences will then be sent to the rovers for execution (see figure 2-2).

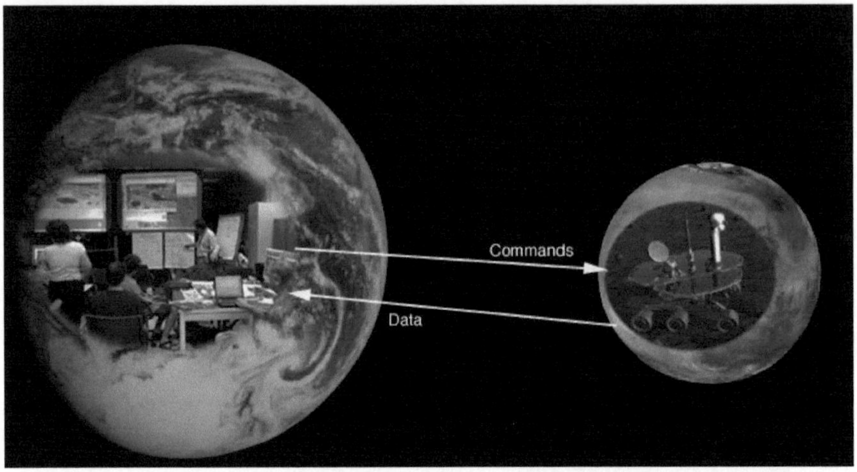

Figure 2-2. Scientists and engineers on Earth communicate daily with the rover on Mars.

As part of a collaborative effort with JPL, NASA's Ames Research Center initiated the Mars Exploration Rover (MER) Human Centered Computing (HCC) Project in the fall of 2000. Since that time, our team of cross disciplinary (computer science, anthropology, cognitive psychology) researchers has worked with MER science and operations team members applying ethnographic and human-computer interaction research methods and offering recommendations for the design of work processes, procedures and technology to help mission participants accomplish their work. Our goal is to help increase the science productivity of rover surface operations and the effectiveness of communication interactions and collaboration. The MERBoard, a new collaborative, situated, large screen technology for creating, accessing, displaying, annotating, sharing, distributing and saving information within the MER mission environment, is the principal technical innovation to come from this HCC effort (see figure 2-3).

The MERBoard platform consists of a collection of large, interactive displays, networked together to share information. The displays will be situated on three floors of the Mission Support Area (MSA) at JPL. The MER HCC team developed custom software for this platform so that it will support users as they (a) create, save, retrieve and share information, (b) collaborate within small groups working around a single board, (c) participate in the collaborative work of large group interactions, as well as (d) share information between personal computers and the large displays.

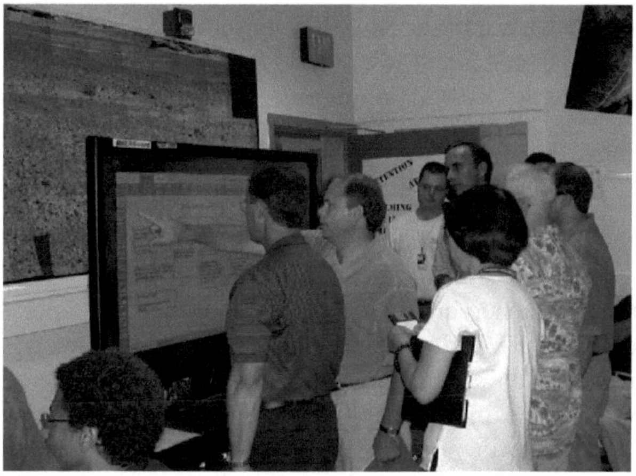

Figure 2-3. The MERBoard's large touchscreen display creates an immersive environment for collaboration. The software is designed to support tasks in the target domain.

This chapter describes the domain in which the MERBoard will be used. We demonstrate how the research process led to the development of the first MERBoard design requirements and comment on how we believe the board's development will come to provide a specialized "common information space" (Bannon 2000) (Bannon & Bødker 1997) (Bannon & Schmidt 1989) (Schmidt & Bannon 1992) within the mission. We describe the functionalities of the MERBoard and its iterative development process as it has been used by the Mars Rover mission team during training events. We then consider the potential use of these displays as new computing platforms, not desktops, but interactive platforms that support collaboration and can become ubiquitous computing platforms.

2. Types of Collaboration that MERBoard Must Support

For our team, the human-centered computing process involves understanding a domain by using a variety of ethnographic methods that include in-situ observations of the domain and working in partnership with domain members to determine information, communication and collaboration requirements. This section first describes the collaborative work processes that have been designed by the MER mission system and science team's for their own use during the MER mission, in anticipation of their daily work of receiving rover data, analyzing it, devising a strategy for doing tele-robotic science and developing plans to carry out that strategy by sending commands to the rover. Then we describe some of our ethnographic findings from the early phases of MER mission design, especially in early test and training events, and we show the role that research played in developing the early design requirements for a new technology, the MERBoard.

2.1 The Mission Operations Team

The combined science and engineering team that will operate the rovers on Mars is called the Mission Operations Team. This team is composed of many sub-groups, such as the science team, the science operations support team, the spacecraft team, the mission planning team, the sequencing team, and others. All of these teams must work together to plan and conduct safe and productive rover operations. Since the focus of our work to date has been the science team, here we describe the science team structure for collaboration in the daily planning process. The Science team has been the major focus of our research, with a special interest in the structure of their work process and the need for collaboration in the daily planning process.

2.2 The Science Team

The MER science team will use the rover and its instruments to carry out the missions' primary science objectives: determine the aqueous, climatic, and geologic history of a site on Mars where conditions may have been favorable to the preservation of evidence of pre-biotic or biotic processes.

During the mission, science team members will formulate and test scientific hypotheses by first analyzing data they have requested from the rover on Mars and then developing new observations and activities for the rover to perform on the current sol. The science team is organized into smaller theme groups according to science discipline. Each theme group has members who work together to set goals and objectives for their discipline. Then a subset of the science theme group members meet together with engineers and other mission personnel in the Science Operations Working Group (SOWG), to develop an integrated set of objectives, observations and rover activity plans. The integrated science activity plan represents the overall goals of the SOWG. Developing these small and large group plans requires extensive communication and collaboration, both within and across the smaller theme groups and within the SOWG. The whole process must be completed each day within a few hours. Successful completion of this process requires access to both current and past information regarding mission decisions and any supporting rationale.

2.3 *Small Group Collaboration: Science Theme Groups*

The science team is organized into five theme groups: geology, geochemistry, soil, atmosphere and long-term planning. The first four are organized according to discipline, but the fifth theme group, long-term planning, has the job of analyzing the science process and rover operations from a strategic (longer term), scientific perspective. This group will keep track of the science decision process and aid in planning for longer-range activities that could cover periods of a few days to weeks or even months.

The science team works in facilities designed to support collaboration in the decision making process. When science data is received from the rovers each day, individual instrument specialists and scientists will view the data and look for information and insights. Those scientists will then come together in a large Science Assessment Room in the Mission Support Area (MSA), specifically designed to support small group collaboration as well as collaboration across the five theme groups. In this room, there are five separate group areas, each with conference tables and good views of a large overhead projection screens that will project information relevant to each theme group's discussions.

The work of the theme groups will be to analyze and discuss the data and relate it to that team's current thinking as well as to any developing hypotheses (see figure 2-4). Then they will create a theme group activity plan consisting of a set of prioritized observations they would like the rover to make on the next sol (a sol is a Martian day). In addition to the collaboration within theme groups, group members will circulate within the room, sharing plans and strategies with other theme groups as they attempt to do some early coordination of their planning.

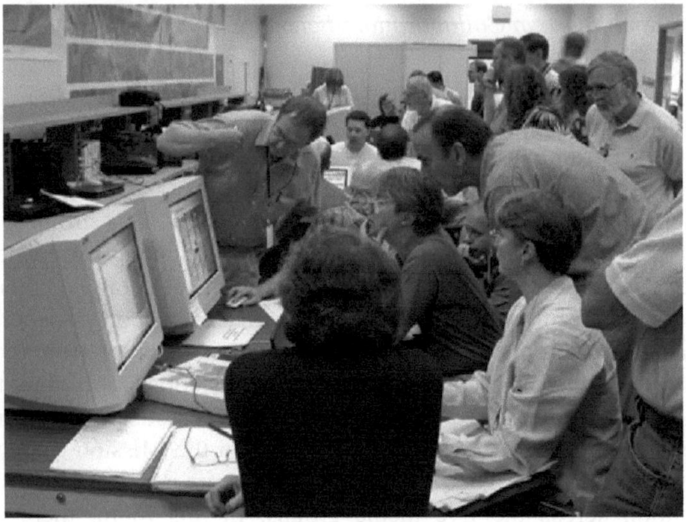

Figure 2-4. Scientists working in a theme group

2.4 Large Group Collaboration: The Science Operations Working Group

The goal of the Science Operations Working Group (SOWG) is to produce requests for an integrated set of observations and activities that represents the science team's priorities for rover activities for the next day. Examples of activities include the gathering of data using a specific instrument and rover drives that take the rover to new areas and features of interest. The science teams' requested plan is turned into commands and sent to the rover by the rover sequence team.

The SOWG meets after the science theme groups have developed their plans and priorities. Here the collaborative process will continue, but it takes on a decidedly different character. The SOWG group will have approximately forty members who can be active participants and another forty who are expected to be observers. To facilitate this large group collaboration, scientists will move to another room in the MSA that again has been specifically designed to support this type of collaboration. The work will be to develop an overall integrated science plan, deciding on which observations, if any, from the plans of individual theme groups will be incorporated. They will make this decision based on a discussion of the scientific rationale, objectives for the next sol's operations, the overall strategic plan, and the need to meet the planning and engineering constraints set by current rover configuration and available rover resources, such as power and the bandwidth dedicated to data downlink.

During this meeting all of the theme groups present their requests and priorities and develop together a single integrated science plan of associated rover instrument activities and movements that is acceptable to all theme groups and achieves agreed-upon scientific objectives. In this meeting, the scientists also work with members of the engineering teams to begin the coordination of science plans and rover engineering plans that are being developed in tandem. This meeting is lead by a single person, the SOWG Chair, who is responsible for delivering a time-ordered list of requested science activities to an integrated team, that will then incorporate science and rover health and engineering plans into an integrated activity plan, do resource planning, turn the plans into commands, validate them and uplink them to the rover on Mars.

3. Observing the Work Practice Domain

Our design philosophy calls for observation of existing work practice before proposing technology additions. In many domains we could simply observe existing work practice. This isn't possible for Mars Rover Surface operations, as the landing doesn't take place until 2004. We have been able to observe two rover field tests (Spring 2001 and Summer 2002), and two associated "Mars Yard" tests. It should be noted that the field tests are only partial representations of the real mission, as the timelines, work process and environments are approximations of real mission events and many of the tools and procedures that will be available for the mission, are still being designed. They are however, a valuable opportunity for gathering data by observing users practicing mission processes. The primary goal of the field tests is to train the science team in tele-robotic operations. For the MER HCC team, the 2001 field tests were a primary source of data used to drive the early MERBoard design requirements. At the 2002 field tests we deployed two MERBoards and observed how they were used. The following summarizes what we observed at the 2001 field test.

In field tests, the scientist engaged in real, not simulated, exploration. What made the explorations "real" was the use of a real rover, situated in the field, with science goals developed in real time for each test. The data used was real images from the field test rover. No simulated data was used. The science teams goal was to determine the location of a rover, which had been placed in a remote desert terrain, and create hypotheses about the geology and geochemistry of the surrounding area. During the tests, scientists worked together to make decisions about the types of scientific observations they wanted to do and worked with engineers, who were collocated in the same area, to create plans for doing science and commanding the FIDO (Field Integrated Design and Operations) rover to traverse and deploy a variety of instruments. During these tests, the JPL test team also introduced a variety of anomalies to train the scientists to deal with conditions they might encounter during Martian surface operations.

During the field test, we used ethnographic methods to gather data, included observing work practice, taking field notes, doing formal and informal interviews, capturing video and still photos, and doing a subsequent analysis of the gathered data, including interaction analysis (Jordan and Henderson, 1994) of the video.

The analysis revealed a variety of constraints on the science team's collaborative process in those early tests. As scientists received data, analyzed it, and made their decisions, we saw limitations on their ability to communicate and exchange information; that is to view, share, present, save and thus refer to important electronic information and material artifacts in both small and large group settings. A 'common information space' was undeveloped. We define the common information space, expanding on Bannon (2000 p. 1,3), Bannon & Schmidt (1989), Bannon & Bødker (1997) and Schmidt & Bannon (1992), as a communication and information space within a work system that is electronic but that can be supported by related communication events in collocated situations. It is a shared space where information 'objects' are accessible to all and communication, sharing and interpretation are supported as participants construct common interpretations and a common work purpose.

The benefits that come through location in physical proximity and a shared work environment were not enough to fully support the work that was being done in these early field tests. Even though the teams were working face-to-face, the pressure of the daily timeline required precise and rapid sharing of information of all kinds, verbal, electronic and hard copies so that the team could make decisions and execute a detailed plan of action. The scientists needed "multiple" and "intense" means of communication (Bossen 2002, p.176) in order to develop the common interpretations (Reddy, Dourish, Pratt 2001) that are important to cooperative work and common information spaces. The fact that the science team shared a common expertise and pre-defined goals contributed significantly to their ability to accomplish those goals (Bossen 2002) and was probably the major reason for their success during these early stages of mission design, when facilities, technology support and procedures were minimal and still in development.

The first tests took place in the single room, among grouped tables, chairs and computer workstations whose configurations went through changes with each successive test based on our feedback and the feedback of others (Norris 2002). This was part of an effort to define the first requirements for the physical space that would eventually contribute to a Mission Support Area. (figure 2-5).

We observed that the scientists had access to the following tools: personal laptop computers; flip charts; notebooks; print outs of schedules, images, and documentation; a twin-screened computer work station in each group area that was running the science activity planning software, still in its early stages of development; and three overhead projection screens that displayed the science activity planning software of the "uplink lead", whose job was to represent the single, common activity plan the team was building each day, along with demonstrating models of rover activity.

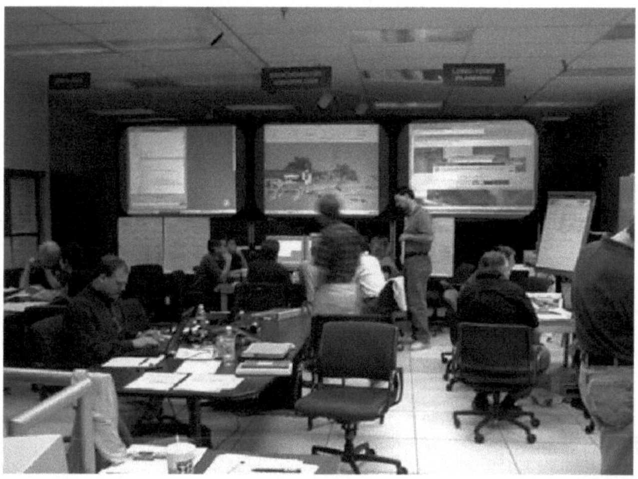

Figure 2-5. The physical layout for the first FIDO Field Test.

3.1 *Identifying Information and Collaboration Needs for a Common Information Space*

It was in the FIDO field test environment that we first identified information requirements that, in combination with design inspiration from IBM Almaden Research Center's BlueBoard (Russell, 2001), would lead to the development of the MERBoard, a technology that we believe will contribute greatly to enhancing communication and developing a common information space during MER surface operations. We began by identifying several areas that needed support: (1) information display, distribution and sharing, (2) a way to generate real time collaborative information representations (3) a way to annotate shared information (4) the ability to save or archive collaborative information generated during the tests and (5) remote viewing and control from one MERBoard to another and from a MERBoard to a personal computer.

3.2 Information Sharing and Display

The need for shared information displays became increasingly obvious over time, as members hung information and images on walls (see figure 2-6), draped images over flip chart stands, laid out large format images on their work tables (see figure 2-7), hung information created on flip charts in permanent display situations and used flip charts as a primary means of developing strategic rover plans and presenting them to the team (see figure 2-8). They also shared information with others simply by "calling out" information about mission updates, meeting times, and science and rover status and updates to the group as a whole. This practice left no information trail and created problems in the test when people who were not in the room failed to hear important information.

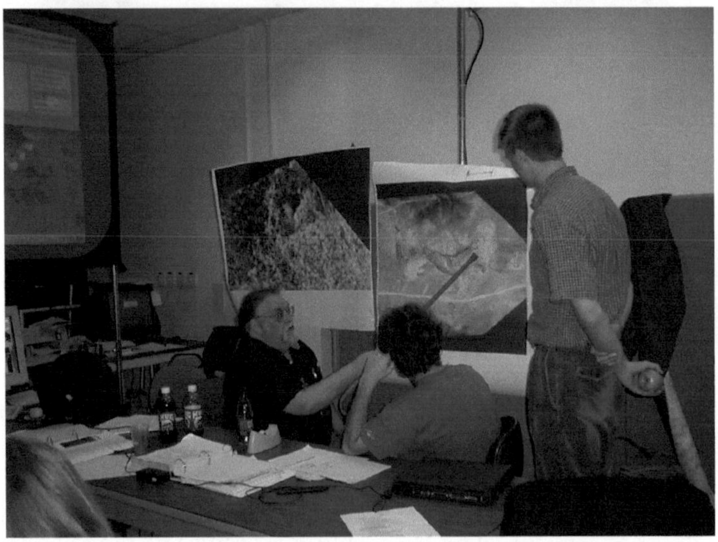

Figure 2-6. The display and comparison of large format images.

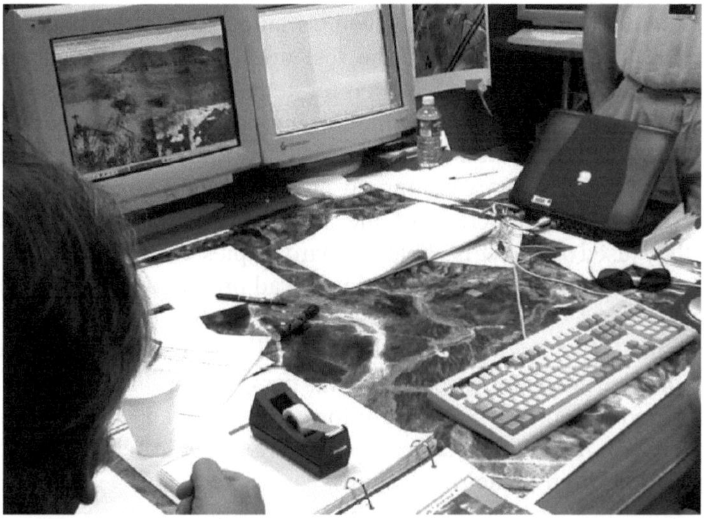

Figure 2-7. Note how the flip chart pages remain posted as a way of allowing information to continue to be accessible

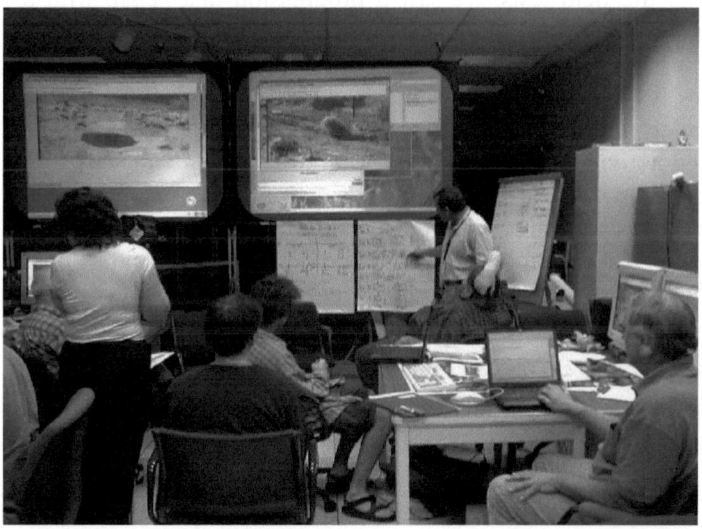

Figure 2-8. A scientist using flip charts to present during the 2001 FIDO Field Tests.

An influencing factor that contributed greatly to our understanding of how important it would be for members to be able to share and display information was that during these tests there was minimal support for the most standard information sharing venues since copiers and printers were not easily accessible. (Note that the test area is quite different from the Mission Support Area being developed for actual Mars operations.)

Scientists needed to share information in both small and large groups. In small groups, they circulated images and printed information sheets; drew on scratch paper and yellow pads; turned notebooks and laptops for others to see; and pointed to the screen of the activity planning software. In large groups, they used flip charts; held up hard copies of images; used a laser pointer to point to information on the overhead projection screens; or simply verbally referred to their findings without the support of shared visualizations. Perhaps the most compelling instance of attempted information sharing from a requirements perspective was when scientists, who often had supporting scientific information on their laptops which they wished to share, held up the laptop for display to the group in an attempt to show the information to their colleagues.

3.3 Creating Real-Time Representations While Doing Collaborative Work

During the field tests, we saw a progression that began with the use of flip charts early in the planning process. The flip charts allow for free-form expression and were used for brainstorming, hypothesis creation and strategies for verification, as well as flow charts for long term planning (the team called these flow charts Sol Trees) (see figure 2-9). For highly structured activities, such as the creation of rover timelines of activities and command sequences, a specialized mission tool was used.

While flip charts support natural, rapid, handwritten representations, they do not allow for the embedding of related information such as images. They are difficult to store, retrieve and search over long periods of time, and they are not easily shared beyond team members who are collocated and in close viewing range.

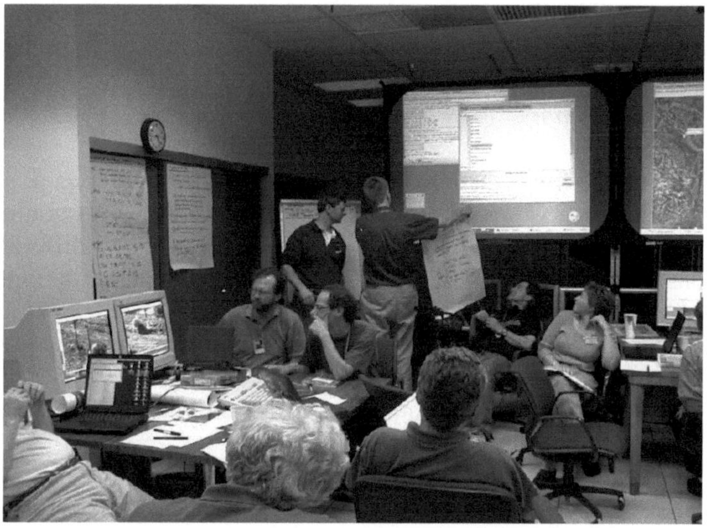

Figure 2-9. The science team brainstorms on flipcharts and hangs the pages for display

3.4 Annotating Information

While we saw scientists mark up notebooks and augment information in their computers, we saw only a few instances where people annotated the large hard copy images that were available. Informal interviews revealed that they were reluctant to mar the single copy of an image and yet they were consistently pointing to information, indicating that there was something of interest in it.

4. Defining the MERBoard

The MERBoard design is intended to assist the mission operations process by addressing the user needs that we observed in the tests, and those that we anticipate for the mission. Note that when we proposed the MERBoard, the critical path tools that would be used to build rover activity timelines and commands were already defined by JPL. By inserting the MERBoard into the mix of mission tools we propose to augment the teams planned work practice.

Success will be measured, not only by acceptance and use, but also by providing needed capabilities that were non-existent or improving ones that were inefficient. As a software platform, its success will eventually be measured as well by the number of groups that adopt it as the mechanism for developing and deploying software in similar collaborative environments.

4.1 Functionality

In deriving the first functional requirements for the MERBoard, we were driven by the observations described above, and design inspiration from IBM's BlueBoard (Russell, 2001). As there are many differences in operations between a field test and a real mission, we had to do our best to account for those differences.

The initial MERBoard design specified the following functionality:

- Data display, annotation and distribution, storage/retrieve capability for individuals and groups
- Ubiquitous access to information anywhere in the MER MSA
- Personal and group storage spaces, with mechanisms for getting information into and out of the MERBoard platform (e.g. from and to a laptop)
- Remote access and control, from board to board, and personal computer to board
- Simple, efficient mechanisms for capturing any data on the screen, and distributing that data using email and personal/group storage spaces

Following initial interactions with users, we added mission specific functionality. A Sol Tree Tool was requested by a science team member. Sol Trees (remember a Sol is a Martian Day) are flow chart representations of rover strategic plans, showing many possible alternatives for rover activities on each Sol. They were done manually on flip charts during the early field tests. We began by adding flowchart-like capabilities to the whiteboard, such as the ability to auto-attach lines between boxes and easily input text. This quickly evolved into a dedicated Sol Tree plug-in tool. The design is based on observed and planned work practice of the long term planning science theme group. Users can build flow charts of plans and then check a path on the plan to see how it affects mission goals. Mission specific features include the ability to track Sol Type (a sol type means what is the rover doing on that day, e.g. driving, approaching or measuring a target).

Throughout the process of proposing the MERBoard to the MER Mission, we emphasized that it would be easy to use, would require minimal training, and would have a level of simplicity comparable to a Palm Pilot. The users are supposed to feel that they are performing tasks, with their focus being the tasks, not the computer interface. Our challenge has been, and continues to be, how to design the collaborative functionality to best help the mission, while keeping the interface simple and providing extensibility.

4.2 Functional Overview

One of the keys to the success of the MERBoard is the integration of functionality into a collaborative workspace. We find issues such as logins and security, that have solutions we take for granted on the personal desktop, require re-design in a situated collaborative workspace.

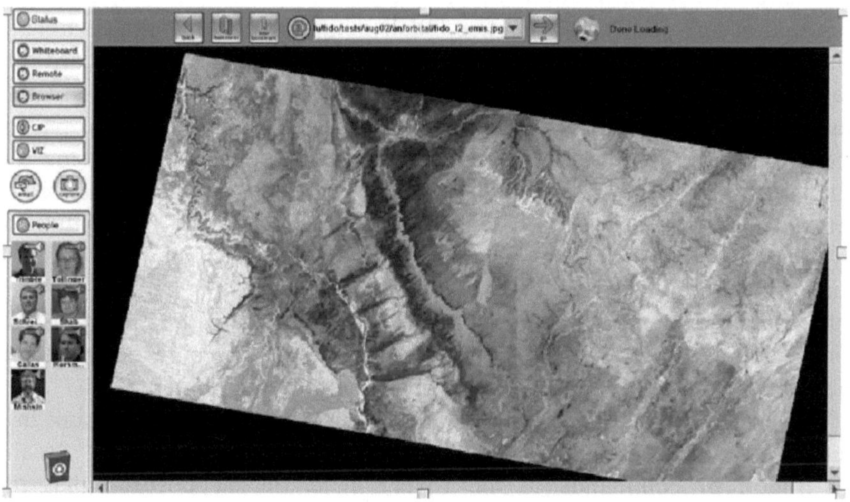

Figure 2-10. The MERBoard user interface showing the display of science data using the browser

Figure 2-10 above, shows the major UI elements. A toolbar on the left side of the screen controls the modes. Functionally, a MERBoard mode is similar to an application. However, we expect that applications on a personal computer go through a startup process and are loaded by the user. For the MERBoard, the user accesses functionality by switching modes, but does not install and startup applications as on a personal computer.

The top three modes, Whiteboard, Remote and Browser, are provided with all boards, as these functions are considered fundamental to any collaborative activity. The next two buttons are reconfigurable and may be specific to a board (the bottom button is user reconfigurable in real time). For example one board might have a data visualization mode for the geology group, whereas another might have a Sol Tree mode for the long-term planners.

Below the mode selection buttons are meta-tools. Meta-tools operate across modes and function as global services. Screen capture and email are shown in the figure. The people button opens and displays a directory to access people to display personal information in the collaborative environment (see Ubiquitous access to information, section 4.5).

4.3 Data, Annotation and Distribution

Based on our observations of the use of flip charts at FIDO, and users descriptions of past work practice, such as annotation of surface images during previous missions, we derived the requirement for a whiteboard that has, in addition to basic whiteboard functions, the ability to display, annotate and distribute data. Observed user work practice at FIDO showed, as part of the daily planning processes, science-brainstorming sessions done using flip charts and whiteboards. Most of the work done on the flip charts consisted of unstructured representations, showing early thinking in the formulation of hypotheses and science strategies. Following the brainstorming sessions, the scientists move to structured representations for integrating activity requests into a timeline, from which commands are generated. Critical path mission tools, such as JPL's Science Activity Planner (SAP), support the structured activities, and indeed, impose mission-required structure on the users.

Given that structured activities, of necessity, require users to think in a certain way (note that this structure is not arbitrary it is required for the generation of commands to the rover), it is our supposition that the MERBoard's free-form tools, integrated with data display and annotation, will provide a means to support free-form thinking and representation for scientists and engineers during the mission, without the imposition of structured by the tools. Combined with the large interactive touch-screen, with its immersive qualities, we expect new types of interactions among team members and groups, in the display and analysis of data.

Initial data access and display capability was provided by integrating a Web browser into the board. This allowed access to existing mission data sources. Figure 4-10 shows data displayed using the browser. We also integrated a mission specific tool called Data Navigator, developed by another group at Ames, to provide direct access to the mission database. Other means to display data on the board include uploading data to a personal or group MERSpace (section 4.4) or using remote access to display data from a personal computer or another board (section 4.6).

Any data that can be displayed on the board, in any mode, can be captured using the capture meta-tool, which automatically captures data to the whiteboard. From the whiteboard users can annotate the data, include it in drawings, brainstorms, hypothesis formation and validation, and any other whiteboard activity.

Whiteboards may be saved to a user's MERSpace (see section 4.4). To distribute a whiteboard to another user, just save it to their space in any public (non-secure) folder. Each MERSpace has an InBox folder; standard work practice for distribution of files to other users is to put it in their InBox. To distribute files outside of MERSpace, an email meta-tool is provided. The whiteboards native file format is industry standard SVG. This allows editing of exported whiteboards in commercial applications that are SVG compatible.

4.4 MERSpace – Individuals in a Collaborative Space

Collaboration for MER requires access to information at many levels, not only from mission data sources, but personal data. At FIDO, we saw users analyze and create data representations on their personal computers. This data, like the mission data stored in the operational mission database, is part of the data set users require access to. To provide individual users with a means to bring their own data and information into the MERBoard's collaborative workspace, we created the MERSpace, a place for users to store and retrieve their personal data. Rather than thinking of a personal computer, the user has a personal space in a collaborative computing environment. The current MERSpace provides folders, with an explorer type interface, a place for personal bookmarks and automatic one-button access to personal remote computers (see Section 4.6). To minimize complexity, we limited the folders to a single level. Users can create new folders, but not folder hierarchies. Figure 2-11 shows a user's MERSpace.

Each MERSpace user has a personal icon. Tapping on the icon selects the MERSpace. The icon also functions as a target, i.e. users can share information by dragging files between their icons. The icon identifies users for remote access requests and email. Users put data into their MERSpace by uploading files from their personal computer using the MERSpace Web Page that provides access to MERSpace over the Web, and provides the user with an interface for uploading files from their personal computer to their MERSpace.

4.5 Ubiquitous Access to Information

MER Mission operations will take place in the MSA (Section 2.3), which occupies three large floors of a building at JPL. It is the Mars Rover equivalent of NASA's Mission Control Center in Houston, seen on TV during Shuttle Missions and the Apollo missions to the Moon. For the FIDO tests, the small physical space provided collocation for collaboration, so access to information across a large physical space was not an issue. This is not true for the mission, with its large MSA.

To address the need for information access across the facility, we provide users and groups with access to their files from any MERBoard, a personal computer running the MERBoard personal client software, and the web. With ubiquitous access, a scientist moving between theme groups need not carry their personal computer with them to discuss their data. An engineer on a tiger team troubleshooting a problem can go from the sequence room to the spacecraft room and have access to the their data.

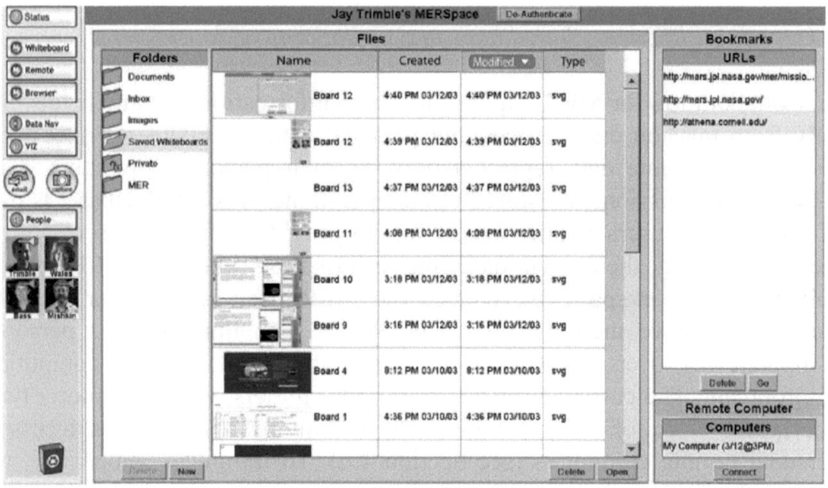

Figure 2-11. MERSpace, showing the file explorer, personal bookmarks, and remote computer connect

4.6 Remote Display and Control

Our observations of team members attempting to show data on their personal computers to large groups, and user requests for being able to view and control one board from another, drove the requirement for remote capability. Remote allows one board to display and control another. The same capability works from a board to a personal computer. A user can display and control their PC from a MERBoard. Recall that user's MERSpace (section 4.4) automatically captures the IP address of users who are logged into their MERSpace Web Site. This allows for one button remote access to personal computers. Figure 2-12 shows a personal desktop being displayed on a MERBoard.

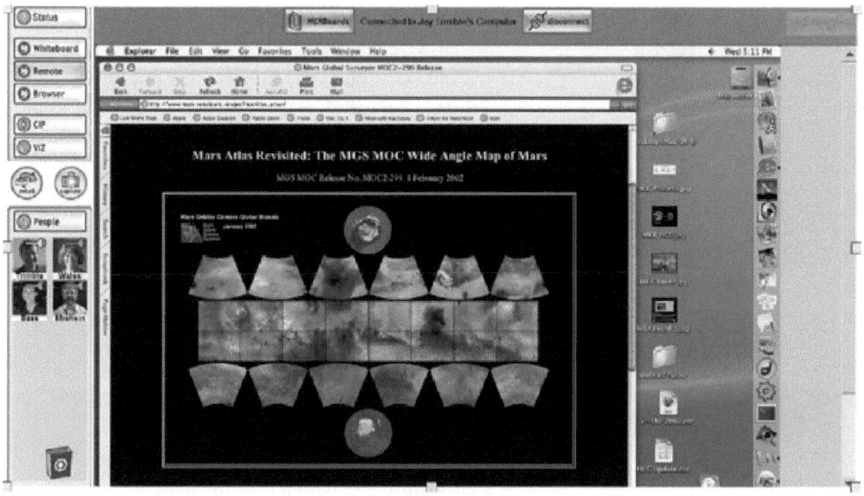

Figure 2-12. MERBoard remote mode, showing a desktop computer on the MERBoard

4.7 Hardware

The MERBoard hardware is commercial off the shelf (with the exception of the stand which is commercially procured, but custom designed). The display is a plasma unit with a touchscreen overlay. A personal computer runs the MERBoard software, which is written in Java and can run on Linux, Mac OS-X, or Windows 2000 (see figure 2-13).

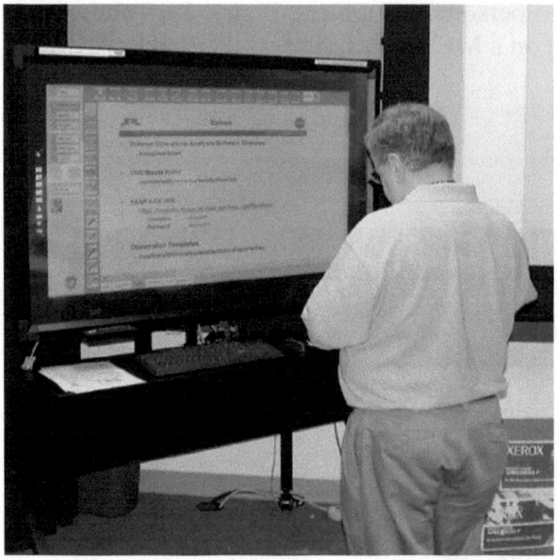

Figure 2-13. The MERBoard hardware, with a user for scale

5. Actual Use

We've had two opportunities to observe the MERBoard in use by the MER Mission operations team in training. The first was in July of 2002, at a mission system thread test. The second was at the FIDO field tests in 2002, this was a follow on to the 2001 test, and provided a good opportunity to compare our design assumptions with actual use. Here's a summary of our observations.

5.1 Mission System Thread Test

The mission system thread test was a test of the uplink processes for planning and sending commands to the rover. The users were a mix of scientists and operations engineers. The goal of the test was a successful uplink of commands. This was the first MERBoard deployment at JPL. As the use of the MERBoard in the mission is discretionary, its use was uncertain. There were several factors that affected MERBoard use relative to what we expect in the mission. First, many mission system tools are not yet complete. This proved to be a plus for MERBoard use, as the MERBoard was able to fill in for some of those tools. For this test, many MERBoard features were either incomplete or partially implemented. For example the remote capability was limited for this test.

The board received extensive use for this test. The primary use was display, capture and annotation of target data. Figure 2-14 shows the actual image used in the test, and the annotations showing target names and direction.

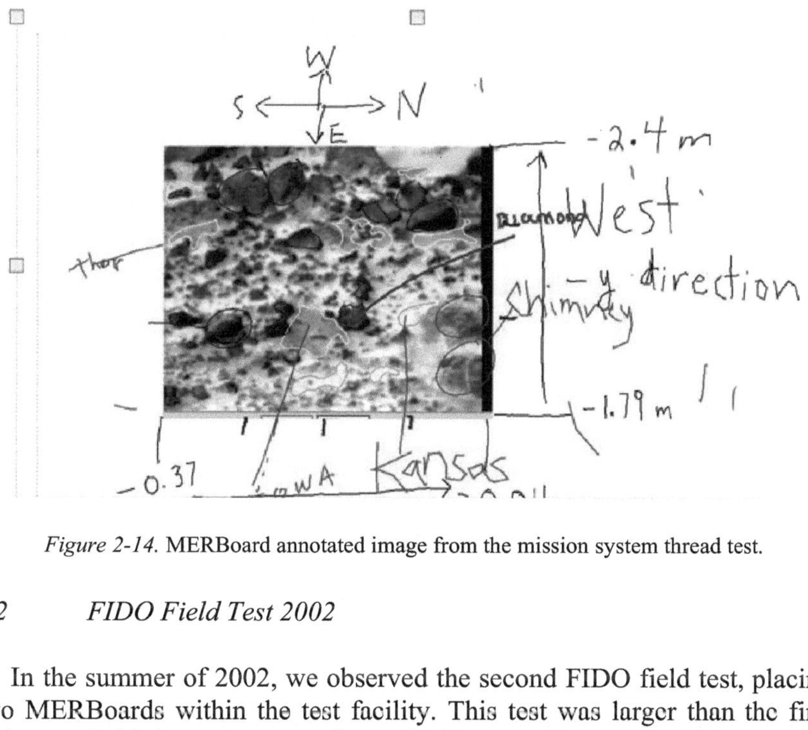

Figure 2-14. MERBoard annotated image from the mission system thread test.

5.2 *FIDO Field Test 2002*

In the summer of 2002, we observed the second FIDO field test, placing two MERBoards within the test facility. This test was larger than the first and was held in two rooms instead of one, with a larger number of participants. The test area now more closely simulated the design of the MSA by putting the larger three of the five science theme groups in one room, where they did their analysis and having them move to a larger room next door, where the other two theme groups were located, for the SOWG meeting. The MERBoard collaboration design assumes that each science theme group has their own MERBoard, however, due to the limitations of the facility, we were only allowed to place one MERBoard in each room.

We used a variety of camera setups to capture interactions around the MERBoard and screen capture and logging setups to capture the activity on the board itself. We were able to observe and capture how the board was used, and to compare the actual use to the expected use.

5.2.1 Group Interactions Around the Board

As we had anticipated, the board in the smaller room supported the work practice of the small groups and was initially used to access, and view images and mission relevant information. In fact, groups sometimes grew from shoulder to shoulder collaborators to over the shoulder collaborators as several people gathered at the boards to view images and create representations of interest. The large size of the board facilitated group interactions around images in several ways. First, the size and height of the board allowed people to easily view and interact with images in groups (Figure 2-15).

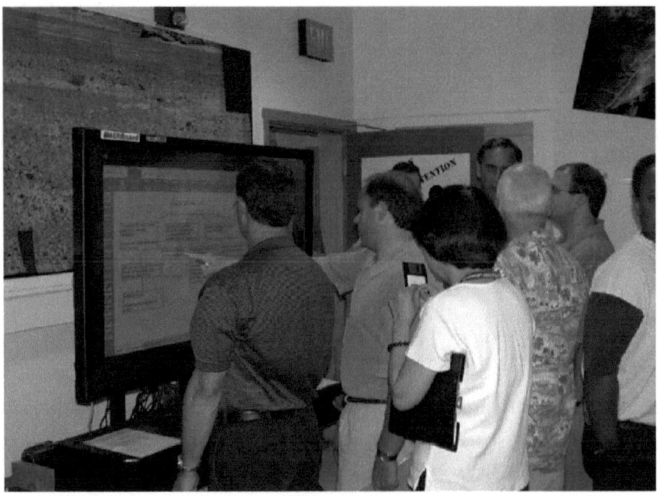

Figure 2-15. Using the board at the second FIDO Test.

The ability of the board to display large scrollable images, combined with the touchscreen that facilitated interactions, allowed groups of scientists to view large terrains such that all of them could scroll through the terrain, point out features of interest and be active participants in the decision process of selecting features to be designated as targets. Contrast this with the more traditional means of a group of people using a personal computer or workstation to examine large terrain images. In that case several people are crowded around a relatively small screen, usually with one person controlling the computer. The size of the screen, locus of control, and type of interaction is changed significantly in this case. It's also worth noting that large terrain and target images are displayed on the wall during field-testing. While this practice continued even in the presence of the MERBoards, the interaction and use of wall-sized images is more constrained and less interactive. Scientists tended to view, rather than interact with, the wall mounted images.

5.2.2 MERBoard as a Pervasive Device and Presentation Tool

With the initial help of some early adopters, scientists used the pervasive set up of the two boards to create and save information in one room and then display it in the second room during the SOWG meeting. Figure 4-16 shows a scientist presenting to the SOWG. Over the period of the tests, the team members adapted their use of the MERBoard during the presentations, using content created on the MERBoards, content created on individual users' laptops and posted to MERSpace, as well as content created on users lap tops then shown and/or captured on the MERBoard using remote mode. Note that the presenter in figure 2-16 can show images to the group, and still be able to directly interact with the image on the screen. This is in contrast to the projection screens where remote interaction using a pointing device is required.

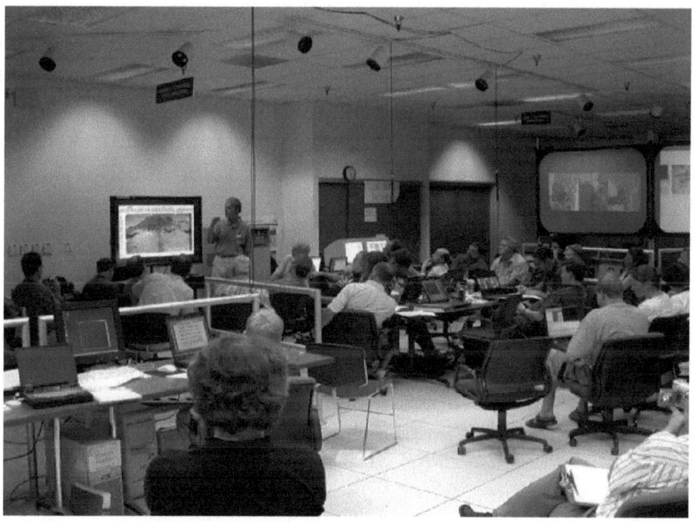

Figure 2-16. A scientist using the MERBoard to present to the science operations working group.

As we had also anticipated, placement of the boards is crucial to their use. The long term planning group that was located closest to the board in the smaller science assessment room rapidly became "owners" of that board. Additionally, we had provided some simple tools on the board (boxes and lines) to help this group create Sol Trees, a science process decision tree representation. Over the period of the test, the consistent day-to-day representation of this "tree" on the board formalized both the representation and the use of the board. From time to time, group members who were creating the tree would move to a large whiteboard to make quick notes before inserting them into the decision tree. When the tree was running on one of the screens, other team members appeared reluctant to minimize it and use the board for other purposes.

5.2.3 MERBoard and Traditional Media

Note in figure 2-8 that flip charts were used as a means of developing content and presenting it to the SOWG at the 2001 FIDO Field Tests. The image in figure 2-8 shows a scientist presenting Sol Trees. As previously mentioned, the MERBoard design includes some basic features in the whiteboard specifically designed to facilitate the development of Sol Trees (this has since been extended to a dedicated sol Tree Tool). A key question for the MERBoard team going into FIDO was to what extent team members would use the MERBoard in place of a traditional medium, such as flip charts. Going in to the test we believed that an electronic medium, such as the MERBoard, must have several advantages to have any chance of replacing traditional media that team members were already comfortable using. The advantages that the MERBoard offered for Sol Trees were a large interactive workspace, the ability to easily save, recall and revise drawings, electronic drawing tools, and the ability to develop the Sol Trees on the board in the theme group area then easily bring the same drawing up on the board in the SOWG area for presentations to the group.

Figure 2-15 shows the Long Term Planning Science Theme Group using the MERBoard to develop Sol Trees. Note how the board facilitates group interaction. For Sol Tree development, the users chose MERBoard over flip charts. The use pattern clearly showed that the MERBoards advantages were enough to get the team members to change their work practice and use an electronic medium in place of a traditional one.

6. The XBoard and Future Work

The MERBoard has evolved into the XBoard, an extensible architecture with an applications programmer interface and a plug-in developers kit. Three developers have started work on plug in applications. The XBoard is a platform for the development of large screen interactive collaborative applications. It is also the foundation for a ubiquitous computing structure for NASA. As part of the XBoard, we have designed a multi-center architecture (MCA). MCA will take the idea of ubiquitous computing beyond the MER Mission Support Area and extend it to conference rooms, design areas and work areas within NASA across NASA centers so that users and groups have access to their data from any XBoard within NASA.

We also plan to develop a personal client. The idea is to have software that runs on a users personal computer to extend the MERBoard/XBoard environment. The client should provide access to the users MERSpace, seamless transfer of data from a personal computer to MERSpace, and easy remote access to the MERBoard/XBoard.

We plan to deploy twelve MERBoards at JPL to support MER surface operations and training. We will observe how they are used and evolve the design based on what we see. No doubt the users will think of many things that we, as designers, have not.

7. Conclusion

The availability of large screen displays at affordable costs has created the beginning of a new class of collaborative interactive computer. The MERBoard, designed for specific tasks in a targeted domain and then deployed in that domain, has begun to accumulate enough use to give valuable data on user reaction to this new class of system. Additionally, based on our initial research, we suggest that this new class of system provides an electronic common information space that helps support collaborative work in intense, collocated situations requiring a variety of information inputs. We believe users will also create new work practices over time that makes maximum use of the MERBoard. Stay tuned for Mars Surface operations in 2004.

8. References

Bellotti, V., Rogers, Y. From Web press to Web pressure: multimedia representations and multimedia publishing. Proceedings of CHI'97 Conference on Human factors in Computing Systems; March, 1997 Atlanta, GA USA: 279-286

Buxton, W., Fitzmaurice, G. Balakrishnan, R. & Kurtenbach, G. Large Displays in Automotive Design. IEEE Computer Graphics and applications, 2000; 20(4): 68-75

Christian, A. D., Avery, B. Digital Smart Kiosk Project: About Faces. Proceedings of CHI '98 Conference on Human factors in Computing Systems; 1998 Los Angeles, CA USA: 155-162

Elrod, S., Bruce, R., Gold, R., Goldberg, D., Halasz, F., Janssen, W., Lee, D., McCall, K., Pedersen, E., Pier, K., Tang, J., Welch, B. Liveboard: A Large Interactive Display Supporting Group Meetings, Presentations and Remote Collaboration Desks, Video, and Screens. Proceedings of CHI'92 Conference on Human Factors in Computing Systems; 1992 Monterey, CA USA: 599-607

Fox A., Johanson B., Hanrahan P., and Winograd T. Integrating Information Appliances into an Interactive Workspace. IEEE Computer Graphics and Applications, 2000; 20(3): 54-65

Grize, F., Aminian, M. Cybcerone: A Kiosk System Based on the WWW and Java. Interactions, 1997; 4(6): 62-69

HID Corporation, http://www.HIDCorp.com

Houde, S., Bellamy, R., Leahy, L. In Search of Design Principles for Tools and Practices to Support Communication within a Learning Community. ACM SIGCHI Bulletin, 1998 30(2) : 113-118

Jordan, B., Henderson, A. Interaction Analysis: Foundations and Practice, Institute for Research on Learning 1994; Report 94-0027

Pedersen, E. McCall, K., Moran, T., Halasz, F., Tivoli: An Electronic Whiteboard for Informal Workgroup Meetings. Proceedings of InterCHI '93 Conference on Human Factors in Computing Systems; 1993 Amsterdam, The Netherlands: 391-398

Russell D.M. and Gossweiler R., On the Design of Personal & Communal Large Information Scale Appliances, Proceedings of UbiComp'01; 2001 Atlanta Georgia USA

SmartBoard. http://www.SMARTTech.com

Stanford Interactive Workspaces Project http://graphics.stanford.edu/projects/iwork/

Streitz, N., J. Geißler, T. Holmer, S. Konomi, C. Müller-Tomfelde, W. Reischl, P. Rexroth, P. Seitz, R. Steinmetz i-LAND: An interactive Landscape for Creativity and Innovation. In: Proceedings of CHI '99 Conference on Human Factors in Computing Systems; 1999 Pittsburgh, PA USA: 120-127

Chapter 3

CONFIGURING SPACES AND SURFACES TO SUPPORT COLLABORATIVE INTERACTIONS

Yvonne Rogers[1] and Tom Rodden[2]
[1]University of Sussex, [2]University of Nottingham

Abstract: This chapter explore how new kinds of displays can be developed to enable collaborative interactions. The chapter explores the research issues surrounding the development of a range of different display systems before focusing on the physical affordances of different display arrangements. In order to this we classify existing systems into three main types before providing detailed discussions of research prototypes drawn from our own work.

Key words: display-based collaboration space, office computing, whiteboards, single display groupware, embedded displays, stand-alone displays, integrated multiple displays; awareness, electronic whiteboards, community, cooperative sharing.

1. Introduction

In the last few years, advances in screen technology have resulted in a much wider range of affordable displays becoming available, providing new opportunities for supporting collocated working, learning and socializing. These include front and back projected wall displays, large flat panel displays, plasma screens, interactive electronic whiteboards like SMARTboards (Smart 2003) and Mimio, and digital tabletop systems. Exploiting these technologies to facilitate collaborative activities raises many research questions. A key question is how can the new kind of displays be developed to enable effective, equitable and socially comfortable

K. O'Hara et al. (eds.), Public and Situated Displays: Social and Interactional Aspects of Shared Display Technologies, 45–79.

collaborative interactions? In particular, how can they be configured to allow collocated and remote activities to be cohesively and seamlessly integrated with the ongoing activities in a given setting? Another key concern is how best to allow multiple people to collaboratively interact with information presented on a single or multiple large displays. Moreover, are there particular kinds of collaborative activities and settings for which the new generation of displays are most suited?

In this chapter, we begin to explore these research issues, considering how various display systems have been designed, assembled and used in different collaborative settings. Our focus in doing so is to pay particular attention to the relationship between the physical set-up of a display system in its context and the socio-cognitive aspects it promotes or constrains. A key concern is the extent to which the physical affordances of different display arrangements affect the way people interact with each other, their physical media and artefacts and the digital information that is shown on the shared displays. We begin by reviewing the literature on shared displays, classifying them in terms of three main types and consider how they have fared in terms of how they are actually used in collaborative settings. Within this framework we provide detailed descriptions of a number of our own projects, where we have designed and evaluated novel shared display systems in social and work settings. We then discuss our conceptualization of the design of large displays in terms of shared 'surfaces' and 'spaces', highlighting aspects of the relationship between the two. Finally, we outline a set of design issues we consider to be important when configuring surfaces to support people in their various collocated and distributed spaces.

2. Developments in display-based collaborative interactions

Current research on shared displays falls broadly into three main types (although they are not mutually exclusive), varying in terms of whether the setting is taken into account, the type of display and the way the displays are integrated with other technologies. In this section, we consider:

1. Embedded displays – where the display is an integral part of a physical space
2. Stand-alone displays – that are placed into existing spaces
3. Integrated multiple displays – where a number of displays and devices are used in tandem

2.1 Embedded Displays

By embedded displays we are referring to approaches that have attempted to configure a whole physical space, like a room, an office or other public building, by embedding various displays within features of that space, to literally become 'part of the furniture'. One of the earliest attempts to embed PCs with new forms of large displays in a room with the purpose of supporting group working was the Electronic Meeting System approach (e.g. Stefik, 1987). Most notable, was the Arizona project (Nunamaker, 1991), where a number of special-purpose meeting rooms were built to facilitate the various kinds of meetings that are held in large organisations. Each room had a series of networked computers embedded in a U-shaped tiered set of desks, facing a large video display (sometimes two or three) at the front of the room, with whiteboards and overhead projectors also being provided. The idea of configuring the displays and supporting technology in the room in this way was to allow everyone to work on their own computer while also being able to contribute their work to the large communal display at the front of the room. Groupware software was installed on the networked machines that allowed the people taking part in the meeting to type comments on their personal workstations and then to copy them over onto the shared display. The comments were subsequently organized by a leader/facilitator, who sat at the front of the room with a master workstation. One of the main attractions of this kind of set-up was the potential for facilitating wider participation in collaborative activities, like brainstorming, through enabling all in the room to generate ideas that could be readily 'heard', copied and shared. However, the downside of making people collaborate around this constrained technology set-up, is the rigid, unequal and formal structure of the meeting that inevitably arises. For example, the facilitator is given an enormous responsibility of integrating and ordering the ideas that the others post to the communal board. This makes the people in the meeting highly dependent on the facilitator. The individual workstations are also substantially apart from each other and a long way from the shared display, having the effect of markedly demarcating private workspaces from the public workspace. In so doing, it places the participants physically a long way away from each other and even further away from the facilitator, making it quite an unnatural way of collaborating. Hence, while the groupware may have been effective at allowing individual input to be shared and seen by all, the physical layout was not conducive to the kinds of informal talking and close working that typically goes on around table meetings.

More recent examples of designing complete meeting rooms include the iRoom and i-land, which have created meeting rooms with a range of embedded displays and interlinked technologies. In contrast with the fixed and formal structure of the earlier genre of electronic meeting rooms, their design is more intimate and informal, allowing people to move freely around the space and be physically close to one another. The iRoom is a project carried out at Stanford University (Johanson *et al.*, 2002), where a meeting room was custom-built, comprising a large interactive table in the centre connected to a number of large interactive wall displays. In addition, the room was set up to allow portable devices to be used in conjunction with the interlinked displays. One of the main motivations for providing 'tiled-wall' displays, i.e. displays that are linked together, side by side, and an interlinked table display was to enable multiple representations of complex data to be dynamically visualised and interacted with, thereby substantially increasing the amount of screen estate available. In so doing, it allows small groups of practitioners (e.g. biochemists, designers, engineers, architects) to view multiple related visualisations of their data concurrently and for all around the table to be able to annotate and point to features of these. Needing to compare and coordinate multiple visualisations is central to many kinds of practitioner's work and so this set-up seems ideal for this purpose. In particular, it overcomes the occlusion problems that arise when restricted by the windowing techniques used by single display systems. However, a downside of this kind of multiple display set-up, is the huge overhead required to coordinate the content across the displays and the orchestration involved in managing the array of collaborative actions and interactions with the content. A key issue is determining who has access and control over which display and how this is switched between the different participants in the meeting. Also there is the question of whether all can see the displays at the same time, given that each person will have a different orientation to the displays, depending where they are sitting around the table.

The i-Land project (Streitz *et al.*, 2002) was also concerned with creating technology-rich, embedded environments, but with more of a focus on how the physical architectural space of a room can affect the way the technologies are used. An instantiation of the i-Land vision was Roomware, which was designed explicitly with the physical space in mind. Electronic walls, interactive tables and chairs were networked and positioned together so they could be used in unison in a way that augmented and complemented existing ways of collaborating. An underlying premise was that the 'natural' way that people work is to congregate around tables, huddle and chat besides walls and around tables. Therefore, the technology should be developed to augment these kinds of informal collaborative activities, allowing people to interact with digital content that was pervasively embedded at these particular locations. The displays should be placed in parts of the room, that allow people to chat, mill around, interact with their work materials together while also communicate remotely with others.

Unfortunately, as with the iRoom, building such a technology-rich room that is usable in a real-life work setting, is at the very least, costly and technically challenging. As, of yet, a functioning i-Land space, which can be used by a group of people to collaborate, has yet to be fully implemented or evaluated. It is difficult to tell, therefore, how people would take to working in such futuristic workspaces; would they mill around, seamlessly moving between the different displays and other people in the room, just as they might do at a party, when moving between different social groups, the food table, the chairs and the drinks counter? Would they, for example, begin by standing at the DynaWall (an interactive electronic wall), talking to remote people via the videoconferencing facility, then move to a ConnectTable (an individual free standing table with flat screen computer embedded in it) to send some email, before switching to a communal desktop table to talk about a project with others? How would individuals and small groups move from one work activity to the next? Who would be doing the coordinating? How would everyone keep aware of what was happening and know what workspace was free? There are many unanswered questions concerning whether the idea of 'hoteling' (as architectural designers refer to it, e.g. Hecht, 2001) – where quiet working, local and remote team meetings, and social interactions are combined temporally and spatially in one environment – is workable or desirable.

In sum, the idea of embedding whole rooms or buildings with a variety of rich-technology displays has many attractions, not least the potential for increasing opportunities for a diversity of collaborative interactions to occur. However, the ability to create novel workspaces of this ilk, that will truly be enabling in the manner hoped, has yet to be realized.

2.2 Stand-Alone Displays

The more common approach to research on shared displays has been to develop stand alone displays, aimed at being placed into existing work, social or learning spaces. These include various kinds of vertical surfaces, collectively known as electronic whiteboards, and horizontal surfaces, collectively known as electronic tabletops. The two basic forms have also been labeled in terms of their attributes or where and how they are intended to be used.

2.2.1 Electronic Whiteboard Systems

Much of the research on electronic whiteboard systems has been to explore new interaction techniques by which to interact with information shown on the large displays. For example, the pioneering work on shared whiteboards (Elrod *et al.*, 1992) was concerned primarily with local interaction issues, such as how to support electronically-based hand-writing and drawing, and the selecting and moving of hand-crafted objects around the display. Since then, there has much interest in using tracking and other sensing techniques, to allow people to gesture to, write on and point at information as a way of interacting with such a display. The move away from the conventional input of a single keyboard and mice was mainly motivated by the perceived need of allowing multiple people to interact with each other and interact more directly with the content on the large displays.

2.2.2 Wall-Sized and LargeTiled Displays

An extension of the early electronic whiteboard research is the work currently being done on wall-sized displays and large-tiled ones using high-resolution screens. A primary motivation is to allow small groups of people to view and interact with large collections of information or visualisations of complex data sets. Similar to one of the aims of the iRoom, an underlying assumption is that showing data as parallel large-scale visualisations can be very useful for comparing, compiling and sequencing different information. Examples include LumiPoint that presents content via multiple tiles, that can be interacted with via a pointing device like a laser pointer (e.g. Chen and Davis, 2002); the Interactive Mural developed by Guimbretiere *et al.* (2001), that allows content to be created and annotated using gesturing and hand-writing; and Flatland (Mynatt *et al.*, 1999), that, similarly, supports handwritten input, by recognizing strokes made on the surface.

So what is the best way of supporting people to interact with these wall-sized displays? Are the more 'naturalistic' gesture-based interfaces more effective than conventional keyboards and mice? Central to this question is how easy and effortless it is to shift from display to interactive device and back again. While many of the gesture-based approaches are promising, they are often unwieldy in this regard. For example, writing on a wall requires the user to be able to reach the different parts of the wall – a feat that can prove to be challenging if the display is several metres high or is placed in order to ensure its users cannot block the view of others. Similarly, the need for gesture-based interfaces to disambiguate between the commands (gestures) and the content (writing on the display) is a difficult problem, both technically and interactionally. This issue becomes even more challenging within cooperative settings when gestures may be part of the non-verbal communication between people rather than directed at the screen.

Remote interaction techniques require users to understand where their point (or points) of interaction are and to manage the inherent action involved at a distance. This can introduce significant interaction overhead. In addition, the separation between the user who initiates an action and its effect on a shared display means that coordination between remote users is made more difficult as their gestures are not visible to others. For example, a user is not able to predict where a remote user is looking as their orientation is not available to them. Providing support for these missing cues without overloading users is a major research driver.

2.2.3 Single Display Groupware

To help think about how to design applications that support people working together at the same time and as a collocated group, Stewart, Bederson and Druin (1999) promoted the notion of Single Display Groupware (SDG). They suggest that providing a large display, with various entry points, can allow more than one person to join in. Their particular focus has been to enable pairs of people to work concurrently on a shared drawing tool on a large display using multiple mice. Using this SDG model, the KidStory project sought to encourage pairs of children to collaborate through using Pad++, a shared drawing tool, that allows children to co-create drawings (Benford *et al.*, 2000). Certain functions are provided in Pad++ that only work when two cursors are used together at the same time (e.g. stretching two sides of an object on the screen). The idea behind this constraint is to encourage pairs to work together on shared objects at the display, rather using their own cursors to create their own individual objects on the same display. Constraining the way software objects can be interacted with in this way requires the users to think quite differently about what is happening on in the display, particularly in terms of ownership and sharing.

A main appeal of this form of shoulder-to-shoulder collaboration is the multitude of interactions enabled to those in a collocated group of people besides the display. In so doing, simultaneous and collaborative interactions are encouraged. This scope, however, is also a limiting factor as it requires people to literally be shoulder-to-shoulder. While it is easy to envisage this model working for small groups of two or three, it is less clear how it scales up. Would this approach work for, say, five users, twenty users, or even two hundred (numbers we could envisage being collocated with large displays)? Also, it is unclear as to how well users take to carrying out computer-based tasks, like drawing or mouse dragging, as co-dependent actions.

2.2.4 Public, Community and Situated Displays

In an attempt to consider how large displays might be used in practice, several researchers have now begun to 'situate' them in public and social spaces. A common application is to place them in offices and other public buildings to provide notices and other information relevant for a particular community (e.g. Agamanolis *et al.*, Chapter 13 this volume; McCarthy, Chapter 12 this volume; O'Hara and Brown, 2001). Systems such as Plasma Poster (Churchill *et al.*, Chapter 10 this volume) and Community Wall (Grasso *et al.*, Chapter 11 this volume) allow communities of users to place, view and interact with information on screens that have been located in specific public places of a building. The forms of interaction provided, are usually via touch screens, pen-based, or gesturing, providing the ability to select information, to expand it and annotate it. The material itself is posted to the situated displays from desktop machines, using conventional keyboard entry, rather than at the board itself.

A key objective is to consider how placing displays in these public settings improves the 'sense of community', through fostering social encounters and an enhanced awareness within the community (e.g. Greenberg and Rounding, 2001). A major challenge confronting these systems, however, is enticing members of the community to voluntarily and spontaneously use them in the first place. There is often an assumption that people will simply walk-up and use them. While the idea of a walk-up and use model has proven successful for getting individual users to interact with information in public kiosks, a situated display presents quite a different set-up. Instead of being a private space – as is the case with public kiosks – a situated display, by its very nature, is public. When people become aware of this and realize that others can see what they are doing on the display, it can have an inhibiting effect. In particular, people are reluctant to use public situated displays. For example, Churchill *et al.* (2002) found that people needed *"constant encouragement and demonstration* to interact with their public display; Greenberg and Rounding (2001) found that co-present use of their public display rarely occurred (although remote usage flourished); while Agamanolis (2002) found that "*half the battle in designing an interactive situated or public display is designing how the display will invite that interaction"* (p.4).

Such a pervasive dilemma needs addressing, requiring us to understand what is causing the resistance. Social embarrassment has been identified as a key factor, especially in determining whether people will interact with a public display in front of an audience (Rogers and Brignull, 2002). In our own research on public displays, we have begun looking at how people move and mill around in social gatherings, and how this changes when an interactive public display is placed in that space. A key observation is that the public display has to be able to be interacted with in a lightweight way and that there should be no obligation to take part. In addition, the space needs to be organized in a way that makes it socially acceptable to take part without feeling embarrassed or overcommitted.

A public display we have developed is the Opinionizer system (Brignull and Rogers, 2003), which is aimed at encouraging people in an informal gathering, such as a welcome party, to share their opinions. In so doing, our objective is to promote the initiation of conversations and socializing between bystanders, who may not know each other. In such settings, there is often a mingling crowd, comprising a mix of newcomers and people who know each other. While the people who know each other may have little problem socialising, it is much more difficult for the newcomers who are to break the ice (Borovoy *et al.*, 1998). The collective building up of opinions on the public display is intended to provide a talking point to others standing besides it, to comment on to their neighbour. People can add their views and opinions to the Opinionizer display, which they and others can observe and then add further comments. This is accomplished by users typing in a few words at a keyboard, which is then projected onto the public display (see figure 3-1).

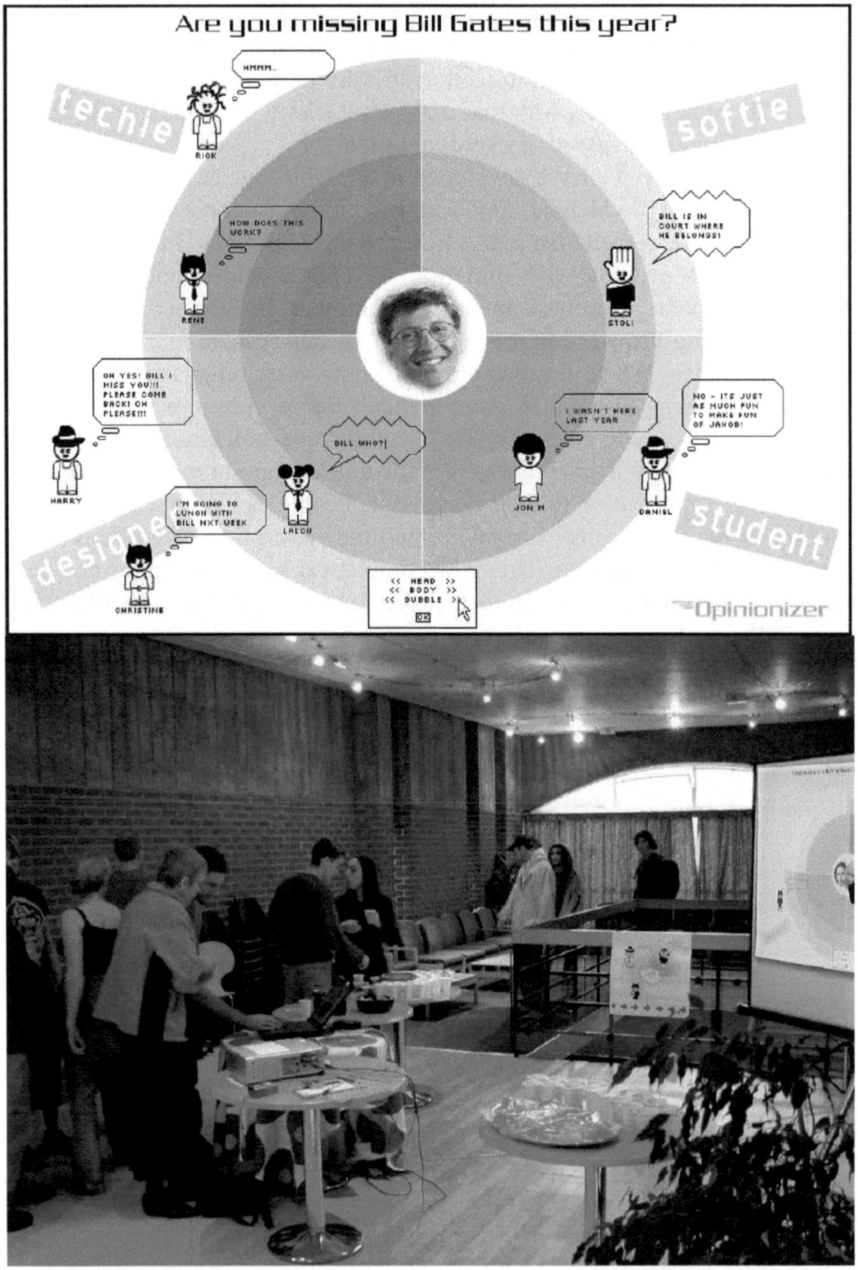

Figure 3-1. (i) A screen shot of the Opinionizer display and (ii) it being used *in situ* at a party

When the Opinonizer was placed in social gatherings we observed the emergence of a 'honey-pot' effect. As the number of people in the immediate vicinity of the Opinionizer increased, a sociable 'buzz' was created in the area. By standing in this space and showing an interest (e.g. visibly facing the screen or reading the text), people seemed to give a tacit signal to others that they were open to discussion and interested in meeting new people. People standing around the display made a number of comments to their neighbours. These included direct references to the opinions being posted on the board, what the Opinionizer was about and whether they had used it themselves.

We also noticed that different activities occurred in the different spaces of the room where the social gathering was taking place, relative to the location of the display. These were:

- Peripheral awareness activities, where people eat, drink and socialize away from the display. In general, people in these activity spaces are peripherally aware of the display's presence.
- Focal awareness activities, where people engage in socializing activities associated with the display, such as talking about, gesturing to and watching the Opinionizer being used. Here they give the display more attention and learn about it.
- Direct interaction activities, where an individual, or a group acting cooperatively, type something onto the Opinonizer display.

A further observation is that most people moved from peripheral activities to focal awareness activities before interacting with the optimizer system. This suggests to us that to entice people to use a public display in a social gathering requires them to make transitions between the different activity spaces. In particular, bystanders need, initially, to cross the *threshold* from peripheral to focal awareness activities (e.g. from chatting to someone on the other side of the room to deciding to move within view of the display to have a better look). In other words, their understanding of what the display is, and what it has to offer, has to entice them forward, to cross the *focal awareness* threshold. This is shown in the schematic diagram in figure 3-2.

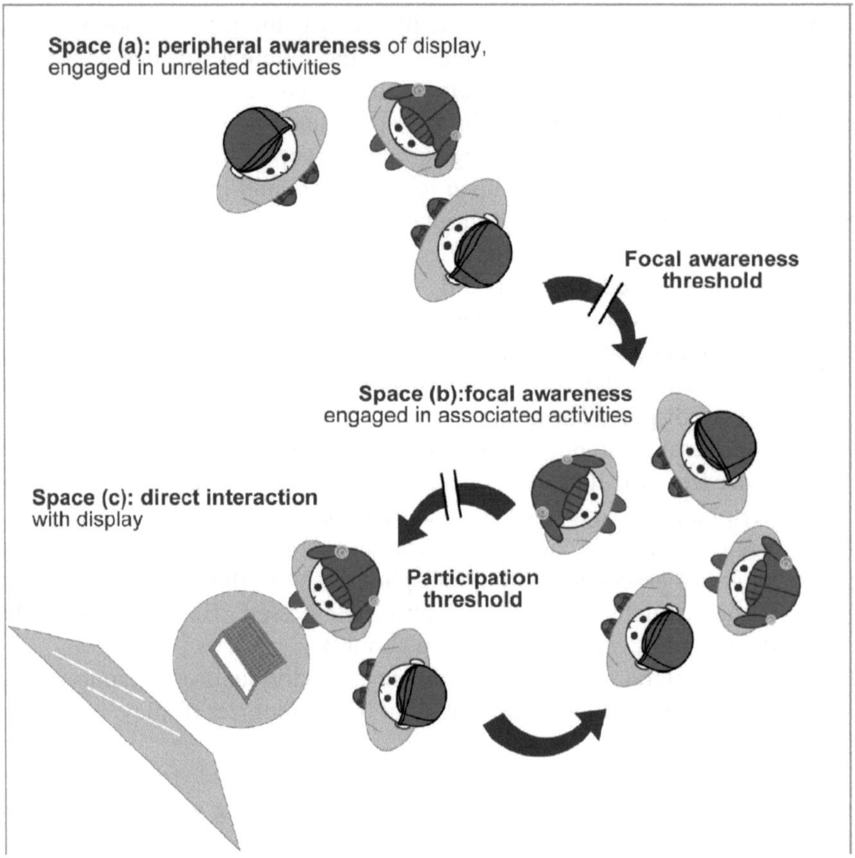

Figure 3-2. A diagram showing a model of public interaction flow across thresholds

Once participants have passed the focal awareness threshold and decided to give the display more attention, their interest needs to be further stimulated to maintain their attention. The display has to provide them with additional cues about what it has to offer, in order for them to become further motivated to cross the *participation threshold.* These cues need to reassure the person that the potential for social embarrassment is low. Key information that needs to be made readily available to someone when deciding whether to cross this threshold is how long an interaction takes; what they will get out of it; what steps are involved; will be a comfortable experience and most importantly, whether there is a quick let out, where they can walk away gracefully, without disturbing the ongoing public activity.

In sum, there is much interest in placing large interactive displays into public spaces to facilitate various forms of social interaction, including conversation initiation, casual chatting, and increased awareness of what is going on in a community. As we have discussed, such a public use of a large display puts very different demands on members of the public or a community than previous kinds of displays. Most notable is the problem of enticing them to interact with the content in a way that they feel comfortable and not socially embarrassed. In our own research, we have been exploring the transitions from being a bystander to an interactor or a member of an audience and how these can be supported.

2.2.5 Tabletop Displays

Much of the work on large displays has focused on vertical boards that are meant to be placed on walls and interacted with by people standing next to them. There has recently been an interest in building horizontal interactive displays that are embedded in tables, with the idea of supporting interactions that take place while seated (or standing). A main advantage of developing displays to be used in this orientation is that sitting or standing side by side around a desk or a table enables a collocated group of people to be closer to the information being displayed than when working around a vertical display. In addition, a table provides a surface that allows people to place their personal accessories on, like papers, books, keys and coffee cups, which they wish to use during the course of the meeting. By capitalizing on the affordances of a table this technology allows groups of people to work and meet in the ways they are more accustomed to.

Early versions of tabletop displays used camera-based recognition systems to sense people's hand and arm movements over the table surface. However, problems of occlusion and lighting means that these systems can be unreliable, making it difficult for people to see or interact with content being displayed. Other systems that also suffer from overhead projection occlusion are pen-based surfaces, such as Smartboards which have been turned on their sides. An alternative approach has been to use back projected displays, in conjunction with pen-based systems (e.g. Mimio), meaning they do not suffer from the same kind of occlusion effects.

A recent innovation is the use of touch sensitive surfaces, that use capacitive sensing to track the position of multiple user's hands. Examples include DiamondTouch (Dietz and Leigh, 2001) and SmartSkin (Rekimoto, 2002). The systems can determine which parts of the table surface are being touched and by whom. However, because they use touch-sensitive technology for recognizing input, it means that people have to be very careful when moving physical objects on the table surface. While for most of the time the systems are not affected by stationary objects placed on the table, they can find it hard sometimes to distinguish between a person's touch and an object being placed on it. This can make it difficult for people to use other artefacts on the table at the same time – which as we mentioned earlier, was one of the advantages of using an interactive horizontal surface as opposed to a vertical surface.

Recognizing the placement of specific objects on a surface, however, can also be exploited, when considering how to enhance collaborative interactions. Systems like PitA-Board (Eden *et al.*, 2002) have specifically been designed to recognize objects, like small wooden bricks, that are placed on a table. These then trigger certain digital events to occur on the table surface, augmenting the physical objects. Placing physical objects onto a surface is a very natural action to do and so easily learned. It also allows multiple people to make rapid choices about where things should be and also to easily change them – allowing alternatives to be explored easily and flexibly. Thus, when used as part of the desktop application, physical artefacts can provide highly familiar ways of manipulating digital content that provides a natural and effortless form of collaborative interaction.

A somewhat novel design for a computer-augmented table is the interactive round dining table installed in a museum of modern art in New York developed by Omojola *et al.* (2000). This piece of dining room furniture was intended to promote fluid interactions between the people sitting around it. The table was designed with eight place settings, each having an individual digital display projected from above. In the centre of the table was a round surface that users could rotate similar to those popular in Chinese restaurants (often referred to as a lazy Susan). This surface was embedded with a number of physical coasters filled with digital content. The design was intended to support social interaction and discussion about the digital content that was contained in the coasters (information about various architectural projects) through supporting fluid movement of the digital content across a physical space. The people that sat at the table could look through the architectural projects on their personal placemat and send any of interest to any of the others sat around the table, via the lazy Susan mechanism. This novel way of sharing information around a table is quite different from the shared display approach insofar as it capitalizes on using the physical surface to send specific kinds of digital content to others who are seated in different locations.

Research into tabletop display systems has focused on developing new kinds of surfaces that supports novel forms of interaction. Similar to the vertical display research, a core motivation has been to provide more direct and natural ways of interacting with the digital content being displayed, namely touching the surface and placing objects on it. How people actually collaborate around such tables is only beginning to be studied. Our own empirical studies suggest that when people have the same visual perspective of a horizontal interactive display (i.e. when they are side by side) they find it easy to coordinate their interactions at the table, taking turns and finding it easy to have the same shared point of reference (Halloran *et al.*, 2003; Rogers and Lindley, 2003). Moreover, it is noticeably more comfortable and easier for them to collaborate and communicate with each other when the display is more tightly coupled with the activity at hand. By this we mean the activity the users are involved in (e.g. editing, writing, browsing) and the information resources used (e.g. websites, files) and created (e.g. documents)

2.3 Integrated Displays

With the advent of Bluetooth, sensing technologies and wireless networking, there has been much interest in creating integrated systems of displays and devices that allow for a diversity of collocated and remote collaborations. A main motivation has been to enable people to seamlessly move information across devices and displays. For example, the PARCTAB system (Shilit *et al.*, 1993) was an attempt, prior to the commercial introduction of wireless and infrared technology, to enable information to be communicated between palm-sized, A-4 sized and whiteboard sized displays (Liveboard). Shared software tools, such as Tivoli (Pedersen *et al.*, 1993) were implemented on the system and this arrangement was intended to be used was in a closely coupled physical-social space; small groups sitting together in comfy chairs around a coffee table, collaborating with each other and remotely located people via videoconferencing on a large display and laptops on their knees.

More recent attempts at integrating displays have sought to provide novel interactions in nomadic and dispersed settings, such as outdoors. A typical set-up is to give individuals who are roaming the space a form of hand-held computer (PDA or cell phone) or a wearable device (e.g. an electronic badge) connected to a large shared display placed centrally in the space. The actions and interactions of the 'roamers' are re-represented as a global or aggregated visualisation on the shared display, providing a bird's eye view of what the individuals have been up to. One such system was CommunityMirrors (Borovoy, 1998) a project that sought to enhance socialising at a party. A large public display was used to depict a set of aggregated visualisations reflecting the ongoing dynamics of a party. The people at the party wore meme tagged badges with LED lights on that changed color depending on how the individuals wearing them had programmed their interests and how these matched up with the interests of another person's badge that they passed by.

In one of our own projects, called Ambient Wood, a playful learning experience was developed where children explore and reflect upon a physical environment that had been augmented with a medley of digital abstractions, that are accessed and presented through a variety of mobile and fixed displays and devices (Price *et al.*, 2003). One particular device the children are given is a probe tool, that enables light and moisture readings to be obtained from anywhere in the wood. Immediate feedback is provided in the form of animated visualisations, showing the relative levels of these variables on a PDA screen attached to the probe. In addition, while the children explore and probe different parts of the wood, their movements and probe readings are all tracked (using GPS). This data is then aggregated to provide a composite visualisation that is then depicted on a large shared display in a classroom setting, providing a bird's eye view of where different pairs of children have been in the wood and what data they have collected. Providing different perspectives on the physical and digital worlds, which result from the children's interactions with them, offers new ways of reflecting and integrating knowledge in a learning experience.

A more complex set of integrated displays has been used in a mixed reality gaming experience called "Can you See me Now" (Flintham *et al.*, 2003). In this game of physical-virtual chase there are two groups of players; online players who try to avoid being caught and their chasers, who physically run around the streets of a city trying to catch them. The players in the streets carry handheld displays, which show the location of the online players. The online players are logged onto a server via a web page and have access to a PC which shows a map of the streets where the 'physical' runners are. To catch the online players, the runners on the street use their handheld displays, tracking and following them as they move across the virtual map on their PC screen. In addition, they have an open-audio link to help them locate the online players. The success of the game is dependant on the ability of the runners to exploit the positional updates delivered to their handheld displays and to orient their actions based on the observations of the movement of the virtual players. Hence, the two kinds of displays used (the mobile handhelds and the stationary PCs) are critical to the coordination of the physical/virtual gaming experience.

In these playful settings, the emphasis has been to create novel, provocative and enjoyable user experiences. In so doing, a key concern has been to examine how people in these spaces reflect and make sense of the mixed-reality experiences provided for them through the integrated arrangement of devices and displays. Another approach is to look at ways of designing and deploying integrated display systems that support collaboration in existing work practices. Here, a key objective is to examine whether their introduction into a work space overcomes or reduces the problems that have been previously identified that exist in the work spaces. Hence, a primary objective in these contexts to support working practices, more effectively by exploiting novel arrangements of display-based technologies. To show how this can be achieved, we describe in the next section three novel display-based systems we designed to support three distinct working practices.

3. Developing Integrated Display Systems to Support Collaborative Work Practices

We have developed a number of integrated systems from the perspective of supporting existing work practices. We describe three of these here, showing how each was designed to enhance collaborative working through being based on a clearly identified problem space that led to a set of design requirements. The first system, called Offloader, was designed to support nomadic team working, providing team members with up-to-the minute information. The goal was to offload some of the mental effort required in figuring out where everyone is and what they are doing onto various interactive graphical representations, shown on interconnected large displays and PDAs. The second system, called eSpace, was developed to support two-party transactions by promoting shoulder-to-shoulder collaboration, through integrating representations via a multiple display console. The third system, called Dynamo, was developed to allow people at a meeting to use communal display surfaces as a virtual extension of their physical setting, enabling them to place, move, add, remove and exchange files, media and other resources in a seamless fashion.

3.1 The Offloader System: Augmenting Verbal Communication with Integrated Visual Surfaces

In this project, we were interested in providing integrated displays for nomadic team working where groups of people have to closely coordinate with each other and be constantly aware of each other's movements, whereabouts and activities. An example is a security team who has to manage and coordinate a large event (e.g. a presidential visit, a conference, a football game) by roaming a large geographical area (e.g. an airport, a convention centre, an arena) while coordinating their whereabouts and movements with each other and a central control base. For this type of work, which is geographically dispersed and often takes place in unfamiliar sites, it is rare for team members to have access to any kind of visual display. Alternatively, to keep in touch with each other and coordinate their work, the teams use public broadcast systems, (i.e. walkie-talkies) backed up by cell and landline phones. While this is an efficient way of keeping in touch, it does put a heavy burden on team members to remember the current state of affairs especially when it is very busy. Our particular interest was what kinds of visual representations could we provide to augment the existing verbal ways of keeping in touch, as a way of helping reduce the cognitive load involved.

The problem space: To understand more fully how nomadic teams keep in touch we carried out an ethnographic study of Audio Visual technicians at a conference, whose job it is to manage the technical support of such events. Our findings showed that while broadcast systems are generally robust and effective at supporting the communication and coordination needs of such nomadic teams, they do have their problems. Sometimes team members miss or mishear messages and consequently do not move to where they are needed or do what is required of the, at a given time. Other times, especially when a lot is happening, discrepancies can arise between what the different members understand of the current situation and what is actually happening. This can be very time-consuming, involving much retracing of steps.

Designing an integrated display system: From our analysis, we decided to focus on supporting team communication and coordination during critical periods of their work, where there is an increase in workload and where communication problems are more likely to occur. Our basic idea was to design an integrated set of small and large shared displays, providing different views of the same information. To this end, we considered how to offload salient aspects of transient verbal communication onto shared visualisations that could readily be accessed by all when needed. An assumption was that re-representing such transient information, as external visual traces, would enable team members to see at-a-glance, who was where and what needed doing, reducing the need for back-tracking and verbal repair work.

Our system, Offloader, was designed around the core activity of maintaining a shared list of the status of problems, i.e. what problems are happening where, who is dealing with them and how urgent they are. The integrated system was made up of two interconnected displays; a mobile 'pocket-loader' display and a fixed 'wall-loader' display. Problems and the way they are solved are represented across both pocket-loader and the wall-loader. Different kinds of information were provided on the same fixed display, enabling team members to compare existing plans of the day's events with overlaid representations of the unexpected events as they unfolded. In so doing, our goal was to enable team members to be able to integrate readily the various pieces of information needed to make rapid decisions from both types of displays.

In particular, the wall-loader was designed to be used as a large touch-screen display, with additional keyboard input, mounted on a public wall in a central location. The display is divided into three parts; (i) current plan views of the day's events displayed in the upper left corner, (ii) a topographical floor plan of the building in the lower left-side and (iii) a job status display, showing jobs as moving strips on the right side (see figure *3-3*). Information is represented on the pocket-loader PDA display as minimalist representations, in the form of text-based, to-do-lists and problem reports.

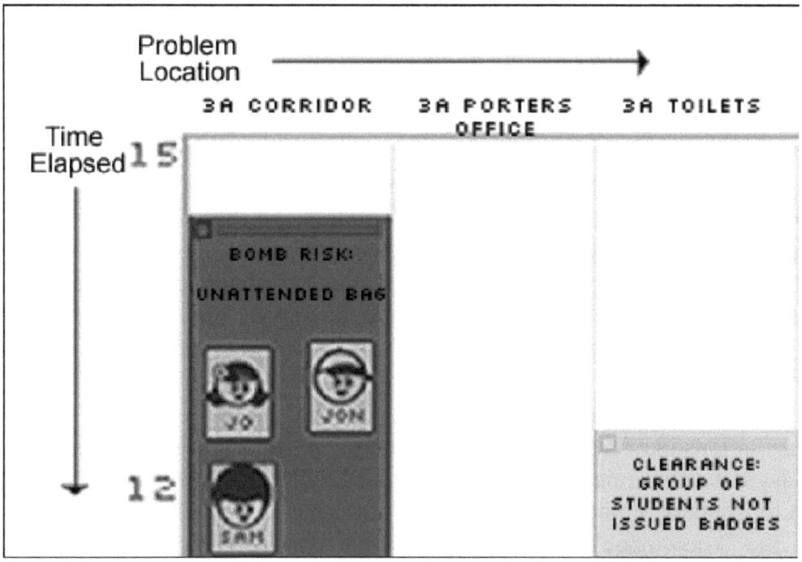

Figure 3-3. Part of the visualization used in the fixed display, showing technicians superimposed on job strips as part of a chart, with location and time elapsed as its axes.

Hence, Offloader was designed to augment existing work practices, providing the team members with an opportunity to record a visual trace of salient events. As such a key requirement was that it should be lightweight to use in conjunction with existing ways of working. Our studies of the Offloader system being used *in situ*, revealed that visually augmenting verbal communication, through providing team members with the ability to track, represent and update salient events as interactive visualizations on handheld and large fixed displays was effective (Rogers and Brignull, 2002). Specifically, it enabled participants to see at-a-glance the key parameters representing the flux of activities and team member's movements, thereby reducing the need to carry out extraneous repair work in order to find this out. In this context, providing novel integrated displays to augment an existing work practice proved to be effective and which the nomadic teams could readily see the benefit of using.

3.2 eSpace System: Supporting Two Party Transactions with Multiple Integrated Displays

eSpace is concerned with supporting more effectively two-party consultations between agents and customers, that take place in a shop setting (Rodden *et al.*, 2003; Scaife *et al.*, 2002). In these settings, the two are typically involved in working up a complex product, like a round-the-world trip, involving much planning and accessing of information. However, our studies showed that these kinds of encounter can often end up being far from satisfactory; typically, the agent sit behind their PC in control of deciding which information to access while the customer is marooned on the other side, very much a passive onlooker to the ongoing interactions with the computer. As an alternative set-up we have been exploring how to change the setting to enable more equitable access to the computer-based information, involved in building up a product. To this end, we have built a shared integrated display system that supports shoulder-to-shoulder collaboration. We have also developed a range of shared representations and interactive computational tools, that are displayed on multiple integrated displays, intended to improve the decision-making and planning that is involved.

The problem space: A problem that we identified with two-party consultations, such as between an agent and a customer, is the emergence of an asymmetrical relationship, where the consultant is very much in charge. While in many situations this may be desirable, especially if the consultant has the 'knowledge', in other situations it can be sub-optimal, where the customer is unable to participate in the consultation as much as they would like. In such dyadic settings, the consultant (e.g. the sales agent) will tend to sit behind their desk, counter or table, facing their computer. It is very much their working space, designed to support them in their work. In contrast, the customer does not have a workspace. Instead they have to enter the consultant's workspace, by either standing or sitting on the other side of their desk/table or counter (see figure 3-4(i)). An effect of this asymmetry is to make it awkward for the customer to fully engage in the conversation. Instead, after asking their initial query (e.g. "I'd like to go to Australia for a month"), they have to watch while the consultant accesses information from their computer and tries verbally to relay possibilities to them. The customer has to decide which information is important from their screen and other resources, and to determine how best to explain this to the customer. This takes a lot of cognitive effort. If there is a lot to explain or it is complex, the customer may also find it difficult to follow. Occasionally, the consultant may swivel their monitor around and show the information they currently have on their screen to the customer. However, this may not help the customer's understanding; not having any experience of how to read the decontextualised information being shown to them in this way they will often take the consultant's word and simply nod.

Hence, having control and access to the information on the computer means that the consultant tends to drive the conversation, with the customer largely being reduced to taking on a passive role, agreeing and accepting what is being said to them.

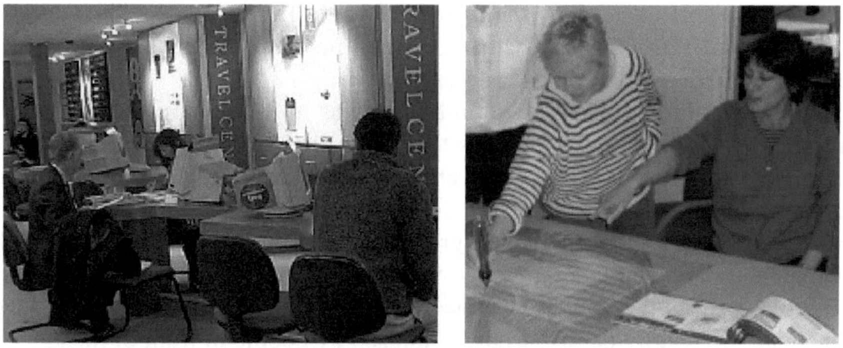

(i) (ii)

Figure 3-4. (i) Typical PC set-up between an agent and customer (ii) Working around a back projected horizontal table display, using a mimio system.

Designing an integrated display system: Our proposed solution for tackling the asymmetrical relationship between the two parties and the resources used to create a product is to consider how to re-design the workspace. In particular, we thought that if we changed the way the physical workspace was set up to allow both agent and customer to sit beside each other, then they would both have equal access to the display. We also redesigned the information presented on the computer, so that it was in a format that was readable by both and provided a novel visualisation planning tool that both could use to co-create a possible itinerary. A key concern was to provide better links between the different external representations needed for this type of planning task to allow for more effective coordination of information.

Our assumption, therefore, was that one way of improving collaborative interactions, especially joint planning, is to change the way information is displayed such that it can be more readily and equitably accessed and shared. Initially, we experimented with using a single large display, using back-projection from a data projector with a mirror arrangement under the table (see figure 3-4(ii)). The size of the table (1m x 1.5m) and the embedded screen was designed to give a space that enabled two or three people to view and work with the display in relative comfort. It was designed to allow them to sit or stand and lean on the surface. An area was also provided for placing brochures and other external resources like paper. Interaction with the display surface was pen-based, using a mimio unit.

One of the main problems we found when using this kind of tabletop display, however, was that it was too public, allowing passers-by to glance at the information being shown. Given that we planned to place our new system in a shop, it was considered that revealing a customer's potentially private information (e.g. their proposed budget and travel plans) in this way was undesirable. We also found that it was difficult to provide multiple informational resources on the same screen because of occlusion problems associated with overlapping windows.

Our solution to these two problems was to design instead multiple interlinked single monitor displays that were tiled and embedded in a table. In one of our initial designs, two were placed horizontally and a third behind these in a vertical position (see figure 3-5). The effect was to create a console display system that small groups could sit or stand in front of, each seeing and being able to interact with the information displayed on the multiple screens. A wireless mouse and wireless keyboard were provided that could be readily passed around and used by people in front of it.

Having three displays placed together in this way provides more screen estate. It also offers an effective way of physically partitioning information. This use of multiple monitors has been found to be an effective strategy by users to facilitate multi-tasking (Grudin, 2001). Here, we found it useful both for separating task-based information and showing the interdependency between different forms of representations. Displayed on the three monitors are three different kinds of information. On the left screen, a visual travel planner is provided where an itinerary can bc built up from different products (e.g. flights, hotels, excursions). On the adjacent screen, various computational visualisations are presented, showing how much of the budget has been spent together with a time-line showing the way the itinerary is being constructed (see figure 3-5 (ii)). In the third vertical screen, brochure information is presented about the products. The three forms of representation are dynamically linked, such that the effects of making certain choices in one screen (e.g. adding a hotel to the itinerary) are shown in the other screens. On the vertical display, the relevant page of information about that product is presented and on the other display the time-line and budget visualizations are updated. The two horizontal screens are interactive, so changes can be made to the travel planner or the visualisations. For example, the customer might want to change their budget or select another hotel.

When placed in a real-life setting, at a large travel trade show, we found that customers and agents readily took to the system. All manner of groupings 'dropped in' to this shared space and planned a round-the-world trip together, using the various online resources and interactive planning tools. There was much evidence of more equitable collaboration taking place, compared with the encounters we had observed of two party consultations taking place around a single PC display. A main observation of the way the two parties worked together was that both the customers and agents focused on the information in front of them while talking with each other. In so doing, the form of collaborative interactions were much less one-sided.

In sum, creating a different kind of workspace where multiple interlinked displays provided the surface for interactions to take place provides a quite different set up. In so doing, the social awkwardness that often arises when a customer enters an unfamiliar workspace, was significantly reduced – for both parties. The agent feels more at ease and is able to invite the customer to participate in the planning activity from the outset. As well as making the customers feel more comfortable, it also improves mood and rapport between the two parties as the transaction between them progresses.

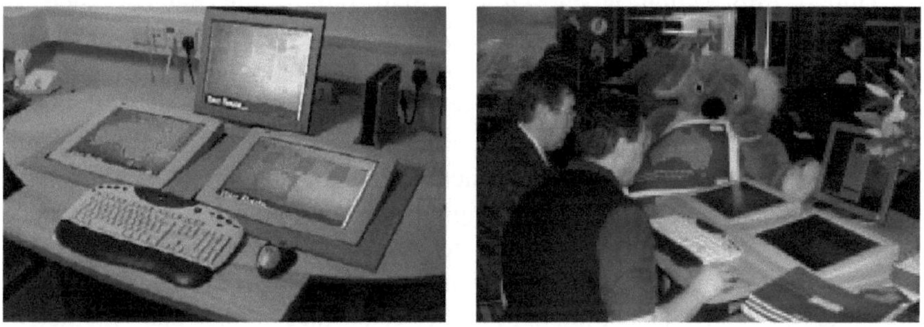

(i) (ii)

Figure 3-5. (i) The design of our physical layout of multiple screens and dyna-linked representations and (ii) system being use at a trade show

3.3 *The Dynamo System: a Public Interactive Surface Supporting the Cooperative Sharing and Exchange of Media*

The Dynamo system was designed more generally than the eSpace and Offloader systems to provide shared interaction surfaces as a communal resource in public spaces for occasional meetings. When people meet up in public spaces, like hotels, lobbies and meeting rooms, they often wish to share and exchange information with others. To achieve this currently, they carry an assortment of physical and digital artefacts, such as laptops and paper documents. The paper-based artefacts can be placed on tables, using the surface to organize items before exchanging it with others. The participants at the meeting are also able to display and share information with each other, using overhead projectors and flip charts. These highly familiar experiences of exchanging physical information via paper-based means are in contrast to the experience of exchanging information via digital media and devices. In particular, it requires moving data from one personal device to another (for example one laptop to another). Besides having to overcome technical problems of incompatibility between devices, such methods of digital exchange can restrict the exchange to the two or three people around that device, and in so doing making it difficult for others in the meeting to see what is happening.

The Dynamo system was developed to make the exchange and sharing of information, via digital media, lightweight and easy to accomplish. A digital shared surface was developed to make it easy and effortless to transfer information between desktops, laptops and other devices. The aim was to provide an experience where the overhead involved in doing this is minimal and the technology does not detract from the spontaneity of the collaborative interactions going on in the meeting.

Digital information is carried on small lightweight devices such as removable USB disks or on more powerful devices such as laptops or PDAs. The Dynamo systems supports the sharing and exchange of information via these devices, and which occurs across a display surface that all participants in the space can easily interact with. Importantly, these interactions do not require people to log onto a remote network. They can simply plug in their physical devices and bring up their digital information on the shared surface – in the same way they do using their personal computers.

To achieve this level of fluidity in collaboration required us to think about large displays as communal interactive surfaces rather than interactive whiteboards or shared drawing/editing/writing tools. Each user plugs into and subsequently interacts with the Dynamo surface through an *interaction point.* An interaction point supports a range of input devices, such as mouse, keyboard, camera, PDA, laptop, PC and MP3 player. These are classified into two broad types:

- *Base interaction points* normally consist of a wireless keyboard, mouse and USB slots for attaching media sources such as removable USB disks, digital cameras, MP3 players and web cameras.
- *Mobile interaction points* that enable laptops and PDAs to act as interaction points as each of these has the capability to provide mouse input (through stylus or touch pads) and text input (through soft or hard keyboards) and deliver media from their internal disks.

The Dynamo system is deployed with a number of base interaction points that allows users to attach a range of input devices or connect their mobile devices to the surface. Users can then drag their digital media onto the surface (e.g. videoclips, text files, digital images, powerpoint slides, MP3 files) to interact with it or make it available to others.

An example of a Dynamo surface is shown in Figure 3-6. The surface provides a multi-cursor environment with each interaction point being represented by a colour-coded telepointer. Users take control of these telepointers to interact with the surface. Associated with an interaction point is a palette. A palette consists of a number of distinct items (represented by an icon to the user) that can act as 'sources' and 'sinks' of media. For example, the files on a removable USB disk are represented as media sources. A media source can be dragged off the palette and displayed on the main surface. Similarly, the user can drop media onto a media sink item within the palette for processing. For example, dropping a PDF file on an email icon located upon the palette results in the document being emailed to that user.

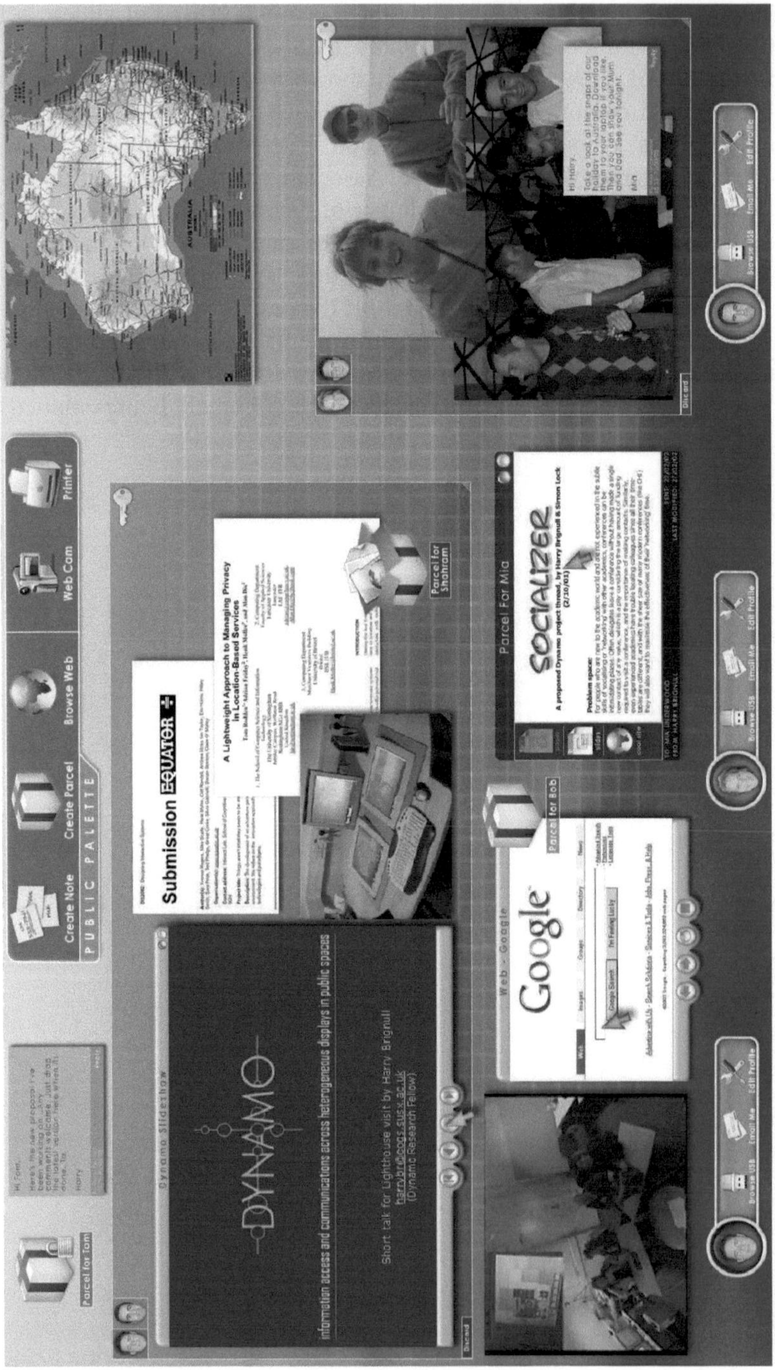

Figure 3-6. The main Dynamo interaction surface with a selection of media and palettes (located at bottom)

Having readily enabled users to place their digital media on the Dynamo surface it was necessary to then let them interact and share it in an easy and intuitive fashion. To this end, we provided various interactive mechanisms to allow users to manage the shared use of the surface. The novel metaphor of 'carving' in the communal space was used; users "carve off" part of the surface, providing them with an area that they can use to arrange and share media and which they manage access to. Users mark an area of the screen by clicking and dragging to indicate the extent of the carved space. On release, interaction with the marked portion of the overall surface is restricted to the creator of the carved off region. Figure 3-7 shows two carved regions on a portion of the surface. On the right a telepointer passing through a circle of a carved region is displayed, indicating that it cannot be interacted with. The creator of a carved region, however, can invite others into their space by dragging a key icon (located at the top right hand corner of the region) onto the palette of the desired user.

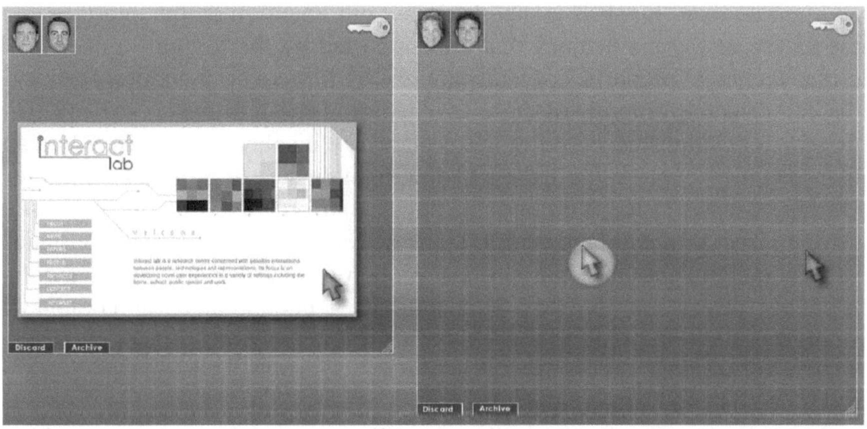

Figure 3-7. Two carved regions displayed on the Dynamo surface, one showing an instantiation of a media type (a webpage) and the other indicating it is not available to others to use

The Dynamo system has been deployed in a number of settings, including an informal workshop within a hotel conference centre and meetings where small groups are collaborating. Initial findings suggest that the Dynamo system supports the flexible and easy sharing of digital information across a shared communal surface that all can see and take part in. The use of multiple and familiar inputs (e.g. keyboards, mice etc.,) means that many of the tensions evident in the use of either gesture or remote control devices are obviated. Rather, users focus on getting onto and interacting with the surface itself by way of moving, arranging annotating and editing their digital media. In so doing, it allows the seamless sharing and exchange of digital media via an assortment of physical devices.

4. Conceptualising Displays in Terms of Configuring Spaces and Surfaces

Our research into developing shared displays for different uses has started us thinking more generally about how to conceptualize this new area of work. As an initial framing, we propose talking about it in terms of *configuring spaces and surfaces*. By a space, we mean the physical location where the display is to be situated and used, such as a work, home or social setting. By a surface, we refer to the display interfaces across which information, visualizations, and other digital representations are presented and interacted with. The reason we consider the term 'surface' to be more appropriate than 'display' is that it focuses our attention on the interface and the nature of the interactions that are supported by the design – rather than on the technical properties of a display *per se*. Moreover, by conceptualizing display research in terms of these two central aspects, it makes explicit that there is a relationship between the design of a display and its use. We can then begin to explore the nature of this relationship in a number of ways. Our approach is to focus on how the physical affordances of a display-based setting affect or encourage certain kinds of social behaviours. This provides us with insights into how the physical properties of a display can have quite profound effects on the way it is used in a collaborative or communal setting.

It goes without saying that spaces vary, depending whether they are a work, home or other one. Hence, a surface developed to support collaborative work activities will not readily transport into a home working or school working space. Each space has different attributes, as do the people who are interacting or collaborating within them. Accordingly, different kinds of surfaces will be needed that augment, support and enhance what people already do in these spaces. Hence, questions concerning the physical attributes of a display, such as the number, positioning, resolution, orientation and best mode of interaction, are best considered in terms of how a surface is to fit into an existing space. In turn, this requires understanding how an existing space is currently used and what form of perturbation will result when placing a new kind of interactive surface in it.

5. Design Issues

As the research area of situated and public displays begins to mature, it will be possible to start generalizing design guidance from the findings. Indeed, such attempts are just starting to emerge. For example, Scott *et al.* (2003) propose eight system guidelines for collocated collaborative working around a tabletop display. They suggest that the technology used in these set-ups must support:

- natural interpersonal interaction
- smooth transitions between activities
- transitions between individual and collaborative work
- transitions between tabletop collaboration and other work
- use of physical artefacts in conjunction with the tabletop
- provide shared access to physical and digital objects
- appropriate physical arrangement of users
- simultaneous user actions

The focus of these guidelines is on ensuring that people can collaborate and interact without too much overhead and disruptions when dealing with the task at hand. In our chapter, we have discussed at length how and why a number of these concerns are important. We would also argue that they can equally be applied to other arrangements of displays, for example vertical displays and integrated displays. Based on our research, we propose a further set of *design issues* that researchers and developers need to be aware of when configuring and designing surfaces for different spaces. These focus on the *uncertainties* and *tensions* that can materialize when introducing novel surfaces into existing spaces. The way in which they should be dealt with is either to reduce them, to transform them into something familiar or to make them explicit to the users, so they become aware of how to overcome them.

5.1 Uncertainty 1: Knowing What to Do

A problem that can arise when setting up new forms of shared surfaces in public, social and work places, is that people can initially feel uncertain as to what to do when entering that space. If there are a number of integrated displays and devices, they may not know where to stand or sit. This can also lead to them not knowing how to interact, or, where and what to look at on a surface. An instance of this uncertainty is the difficulty people have determining who has access and who is controlling what, when using multiple cursors on a shared surface.

One way to reduce such uncertainty is to capitalize on well-learned user-interaction behaviors that people feel socially comfortable with. For example, keyboard and mouse and pen-based entry, even though they are less direct than gesture or touch input, can provide more socially acceptable ways of interacting with information and inputting data onto a shared surface. A mistaken gesture in a public place that leads to the wrong information coming up on a display is all it takes for someone to become highly self conscious of their actions, leading to high levels of social embarrassment.

Another well known interaction design method that can be capitalized on is the provision of various forms of visual and auditory cues, that people are familiar with (e.g. use of color, highlighting, beeps), that can guide users as to know what to do next, which part of the display 'belongs' to others or that others are working on.

Constraining the location and orientation of the shared displays and devices can also makes it more obvious to participants as to how they can join in and interact with the shared information in the physical space they have entered. Designing the physical space to explicitly show people on first entering it, where to sit or stand, can also position them in relation to each other such that they have equal access to input devices and the displayed information.

5.2 Uncertainty 2: Moving Between the Physical and Digital

It is important that people can use their existing repertoire of representations and artefacts when interacting with shared displays. This includes everyday physical tools like pens and paper, communication devices, resources like notes and documents. As we saw with the new generation of tabletops that uses touch-sensitive technology, conflicts can arise in detection of touches and other noise caused by placing objects onto the surface. Making a part of the table, such as the periphery, non-sensitive is one way round this. This allows people to carry on their usual social and personal activities, like drinking coffee, making notes while also collaboratively interacting with the digital content. Enabling people to seamlessly create new physical and/or digital content (e.g. notes, diagrams, plans) while at the same time accessing digital content via a surface (e.g. web, files) and other physical artefacts (e.g. books) can also be problematic. Providing seating and physical support structures that people can move and set up themselves to meet their different needs while working can enable them to move between physical and digital displays and devices.

5.3 *Tension 1: Social and Personal Space in Front of a Display*

A tension that can emerge with situating shared surfaces in work and other spaces is the extent to which the new arrangements contravene existing norms of social acceptability, comfort and physicality. For example, in one of our empirical studies investigating the effect of orientation on interactive whiteboards (Rogers and Lindley, 2003), an observation was that people felt socially awkward having to stand in a line, side-by-side to view and interact with the information on a vertical shared display. The participants in the study said it felt like they were invading each other's personal space, while also not being able to see what other people were doing besides the person adjacent to them. Other research has also shown that vertical boards afford only one person interacting with them and that when a pair or group of people are situated around a display, one person will tend to become the driver or interactor and remain so, while the others take the role of 'audience' (Henderson and Jordan, 1995; Trimble *et al.*, Chapter 2 this volume; Russell and Sue, Chapter 1 this volume). This suggests that, if collaborative activities are being promoted around a vertical display that requires multiple interactions, then interaction techniques and the physical setting will have to be designed to overcome this social tension.

5.4 *Tension 2: Social Embarrassment in Front of a Public Display*

Overcoming the well known tension of people's reluctance to join in and make a fool of themselves in public, can be considered in terms of how best to design the transitions between private/public spaces and the thresholds between peripheral and focal activities. One technique is to provide a buffer zone for users to enter their contribution onto before it is placed on a public surface. For example, mobile input devices (e.g. cell phones, PDAs, wireless keyboards, digital cameras) can be provided that have an associated private display space, where content can be entered and edited, before being placed live on the public surface.

Other considerations are that the form of interaction must be lightweight and offer a means of graceful departure so that the participants can leave without it disrupting the ongoing collaborative activity.

6. Conclusions

We have provided an overview of the burgeoning literature on shared displays, classifying it into three main categories. The first type, 'embedded displays', covers the tranche of research that has concerned itself with developing whole new rooms or buildings, to promote quite different ways of working or socialising, The second type, 'stand-alone displays' covers the bulk of the research that has been carried out on displays, where many innovative types of surfaces have been built, supporting novel modes of interaction, The third type, 'integrated display systems' covers research that combines different kinds of displays and devices, with the purpose of providing inter-related and dynamically-linked information. These have often been developed for people who are moving around a space (as opposed to standing or sitting), supporting multiple perspectives on the information being presented.

Much of the research on situated and public displays has so far been exploratory and led by the desire to create new functions and new interaction techniques. There has been less research directly concerned with how display technologies can be designed and exploited to support new kinds of user experiences, especially those that involve collaborative interactions. There has been even less research that has focussed on the social tensions and uncertainties that emerge when creating new kinds of collaborative spaces.

Our own research agenda has been to carry out three main research strands: (i) to understand what kinds of existing and new user experiences shared surfaces can promote, augment and support; (ii) to understand the relationship between the physical, the social, and the cognitive so as to inform the design of shared surfaces that provide appropriate physical affordances that promote the desired communal, social and cognitive activities and (iii) to develop novel arrangements of displays and interaction modes

7. Acknowledgements

This research was carried out as part of the Espace and Dynamo projects, awarded jointly to us by the EPSRC. We thank our research fellows working on these two projects: Harry Brignull, John Halloran, Shahram Izadi and Ian Taylor.

8. References

Benford, S., Bederson , B., B., Åkesson, K., Bayon, V., Druin, A., Hansson, P., Hourcade, J-P., Ingram, R., Neale, H., O'Malley, C., Simsarian, K.T., and Stanton, D. Designing Storytelling Technologies to Encourage Collaboration Between Young Children. In Proceedings of the CHI '00 Conference on Human Factors in Computing Systems; 2000; Amsterdam, The Netherlands: 556-564.

Borovoy, R., Martin, F., Vemuri, S., Resnick, M., Silverman, B., Hancock, C. Meme Tags and Community Mirrors: Moving from Conferences to Collaboration. In Proceedings of CSCW '98 Conference on Computer Supported Cooperative Work; 1998; Seattle, WA, USA: 159-168.

Brignull, H. and Rogers, Y. Enticing People to Interact with Large Public Displays in Public Spaces. To appear in INTERACT'03; 2003; Zurich, September.

Chen, X. and Davis, J. LumiPoint: Multi-User Laser-Based Interaction on Large Tiled Displays, Displays, 2002; 23(5).

Dietz, P. and Leigh, D. DiamondTouch: A multiuser touch technology. In Proceedings of UIST'01; 2001; San Diego, CA, USA: 219-226.

Eden, H. Hornecker, E. and Scharff, E. Multilevel design and role play: experiences in assessing support for neighbourhood participation in design. In Proceedings. of DIS'02; 2002; London, UK: 387-392.

Elrod, S., Bruce, R., Gold, R., Goldberg, D., Halasz, F., Janssen, W., Lee, D., McCall, K., Pedersen, E., Pier, K., Tang, J. and Welch, B. Liveboard: A large interactive display supporting group meetings, presentations and remote collaboration. In Proceedings of the CHI '92 Conference on Human Factors in Computing Systems; 1992; Monterey, CA USA: 599-607.

Flintham, M., Anastasi, R., Benford, S., Hemmings, T., Crabtree, A., Greenhalgh, and Rodden, T. Where on-line meets on the streets: Experiences with mobile mixed reality games. In Proceedings CHI '03, Conference on Human Factors in Computing Systems; 2003; Ft Lauderdale, FL, USA: 569-576.

Fox, A, Johanson, B., Hanrahan, P. and Winograd, T. Integrating information appliances into an interactive workspace. IEEE Computer Graphics and Applications, 2000; 20(3): 54-65.

Greenberg, S. and Rounding, M., The Notification Collage: Posting Information to Public and Personal Displays. In Proceedings of CHI '01 Conference on Human Factors in Computing Systems, 2001; Seattle, WA, USA, 515-521.

Grudin, J. (2001) Partitioning digital worlds: focal and peripheral awareness in multiple monitor use In Proceedings of CHI '01 Conference on Human Factors in Computing Systems, 2001; Seattle, WA, USA: 458-465.

Guimbretiere, F., Stone, M. and Winograd, T. Fluid Interaction with high-resolution wall-size displays. In Proceedings of UIST'01; 2001; San Diego, CA, USA: 21-29.

Halloran, J., Rogers, Y., Rodden, T. and Taylor, I. Creating new user experiences to enhance collaboration. To appear in INTERACT'03, 2003; Zurich, Switzerland.

Hecht, S. (2001) Cited in Workspheres: Design and Contemporary Work Styles, Paoli, Antonelli (ed). The Museum of Modern Art, New York. 2002.

Johanson, B., Fox, A. and Winograd, T. The interactive workspaces project: experiences with ubiquitous computing rooms. IEEE Pervasive Computing, 2002; 1(2): 67-75.

Jordan, B. and Henderson, A. Interaction Analysis: Foundations and Practice. The Journal of the Learning Sciences, 1995; 4(1), 39-103.

Mimio Virtual Ink Corporation htttp://www.mimio.com

Mynatt, E.D., Igarashi, T., Edwards, W.K. and LaMarca, A. Flatland: New Dimensions in Office Whiteboards. In Proceedings of CHI '99 Conference on Human Factors in Computing Systems; 1999; Pittsburgh, Pennsylvania, USA: 346-353.

Nunamaker, J. F., Dennis, A. R., Valacich, J. S., Vogel, D., George, J. F. Electronic Meeting Systems to Support Group Work. Communications of. ACM, 1991; 34(7): 40-61.

O'Hara, K. and Brown, B. Designing CSCW Technologies to Support Tacit Knowledge Sharing Through Conversation Initiation Workshop on Managing Tacit Knowledge at ECSCW '01 Conference on Computer Supported Cooperative Work; 2001; Bonn, Germany.

Omojola, O. Post, E., Hancher, M., Maguire, Y., Pappu, R., Schoner, B., Russo, P., Fletcher, R. and Gershenfeld, N. An Installation of Interactive Furniture. IBM System Journal.2000; 39 (3/4): 861—879.

Pedersen, E., McCall, K., Moran, T. and Halasz F. Tivoli: an electronic whiteboard for informal workgroup meetings. Proceedings of InterCHI '93 Conference on Human Factors in Computing Systems; 1993 Amsterdam, The Netherlands: 391-398.

Price, S., Rogers, Y., Scaife, M., Stanton, D., and Neale. H. Using 'Tangibles' to Promote Novel Forms of Playful Learning. To appear in Interacting with Computers, 2003.

Rekimoto, J., SmartSkin An Infrastructure for Freehand Manipulation on Interactive Surfaces. In Proceedings of the CHI '02 Conference on Human Factors in Computing Systems; 2002; Minneapolis, MN, USA: 113-120.

Rodden, T., Rogers, Y., Halloran, J., and Taylor, I, Designing novel interactional workspaces to support face to face consultations. In Proceedings of CHI '03 Conference on Human Factors in Computing Systems; 2003; Ft Lauderdale, FL, USA: 57-64.

Rogers, Y. and Brignull, H. Subtle ice-breaking: encouraging socializing and interaction around a large public display. Workshop on Public, Community and Situated Displays. CSCW'02 Conference on Computer Supported Cooperative Work; 2002, New Orleans, LO, USA.

Rogers, Y. and Brignull. H. Computational offloading: Supporting distributed team working through visually augmenting verbal communication. In Proceedings of CogSci 2003: 25th Annual Meeting of the Cognitive Science Society, 2003; Boston, MA, USA..

Rogers, Y. and Lindley, S. Collaborating around large interactive displays: which way is best to meet? Submitted to Interacting with Computers.

Rogers, Y., Brignull, H. and Scaife, M. Designing Dynamic Interactive Visualisations to Support Collaboration and Cognition. First International Symposium on Collaborative Information Visualization Environments, IV 2002, IEEE, 39-50.

Scaife, M., Halloran, J. and Rogers, Y. Let's work together: supporting two-party collaborations with new forms of shared interactive representations. In Proceedings of COOP'02; 2002; IOS Press, The Netherlands, 123-138.

Schilit, B. Adams, N. Gold, R., Tso, M. and Want, R. The PARCTAB mobile computing system. In Proc. of Fourth Workshop on Workstation Operating Systems (WWOS-IV); 1993; IEEE, 34-39.

Scott, S.D., Grant, K.D., and Mandryk, R.L. (2003) System Guidelines for Collocated, Collaborative Work on a Tabletop Display. To appear in Proceedings. of ECSCW'03, European Conference Computer-Supported Cooperative Work; 2003; Helsinki, Finland

Smart (2003) Smart technologies http://www.smarttech.com/

Stefik, M., Foster, G., Bobrow, D.G., Kahn, K., Lanning, S. and Suchman, L. (1987) Beyond the chalkboard: computer support for collaboration and problem solving in meetings. Communications of the ACM, 1987; 30(1): 32-47.

Stewart, J., Bederson, B., and Druin, A. (1999) Single display groupware: A Model for Co-Present Collaboration. In Proceedings of CHI '99 Conference on Human Factors in Computing Systems; 1999; Pittsburgh, Pennsylvania, USA: 286-293.

Streitz, N., Tandler, P., Müller-Tomfelde, C., Konomi, S. "Roomware: Towards the Next Generation of Human-Computer Interaction based on an Integrated Design of Real and Virtual Worlds". In: *Human-Computer Interaction in the New Millennium, Carroll*, J. ed. Addison-Wesley, 2002

Chapter 4

LARGE DISPLAYS FOR KNOWLEDGE WORK

Elizabeth D. Mynatt, Elaine M. Huang, Stephen Voida, and Blair MacIntyre,
College of Computing & GVU Center, Georgia Institute of Technology

Abstract: Knowledge workers, a growing component of our modern workforce, have specialized work practices not well served by existing office technology solutions. Our research in designing office systems that better support this class of workers has included an in-depth study of traditional whiteboard use and the development of three large display systems, each addressing different aspects of and work practices involved in knowledge work. We have identified three cross-cutting themes in making these kinds of large display applications effective for supporting a variety of information management activities: context-awareness, privacy and content relevance, and informal and casual interaction techniques. In this chapter, we reflect on the ways in which each of these themes guided the design of our system prototypes and how they may inform future efforts in integrating large displays into the office environment.

Key words: computer-supported cooperative work, large displays, knowledge work, context-awareness, privacy, informal interfaces, information visualization, peripheral displays, ubiquitous computing, office computing, whiteboards, groupware

1. Introduction

Our research seeks to design office systems that better support knowledge workers, the growing number of business professionals whose job it is to interpret and transform information. Knowledge workers are individuals who "put to work what [they have] learned in systematic education, that is, concepts, ideas and theories, rather than…manual skill or muscle" (Drucker, 1973). Successful knowledge workers manage multiple tasks, collaborate effectively among several colleagues and clients, and manipulate information that is most relevant to their current task by leveraging the spatial organization of their work area (Kidd, 1994; Malone,

K. O'Hara et al. (eds.), Public and Situated Displays: Social and Interactional Aspects of Shared Display Technologies, 80–102.

1983; Mynatt, 1999). The diversity of these work practices and the complexity of implementing flexible computing tools make it difficult to meet all of these workers' needs.

Further complicating the design of systems for knowledge workers is the variety and distribution of tools and information in a modern knowledge work environment. In a typical office, workers use desktop and laptop computers, PDAs, and wired and mobile telephones. They also make use of non-electronic tools, such as filing systems, whiteboards, and desk surfaces. Sources of important work-related information are frequently distributed throughout the office environment, both within and beyond the individual office walls. Finally, colleagues often act both as additional information sources and as collaborators. It is up to the individual knowledge worker to make sense of all of these informational resources, coordinate and organize them so that higher-level abstractions emerge and the relationships among pieces of information become clear, and then act on this comprehensive understanding appropriately.

In our research, we have focused on leveraging large interactive surfaces, such as electronic whiteboards, as an effective platform for supporting spatial organization of information, task management, and collaboration. We have expanded the scope of this research over time from supporting informal manipulation of information on a whiteboard (Mynatt, Igrashi, Edwards & LaMarca, 1999, 2000), to supporting multi-tasking and background awareness with an integrated whiteboard and desktop system (MacIntyre, *et al.*, 2001; Voida, Mynatt, MacIntyre & Corso, 2002), and to enhancing awareness and asynchronous collaboration of small groups of co-workers using a shared board (Huang & Mynatt, 2003).

Some of the recurring themes that have emerged in all of these projects are the importance of context-awareness in supporting knowledge work, the necessity of addressing user concerns about content relevance and information privacy on large interactive surfaces, and the usefulness of informal interaction techniques that match the flexibility of knowledge workers' practices.

2. The Writing on the Wall: A Study of Whiteboard Use

Our initial research exploration in this area was completed at (then Xerox) PARC. This project focused on understanding the use of common office whiteboards in individual offices. Using observational data and interviews, we collected information about personal whiteboards from a diversity of participants, ranging from senior managers to visiting researchers and support personnel. Daily photographs of office whiteboards provided useful clues in understanding how whiteboard content changes on a day-to-day basis and proved incredibly useful for grounding subsequent discussions with study participants. Although whiteboard use has been studied in other settings (Abowd, 1999; Moran, *et al.*, 1996) such as meeting rooms, classrooms, and production environments, our observations (Mynatt, 1999) indicate that whiteboard use in the office differs from its use in more public spaces:

- In contrast to meeting room or production environments, office whiteboards tend to be used for a heterogeneous set of tasks in parallel.
- Whiteboard content seems to group in natural clusters or segments. These segments may correspond to different tasks, different people, or writing at different points in time.
- Personal whiteboard content in particular seems heavily context-dependent. Although an office visitor would have great difficulty interpreting a whiteboard, its owner invariably recalls a substantial amount of context when working with each cluster of content.

These characteristics underlie our model of informal whiteboard use for knowledge workers and are relevant to shared whiteboards when the content can be persistent and owned by the group.

3. Supporting Informal Whiteboard Interactions With Flatland

Our next step was to create an augmented whiteboard, called "Flatland," to better support typical whiteboard use in an individual office (Igrashi, Edwards, LaMarca & Mynatt, 2000; Mynatt, *et al.*, 1999, 2000). In our design, we extended the existing whiteboard look-and-feel with an interface that matches its role in informal office work. Using a touch-sensitive surface and projected display, our design goals were:

- To support a low threshold for initial use while making increasingly complex capabilities available. At the simplest level, Flatland should act like a normal whiteboard, so that users can walk up to it and write on it.
- To provide a look and feel appropriate for informal whiteboard tasks and distinct from production-oriented tools typically found on a desktop computer.
- To support informal whiteboard tasks such as to-do lists and sketching.
- To support clusters of content on the whiteboard. These clusters, or segments, may be created for different purposes, at different times, and by different people.
- To support the use of informal and context-dependent information. For example, content could be stored and retrieved based on its salient

context (e.g. time of creation, people present) instead of requiring a file name.

- To support the flexible management of a dynamic whiteboard space, such as freeing up white space for new input while maintaining the visibility of current content.

The conceptual building blocks in Flatland are called segments. Segments are clusters of whiteboard content that are automatically created based on grouping of input strokes, and that can be enhanced with special, task-specific behaviours, e.g. to-do lists, a calculator utility, and stroke clean-up or enhancement. The notion of segments mirrors the existing work practice of clustering like information together in blocks on the whiteboard surface, and allows for straightforward manipulation of the board's content in an intuitive manner (see Figure 4-1).

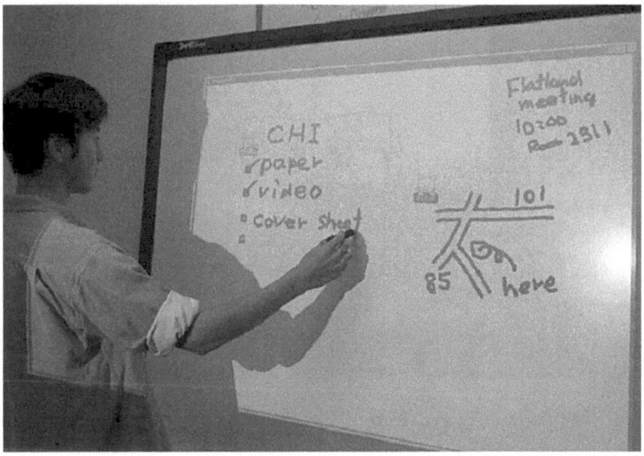

Figure 4-1. Typical use of Flatland.

Although evaluation of Flatland indicated that the system design successfully supported knowledge workers in leveraging an enhanced whiteboard, many of the subjects expressed an interest in integrating Flatland with other existing technologies such as desktop computers and PDAs. Moreover, just as traditional whiteboards are fluidly used for individual and small group tasks, Flatland also enabled informal collaboration in limited ways. However, the potential to leverage content associated with multiple people as a springboard for asynchronous collaboration and awareness remained.

4. Leveraging an Integrated Whiteboard and Desktop with Kimura

In our more recent work, we sought to augment and combine many of the common tools used by knowledge workers – desktop computers, whiteboards, and networked peripheral components – into an integrated, pervasive computing system called Kimura (MacIntyre, *et al.*, 2001; Voida, *et al.*, 2002). Moreover, we explored ways to make the content of the whiteboard context-aware to support individual and collaborative work.

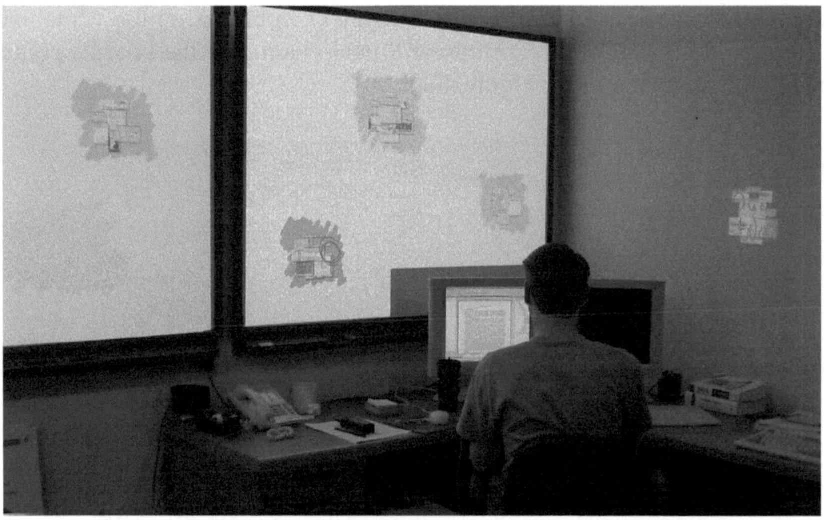

Figure 4-2. The Kimura system in an office environment, including the monitor and peripheral displays.

Kimura separates the user's computer desktop into two regions: a focal region, displayed on the desktop monitor; and one or more peripheral displays, projected nearby on the office walls. Each of the user's work activities are associated with a unique virtual desktop that is displayed on the monitor while the user is engaged in the activity. Background activities are projected as visual montages on the peripheral displays, implemented here as an electronic whiteboard (Figure 4-2). The peripheral display allows users to monitor each ongoing work activity, transition smoothly between activities, access a wide variety of contextual information, and maintain awareness about relevant activity changes. The interactivity provided by the electronic whiteboard surface allows the user to informally annotate and spatially organize the visual montages.

From Kimura's point of view, a work activity—such as managing a project, participating in a conference, or teaching a class—is modeled as a cluster of documents and a collection of cues representing ongoing interactions with people and objects related to that activity. We refer to this cluster as the activity's *working context*. Each working context may have numerous documents—including text files, Web pages, and other application files. A working context may also include indications of ongoing activity, such as email messages without replies and outstanding print jobs. Kimura automatically tracks the contents of each working context and tags documents based on their relative importance. As in previous systems, such as Rooms (Henderson & Card, 1986), users define the boundaries of working contexts manually—in our case, by creating virtual desktops. We chose this strategy because these operations are easy for the user to perform and can be easily monitored to detect working-context changes, and because this strategy avoids relying on the system to infer these transitions.

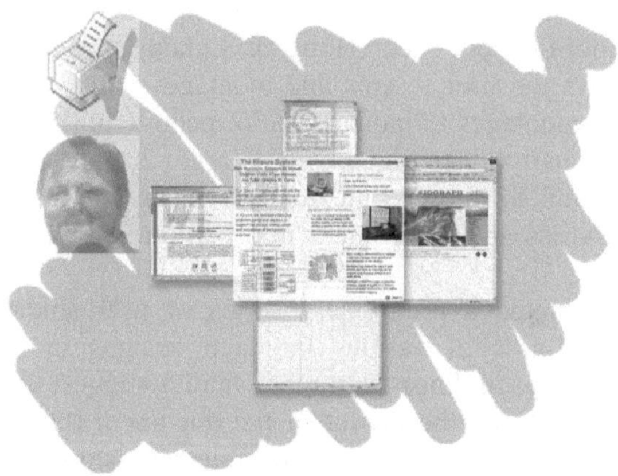

Figure 4-3. A montage of a working context, including a number of application windows and two external context notification cues, representing both virtual- (completion of a print job) and physical-context information (the availability of a colleague).

Each working context is displayed as a *montage* of images garnered from system activity logs (Figure 4-3). These montages are analogous to the "room overviews" provided by other multi-context window managers. But where these systems show the exact layout of the windows in each room, our goal is to provide visualizations of past activity in context. These visualizations are designed to help remind the user of past actions; the arrangement and transparency of the component images automatically create an "icon" for the working context. Additionally, montages can serve as anchors for the background awareness information that is gleaned from our context-aware infrastructure.

The montage design is intended to relieve the user of some of the cognitive load associated with remembering a large amount of information—information about each work activity and its related contextual information—and with synthesizing that information on the fly from a potentially overwhelming number of sources. Furthermore, they are designed to present this information without intruding on the user's focal activity and in a manner that specifically supports the needs of knowledge workers. Future work in this area can and should include further iterations on these kinds of work activity visualizations based on usability evaluation.

As in Flatland, Kimura's electronic whiteboard—the primary display surface for the montage visualizations—supports common whiteboard practices (Mynatt, 1999). This surface is also well-suited to supporting informal information management activities. Our system implementation incorporates existing electronic whiteboard interaction techniques with montages and notification cues (Hong & Landay, 2000; Mynatt, *et al.*, 1999). This allows the user to annotate montages with informal reminders and to reposition montages to indicate the respective priority of background activities. Additionally, the whiteboard's large display area is an ideal, unobtrusive location to show contextually relevant information about the user's work activities and the context information sensed from around the office.

We have completed a preliminary series of user studies designed to evaluate the usefulness of various montage designs in supporting task resumption. The initial findings from these studies suggest that there may be some correlation between the layout of the document thumbnails within a montage and the ability of users to resume a postponed work activity represented by the montage. We have also run a number of psychophysics experiments to determine if a relationship exists between the speed of changes in the peripheral display and humans' ability to detect those changes when involved with a demanding focal task; analysis of the results of these experiments are forthcoming.

5. Supporting Collaboration with Semi-Public Displays

In addition to the use of large interactive displays to support the information needs of individual knowledge workers, we have also been exploring the use of these surfaces to support awareness and collaboration among group members collocated within a shared space. Like the Kimura system, the Semi-Public Displays project (Huang & Mynatt, 2003) aims to help users integrate and manage information from a wide range of sources; the primary goal of the system is to help group members maintain an informal work/social awareness of each other's activities by taking advantage of the various affordances of persistent, group viewable displays. The system aims to provide some of the properties or group viewing that public displays afford, but in the context of a shared space available only to individuals within a tightly-knit group. Therefore, while the information on the display is available to members of the collocated group, it is generally unavailable to passerby or people who are not members of the workgroup. As these displays are neither truly public in their availability, but are still group viewable within a set of people, we have termed them "Semi-Public."

Small group settings are often already equipped with the means to display information, such as projection displays, electronic whiteboards, or large monitors, but these tend to be used only in certain circumstances, such as during a meeting or a presentation. Our aim is to take advantage of these resources by using them as persistent sources of group information and shared workspace. However, determining what content and interactions are most effective for these large displays still remains a challenge.

The members of a collocated lab are likely to be highly aware of each other's activities; even so, we have identified several benefits that shared interactive displays can offer in a small group setting. By making certain types of relevant information persistent in the environment, these displays can provide information about group members, and foster coordination and collaboration. We have found them to be a potentially effective medium for making information from other channels persistent in the environment, thus making information easily available and reducing the need for group members to remember or retrieve it from overloaded channels, such as email.

Based on observations of practices for maintaining awareness and collaborating, we identified potential content for the system, limitations of current methods for sharing this information, and then sought to adapt this content to be effective and appropriate on a large shared display. In exploring the current methods the lab members used to maintain awareness of each other, we found they used information distributed across several methods and tools. In designing the system, we also aimed to provide users with a display on which they could have easy access to this type of information all at once.

The use of Semi-Public Displays supports a heightened awareness of group interests and activities by making information persistently visible in the environment. Additionally, the group viewable properties of the displays promote the use of the board not just as an information source, but as a catalyst for face-to-face collaboration and interaction as well.

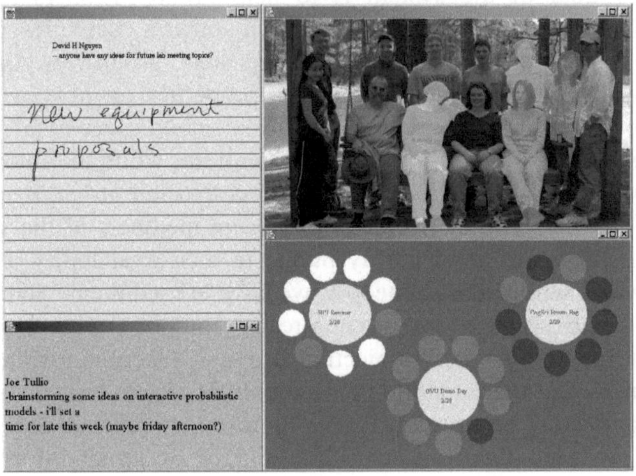

Figure 4-4. The Semi-Public Display prototype. Clockwise from top left: (a) Collaboration Space, (b) Active Portrait, (c) Attendance Panel, and (d) Reminders.

Our first design of a Semi-Public Display (Huang & Mynatt, 2003) aims to compensate for overloaded individual communication channels and to provide desired awareness information via four applications (Figure 4-4):

- Reminders: a slideshow-style application to display help requests and reminders that have been extracted from group members' weekly status reports, in order to provide constant access to the information in the environment.
- Collaboration Space: an interactive application that cycles through lab members' requests for assistance or brainstorming and allows lab members to create and edit ink annotations.
- Active Portrait: an abstract representation of group activity, consisting of a group photograph of the lab members in which each group member's image fades slowly over time when he or she leaves the lab.
- Attendance Panel: an application that provides lightweight group awareness through flower-like representations of upcoming events and the group members' intended attendance of those events.

6. Recurring Themes in Large Display Design for Knowledge Work

Although our research has focused on understanding and supporting many varied information activities, we have identified some common cross-cutting themes in making large display applications effective for supporting all of these activities. Among these themes is context-awareness, which allows interfaces to provide richer and more useful information. Additionally, we have also sought to tailor information to be appropriate for its audience through the maintenance of information privacy and the emphasis on content relevance. Finally, the design of large displays need to match their mixed roles of primary and peripheral display and the need for informal and casual interaction.

6.1 Context-awareness

Several researchers have recommended integrating physical and virtual context to provide a better understanding of user activity in future pervasive computing environments (Dey, Abowd & Salber, 2001; Edwards, 1995). However, an overwhelming amount of the actual work in context-aware computing has focused exclusively on collecting and applying physical information—specifically location—in a variety of applications (Dey, *et al.*). Likewise, intelligent user interface community members have often used virtual context to tailor user interfaces and information presentation to match the user's activity or abilities (Maes, 1994), but rarely is physical context-awareness integrated into these systems. Some projects might be considered to have focused on integrating physical and virtual context to a limited extent (Maes, 1994; Tang, *et al.*, 2001; Horvitz, Jacobs & Hovel, 1999) but none, to the best of our knowledge, extend beyond the bounds of a single application.

In Flatland, we explored the utility of context-awareness as the primary means for storing and retrieving whiteboard content. The notion of "un-filable" content typical of knowledge workers is strongly evident in typical whiteboard content. Requiring users to name, organize, and store this content runs against these flexible work practices. In Flatland, all material is automatically stored with a series of context tags, including virtual context information such as when each segment was created, when it was last edited, and what behaviours and colors were used. Additionally, if possible, physical context information is also stored when changes are made, such as what people were in the room at the time. Users can then search for past segments either by submitting context descriptions (e.g. a map created during the last month) or by searching backwards in time with a timeline scrollbar.

Table 4-1. The kinds of virtual- and physical-context information the Kimura system collects, the effect each has on the montages' appearance, and the specific user goals each supports.

Context description	Context type	Effect in task representation (montage)	Work. practice supported
User interaction with windows on a desktop computer	Virtual	Presence, size, and opacity of window images	Multitasking, task awareness
Email messages	Virtual	Colleague availability notification cue	Collaboration
Documents printed by the user	Virtual	Peripheral notification cue	Task awareness
User interaction with Kimura on the electronic whiteboard	Virtual	Size and (initial) location of montage on electronic whiteboard	Multitasking, task awareness
Location (availability) of the user's colleagues	Physical	Colleague availability notification cue	Collaboration
Presence of multiple individuals in the user's office	Physical	Presence, size, and opacity of montages on electronic whiteboard	Collaboration
User's presence at or near peripheral devices	Physical	Peripheral notification cue	Task awareness
User's presence and physical activity at the computer (mouse and keyboard use, conductive paint, eye gaze tracking)	Physical	Rate of peripheral display change, intensity of alert notifications	Task awareness

The Kimura system is designed as a series of distributed components that fall into three classes: context acquisition, context interpretation, and user interaction. As the system acquires context information, it posts it to an activity database. Then, the context interpreter transforms the raw activity data into one or more working contexts and augments these working contexts with relevant cues about how other events in the office environment relate to them (see Table 4-1). Finally, user interaction components running on the whiteboard and the desktop computer display different visualizations of the working contexts. The user can manipulate (and, in the case of the whiteboard, annotate) those representations. The user interaction components on both the desktop and electronic whiteboard displays also act as an interface to a virtual window manager system.

Kimura's context acquisition components capture a wide variety of information garnered from sensors placed throughout the office and from virtual-context sources, such as keystroke and mouse monitoring utilities and mail and Internet use proxies. This integration of context information is an important contribution because the research in context-awareness focuses so heavily—and often, exclusively—on applying the use of physical-location data. A concerted effort is made to capture the user's activity while they run software applications, use documents and networked electronic information, and interact with peripheral devices distributed throughout the office environment.

The Kimura system uses the context information it collects in two ways. First, it creates a high-level framework of working contexts based on the user's activity, within which other virtual- and physical-context information is classified and interpreted. Second, it produces interactive visualizations of the user's working contexts. The system's context interpreter constantly updates the framework and the montage visualizations based on the stream of virtual and physical context captured by the context acquisition components.

The Semi-Public Displays leverage context in much the same way as the notification cues do in the Kimura system. Keystroke and mouse-movement monitors are installed on computers throughout the collocated group's work area to estimate the activity of each group member. This virtual context information is translated into a visualization supporting social awareness in the Active Portrait component. The use of keystroke and mouse-movement provides an inexact approximation of presence information, as it is conceivable that group members are present but not active at their computers. The Active Portrait application therefore provides viewers with approximate data about the presence of their colleagues, while the potential for ambiguity offers plausible deniability and privacy about the specifics of activity to individuals.

6.2 Privacy and Content Relevance

Large displays for groups can often suffer for lack of content that is relevant to its audience, that can be automatically gathered or easily authored, and that is appropriate given differing privacy concerns.

We have analyzed many of the existing and past projects that address awareness among people and have found that they can be meaningfully subdivided along two dimensions (Figure 4-5). First, awareness applications can be categorized by the type of audience they are intended to support.

Applications have been built to facilitate awareness between pairs of people, as well as among groups of people. Applications that support groups typically target different types of groups such as a workgroup of five people, or a company of a hundred. Applications typically are intended to support only one of these audiences—pairs, small groups, or large groups.

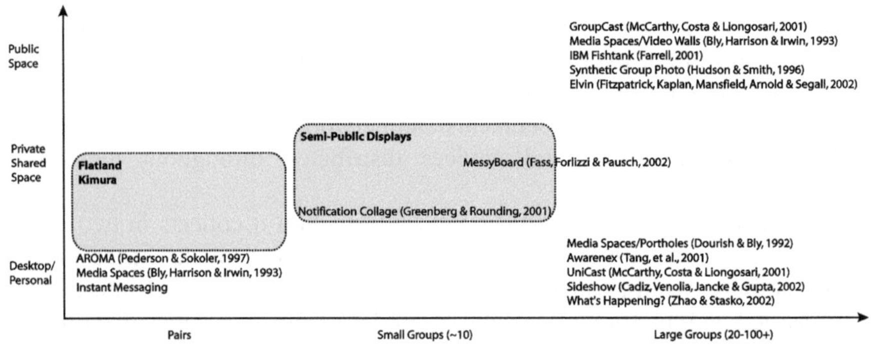

Figure 4-5. An illustration of the current design space of awareness applications categorized by the group size they are designed to support and the type of space in which they are meant to be viewed. Flatland and Kimura explore the space of shared public and personal displays to support very small groups, illustrated by the box on the left. Semi-Public Displays addresses the space of shared public displays to support small, collocated groups, delineated by the box in the center.

Additionally, we have examined the environments in which the applications are intended to be viewed and used. Applications typically reside on the desktop or other individually viewed display such as a PDA, within a shared private space such as an office or lab, or within a public space, such as the kitchen or lounge area of a building.

Looking at the space, we can see that much of the work on awareness applications falls into three areas: applications for pairs on desktop or individual displays, applications for large groups on desktop or individual displays, and applications for large groups in public spaces.

The success of these applications is primarily dependent on two issues: the ability of the application to provide *relevant content*, and the extent to which the application addresses *privacy* concerns.

Applications deployed in public spaces intended for supporting large groups that provide low levels of general awareness have been most effective. Displays that indicate the presence or absence of group members (Farrell, 2001) or video walls that allow for opportunistic conversations (Jancke, Venolia, Grudin, Cadiz & Gupta, 2001) aim to provide low-level or general information awareness. These types of applications have usually been successful in fostering low-level awareness because the lack of information specificity combined with the generality of audience to which the information is targeted mitigate some of the challenges of personal privacy and information relevance.

Applications intended for large groups that attempt to provide higher levels of awareness by providing more detailed information about individuals often face difficulties because of privacy concerns. It is difficult to make personal details available to large groups without impinging upon individuals' privacy. Because of the tradeoff between privacy and depth of awareness, the applications that have been most successful and useful for large groups have been those that provide less information. Another challenge for presenting detailed awareness information to large groups lies in the relevance of the information to its audience.

Because it is unlikely that detailed information will be of general interest and relevance to all members of a large group, rather than a subset of that group, it is difficult to provide appropriate content for these systems. A further challenge is presented when such systems rely on the users to supply content explicitly. Because the information an individual can provide about herself and her activities and interests is unlikely to be of interest to the large group in general, individuals tend not to be motivated to supply content, or else have difficulty identifying appropriate content. As a result, systems for promoting awareness among large groups that rely on user-submitted content tend to be uninformative because of a paucity of content, and because the content is not of interest to much of its audience (McCarthy, Costa & Liongosari, 2001; Tang, *et al.*, 2001).

Desktop displays of applications for large group awareness exacerbate privacy concerns because it is difficult to assess who is looking at what information and how often. In contrast, public displays that exist in a shared social space that bring with them shared social mores and mechanisms for preventing abuse. Moreover, desktop interfaces for pairwise connections have the opposite effect. The privacy garnered by the personal display supports the depth and details appropriate for disclosure by a pair of users. Flatland and Kimura were designed to take advantage of this region of the design space, since their deployment was intended for individual offices – environments which exhibit characteristics of both desktop and private shared space displays, but have limited access, which is typically controlled by the display's owner.

In Kimura, we rely on the techniques underlying ambient and peripheral displays (e.g., the ambientROOM, Ishii & Ullmer, 1997) to determine what content to display on the electronic whiteboard and how to display that content to mitigate privacy issues. Our montages consist of thumbnail-style images of the user's actual work, which have been manipulated to provide a quasi-summary of past activity. These montage styles are reminiscent of the "piles" (Mander, Salomon & Wong, 1992) that conveyed the age and type of items in desktop folders. However, due to the small size and limited resolution of the montages' component images, the content is largely undecipherable to an office guest who is unfamiliar with the details of the work that the montages represent. Like other ambient displays, the montages provide meaningful information to the initiated, but much less so to a casual observer.

Because of such privacy concerns, for example, it makes little sense to design for some unexplored areas of the audience-environment design space. If the intention of a system is to increase pairwise awareness between people, using a display in a public space is unlikely to be a good choice to support that goal.

However, not all areas with potential for design have been explored in depth. We posit that the space of applications for small groups supported by displays in shared group space has been largely unexplored. Designing applications for this space is an important area of research for several reasons. First, detailed information about individuals is more likely to be of relevance to the group as a whole. It is easier to identify and present content that is going to be both informative and appropriate to its audience. Additionally, whereas the presentation of personal information to a large group may intrude upon an individual's privacy, such information may be more appropriate among a group of collocated co-workers, who are likely to share context and have more personal knowledge of each other. Finally, because the need for communication and collaboration within small groups is often greater than that of large, distributed groups, it may be more important for individuals in a small group to have access to information about their co-workers. The small group audience may benefit more from having access to awareness applications and their content than the larger groups for which most applications have been designed.

The shared public display setting also matches the privacy and collaboration needs of small groups. The use of the display can be integrated into the practices and social customs of the group. The shared space encourages collaboration, especially semi-asynchronous collaboration, without competing for valuable desktop real estate.

The Semi-Public Displays application that we use to display an abstract representation of group activity consists of a group photograph of the lab members (Figure 4-4b). In this "active portrait," each person's image is displayed in full color if he or she is present in the lab. A person's image fades slowly over time when he or she leaves the lab. The resulting composite image provides viewers with a quick, at-a-glance picture of colleagues' recent presence in the lab. It allows the viewer to have some context about lab activity, especially when she has just entered the space. Unlike tools such as shared calendars or in-out boards, however, the image does not provide specific information about the exact times when a person left or entered the space, or a person's current whereabouts.

Our design provides low-fidelity presence information to give an overall picture of group presence, unlike instant messenger status, which gives high-fidelity information about presence, usually accurate to within minutes. Like instant messenger status cues, our design also monitors keyboard activity on desktop machines to measure idle time. However, rather than conveying information such as "Beth has been away from her computer for 7 minutes," the Active Portrait allows users to make inferences such as "The lab has been mostly empty for the weekend" or "Most people seem to be around this morning."

The application that we use to provide lightweight group awareness is the Attendance Panel (Figure 4-4c) on the Semi-Public Display, which uses a flower metaphor to provide an aesthetically attractive and easily interpretable abstract visualization to provide information about group members' upcoming plans. The panel displays several "flowers," which consist of a large circle with an event title as a label, surrounded by a ring of smaller circles. Each flower is a representation of an upcoming event, such as a seminar or a talk. The center circle represents the event description; the smaller circles, or "petals," represent users. Each petal has three states: blue for "not planning on attending," bright pink for "planning on attending," and white for "haven't decided yet." When a new event is added to the panel, it creates a flower whose petals are all white on a blue background, signifying that no one has yet updated his or her status. If a user elects not to attend the event, he toggles one of the petals to the "not attending" state, which is a slightly darker blue than the background, therefore blending with it. If a user chooses to attend the event, she toggles a petal to the "attending" state, which is a bright pink, contrasting significantly with the background. Users are free to select any petal that has not already been taken; they are not bound to any particular position on the flower. Their identities, therefore, cannot be discerned by the position of the petal on the flower, thus protecting their privacy.

The colors of the states create a visual image that brings the petals in the attending state to the foreground, while camouflaging the petals in the not attending state. A viewer can easily discern what events are of importance or interest to the group, or of potential relevance to her, by noticing how "complete" the flowers are. This simple interaction and visualization allows users to view planned attendance at near future activities, without compromising group members' privacy.

6.3 *Display Design and Interaction Techniques*

There has been substantial research in developing adequate interaction techniques for augmented whiteboards in conference room settings, including Tivoli (Moran, *et al.*, 1996) and i-LAND (Streitz, *et al.*, 1999). Some of the interaction techniques presented as a result of these projects – for example, the ability to "throw" content from one side of the board to the other in i-LAND – are clearly applicable for our projects, and many other large surface interactions. In general, our systems, like these conference room whiteboards, require informal interaction techniques to provide a fluid match between work practices and the interaction medium.

However, the unique work practices exhibited by knowledge workers and the specific environments that our projects are designed for lend themselves to additional kinds of informal interactions not well addressed by previous work. The whiteboard surfaces often serve as persistent displays of information in the work environment and thus incur additional requirements regarding information structure, readability, and privacy. Also, because these whiteboards often function as peripheral displays, various visualization techniques are needed so that the interface is appropriately obtrusive.

Our explorations into informal interaction techniques began in Flatland, where we designed and implemented a few behaviours to support typical office whiteboard tasks. Flatland's design goals of simple, informal interaction extend past the general look-and-feel of the interface into the design of individual behaviours themselves. Since the purpose of the behaviours is to support informal, preproduction tasks, we strongly favored ease of use over providing features for producing a detailed artifact. Common themes in designing individual behaviours were:

- Few explicit commands exist; strokes are interpreted on-the-fly.
- Generated output is rendered in a "hand-drawn" style.
- Minimal (if any) control widgets are added to the segment.
- "Infinite" undo-redo supports easy error recovery.
- Handwriting recognition is generally not used, to limit the need for error correction and recovery. The one exception was the calculator behaviour, which favors handwriting in lieu of push buttons.

This final design choice limits some potential uses of the system, but significantly simplifies user interaction.

The difference between behaviours and traditional applications becomes more apparent when combining multiple behaviours over time. For example, starting first with the map behaviour, a user can sketch out relevant streets and intersections. After removing the map behaviour and applying the 2D drawing behaviour, the user can sketch relevant buildings and other landmarks. Finally, with no behaviours present, the user can label the map.

Kimura was designed to compliment Flatland's interface. Each of the montages displayed on the electronic whiteboard is essentially a Flatland segment with a special rendering behaviour that creates a visualization of one working context on the desktop computer. Montages can be manipulated in many obvious ways on the wall display: they can be moved, deleted and so on using simple gestures. Montages also respond in many of the same ways as hand-drawn segments do in Flatland. For example, montages adjust their size to fit their contents, particularly user annotations, and they "push" neighboring montages when moved to prevent segments on the wall display from overlapping. Currently, the behaviours connected to montages are *moving* when selected, and *annotating* when de-selected.

We present two primary day-to-day uses for Kimura's large interactive display surface. First, and most importantly, users can use the wall display as a peripheral interface for keeping track of the existence of, and changes in, background activities. Second, users directly manipulate the montage images, in conjunction with other whiteboard tasks, while standing at the wall display.

Tapping a selected montage triggers a task switch, an operation that can also be performed from the desktop computer. The contents of the past activity disappear from the desktop and reappear as a montage on the wall display. Simultaneously, the contents of the new task appear on the desktop. The montage for the current task is also displayed near the desktop monitors. This "near-periphery" display allows the user to remain aware of contextual cues, such as a past browsing activity, that are no longer part of the active desktop, as well as the annotations that the user may have made to the montage on the electronic whiteboard. Montages retain their position on the wall display so that a background task will return to its prior location unless the user explicitly rearranges the montages.

Annotating montages is an example of an interaction that is particularly well-suited to the wall display: using the dry pens of various colors provided with the SMART Boards, the user may annotate montages with simple electronic ink.

In keeping with the Flatland design guidelines, and in order to suggest that the information on the wall display is peripheral to the user's active working context, we have tried to create an informal look for the montages. Montages are shown with sketchy backgrounds in soft colors using a separate color for each montage (see Figure 4-3).

The Semi-Public Display project also required the development of informal interaction techniques, although the goals for these techniques differ somewhat from those underlying the Flatland and Kimura projects. Because the Semi-Public Display is designed for a shared, group setting, its interactions must be lightweight enough to encourage casual, walk-up use, and be comprised of observable, easy-to-learn actions so that a novice user is not intimidated by a steep learning curve.

By creating a Collaboration Space component on the Semi-Public Display, our aim was to provide a dynamic, captured space that was clearly designated as editable and viewable by anyone at anytime (Figure 4-4a). Using help requests extracted from the group members' weekly status reports, the Collaboration Space cycles through each request, displays each one for several minutes at a time, and provides a space in which users can create and edit ideas. Users add content using freeform ink and a variety of common gestures provided by the SATIN toolkit (Hong & Landay, 2000). The annotations affiliated with each item are captured and redisplayed every time the item is shown. Unlike conventional whiteboards, whose content group members are often wary of erasing, editing, or adding to outside of brainstorming sessions, our design keeps the request visible and provides an explicit space for brainstorming and scribbling at all times.

Similarly, the Attendance Panel allows users to view other group members' intended participation in an upcoming event, and to add their own preferences with a minimum amount of additional effort. Because the center of each "flower" and its petals are displayed on a touch-sensitive surface, users do not need to interact with the board using additional technology or specialized implements – they simply touch the portion of the board with which they want to interact. Furthermore, the fact that individual users are not permanently associated with any particular "petal" means that users can simply pick any uncolored petal to encode with their planned activity attendance. Based on our informal observations, a user could approach the board and provide their attendance intentions for three to four upcoming activities in a matter of seconds. This low-effort interaction helped to foster use of the Attendance Panel, which increased the informational value of the Semi-Public Display as a group resource.

7. Conclusion

In this chapter, we have provided glimpses of the future for large interactive displays and, in particular, their utility for knowledge workers.

The use of large interactive displays follows a similar historical path as the use of previous computing technologies. Due to their expense, the deployment of early large interactive displays was limited to formal situations and required the use of specialized applications and expert system operators. In the past decade, these displays have seen more widespread deployment in specific environments – most commonly, meeting rooms – and, while typically controlled by a technical expert, offer novice users the opportunity to explore the use of these displays with general-purpose software. We are now at the point where these large interactive displays are becoming commonplace and will materialize as a general resource for individuals and informal groups.

This shift to commonplace use requires new software infrastructures and user interface techniques to make large interactive displays a useful office tool. This need is particularly evident when we investigate the work practices of knowledge workers. When large interactive displays become a fixture in these workers' office environments, they must complement the informal, flexible and improvisational practices of knowledge workers, in contrast to forcing the workers to shape their practices around the use of a specialized tool. One distinction is the shift to providing persistent information on large displays, in contrast to their common use as a typically blank display harnessed for focused interactions. By using these displays as a persistent source of information, the content on the display becomes an additional resource for manipulating information. Additionally, the interaction with these displays needs to exhibit informality to meet the flexibility of knowledge work and mirror the transient nature of information more likely to be modified than filed. Finally, this resource must become part of a distributed network of information sources. It can no longer serve as a stand-alone technology. By leveraging a context-aware infrastructure, the content displayed on the board can provide additional benefit by lowering the burden of retrieving information and supporting awareness.

Similar benefits accrue to groups of knowledge workers. As a persistent source of information, large interactive displays are an excellent resource for coordination, information sharing and awareness. However, these displays face a variety of challenges in providing benefit to a group while avoiding pitfalls of requiring too much effort to use or breaching privacy concerns.

Acknowledgements

This work was completed under NSF IIS grant 99-88712, and with additional support from IBM Research, the Sloan Foundation and Ricoh Innovations. We would like to thank the individuals who participated in our numerous studies, and Dr. Gregory Corso and the members of the Everyday Computing lab for their patience and feedback. Thank you to Jaroslav Tyman for his valuable assistance in the development of the prototypes. We would also like to recognize the valuable comments provided by the organizers and participants of the Large and Situated Displays workshop at CSCW 2002. Thanks to Amy Voida and the book editors for reviews of earlier versions of this chapter.

References

Abowd, G.D. Classroom 2000: An experiment with the instrumentation of a living educational environment. IBM Systems Journal, 1999; 38(4): 508–530.

Bly, S.A., Harrison, S.R., & Irwin, S. Media spaces: Bringing people together in a video, audio, and computing environment. Communications of the ACM, 1993; 36(1): 28–46.

Cadiz, J.J., Venolia, G., Jancke, G., & Gupta, A. Designing and deploying an information awareness interface. Proceedings of the CSCW '02 Conference on Computer Supported Collaborative Work; 2002; New Orleans, LO USA. New York: ACM Press: 314–323.

Dey, A.K, Abowd, G.D., & Salber, D. A conceptual framework and a toolkit for supporting the rapid prototyping of context-aware applications. Human-Computer Interaction 2001; 16: 97–166.

Dourish, P., & Bly, S. Portholes: Supporting awareness in a distributed work group. Proceedings of the CHI '92 Conference on Human Factors in Computing Systems; 1992; Monterey, CA USA. New York: ACM Press: 541–547.

Drucker, P.F. *Management tasks, responsibilities, and practices.* New York: Harper & Row, 1973.

Edwards, W.K. *Coordination infrastructure in collaborative systems.* Unpublished doctoral dissertation, Georgia Institute of Technology, Atlanta, 1995.

Farrell, S. Social and informational proxies in a fishtank. In Extended Abstracts of CHI '01 Conference on Human Factors in Computing Systems; 2001; Seattle, WA USA. New York: ACM Press: 365–366.

Fass, A.M., Forlizzi, J. & Pausch, R. MessyDesk and MessyBoard: Two designs inspired by the goal of improving human memory. Proceedings of DIS '02 Conference on Designing Interactive Systems: processes, practices, methods, and techniques; 2002; London, UK. New York: ACM Press: 303-311.

Fitzpatrick, G., Kaplan, S. Mansfield, T., Arnold D., & Segall B. Supporting public availability and accessibility with Elvin: Experiences and reflections. Computer Supported Cooperative Work (CSCW): The Journal of Collaborative Computing, 2002; 11(3-4): 447–474.

Greenberg, S., & Rounding, M. The notification collage: Posting information to public and personal displays. Proceedings of the CHI '01 Conference on Human Factors in Computing Systems; 2001; Seattle, WA, USA. New York: ACM Press: 514–521.

Henderson, J.D.A., & Card, S.K. Rooms: The use of multiple virtual workspaces to reduce space contention in window-based graphical user interfaces. ACM Transactions on Graphics, 1986; 5(3): 211–241.

Hong, J.I., & Landay, J.A. SATIN: A toolkit for informal ink-based applications. Proceedings of the 13th annual ACM symposium on User Interface Software and Technology; 2000; San Diego, CA, USA. New York: ACM Press: 63–72.

Horvitz, E., Jacobs, A., & Hovel, D. (1999). Attention-sensitive alerting. *Proceedings of UAI '99: Conference on Uncertainty and Artificial Intelligence* (pp. 305–313). San Francisco, Morgan Kaufmann.

Huang, E.M., & Mynatt, E.D. Semi-public displays for small, collocated groups. Proceedings of the CHI '03 Conference on Human Factors in Computing Systems; 2003; Ft Lauderdale, Florida, USA. New York: ACM Press: 49-56.

Hudson, S.E., & Smith, I. (1996). Techniques for addressing fundamental privacy and disruption tradeoffs in awareness support systems. *Proceedings of the 1996 ACM conference on Computer supported cooperative work* (pp. 248–257). New York: ACM Press.

Igrashi, T., Edwards, W.K., LaMarca, A., & Mynatt, E.D. (2000). An architecture for pen-based interaction on electronic whiteboards. *Proceedings of the Working Conference on Advanced Visual Interfaces* (pp. 68–75). New York: ACM Press.

Ishii, H., & Ullmer, B. Tangible bits: Towards seamless interfaces between people, bits, and atoms. Proceedings of CHI '97 Conference on Human Factors in Computing Systems; 1997; Los Angeles, CA, USA. New York: ACM Press: 234–241.

Jancke, G., Venolia, G., Grudin, J., Cadiz, J., Gupta, A. Linking public spaces: Technical and social issues. Proceedings of the CHI '01 Conference on Human Factors in Computing Systems; 2001; Seattle, WA, USA. New York: ACM Press: 530–537.

Kidd, A. The marks are on the knowledge worker. Proceedings of CHI '94 Conference on Human Factors in Computing Systems; 1994; Boston, MA, USA. New York: ACM Press: 186–191.

MacIntyre, B., Mynatt, E.D., Voida, S., Hansen, K.M., Tullio, J., & Corso, G.M. (2001). Support for multitasking and background awareness using interactive peripheral displays. *Proceedings of the 14th annual ACM symposium on User interface software and technology* (pp. 41–50). New York: ACM Press.

Maes, P. (1994, July). Agents that reduce work and information overload. *Communications of the ACM, 37*(7), 31–40.

Malone, T.W. (1983, January). How do people organize their desks? Implications for the design of office information systems. *ACM Transactions on Office Information Systems, 1*(1), 99–112.

Mander, R., Salomon, G., & Wong, Y.Y. A 'pile' metaphor for supporting casual organization of information. Proceedings of CHI '92 Conference on Human Factors in Computing Systems; 1992; Monterey, CA, USA. New York: ACM Press: 627–634.

McCarthy, J., Costa, T., Liongosari, E. (2001). UniCast, OutCast & GroupCast: Three steps towards ubiquitous, peripheral displays. *Proceedings of UbiComp 2001: Ubiquitous Computing* (pp. 332–345). Berlin: Springer-Verlag.

Moran, T.P., Chiu, P., Harrison, S., Kurtenbach, G., Minneman, S., & van Melle, W. (1996). Evolutionary engagement in an ongoing collaborative work process: A case study. *Proceedings of the 1996 ACM conference on Computer supported cooperative work* (pp. 150–159). New York: ACM Press.

Mynatt, E.D. (1999). The writing on the wall. *Proceedings of INTERACT '99* (pp. 196–204). Amsterdam, IOS Press.

Mynatt, E.D., Igrashi, T., Edwards, W.K., & LaMarca, A. Flatland: New dimensions in office whiteboards. Proceedings of CHI '99 Conference on Human Factors in Computing Systems; 1999; Pittsburgh, PA, USA. New York: ACM Press: 346–353.

Mynatt, E.D., Igrashi, T., Edwards, W.K., & LaMarca, A. (2000, July–August). Designing an augmented writing surface. *IEEE Computer Graphics and Applications, 20*(4), 55–61.

Pedersen, E.R., & Sokoler, T. AROMA: Abstract representation of presence supporting mutual awareness. Proceedings of the CHI '97 Conference on Human Factors in Computing Systems; 1997; Losa Angeles, CA, USA. New York: ACM Press: 51–58.

Streitz, N.A., Geißler, J., Holmer, T., Konomi, S., Müller-Tomfelde, C., Reischl, W., Rexroth, P., Seitz, P., & Steinmetz, R. i-LAND: An interactive landscape for creativity and innovation. Proceedings of CHI '99 Conference on Human Factors in Computing Systems; 1999; Pittsburgh, PA, USA. New York: ACM Press: 120–127.

Tang, J.C., Yankelovich, N., Begole, J., Van Kleek, M., Li, F., & Bhalodia, J. (2001). ConNexus to Awarenex: Extending awareness to mobile users. Proceedings of CHI '01

Conference on Human Factors in Computing Systems; 2001; Seattle, WA, USA. New York: ACM Press: 221–228.

Voida, S., Mynatt, E.D., MacIntyre, B., & Corso, G.M. (2002, July–September). Integrating virtual and physical context to support knowledge workers. *IEEE Pervasive Computing, 1*(3), 73–79.

Zhao, Q.A., & Stasko, J. T. (2002). What's happening?: Promoting community awareness through opportunistic, peripheral interfaces. *Proceedings of the Working Conference on Advanced Visual Interfaces* (pp. 69–74). New York: ACM Press.

PART II:

AWARENESS AND COORDINATION

Chapter 5

SITUATED WEB SIGNS AND THE ORDERING OF SOCIAL ACTION

Social co-ordination around a public room reservation display appliance

Kenton O'Hara[1], Mark Perry[2] And Simon Lewis
[1]The Appliance Studio, [2]Brunel University

Abstract: Advances in display technology are creating more opportunities for situating displays in our environment. While these displays share some common design principles with display-based interaction at the desktop PC, situated displays also have unique characteristics and values that raise particular design considerations and challenges. In order to further understand situated display design we present a field study of RoomWizard, an interactive room reservation display appliance designed to be mounted outside meeting rooms. The findings illustrate important ways that individual and social behaviours were oriented around the persistent situated displays. These observed behaviours are discussed in relation to particular design characteristics of RoomWizard. We conclude by highlighting more general themes supporting the design of other situated display technologies.

Key words: Situated display, peripheral display, appliance, field study, room reservation

1. Introduction

Displayed information and signs are not simply read-write mechanisms for communicating information over; they also provide affordances for manipulating and interpreting social action in the spaces around them. This is an important factor that has to be addressed in the design of public and situated displays – displays are created and used within social and

K. O'Hara et al. (eds.), Public and Situated Displays: Social and Interactional Aspects of Shared Display Technologies, 105–140.

organisational contexts and may be appropriated for purposes other than for which they were primarily designed. This chapter addresses the design and use of a display appliance used to book rooms, illustrating how simple design features of the technology were exploited by users in the management and use of the shared spaces that the displays were located in.

As we look around our environment we are constantly made aware of displayed information and signs. This displayed information is designed to help us identify space, help understand the purpose of a space, support navigation through space and to inform what is happening in that space (Sims, 1991). There is an inherent two-way relationship between the space and the information displayed in that space: the meaning of a sign can be derived from its location, whilst it simultaneously provides information about that space itself.

Much of the value of signage lies in its presentation of static information with the information remaining relevant over a long period of time. However, other signage is designed to be more dynamic in terms the information it provides about a location. For example, as one enters a city centre there is often signage to dynamically indicate which public car parks have free spaces or are full. Likewise, a train departure display dynamically presents information that designates a particular space, namely a platform, at a particular time, as being dedicated to a particular destination. Thus it helps people understand and use space, the status of which is shifting over time. However, the nature of signage in not simply in its role delineating the nature of a space – it can also act as a resource for organising that space. In this chapter discusses this aspect of signage in acting as a resource in social action around the use of space, and the design of signage technology to support the effective use of shared and public spaces.

Increasingly, technology is playing an important role in the presentation of these environmental graphic elements. Architecturally placed interactive signage - liquid crystal displays, light reflecting displays, split-flap displays (electronic rolodex-type displays), TVs and large Plasma displays - are often used to provide spatially relevant information being both defining of and defined by their position within an architectural structure. An important characteristic of these existing electronic signage technologies is that they are updated remotely via a central computer. As such, they operate within a model of control that is authoritarian, in the sense that a nominated individual/s are responsible for updating the information that consequently informs the users of that space – control over content is denied from the everyday users of the space. This authoritarian model can be entirely appropriate in many situations. For example, in the railway station signage example, one can easily envisage a chaotic outcome if the permission to alter the signage was opened up to all users of that space.

Whilst maintaining control over content is clearly an issue, there are other situations where the authoritarian model of signage may not be appropriate and would restrict the patterns of use. Consider the ways, for example, that people stick pieces of paper on or adjacent to doors to provide information about what is going on within that space. For example, "Do not disturb", "to reserve this room please call x5555 ", and "back in 5 minutes". These examples are clearly indicative of a need for the people who use certain spaces to be able to control the signage of those spaces. Harrison and Dourish's (1996) comments on space and place reflect this: space is a physical location, whilst "a place is a space which is *invested with understandings* of behavioural appropriateness, cultural expectations, and so forth. We are *located* in "space", but we *act* in 'place'". Signage is one of those extensions that help create a social context through which the space can be interpreted and used effectively in social action. More active participation in the signage of space by its users offers new ways for incorporating it into everyday behaviours and practices. A more decentralised and democratic model of electronic signage updating is clearly an approach that could provide benefits to users.

How best to implement this, though is unclear as it is an uncharted area. The vast majority of understanding of display-based interaction within the field of Human-Computer Interaction, centres around interaction at a desktop PC display where an individual is in a relatively bounded context in terms of proximity to the displayed information and where the interactions are typically a central focus of user attention. By contrast, the value of situated display technology and interactive signage is not dependent on it being constantly at the focus of our attention. Rather, much of the time, this information remains peripheral to our primary goals and attention (cf McCarthy *et al.*, 2001). But being situated in particular contexts and locations, these displays move fluidly into focus at appropriate points in our activity contexts. Situated display technologies cannot simply be regarded within the same interaction paradigm as displayed-based interaction at the desktop. While there are undoubtedly some common principles, there are also many unique characteristics of situated displays that present us with particular design considerations and challenges. There are also many unique affordances of these display technologies that can have an important impact in the way they shape both individual and social behaviour.

In this chapter we present our own attempts to contribute to this body of knowledge by discussing ethnographic fieldwork observations around a new situated display appliance called RoomWizard that displays basic room reservation information outside a meeting room. Whilst we recognise that room reservation software in itself is no longer a hugely interesting design question, our aim here is to explore the effects of persistently presenting a subset of information from the reservation software at an appropriate location in the environment. To do this we use ethnographic observations to offer insights into how people orient to such situated display technology as a resource for guiding their behaviour, and the values this brings to their work. More importantly, we aim to use such observations to reveal key dimensions of interest to designers of other situated display technologies by highlighting how particular design characteristics of this particular situated display relate to the observed behaviours and values.

2. Related Work in Situated Displays

Within the HCI and CSCW communities there have been a number of efforts contributing to our understanding of peripheral situated display of information (e.g. Houde *et al.*, 1998; Farrell, 2001; Gruen *et al.* 2001; McCarthy *et al.*, 2001; O'Hara and Brown, 2001; Snowden and Grasso, 2002). This research has demonstrated a number of important points about the situated nature of peripheral information display importance. For example, the location of the technology defines a certain catchment area of interest and relevance to its users. Placing these technologies in different locations changes on the type of information that people find useful to display (e.g. Snowden and Grasso, 2002). Different locations of the situated technologies also present different behavioural contexts within which the displays operate. Thus, in Houde's (1998) work, the placement of a newspaper display was important because it was an area where people would come to make a drink and have spare time in which to engage with any noticed content of interest. What these studies demonstrate is that the relationship between the technological functionality and the behavioural context associated with that particular location was the key determinant of the value of the situated display to its users. These studies also demonstrate that making information persistently visible in the environment dramatically affects its value to users. In Snowden and Grasso's (2002) work, for example, people who found useful information from the CWall would not have bothered to search for the same information directly from the web. The persistence and immediate availability is critical here, and makes such peripheral displays useful as resources for initiating and supporting ongoing general conversations around general content (cf McCarthy *et al.*, 2001; Snowden and Grasso, 2002). The effects of persistent visibility have also been observed in relation to other situated display technologies aimed at promoting presence and awareness across disparate work and social groups (e.g. Gaver *et al.*, 1992; Pedersen, 1998).

Of more specific relevance to our concerns here is the work done on situated displays where their content is not as tightly bound to that specific location in the same way as with the RoomWizard. Much of this work has been done within the context of people's personal workspaces within the office place and in particular dynamic door displays (McCarthy *et al.*, 2001; Nguyen *et al.*, unpublished; Nichols *et al.* 2002; Cheverst *et al.*, this volume). For example, OutCast is a situated display designed to be placed outside the office or workspace of a particular individual displaying information such as calendaring information, messages or contact details. When a visitor comes to an office and finds the person not there, the situated display provides information to hand that can help them interpret the situation and support judgements about, for example, where to locate them, or when to come back. IBM's BlueSpace (Chou *et al.*, 2001) provides some similar functionality but also explores ways of simplifying the display of availability information through using colour-coded lighting (depending on whether the person was in or out). Other efforts within this area have explored how situated digital door displays offer interesting new ways for managing the complex space between public, semi-public and private information. Such displays can present or receive content according to who is outside the place looking at the display (e.g. Nguyen *et al.* (unpublished); Nichols *et al.*, 2002; Cheverst *et al.*, this volume)

3. RoomWizard

3.1 RoomWizard as Web Appliance

RoomWizard is a situated display appliance that is designed to be mounted outside a meeting or conference room to provide a reservation management capability for that space (see figure 5-1).

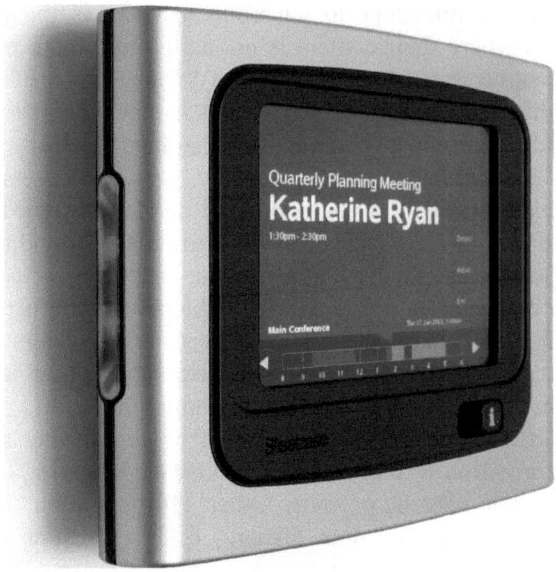

Figure 5-1. RoomWizard web sign appliance: local interface

The device has an 8-inch colour touch screen display that displays information about that room's reservations. Each RoomWizard contains a *web-host* capability which, when placed on the network, generates and serves a reservation web page. This web page is visible via any standard web browser simply by surfing to the URL of that particular RoomWizard. Being a self contained appliance in this way is an important property of RoomWizard in its function as a situated display since once positioned outside the room and connected to the network it is immediately functional in a way that gets close to the immediacy of physical signs and notices attached to architectural elements (such as, for example a name plate or a paper "do not disturb" sign[1]).

Being web appliances, multiple RoomWizards also work together. When several RoomWizards are connected to the same network, they "buddy" together to create a unified user-interface for all the associated rooms. This allows bookings for a whole set of rooms to be managed together in a

[1] Indeed this becomes more important when we consider this in terms of wireless connectivity. Wireless versions of the RoomWizard will simply require a power socket allowing greater flexibility for placement of the devices.

convenient way, and the RoomWizard appliances to be managed as a unified system across the web. Rather than seeing a single timeline for each room, this federation of RoomWizards presents all the timelines for the "buddied" rooms on a single web page (see figure 5-2).

3.2 RoomWizard Interfaces

The RoomWizard then has two interfaces: a "local" one, which is presented on the situated display outside the meeting room; and a "remote" one that is viewable via the web with a standard web browser. The concerns of this chapter are primarily with the situated display of information. However, we want to argue that you cannot understand the role of the situated display without considering it in the context of the remote browser-based display and the affordances that this offers. The way the situated display is incorporated to the people's everyday behaviours is intimately bound to the properties of the remote interface – it is the relationship that is key to the use and value of the technology.

3.2.1 Remote Interface

For all intents and purposes, the PC browser-based reservation interface offers much the same type of functionality as a range of commercially available reservation systems. As can be seen in figure 5-2, the interface consists of a calendar through which people can choose which day they wish to view. There are also timelines, one for each room clustered into a "buddy" set. On the timelines, red blocks indicate those periods when the room has been reserved. Hovering over these red blocks provides some pop-up information about who has booked the room. Clicking on the blocks takes you to the booking form for that reservation from which the reservation can be edited if necessary.

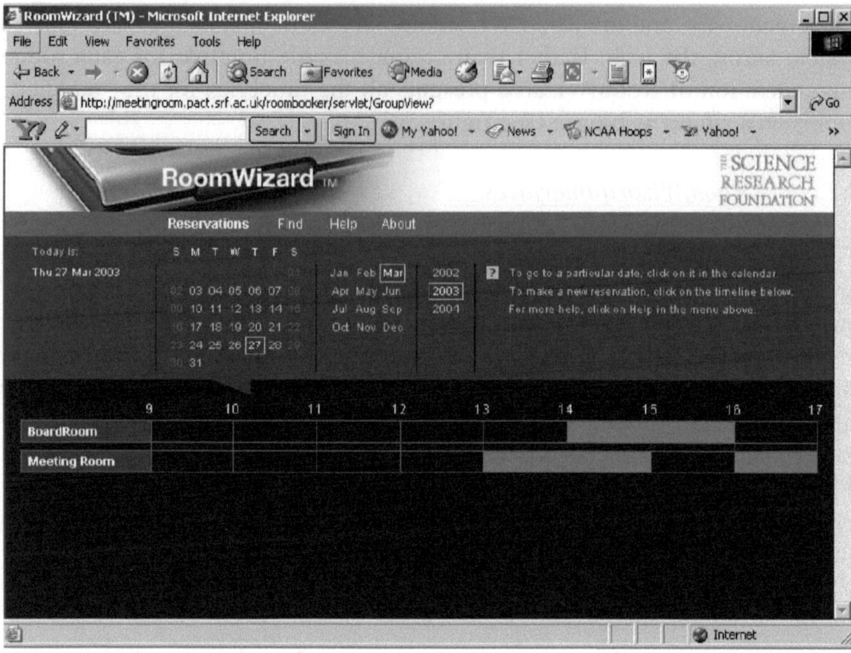

Figure 5-2. RoomWizard remote interface: overview

In order to make a booking the person reserving the room clicks on the timeline at the relevant point where they wish it to start. This brings up the view shown in figure 5-3 which we call the *simple booking form*. This view reverts to a single timeline and a few fields – the "Host" field, "meeting purpose" field, start time and end time. The "host" fields and "meeting purpose" fields are essentially free text fields in which the user is given discretion to enter any information they see fit. When en end time has been specified the user presses save and the reservation is made. The information in these two fields will then be displayed outside the meeting room concerned from the specified start time to specified end time. A deliberate design choice with this simple booking form was to present only the minimal elements necessary to make a reservation that we felt would accommodate the majority of room reservation instances. Advanced functionality is available on the system but this remains hidden in this view so as not to compromise the simplicity and low effort of the interaction for the majority of cases. This advanced functionality is reached by clicking on the hyperlink to the *advanced booking form* for this particular reservation. In this advanced view it is possible to set-up repeat bookings, password protect the booking from being edited by others and set-up email reminders and invitations etc.

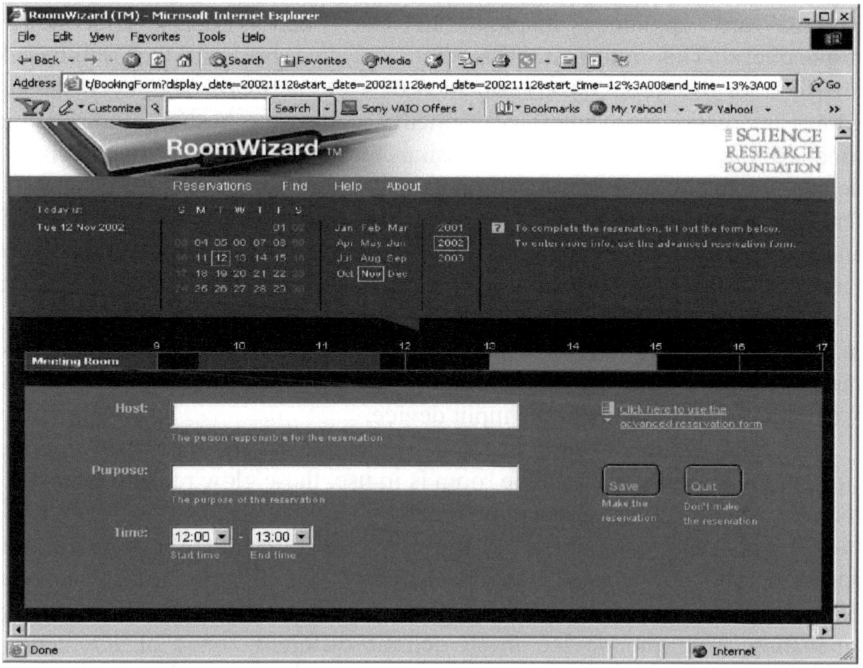

Figure 5-3. RoomWizard remote interface: simple booking form

3.2.2 *Local Situated Interface – Grabbing and Zooming*

As can be seen in figure 1, the information on the situated display reflects the look and feel of information from the remote browser interface borrowing interface elements that help demonstrate the relationship between the two. A timeline for the day is shown at the bottom of the screen again showing the blocks of reserved and "free" time. Above this is positioned several lines of structured information about the status of the room. During those periods when a reserved meeting is taking place the larger text line displays the contents of the "meeting host" text field on the remote browser-based reservation form. The smaller text line displays the contents of the "meeting purpose" text field on the remote browser-based reservation form. When the room is not reserved, these large and small text lines respectively display "free" and "available for use" on the appliance display.

The 8-inch colour display is also an interactive touch screen, allowing a free room to be "grabbed" *in situ* for an *ad hoc* meeting. To do this the user presses the "use now" button, which reveals a time period that can be quickly adjusted in 15-minute increments through simple button presses. When such an *in situ* reservation is made, the two text lines on the

RoomWizard appliance display "In Use" and "Local Reservation" respectively. This information is then reflected back in the web-based interface for the RoomWizard, updated over the network. The touch screen allows interaction with interface elements such as the host's name and the timeline for the purposes of accessing further information (e.g. contact details, details about other meetings that day, or room facilities) or control features. The top-level display however is designed to be simple, uncluttered and clear, reflecting its primary status as signage. An important point to recognise is that the capabilities of the local interaction are less sophisticated than those of the remote interface. One cannot use the situated display to make future reservations or even to enter a name. The point here was to make deliberate decisions that were appropriate to the situated context and the particular constraints of the input device.

The final features of note in terms of signage are the light strips on the sides of the appliance. When the room is in use, these glow red and when the room is available to use these glow green.

An important component of RoomWizard lies in the design of the hardware and software to support different *spatial zones* of interaction around the device. If one can imagine ever increasing concentric circles emanating from the device these delimit different zones of interaction around the device. Supporting awareness in an elegant fashion is based on consideration of the different behaviours that take place or need to take place in these different spatial zones and the associated cognitive and social constraints associated. Consider some examples from RoomWizard. The green and red status lights and their placement on the sides of the device support behaviour in the outermost zone. While people are walking about, simple binary judgments can be made quickly with minimal cognitive effort to determine room availability and to monitor status change without need for more detailed analysis of the booking information on the display. No other information was available to support other user behaviour in this zone. In a zone closer in, the next set of behaviours centre around the visibility of the meeting host's name. The larger font size of this information allowed it to be resolved from a greater distance while other aspects of the display are too small to be resolved and therefore blend into the background at this distance. This means that primary information (the name of the meeting host) can be extracted at this distance without distraction from other interactive interface elements. This was an important design consideration in that RoomWizard's purpose was not primarily about attracting people in from a distance as might be the case with other situated displays. Rather, it allowed key information to be perceived quickly at a distance while walking by. Consequently, the graphical elements designed in support on this zone were deliberately static rather than animated, giving it a more sign-like quality –

we had explored animation in earlier versions of the interface and found unsuitable from this perspective.

As you move to a closer zone around the situated display, more of the information becomes visually resolvable, affording a greater number of behaviours and values that are dependent on these more detailed interface elements – e.g. pointing at the display in support of conversation. Again, there is an interesting point to be made about the use of animated interface elements here. In earlier versions of the interface, we had considered presenting more information about meeting hosts for the other meetings on the timeline. In order to do this, the interface would scroll along the timeline and briefly flash the name of the other meetings along the timeline. What was difficult about this however was that it was a continually changing conversational resource that was difficult to point to in support of negotiations about room use.

Finally, there is an interactive zone when the user is stood right in front of the display. An important aspect of designing for these zones is to think about the key information in a pyramidal manner where gradually more layers of detail are revealed. This affords another important principal of situated display design for elegant peripheral awareness, namely "Zooming by walking in". While this may sound somewhat flippant and technically unsophisticated, it is nevertheless significant. Cognitively speaking, it can provide a much more elegant solution to the provision of greater information access than is possible with more discrete and explicit interactions.

For the designer of situated displays, these "zones" have an impact on choices of physical form factor as well as properties of content and information architecture and so needs to be defined and considered in the design process.

4. The Study

In order to further understand the impact of RoomWizard, we conducted a field study of the technology in use in a large multinational petroleum organisation in the UK. The site of the organisation housed several thousand employees distributed across many buildings on the campus. For the practical purposes of the study we chose to limit the deployment of the technology to two adjacent buildings on the campus and more specifically to two groups comprising about 50 employees (of differing levels of seniority, ranging from office administrators to engineers and managers). The first department was made up purely of employees from the main organisation; the second department comprised a mixture of employees from the main organisation and employees from an auxiliary organisation permanently contracted and housed by the main organisation to manage campus wide issues such as health and safety, facilities and maintenance. Visits from external contractors were also commonplace. In total, 5 RoomWizards were installed in the two buildings. In building 1, RoomWizards were installed outside two meeting rooms on the same floor, (one for 5 people) located off the main corridor of that floor; the other (for 8 people) located within the open plan office space itself off the main corridor (see figure 5-4a). In building 2, which housed people from both departments, RoomWizards were installed outside 3 dedicated meeting rooms off the main corridors of two floors (one for 10 people, the other two rooms for 4 people – see figure. 5-4b).

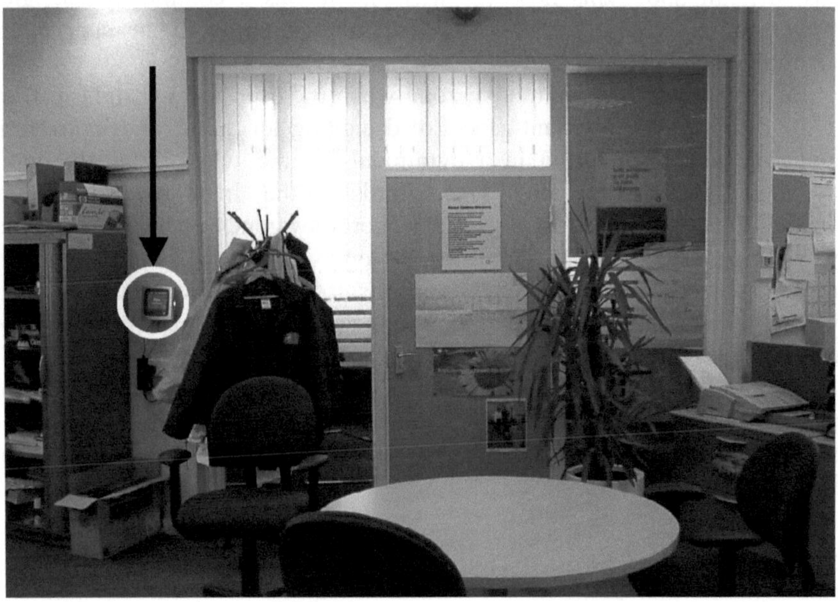

(a)

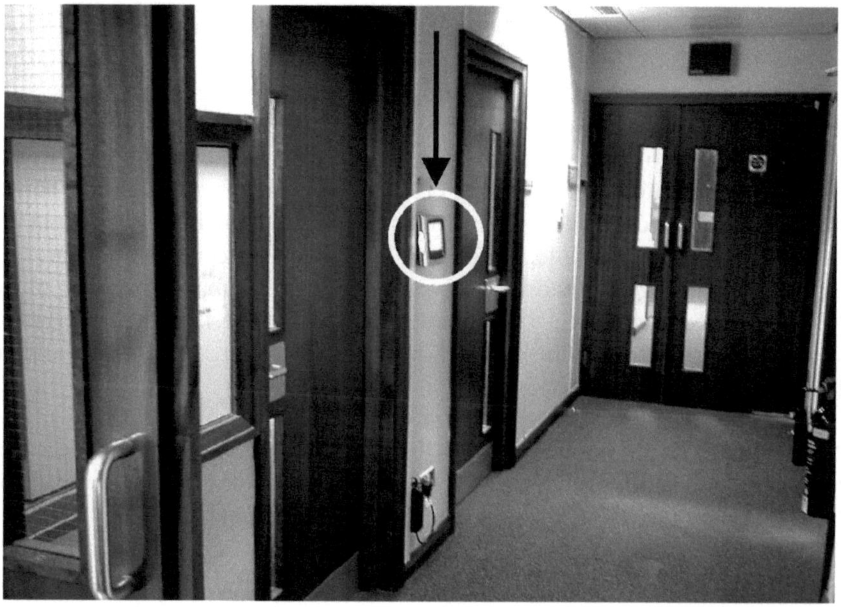

(b)

Figure 5-4. RoomWizard *in situ* in field trial: a) in building 1; b) in building 2

Data collection took place in two phases. The first phase prior to the RoomWizard installation involved a series of interviews with a subset of trial participants and was used to establish some background context about the organisation, the individuals and an understanding of the current meeting practices within which RoomWizard was going to be immersed. Contacts at the organisation helped identify and arrange preliminary interviews with 10 key personnel responsible for the management of the current booking system and monitoring patterns of use (the office administrators) and people who booked and used meeting rooms for their own purposes (surveyors, managers, contractors). Participants were interviewed for 30 minutes about general meeting behaviour – such as how often they used meting rooms, whether they booked them for themselves, or on behalf of other people, whether the meetings they booked were regular, *ad hoc*, on the fly; formal or informal and how they informed others that they had booked a meeting.

The second phase of interviews took place after the RoomWizards had been installed. The same participants were asked to keep a journal of their meeting room usage – who was invited, when and how they booked rooms, used rooms, or were invited to meetings. The journals were used as the basis for in depth interviews, lasting between 30 to 90 minutes that were carried out over the first 4 weeks of the trial. Interviewees were separated into two groups (we were limited by participant availability), the first group interviewed one week after installation and the following week, the second for the subsequent two weeks.

Several days of observation also took place in the two buildings in the offices and around the meeting rooms to collect data about actual interactions around the RoomWizards, and the kinds of information put on the system. Where possible, observation episodes were elaborated through further questioning with those observed using the system, often taking place during or directly following room reservations. Briefer informal interviews were also carried out with a wider range of trial participants to validate details from in-depth interviews.

While the fieldwork revealed a vast array of findings in relation to the RoomWizard Technology, we focus here on those involved in the *in situ* display of information in relation to the meeting spaces, and the impact of these from an individual, social and organisational perspective.

5. Pre-Installation Context

Prior to the introduction of RoomWizard, room reservation was handled by two paper "booking" diaries, one governing the meeting rooms in one building, and one governing the meeting rooms in the adjacent building. These diaries resided on the desks of the senior administrative assistant for each group. In theory the diaries were openly available for use by everyone in the departments. Anyone could use the diaries to make a reservation or consult them to check room availability. However, having a reservation system embodied in paper diaries at fixed physical locations meant that there was an effort cost associated with physically moving to them. Obviously this was particularly acute if the diary concerned was located in another building. As a consequence, a number of interesting phenomena and difficulties were apparent that contributed to inefficiencies in the way that the meeting spaces were reserved, used and understood by its users when using the paper diary system:

1. *Room administration*: while some people would make the effort of doing the reservation themselves, a disproportionate amount of people would try and avoid this effort by contacting the administrative assistant holding the particular diary to make a reservation on their behalf. This created an unnecessary burden for the administrators involved. It also prevented task closure being achieved by the individuals if the administrator was not available at the time when the need arose. This lack of closure was

seemingly of minor significance to the individuals concerned but actually had significant consequences elsewhere. The inability to achieve closure in the local meeting rooms would encourage people to phone up the central site-wide meeting resource in order to transfer their reservation attempts to these centralised meeting room resources. These centralised meeting resources were already under considerable pressure and so there was some organisational desire to try and reduce this.

2. *Room administration:* by virtue of its physical location and the behaviour described above, the administrators acquired a lot of territorial control over room use. The consequence of this was some strategic protectionism over "their" rooms whereby they would hinder reservations made by people external to their building unless it was an emergency. For example, they might not allow a reservation from outside the building to be made too far in advance if their own group might have an emergent need for it. By having the information "hidden" in the diary they were able to be liberal with the truth in how much they revealed to the outsider requesting a reservation. Giving permission for external people to use the rooms would require special circumstances and be seen as a favour, rather than routine. While these local tactics were of some benefit to the individual administrators and local group, it was not always the most efficient way of managing space for the organisation as a whole because the protected rooms would go unused by the local groups when they could have been used by others. This again put further pressure on the site's centralised meeting rooms.
3. *Ad hoc use*: impromptu availability of rooms was difficult to check for. The effort cost[2] of using the information in the diaries to check immediate availability was often too high to bother with. As such, people would typically do a 'corridor cruise' to look for a free room in their own building or met in the cafeteria. If they found a room that was free they would simply walk in and use it. The problem with this was that they had no idea about how long the room would be free for, making it difficult to make decisions about whether it was appropriate to use or not. This difficulty was recognised to an extent by those on charge of the organisations' centralised meeting rooms and in response they would physically place printed paper signs of reservation overviews in a slot outside the meeting rooms for the particular period of use (see figure 4-5a). The other issue was that this impromptu type of room usage was not reflected back into the diary system, further reducing the ability to manage the space effectively. This was despite the important fact that

[2] This cost was partly the physical effort but also the cost of social interaction with the administrator and likely questioning about room use that would ensue.

there was that there were signs situated on the doors saying "to book this meeting room please telephone x64699" (of the type shown in figure 4-5b). However, this request was rarely followed for impromptu meetings, indicating the low effort threshold that people would tolerate in systematically propagating this information back to the physical situated diaries. Even making a quick phone call was regarded as too effortful for them to bother with.

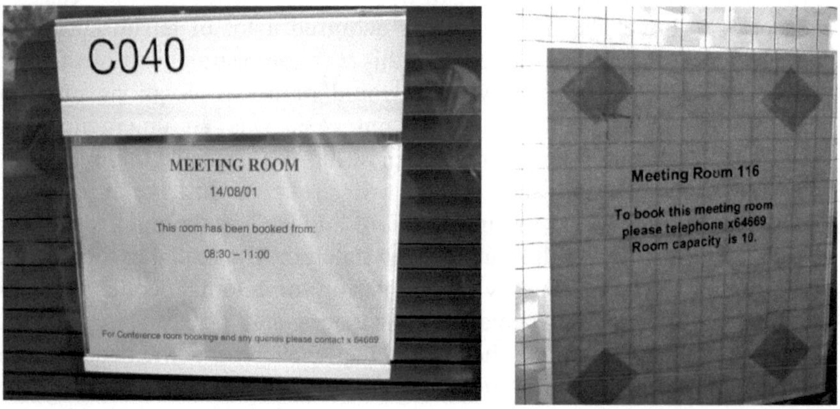

(a) (b)

Figure 5-5. Paper printouts on meeting room doors – a) booking times and b) contact details

4. *Invisibility and responsibility:* with shared meeting rooms there was potential for selfish or inefficient use. For example, people would make reservations *just in case* they would need it; reserve a room for a longer period than necessary; reserve what was regarded as a "plush" room with capacity for 10 people when only needing a simple room for 2 people; not cancel a reservation if a meeting was moved or the meeting was shorter than the reservation, and so on. These behaviours are a natural part of the utilisation of any shared resource and are due to a variety of factors such as social selfishness (with the knowledge that there would be no comeback on this), forgetfulness and the high effort costs of making changes to bookings. With the paper diaries, people were supposed to write the bookings in pencil for the very purpose of trying to overcome some of these behaviours. However, it was typically the case that people would not bother to remove unwanted bookings or would not alter bookings that had finished early. The invisibility of the information meant that people were not reminded to do make these alterations nor were they held accountable for these behaviours.

6. Visibility and Social Co-ordination

6.1 Ownership of Space and Resolution of Conflict

In time-shared spaces such as meeting rooms, there are often difficulties and conflicts in terms of who has legitimate use of the space. Reservation systems attempt to alleviate these breakdowns to a certain extent, but problems still frequently arise due to *ad hoc* use of spaces without reservation, genuine uncertainties about correct times and spaces for meetings and genuine uncertainties about whether a reservation has actually been made or not. The display of the booker's name *in situ* outside the meeting room at a particular time provided people with the necessary sense of ownership over that space giving users the *ammunition* to enforce the booking times: they could simply point to the display to reinforce their request for ownership. For example, while some people were looking at the display outside a meeting room, the meeting owner (a manager) came along the corridor and good-naturedly bellowed:

> "That's my name, that's my meeting room"

Clearly, the room owner was referring to the display, and to the fact the people looking at the display could demonstrably see that it was booked in his name – it was *reserved for him*. The important value of this was the provision of a resource at the appropriate point in space and time where potential conflict could occur. Generally speaking, this applied to overrunning of meetings or people using meeting spaces without prior reservation. Before the adoption of the RoomWizards, there was a social asymmetry around space use with people already occupying a space having a stronger sense of ownership that made it awkward for the "legitimate" bookers to ask them to leave the room. Having the information there and then increased their level of confidence to be able to deal with these situations fairly. As a junior member of staff reported in an interview:

> "People ignore it and sit in your room when you have booked it. Having the system there has given me the confidence to go in and turf them out."

RoomWizard did not completely remove this overrunning behaviour or use of space without reservation. Indeed, it is not designed to do this. There are all sorts of organisational contingencies that need to be managed in relation to space use, and these need to be mediated by people on the basis of locally interpreted information.

The use of *local context* in the interpretation of information on the display can be seen in an example drawn from our fieldwork. During one of the lunch breaks, the people in the meeting left the room, but did not cancel the session on the RoomWizard, as they were going to return in the afternoon at some point. Whilst the room was empty, two senior managers walked in to use it for 10 or 15 minutes for an impromptu meeting. This example extends the idea of ownership to show how RoomWizard bookings are interpreted as resources for action, rather than followed as rules to direct their action.

So we see here that the RoomWizard does not *stop* people using the room. We do not see this as a limitation of the utility of the RoomWizard system – what it points to is that the use of local knowledge about activities in the office is used to interpret what the information on the RoomWizard really means. In this case the senior managers knew that most people would be out of the office, because there was a team meeting that morning, and also made a judgement that the other room users would be at lunch (and that their own meeting would likely be finished before the original room bookers returned). This intermixing of local knowledge with information on the *in situ* display is interesting, because it allows an even more effective use of space than would have been expected using a simple rule-enforced booking system.

The example above had an additional dimension that makes it interesting in another, related way: whilst the managers were in the room, J (an external contractor) returned from her lunch and wanted to get into the room in order to have a look through her slides on her laptop. She did not go in (even though the room had been booked for her meeting) because it was socially difficult, given that the occupants were on home territory, visibly engaged in deep discussion and that they were important figures (she had recognised them as managers from a previous visit), but also because it was not important enough to interrupt the meeting just so that she could get her laptop. So, the RoomWizard's situated display enables judgements to be made on the basis of local context and allows 'lean' social mediation over room use when necessary, without breaking important organisational protocols. This lean social mediation is relatively effort-free to maintain, and allows a high degree of flexibility in its application, thus supporting what are judged as the most appropriate of follow on activities (cf Palen, 1999).

RoomWizard, then, is not the only and absolute resource for booking and using rooms. People who have booked can be kicked out, and people may use the room without booking. This introduces lots of social interactions around the use of the device. People will use the room for longer than their booking, or conduct other time-related activities that are not directed by the room booking system. Some people are more affected by this than others, as, for example, the level of the user's organisational seniority affects interpretation of rules.

The RoomWizards were also seen as something that could help negotiate changes for meeting rooms when necessary. This swapping of room use was always seen as a socially mediated process. Showing who was the temporary owner of a particular space on a public display at a particular time provided the information to help initiate conversations for this negotiation. As a junior member of staff described in an interview:

> "I have been looking – if there is someone in the room you want to go - or who has nicked it already... and you have a look to see who it is... It could be useful because you think well maybe if I ask really nicely then maybe they would swap".

This notion of the visibility of resources for exchange is extremely important – without it, there is no possibility of managing the process in a reasonable way. Even the previous diary-based system allowed a low level of visibility, but by increasing the level of visibility, users can make more effective use of the social spaces that they have, and can manage resources these in a manner that is appropriate for the organisational context. Imagine the frustration an automated system that booked and managed rooms in this way, bumping people out of rooms on a rule-based system ordered through booker seniority and meeting criticality. By making the system visible and allowing room management to be negotiated through social mechanisms, the resource allocation model becomes transparent and can be moderated through appropriately through more context-sensitive social interaction.

6.2 Supporting Interruption

The RoomWizards did not simply allow the improved management of reservation times, but also supported some other features of co-ordination and collaboration behaviour. A particularly important by-product of the displays was the provision of useful information for judging the interruptability of a meeting. The interruptability status of a meeting or a person in a meeting is not something that is absolute by definition. Rather, it is dependent upon factors such as the status of the meeting interrupter in relation to the status of the interruptee, the type of meeting, or the reason for interruption in relation to the reason for the meeting.

The data show that interruption judgements were made using knowledge of local context. The information on the RoomWizard displays about the meeting's owner and its purpose supported these situated judgements about interruption. For example, the subject header "Quiet working" had a completely different level of interruptability to that indicated by a "one-to-one" meeting. This information would not have been practical to ascertain using the previous, paper-based system (or even a solely web-based system) because of the high level of effort required to locate the room's calendar and identify the nature of the booking. A "one-to-one" meeting was regarded as largely non-interruptible, except in urgent circumstances or by the most senior of people, whereas the note "quiet working" was something that was generally interruptible for less serious reasons. An example of this was given where the organisation's vice-president was in a meeting, and because the RoomWizard had his name on it, people interpreted this as definitely a non-interruptible situation – even though they had overrun their booking. When the administrator had booked this meeting she (unusually) typed the names of the three people in there so that people would know it was an important meeting, and who was attending it, all adding to the richness of context for interpretation. Interestingly, this was not something just interpreted by viewers; the office administrator was aware of this and made use of the display's affordances to alert others about the meeting's interruptability.

7. Visibility and Awareness

7.1 Navigation and reassurance

The display of *in situ* information about the use of a space was also important as confirmation that members of the meeting were in the right place. While this may appear almost trivial, the role of the RoomWizard as a confirmation device was regarded as important, in the sense that room information is often abstract and easy to forget or confuse with other similarly labelled rooms. It was particularly important in reassuring external visitors, who were unfamiliar with a building, that they were in the right place – the name of the meeting host and meeting purpose were meaningful and recognisable to them more so than an abstract room name.

7.2 Peripheral Awareness

The situated display of information outside the meeting rooms provided a level of incidental awareness of ongoing activities in the office. While this information was not something people would have explicitly sought out elsewhere, RoomWizard's visual immediacy and people's general sense of curiosity meant that office workers would frequently look at the information on the displays as they went about their business. For example, a number of people commented how by casual intermittent looking at the displays they had acquired information that had subsequently allowed them to answer questions about people's whereabouts and to build up understanding of habitual work patterns of others. As one office administrator described:

> "Every time I walk into the office, if anyone's in there, I tend to just check the screen, just as I walk past, just to see if they've actually put anything in because ... it's helpful to me ... because then I know who's in there. Other people do this as well…It's a good way of giving people information about what is going on. We have a lot of people coming in saying "Have you seen P, have you seen M?" – and having walked past and looked at the display I know how to answer them".

What is important about the provision of this awareness information, compared with some other approaches to awareness, is that it is provided on the back of a genuine need for room reservation, rather than being based on any sense of moral obligation to make this information available. As such, it remains up-to-date and relevant, without requiring extra work to provide this information.

7.3 Not Just Reserving But Informing

Users were very much aware of the link between the reservation information entered into the remote interface and what was displayed at the local interface. Users creatively adapted what they wrote in the reservation fields on the Web-based booking form because they knew it would be visible on the RoomWizard displays outside the rooms. In an incident previously noted in section 6.1, the "meeting host" text field was filled out as "R <name of office administrator> for J <name of external visitor>". The reservation was actually for J who was a visitor and not known well by the rest of the people in the office. R put her name down to make herself visible as a contact person. Because people would not know who J was, R judged that they would be more inclined to bump her, or act in an inappropriate way towards her booking. To prevent this, she put her own name on the RoomWizard as well as J to indicate this was a legitimate booking and legitimate use of the room. The creative use of the free text field allowed R to anticipate a certain reaction and inform others with the necessary information to overcome their concerns. So, RoomWizard users were doing more than just reserving meetings: they were also aware that they were providing information to others. On the other hand, there were other times when people wanted to restrict the information they were giving to others. In the case of confidential meetings, or when people did not want others to know what they were doing, they would put something deliberately cryptic and difficult to interpret thereby overcoming privacy concerns of increased information visibility through social mechanisms.

An important part of the design of the RoomWizard was to give users freedom over the information they put in the text fields. Although the text fields were labelled as "meeting host" and "meeting purpose" it was clear that users were creatively appropriating these fields for their own purposes (however, for ease of data entry, user details are recorded as a default value for RoomWizard on an individual's PC). Alternative design possibilities were based around integration with a corporate directory that would have automatically entered the user's name in the meeting host field. Likewise, we could have devised a series of meeting categories from which people could quickly choose, again ensuring that organisationally classifiable information would appear in this field. While this stricter approach may have led to some benefits later in terms of categorising information for visualisation or search purposes, we felt it was more important to give people the freedom to use the fields in the way that they saw fit for the contingencies of their particular circumstances. That is, we have attempted to mediate rather than automate activity, allowing flexible appropriation and evolving strategies of use to support contingencies.

7.4 Assessing Availability

The RoomWizard's red and green room availability status lights were useful in assessing a room's availability for impromptu meetings at a distance; as one user said, it is:

> "easy to see when the room is free or in use for those on-the-spot meetings."

This feature of the device provides important affordances in relation to its role as signage since it supports what we have come to describe as "drive by" usage as opposed to "walk up" usage. That is, it afforded quick glance assessment of high-level device/room status without the need to interact with the more detailed information up close. As the above example shows, this is often all that is needed as a resource for making a decision about action.

Whilst useful for assessing room availability, some participants also used it to monitor the availability of other people. For example, a participant needed to see her boss about a particular issue. She knew her boss was in a particular room down the corridor in a meeting of unpredictable length but was able to intermittently peer down the corridor to monitor the light colour. This allowed her to determine whether the meeting was finished so that she could initiate a conversation with him. The indicator light was not just a simple indicator of room use, but was adopted here as an organising resource for locating people.

Assessing a room's availability before the introduction of the RoomWizard system could sometimes create a sense of social awkwardness. Looking into a meeting room through a glass window had some benefits in terms of providing information about room use. Catching someone's eye was also useful in some respect in terms of initiating a potential interaction, e.g. to remind someone they should finish the meeting up. However, for those instances when people were just checking room availability for impromptu use, this could be socially awkward, not wishing to discomfort the room occupants, or pressure them to finish up unnecessarily. In an example that illustrates the difficulties associated with this, one of the meeting rooms at the fieldwork organisation had a glass door panel allowing passers by to look in and see inside the room (and therefore to make judgements about its use). However, this glass panel had been covered over with an opaque plastic sheet that we surmised had been necessary to stop prying eyes from seeing everything that was going on inside the room. Further to this, a small hole had been roughly cut in the plastic sheet so that it was now possible to look into the room, but without greatly disturbing those inside and requiring more of an effort to do so. Clearly, this was an issue that had been deemed important enough to necessitate considerable effort and thought to have come up with such (indeed so inelegant) a solution.

The information provided on the RoomWizard display helped alleviate some of this social awkwardness by allowing some judgments without peering into the room. Nevertheless, the RoomWizard's displayed information was not always a perfect reflection of what was actually happening in the room, and could not be relied upon completely in making these judgements. Somctimes there was still a need to look through the windows to confirm the information if there was a really strong immediate need for the room:

> "People in the office do tend to look in the glass, but it can be hard to stand outside looking in" (because the people in the meeting can also see out). "So the RoomWizard is useful for that…I think it's just curiosity most of that time. I wouldn't like it like it if we had a meeting room with the door completely closed off ... there are some meeting rooms like that, and it's awful because you can never tell if the room's being used - sometimes they may just shut that door, and you could just walk straight in and there's a massive meeting going on."

There were some examples when having the RoomWizard on red outside an empty and unused room would actually stop people going in and making use of that room in an *ad hoc* way. On the other hand, some people did not mind going to an empty room on red with the understanding that they might be kicked out if the legitimate user of the room returned. Similarly, people were using the situated information to help make decisions about whether these "illegal" occupations were appropriate or not, e.g., people would be less inclined to go into the empty room if the RoomWizard indicated it was the beginning of the supposed meeting (assuming that people were late). On the other hand, they would be more inclined to go in nearer the end of the booked time, assuming it to be over early but without the reservation having being cancelled on the RoomWizard.

8. Policing, Morality and Accountability

8.1 Hall of Shame: Visibility and Accountability

The visibility of the reservation information made people more accountable and socially aware that they were using shared resources that others might need. This promoted a sense of moral anxiety in some people if they forgot to cancel a reservation they were not using. There was not complete improvement in this respect since people still forgot to do this on occasion, but the RoomWizard displays made this behaviour more publicly visible. This encouraged others, particularly office administrators, to remind people to cancel. The displayed name also made it easy to attribute responsibility for the behaviour, making policing easier.

There were clear expressions of annoyance at the behaviour of people having their name outside an empty room and, with repeated instances over time, they would be likely to say something about this to the offenders. In this sense, there was an emerging "Hall of Shame" phenomenon in which people's now *visibly* antisocial reservation behaviour was being monitored by others over a period of time. As one senior office administrator commented:

> "You can see who has been booking them and not using them so if you see repetitive names then you would be able to go and tell them off – but people can take individual responsibility as well – so someone wants to use the room and it is already booked but the booker is not there the person can always locate the booker to see if they are going to use the room – that is the nice thing about the system."

This information was useful to her in that it allowed her to manage room space more effectively – but also because it allowed other people in the office to manage room space more effectively. This was repeated numerous times in interviews. The interviewees reported that by making this information more visible, individuals would become more aware of their own anti-social use of space and would lead to a degree of self-policing. At the same time, room bookers would also be made aware of other people's unsocial behaviour, leading to potential policing by them, rather than by the traditional enforcers of the room booking system, the office administrators. The evidence from participants suggests that there were less unattended meetings than on the paper-based system, which distanced planning from action and which kept behaviour hidden.

The situated display thus had begun to encourage the cancellation of meetings, freeing up the room for others to use through the ability to end the current meeting booking upon leaving the room. The impulse to cancel could be acted upon as soon as people were leaving the room, making it very low effort. Unfortunately this ability to bridge the intention-action gap through the situated functionality did not extend to other meetings reserved for that room: the interface limited this to editing current room bookings only. However, the observations showed that the situated displays also provided a visible prompt to users to cancel meetings that were initially due to take place in that room at a later date. For example, one participant relayed an episode where she had changed a meeting time and made new reservations while forgetting to cancel the original bookings. She was reminded of this only when she walked past the display outside the meeting that room she had reserved and wanted to act on that reminder there and then (although she could not). This suggests that meeting reservation behaviour is sometimes prompted by the physicality of the RoomWizard display itself (perhaps similar to paper reminders being more effective than electronic documents). Extending the functionality to allow reservation on the current day is something that can likely be done within the bounds of the simplified interaction model of the local display interface, and is currently vying for inclusion on the device's feature list.

Interestingly the extend meeting time feature of the *in situ* device was not used despite the fact that people were aware that it was an interactive part of the display. There were a number of reasons for this. While immersed in a meeting, people remain unaware that a change needs to be made. They cannot see the device and are thus not visually prompted. More importantly, though, the social and effort cost of interrupting a meeting remains too high in terms of stopping the conversation, getting up and going outside to extend the booking. Anecdotal evidence suggest that at any point during the overrun, people tend think they will be finished in a few minutes (even if this is not always the case) – so the need to adjust may not be something that is even apparent, as noted by an office administrator:

> "People do not bother extending meetings: they will tend stay in there as long as they cannot, until someone kicks them out. They wouldn't necessarily think - OK, it's 10 o'clock - I'd better extend it…half the time, they're so engrossed in what are they are talking about, they won't even notice. They don't even notice the time: quite a lot of the time I'll have to pull M out of the meeting because he supposed to be attending another one."

One solution used by a group within the organisation for management of booked but unattended meetings was to devolve the policing role from an administrator to users through the proposed creation of a '15 minute rule': *use it or lose it*. This was only proposed by one of the two buildings observed, so would only be a locally enforced rule. It is interesting that the rule was not intended to be used in the office where contractors and non-office staff were frequent visitors: these were often late and their visit might involve a break in the middle for other visits to be made to other locations on the site. This demonstrates the importance of *not* enforcing rules within the technology – local conditions may preclude the usefulness of this type of functionality – but rather, designing the technology to allow socially mediated (and contextually appropriate) policing of this rule.

8.2 Overcoming Visibility

The impact of this increased visibility of use was also seen in people's attempts to make their antisocial behaviour less visible. To elaborate with an example relating to policing of intrusion and the visibility of the booking behaviour, there was a difference in the status of bookings with planned meetings based on advanced web reservations (i.e. recording the meeting host and title) being perceived as more important than *ad hoc* meetings (labelled as "In Use/Local Reservation"). While this was typically respected, people would still employ tactics for their own gain, e.g., if a RoomWizard was 'on green' but the meeting still going on, people would not use the RoomWizard display to make a local reservation even though in theory this would give them the right to use the room. To grab the room locally under such circumstances was considered rude and the visibility of this fact on the screen prevented people from doing this. There was therefore a strong social imperative for these *ad hoc* intruders to go elsewhere. However, the technology allowed them to go back to their PC and book the room remotely for immediate use. This made their behaviour less *visibly* anti-social, as it obscured the time that the booking had been made, and whether it was *ad hoc* or planned

8.3 Trust and security

With RoomWizard, the space/resource control model is decentralised so that the whole community of users has direct responsibility over the contents on the display. A decentralised model like this is dependent on trust among the users and is open to certain abuses. As such, while it might not be appropriate for more critical information, it is suited to the information associated with room reservation – indeed it is this decentralised model that allowed many of the creative behaviours to develop and the technology to be effectively incorporated into people's everyday social coordination and work practices. Placing responsibility on the users, allowed lightweight socially mediated coordination to *emerge* without training or enforcement, through the provision of social affordances.

Related to trust was the notion of security. Prior to the design of RoomWizard, our ethnographic interviews consistently highlighted security as a concern for people over their bookings. The notion that someone else could change the content of another person's booking or overriding it was clearly of concern to people and they stressed the importance of having their bookings security-protected. Our concern from a design point of view was that this would introduce additional effort cost into making a booking which would have made it cumbersome to make and edit reservations. The intuition here was that the consequences of these potential abuses was serious enough to distort people's perceptions of their likely frequency. As a consequence, security was perceived as an important requirement at the expense of compromising simplicity of interaction for what would in actuality be the vast majority of needs. The design solution was to offer a security facility in which people had the option to lock a booking with a password if necessary but this feature was hidden two layers deeper than the simple booking form. Having this option gave the administrators and users of the system peace of mind even though, as we intuited, in actual usage they made no use of the functionality – with no problems reported following its introduction. Rather, the management of this issue was left down to social mediation. This has parallels with other awareness systems where the only distinction between awareness and monitoring is the social culture in which they are immersed (e.g. Xerox media space, Gaver *et al.*, 1992). In order to maintain elegance of the peripheral awareness, where possible, one should attempt to design for socially mediated control of the system, rather than introduce heavyweight interaction element.

9. Usage Patterns

9.1 *Local and Remote Reservations*

As discussed, prior to the installation of RoomWizard, it was only possible to make reservations remotely via a paper diary system. Impromptu use of the meeting rooms was not something that was recorded leading to discrepancies between the information in the diary and its actual use. As noted, this could result in inefficiencies in space management. Given that it was possible to use meeting rooms without reservations an important question for RoomWizard was whether it would lead to any behaviour change in impromptu use. Would people still continue to walk into rooms without "grabbing " it at the local interface, or would the *in situ* display encourage people to book the room in the moment. In figure 5-6 we can see the distribution of how room reservations were made over a 2-week period mid-trial: the data clearly show that people *were* making use of local on-the-spot reservations. This illustrates how placing the information *in situ*, at the point where the intention to use the room arose, significantly shifts the cost barrier to updating the reservation information. People were therefore willing to perform some interaction to more officially "grab" the room. The consequence of this was that the information in the diary about room use was more up to date both outside the meeting room and in the browser-based timeline. Having more accurate reflection of the current status of the room would improve judgements made about intended room use.

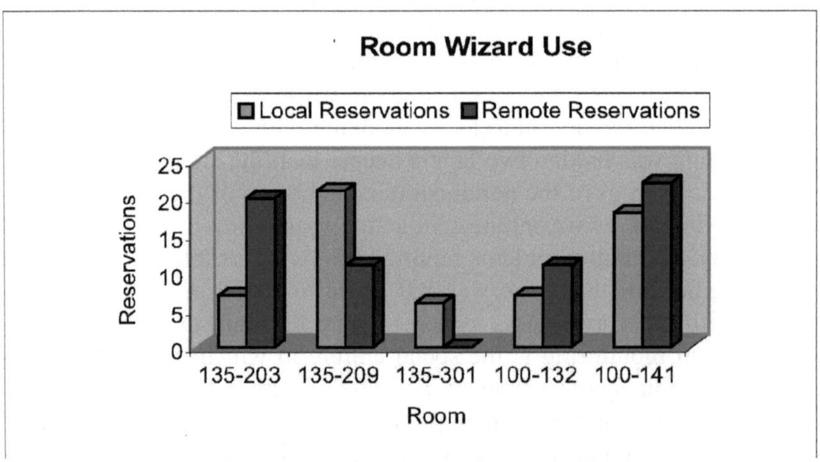

Figure 5-6. Pattern of local and remote reservations showing good use of both reservation methods (taken over a two week period mid-trial)

The other important consequence of this was that it provided a more accurate account of room usage from an organisational perspective. During the time of he field trial, the organisation was asking questions about space usage in order to determine how best to allocate functionality. For example, if certain meeting spaces were not being used could they be better utilised as office space? Room 135-301 was particularly in question because it was understood to be unused according to the information in the previous diary system. This lack of planned reservation is indeed reflected in the data shown in figure 8. But what we also see though is that it was being used primarily for impromptu meetings. This type of use was thus made more visible to those in the organisation making space-planning decisions allowing more informed choices to be made about functional allocation of this space.

9.2 Local Ownership and Territoriality

One of the potential affordances of the RoomWizards was the ability to open up meeting rooms to a wider audience by providing remote reservation access across the different buildings. That is, people in one building are in theory able to book and use meeting rooms in the other building. Throughout the period of the field trial there still remained a strong respect of territory and understanding of the needs of others to have local ownership, despite not being forced having to go through spatial and social controls. Cross building reservations therefore still retained a high element of social negotiation. However, by making the reservation visible between buildings by removing the spatial constraints of the paper diary system, it was possible for visitors to see suitable slots that might be available on which to base their negotiation with the space's owners. While this obviously removed the some of the "plausible deniability" to the room controllers afforded by hidden information, in other ways it was deemed to support the negotiation process through preplanning and shared visualisation of the information[3]. Indeed it also shifts some of the time selection burden onto the person making the request. So again, RoomWizard did not violate these other organisational factors underlying room allocation but rather offered new possibilities of resource management and use.

[3] This has parallels with the shared calendaring literature in which the information about personal schedules of colleagues becomes a resource for narrowing down the possibilities for meeting times prior to the social process of negotiating of meeting invitation (e.g. Palen, 1999).

Interestingly, for impromptu meetings, there was a hint of psychological shift in attitude for some people regarding cross-building room use. Having the displays outside the meeting room legitimised room usage in someone else's building in a way that they didn't have before.

> "We wouldn't have gone in to that meeting room if it hadn't had that thing on the front but because it did and we booked the room [grabbed locally] we felt that we were allowed to go in there. Because it is not our meeting room it's the site management meeting room but because I knew that was on the door I was happy to be in there – I wouldn't have gone in there otherwise probably because I would have felt that I shouldn't have been but because I had booked it as far as they were concerned then it was OK – I wouldn't have booked it remotely, never in a million years."

9.3 Self Reservations and Administrator Reservations

An important value of the RoomWizards was that they helped devolve responsibility for bookings from the intermediary administrators to individuals. Prior to the installation of the RoomWizards, the administrators commented that they would often have to make room reservations for other people in the office or would be asked about availability of the rooms – despite the fact that these users were allowed access to the paper diaries and could have done this themselves. While this behaviour has not disappeared completely, and is unlikely to, it was felt that there had been a shift in this behaviour over the course of the trial, with people taking more responsibility to book their own meetings and check room availability.

> "This is really good. We can now be more self sufficient and not have to ask people to book the rooms for us." *(RoomWizard user)*
> "People used to swarm around the desk with the paper diary – can you do this, can you quickly book this in – but now it is not – I am free of it" *(office administrator)*

This is not just important in helping the administrators. It also helped individuals to reach closure more quickly on reservation tasks. They no longer had to go through an email loop with the administrators and wait for confirmation that the room was booked. Rather, they could complete the task more immediately from their own machines.

10. Discussion

In conclusion, what might initially have been regarded as a simple room reservation application actually turns out to have important behavioural consequences by virtue of its situated display component. The field study observations have shown how a situated display technology can create a more socially translucent system around which important user behaviours and values emerge (c.f. Erickson and Kellogg 2000). By studying the ways that individual and social activity is oriented towards this device, it has been possible to identify important issues of concern to designers of other situated display technologies.

The elicitation of the observed value with such a situated display technology was not simply due to the *display* of appropriate information in space. Rather there is an important relationship with the situated interface and the remote (web) information source for the display. In this respect, the behaviours associated with the display and its ability to remain a "living" system are dependent upon the time and effort costs associated with getting the information there. As we have seen, an important characteristic of RoomWizard was that the useful displayed information was built on an already required behaviour – namely, reservation of a room by entering your name into the reservation system. The situated display of this information was not dependent upon any additional effort or moral obligation on the part of the user. The nature of this cost and extent of moral obligation is something to consider. There is an interaction her between effort costs, perceived value to self and perceived value to others. For example, in other situated display applications the same input mechanisms via a web based form can have a different feel depending on the application, frequency of use and perceived value to self and others – thus, in a personal web sign designed to be positioned outside a person's workspace, the manual filling in information about whereabouts is much more of a social obligation since the benefit is primarily for people coming to the space rather than the person who works there. Under such circumstances, the RoomWizard's interaction model appears less acceptable and less effortful mechanisms need to be considered to compliment these other mechanisms.

A further point about RoomWizard, in contrast to some other situated display applications is that is that it is a single functionality device. While the basic technology of the RoomWizard appliance can potentially host a whole variety of web-based content and functionality, the single functionality of the RoomWizard was an important component of its utility in a social context for many reasons. Most notably, the display space on the RoomWizard is not competed for by multiple sources of content. As such, information is persistently visible. If this display was time-shared between different sources of content, it would dilute the value derived from such persistence – it is *always* present for *ad hoc* conversational and awareness support. The importance of this lies in its role as a shared resource for the whole user community.

The dedicated functionality of the RoomWizard situated display also contributed to a stronger sense of simplicity and predictability around the device that was important in an individual and social context. Its predictability allowed users to develop a reasonably well-defined set of normative rules around their use of the device that would be more difficult in a multi purpose situated display. At HP laboratories where a related system was installed, the casual suggestion that someone was going to use the meeting room displays to display some photographs was met with considerable resistance since this would interfere with its primary role of informing people about room reservations. Predictability also supported understanding the relationship between the remote and local interfaces helping avoid uncertainties that can arise in other systems in terms of how and when remotely entered information will appear on the situated display (e.g. Houde, 1998).

Situated displays can also be thought of as having catchment areas of interest. For RoomWizard, these areas are simply defined by the people who use the meeting rooms. The notion of catchment area is one of particular importance to situated displays because it is intimately bound to the type of information that can be put on there and expectations on how it can be interpreted. With the RoomWizard the catchment was well bounded allowing relatively minimal content to be interpreted, understood and embellished with local context. Different applications and catchment areas will create different design requirements, but this is a general dimension that should be considered in situated display design.

Another important dimension of interest is spatial specificity. With RoomWizard, content was closely coupled to its spatial location. It was both defining of the activities that were going to take place in that space and defined by that space. Moving the device to another location would completely change the value and use of the device and its content. With RoomWizard, association with the space was by virtue of proximity. This association was somewhat sensitive and in some circumstances was weakened or confused by inappropriate placement (see figure 5-7).

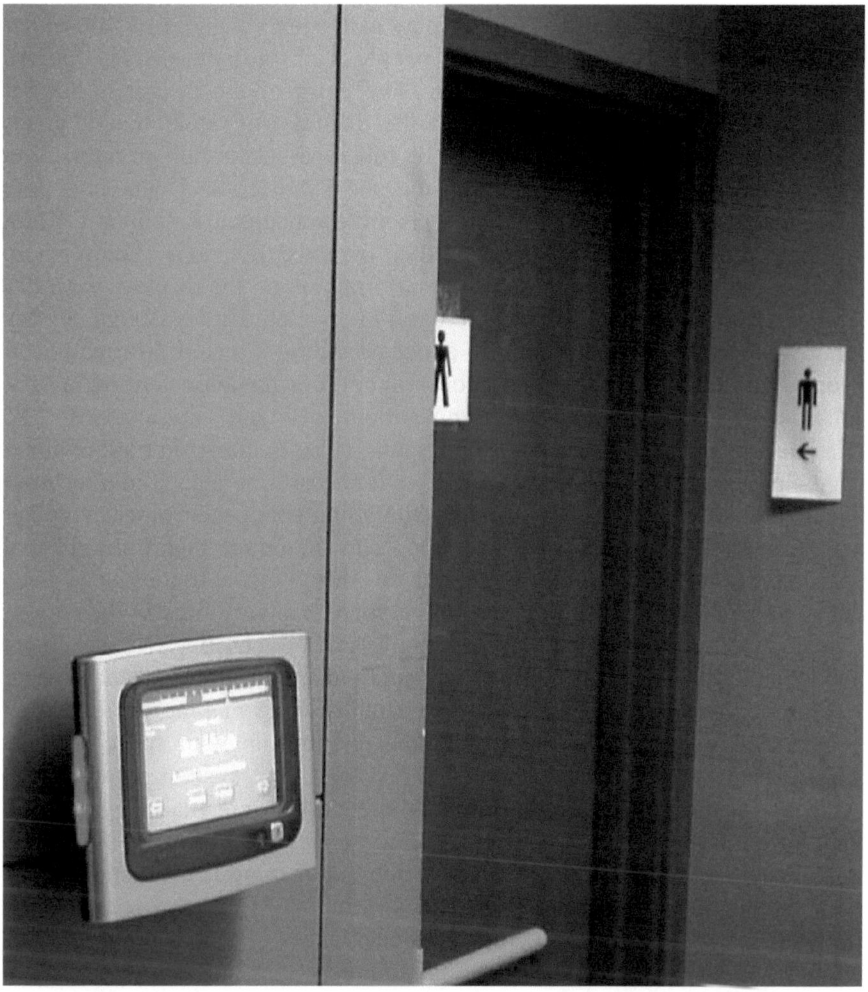

Figure 5-7. RoomWizard outside a meeting room adjacent to the restrooms.

While important in its impact on use, location may be less closely coupled with location with some other situated displays. Location may be more important in defining user catchment area and also the relationship between the device and typical activities in that area. An example of this can be seen with the "notice board" display appliance (O'Hara and Brown, 2001). This technology allowed people within a locally distributed team to email a URL to the display that they think may be of interest to the group. The display appliance then presents the web page denoted by the URL along with any contextual information as to why the page is of interest that the sender included in the email. The display also shows a photo of the sender and their various contact details. As people walk past the display, posted information may catch their attention. The point of the design is not for engagement in extensive browsing at the display but rather that it raises interest in certain issues that can then be followed up through an interaction with the sender – knowable through the photo and contact details. It also promotes *in situ* discussion by acting as a conversational resource. O'Hara and Brown report seeing examples in their own use of such a display where there is both a conversation around the information on the display *in situ* as well as its use in a later follow up activity. In creating display designs of this kind, we need to think not simply about providing situated information to people but also (and perhaps more) about conversation initiation that subsequently encourages the propagation of tacit knowledge. The relationship between technology and space is particularly important for a technology such as the notice board since it needs to be placed in a location where people will be able to view it while going about their other everyday activities. In O'Hara and Brown's example of the notice board, the display was initially poorly located in relation to other work activities in a place where people did not naturally flow to, so there was very little in the way of casual glancing at it in the course of people's other activities. The designers had toyed with the idea of putting the display in a more informal shared area where people would glance at it, for example while making coffee – this would have allowed them to explore the relationship with space and see what impact this relationship had on the value of the system. However by accident, as the group became larger, more desks were placed within the vicinity of the display. This changed the nature and purpose of the space immediately surrounding the display, thereby immersing it within a different activity context. Now that people were working close to it, there was more flow to that space leading to more casual glances at it and conversations around it. Space use then shifted again, and the display became orphaned in a corner of the room. As a consequence, no new information was posted to it and it became an essentially dead resource.

A final point arising from observing this use of a networked technology (i.e. RoomWizard) in managing a shared resource, such as space, is the importance of designing to support social mediation rather than automation (cf Zuboff, 1988). In designing RoomWizard, we have not built in formal rules that force its users to act in a certain way (e.g. booked rooms that physically lock out other users): it has normative rules built into it that its users *orient* towards. These normative rules can be 'broken' to achieve different outcomes, and this aspect of the design allows social mediation. As places and things are increasingly becoming networked, they will need some method to manage their control and availability, and as we have seen, this cannot be easily managed through a purely technical solution. Consider, as a simple example, a networked printer that can be accessed locally (e.g. over infra-red or Bluetooth). If multiple users need to use the device simultaneously, which print jobs should be given priority? The organisationally senior person? The most urgent? The shortest document? No clear answer is likely to be applicable in all cases. Technologies that allow socially mediated co-ordination protocols to develop around them are likely to fit the needs of their users better than those that enforce rigid application of embedded rules. One of the ways that this social mediation can be operated is through the use of easily visualisable system states - not just of the systems' current internal modality, but also of their social states and status.

11. Acknowledgments

This work was funded by Steelcase. Thanks to the RoomWizard team at The Appliance Studio, Steelcase & IDEO. Work by Mark Perry was supported, in part, by EPSRC grant GR/R09503/01 (Designing for mobile and distributed work).

12. References

Chou, P., Gruteser, M. Lai, J., Levas, A.McFaddin, Pinhanez, C. Viveros, M., Wong, D. and Yoshihama, S. BlueSpace: Creating a Context-Aware Workspace. IBM technical Report, 2001, T. J. Watson Research Center

Erickson, T. and Kellogg, W. Social Translucence: An Approach to Designing Systems That Support Social Processes. ACM Transactions on Computer-Human Interaction 2000; 7(1): 59-83.

Farrell, S. Social and informational proxies in a fish tank Extended Abstracts of CHI '01; 2001; Seattle WA, USA.

Gaver, W., Moran, T., MacLean, A. Lovstrand, L., Dourish, P. Carter, K. and Buxton, W. Realising a video environment: EuroPARC's RAVE system. Proceedings of the CHI '92 Conference on Human Factors in Computing Systems; 1992; Monterey, CA USA. New York: ACM Press: 27-35.

Greenberg, S. Designing Computers As Public Artifacts. International Journal of Design Computing: Special Issue on Design Computing on the Net (DCNet'99), Nov 30 - Dec 3, University of Sydney.

Gruen, D., Rohall, S. Petigara, N. and Lam, D. "In Your Space" Displays for Casual Awareness. In Demonstrations of the CSCW 2000 Conference Computer Supported Cooperative Work; 2000, December 2-6; Philadelphia, PA.

Harrison, S. and Dourish, P. Re-Place-ing Space: The Roles of Place and Space in Collaborative Systems. Proceedings of CSCW 96 Conference on Computer Supported

Cooperative Work; 1996, November 2-6; Boston, MA. ACM Press. Cambridge, MA., ACM Press: 67-76.

Houde, S., Bellamy, R., Leahy, L. In search of design principles for tools and practices to support communication within a learning community. SIGCHI Bulletin, 1998; 30(2): 113-118.

Ishii, H. Wisneski, C.Brave, S. and Dahley, A., Gorbet, M. Ullmer, B. and Yarin, P. ambientROOM: Integrating Ambient Media with Architectural Space. In Extended Abstracts of CHI '98; 1998; Los Angeles, CA, USA: 173-174.

McCarthy, J.F., Costa, T.J. and Liongosari, E.S. UniCast, OutCast and GroupCast: Three Steps Toward Ubiquitous Peripheral Displays. Proceedings of UbiComp'01 Conference on Ubiquitous Computing; 2001; Atlanta, GA, USA; Springer: 332-345.

Nguyen, D.H. Tullio, J., Drewes, T., Mynatt, E. Dynamic Door Displays. Georgia Institute of Technology unpublished Technical Report.

Nichols, J., Wobbrock, J., Gergle, D., and Forlizzi, J. Mediator and Medium: Doors as Interruption Gateways and Aesthetic Displays. In Proceedings of DIS '02; 2002; London, UK: 379-386.

O'Hara, K. and Brown, B. Designing CSCW Technologies to Support Tacit Knowledge Sharing Through Conversation Initiation. Workshop on Managing Tacit Knowledge, ECSCW'01 European Conference on Computer Supported Cooperative Work; 2001; Bonn, Germany.

Palen, L. Social, individual and technological issues for groupware calendar systems. Proceedings of CHI'99 Conference on Human Factors in Computing Systems; 1999; Pittsburgh, PA, USA. New York: ACM Press: 17-24.

Pedersen, E.R. People Presence or Room Activity supporting peripheral awareness over distance. In Extended Abstracts of CHI '98 Conference on Human Factors in Computing Systems; 1998; Los Angeles, CA, USA.

Sims, M. *Sign Design: Graphics Materials, Techniques*. London: Thames and Hudson, 1991

Snowden, D. and Grasso, A. Diffusing Information in Organisational Settings: Learning from Experience. In Proceedings of CHI'02 Conference on Human Factors in Computing Systems; 2002; Minneapolis, MA, USA. New York: ACM Press: 331-338

Zuboff, S. *In the Age of the Smart Machine. The future of work and power*. New York: Basic Books, 1988.

Chapter 6

EXPLORING THE EVOLUTION OF OFFICE DOOR DISPLAYS

The Hermes System

Keith Cheverst, Dan Fitton and Alan Dix
Lancaster University

Abstract: Within the field of ubiquitous computing, many of the issues related to the notion of 'situated interaction' remain very much under explored. For example, there is little understanding of the kinds of interactions or uses that are likely to occur when large numbers of interactive displays are publicly situated throughout an office environment. In this chapter, we describe the development, deployment and initial evaluation of the Hermes system, a system that comprises a collection of small interactive display units placed outside a number of offices within a University department. The placement outside offices is enabling us to explore some of the issues, such as appropriation control, that arise when interactive displays are situated in places that exhibit both public and private properties. To date, the development of the system has been guided by the principles of participatory design and our intention is that the use of the Hermes system will continue to evolve over a longitudinal period of time as it is used on a day-to-day basis by university staff and students alike.

Key words: Situated displays, ubicomp, remote interaction, messaging, participatory design.

1. Introduction

Many researchers argue that we are still some way away from understanding the implications of Weiser's vision of ubiquitous computing, with computers "interwoven into the fabric of everyday life" (Weiser, 1991). Indeed, studies based on deployed ubiquitous systems are still relatively rare. Furthermore, although the definition of ubiquitous computing clearly

K. O'Hara et al. (eds.), Public and Situated Displays: Social and Interactional Aspects of Shared Display Technologies, 141–169.

includes (and perhaps even implies) systems based on highly-available 'situated' or 'placed' technology, the majority of ubicomp systems that have been studied have been based on systems oriented towards mobile 'connected' and 'location-aware' systems.

One of the goals of our current research is to explore the use of asynchronous messaging systems that are situated in places that posses both private and public elements. In the University department where we work, one place that exhibits both these elements is the area outside an office. In more detail, this place may be used by the owner(s) of the office in order to leave publicly viewable messages (in the form of post-it notes etc.). Similarly the same area may also be used by visitors wanting to leave a message for the owner to read on his or her return.

We wanted to explore whether this traditional way of leaving messages on post-it notes in 'semi-private' places could be enhanced with a digital equivalent, e.g. one that supports remote interaction. In order to explore this area we have designed and deployed a digital asynchronous messaging system (called Hermes) within the main computing building at Lancaster University. The Hermes system supports remote interaction by allowing messages to be created and read via the web or a mobile phone. We hope that by supporting remote interaction and observing how the new system is used over a significant period of time we will gain useful insights into the importance of 'place' within this application domain. For example, will members of university staff be prepared to allow anonymous users to leave messages 'remotely' or will they insist that the person leaving a message be situated outside of their office when the message is created?

1.1 Deployed System vs. Lab Prototype

One of our key goals has been to develop the system using a participatory design based approach and then observe how the system is actually used by staff and students on a day to day basis and how this use evolves over a longitudinal period of time. In this respect, we see the aims of our work as similar in motivation to previous projects such as the Portholes project (Dourish and Bly, 1992) where a system was deployed in the workspace in order to enable a longitudinal study of the actual use of shared media spaces.

1.2 Related Work

A number of systems related to Hermes have been developed previously. However, the research agenda of much of this previous work appears to be in marked contrast to the agenda associated with our work on Hermes. In particular, the emphasis of previous work seems to be on the "one off" production of a proof of concept demonstrator in order to gauge technical feasibility and initial user feedback.

For example, McCarthy developed the 'OutCast' service to provide "a personal yet shared display on the outside of an individual's office"(McCarthy *et al.*, 2001). In contrast to the relatively small screens utilised by the Hermes system, the OutCast system utilizes a twenty inch NEC 2010 flat-panel monitor augmented by a MicroTouch touch-screen, which is embedded in a cubicle (office) wall and connected to a Pentium II computer situated inside the owner's office. The OutCast system can be configured by its owner to display a range of content, including: information from the owner's personal web page, public calendar entries in the owner's 'Outlook' calendar, location information obtained from the owner's infrared badge, descriptions of the owner's projects and even online demonstrations.

In common with the Hermes system, OutCast supports both a passive display mode and an active mode. In active mode, a visitor to an OutCast display can leave the owner a text message using a touch-screen virtual keyboard. Also in this mode, visitors can actively navigate through the content that has been made available by the owner.

Unfortunately, at the time of writing the OutCast system only has one unit deployed but this has still enabled some qualitative results to be obtained based on feedback obtained from visitors to the OutCast display (McCarthy *et al.*, 2001). The feedback suggests that visitors appreciate the ability to view the owner's calendar information and his or her location via information obtained from the owner's active badge. However, it is unclear how owners would feel about making such information available on their OutCast display.

Interestingly, McCarthy notes that in general visitors to the OutCast display were skeptical about the reliability of leaving messages for the owner using the messaging facility. During our experiences with Hermes, we have also found that some members of staff still prefer to leave a physical post-it note on an owner's door. However, we have also observed that many members of staff and students are happy to forgo the use of a post-it note wherever a Hermes display is available and (although no in depth analysis has yet taken place) there appears little evidence to suggest any particular stereotypical behaviour in this respect.

Research on the development of 'dynamic' door displays has also been conducted at Georgia Tech (Nguyen, unpublished). Technologically, the Hermes system is very similar to the prototype door displays developed at Georgia. Both systems provide a self-contained solution, based around a small PDA display with wireless LAN card and (optionally in the case of Hermes) an iButton reader. In common with the OutCast system, the Georgia displays are automatically updated to reflect the owner's current location and also his or her calendar information. Visitors to a dynamic door display can also leave voice messages for the owner.

The dynamic door displays were also designed to enable owners to control the content displayed to a visitor based on the actual identity of the visitor. In common with the developers at Georgia, we are also interested in exploring the extent to which owner's may wish to control the information presented to a visitor based on the visitor's identity, especially where this information represents some form of personal context such as location.

Unfortunately, the work at Georgia on deploying the dynamic door displays came to an end before any significant deployment or reasonable evaluation of the system was able to take place.

A project at Carnegie Mellon University is exploring how office doors can be augmented with computer generated displays in order to support the functions of 'aesthetic display and 'interruption gateway' (Nichols, *et al.*, 2002). This latter 'mediator' function arose from the researchers' observation that people often use their door to signify their availability or interuptability, e.g. a closed office door might indicate that the owner of the office does not wish to be disturbed.

In contrast to the other systems described, the system deployed at CMU does not utilize a tangible display that is somehow fixed to the office door or wall. Instead, the CMU system actually projects an image onto a window in the office door from a projector located in the office. This approach produces a relatively large image which is viewable on the public side of the office door. The information projected onto the office door is of three main types: virtual notes, digital art (such as web pages, personalized graphics etc.) and awareness information. The presentation of awareness information utilizes a system called 'StatusLight' which utilizes a simple traffic-light metaphor in order to enable users located in the office to stipulate their interuptability.

At the time of writing, the system at CMU has only been deployed on a single office door (the office of a group of PhD students, including some of the researchers working on the system). However, as part of their future work the researchers describe their intention to deploy more systems in order to carry out more comprehensive field trials and a more iterative development cycle.

Location-aware community systems are also related to our work on Hermes. These systems utilize wireless mobile devices in order to enable users to place digital notes at particular locations. Users of the system can then discover and read these digital notes when they enter the appropriate location. Examples of evaluated location-aware community systems include E-graffiti (Burrell and Gay, 2002) and GeoNotes (Espinoza *et al.*, 2001) The way in which these systems are designed means that the 'situated' nature of a message is to a large extent dependent on the accuracy of the user's location as sensed by the system, e.g. using GPS or the coverage area of an 802.11 wireless communications cell. Consequently, it is possible for there to be some geographic mismatch between the actual location where a message was created and the location where a message is read.

At a conceptual level, the notion of 'infoDoors', described by Ben Schneiderman in his book 'Leonardo's Laptop' (Schneiderman, 2002), bares a striking similarity to the ideas behind Hermes and envisions a future in which buildings may contain displays outside every office supporting a variety of different applications, e.g. personal message posting, support for visitor navigation etc. In common with Hermes, Schneiderman recognizes the suitability of off-the-shelf PDAs with wireless connectivity capabilities as a readily available and affordable technology for deployment purposes.

2. The Evolution of the Hermes System

Development work on the Hermes system commenced in October 2001 and has continues to evolve since the first two units were deployed outside offices in March 2002.

In order to describe the evolution of the Hermes system the following sub-sections describe and analyse the key phases of development and our current ideas for potential future developments.

2.1 Phase 1

During this early phase the core functionality of the system was developed and this functionality was tested on two Hermes displays that were deployed outside the offices of two of the system's developers.

2.1.1 Initial Design/Deployment Requirements

The design of Hermes displays was required to meet a number of separate installation requirements. For example, the fact that Hermes displays were to be mounted outside offices and were required to run permanently meant that the system had to comply with the University's health and safety regulations. Previous attempts to experiment with the use of ubiquitous displays within the department (e.g. the Flump system, Gellersen, *et al.*, 1999) had been thwarted at an early stage by the health and safety regulations which forbade the deployment of 'permanently on' High Voltage equipment within the University's corridors. Effectively this restriction meant that the Hermes displays would have to be based on a low voltage (LV) unit, such as a PDA.

An additional requirement was the need for the deployment of Hermes displays to comply with current U.K. Disabilities Legislation. This legislation states that public facilities need to be positioned at a height that does not unduly discriminate against people using a wheelchair. For this reason, it was necessary to place the units at a fairly low height (approximately 150 cm) off the floor. However, one of the implications of this is that the device is quite awkward to use for taller people. For this reason, we are considering designs that will enable the unit to be 'dragged' to the appropriate height by the user. This problem highlights an interesting variation on the theme of private ownership vs. public use.

A further and much more general requirement for the Hermes displays was that they should be easy to deploy. We felt that this requirement would be best met by deigning the Hermes display as a self contained unit. We also wanted a reasonable application development environment and so we chose to adopt a Pocket PC PDA based solution. We had hoped that the use of wireless communications would mean that no cabling would be required from a Hermes display to its associated office. Unfortunately however, the battery life of a PDA is still relatively short and so it has proved necessary to take (LV) power from offices through a small drilled hole in the door mounting.

Although access to the department is restricted during evenings and weekends the department has unrestricted access at all other times. For this reason, we needed to mount displays in such a way that opportunistic theft of the device would be difficult.

2.1.2 The Chosen Hardware Solution

Having decided to develop a system using an off-the-shelf Pocket PC based PDA, we considered two candidates, namely: the Compaq iPAQ and the HP Jornada 568. After much deliberation we decided upon using the HP Jornada for two main reasons. Firstly, at the time, only the Jornada came equipped with a built-in compact-flash slot and therefore could support wireless 802.11 networking without requiring an additional expansion jacket. Secondly, the unit has a relatively square shape (compared to the rounded back of the Compaq iPAQ with expansion jacket) and we felt that this would simplify case design. The case for holding the unit is made from aluminium and illustrated (together with a Jornada) in figure 6-1. Note how the case is designed to restrict access to the buttons on the PDA in order to prevent malicious or accidental termination of the application.

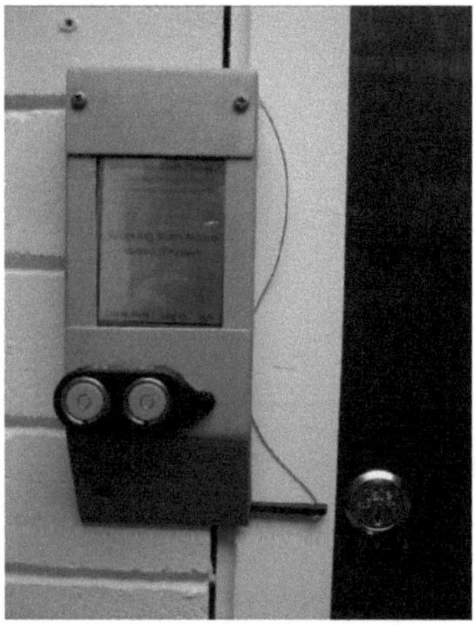

Figure 6-1. The first deployed Hermes display.

2.1.3 The Chosen Software Solution

At an early stage, we decided to use a Java based implementation. However, finding a version of Java that met our particular requirements was a frustrating process. In particular, it was difficult to find a version supporting the PDA's COM port. Such support was necessary because from a very early stage in the design process we thought that the use of iButtons could prove to be a useful tool for achieving user authentication.

Eventually, we chose to adopt CrEme version 3.2 (see CrEme home page) running on the PocketPC operating system as our software platform.

2.1.4 Overall System Architecture

The overall system architecture of the Hermes system is illustrated in figure 6-2. At the heart of the system is a single central server application written in Java 2 that runs on the Linux platform and provides the following key functions:

- centralized storage for messages and user profile information,
- communication with the SMS terminal,
- hosting of the web portal which is implemented using Java servlets to enable the dynamical generation and publication of HTML web pages

The system utilizes both wireless (802.11b) and wired Ethernet network infrastructures. In order to support the reception of SMS messages, the central server also communicates with a Wavecom DB02 GSM terminal. Communication between the components in the system is achieved using Java RMI (Remote Method Invocation) calls.

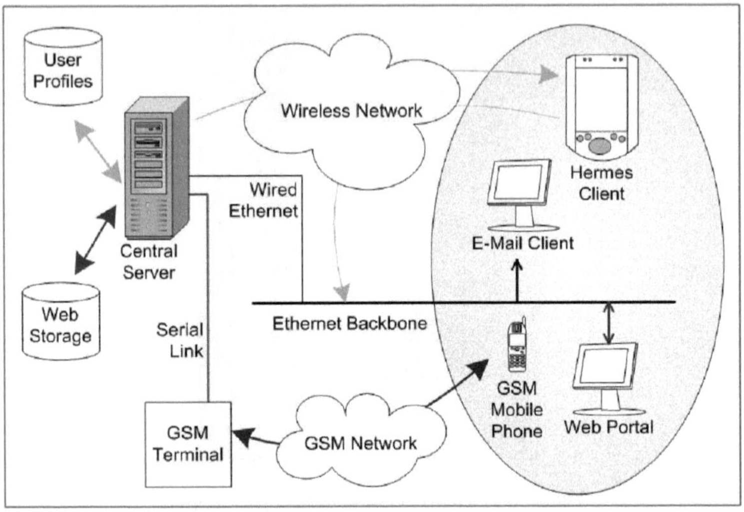

Figure 6-2. The Overall System Architecture of Hermes.

2.1.5 Functionality Available to the Owner of a Hermes Display

The system provides the owner of the Hermes display with several functions, notably:
- the ability to create and post a message via a web page,
- the ability to create and post a message be sending an SMS message,
- the ability to read messages left by visitors.

Posting a Message via a Web Page

Our initial idea for displaying messages posted by the owner of a Hermes display was to support two types of messages, namely: public messages and private messages. A public message would be the default message that would appear on the Hermes display. Conversely, the private message would only appear to those users that authenticated themselves with the system. Figure 3 shows the web interface for setting these two types of messages.

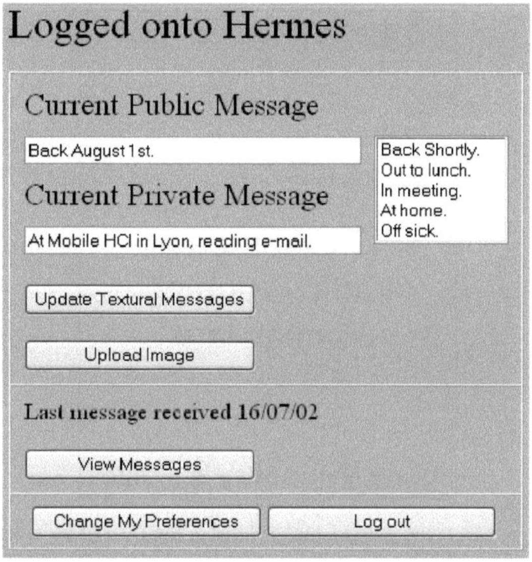

Figure 6-3: An Early version of the Hermes Web Interface.

The idea behind this approach was to enable the owner to have some control over the 'public' nature of messages. A typical example of how this could be used is illustrated in figure 6-3 where the public message contains low-fidelity information, i.e. "Back August 1st", and this information would be seen by those visitors that do not (or cannot, e.g. students) authenticate themselves with the Hermes system. Those visitors that do authenticate themselves with the system would be able to view the high fidelity information, i.e. the owner's reason for being away. Another motivating reason behind this approach was that we wanted to explore issues concerning the sharing of personal context, e.g. location, and, clearly, providing the user with some degree of control over who should have access to his or her personal context in an important aspect for consideration.

Posting a Message by Sending an SMS

One of the issues that we want to explore with the Hermes system is the implications of supporting remote interaction with Hermes displays. Consequently, we have designed the system such that, in addition to using the web interface to post a message, the owner of a Hermes display can also use GSM's SMS (or Short Message Service) in order to text a message to appear on his or her Hermes display. An example of a display showing a typical message received via SMS is shown below in figure 6-4.

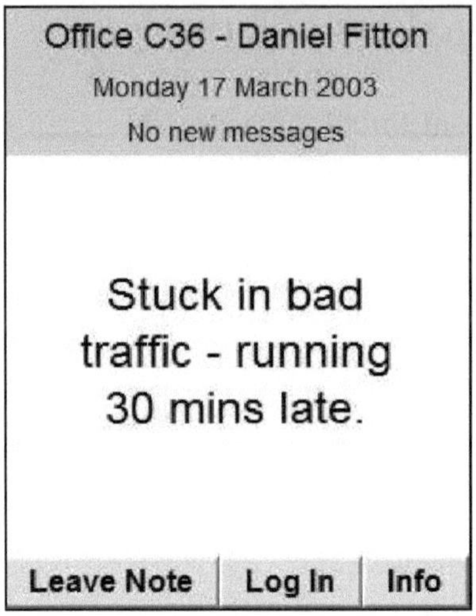

Figure 6-4. Example of message sent via SMS.

This particular remote messaging feature was originally motivated by one of the author's fears of being delayed during his daily commute to work and consequently missing appointments with students.

Reading Messages left by Visitors

The web portal (shown in figure 6-3) also enables the owner of a Hermes display to read the messages that have been left outside his or her door. In more detail, by clicking on the 'View Messages' button, the system generates a web page containing any notes which have been left on the owner's Hermes display and not yet deleted. As can be seen from figure 6-5, this web page also identifies the time and date that each message was left. The identity of the person who left each message is also presented but, as with its traditional 'post-it note' counterpart, the Hermes system does not require visitors to authenticate themselves in order to leave a message. However, if the user does authenticate him or herself (using an iButton or using the pen to select a user name and enter a PIN) then the owner's task of replying to the message is simplified. In more detail, by clicking on the appropriate button positioned alongside the authenticated message (e.g. the bottom message shown in figure 6-5), the owner is presented with a partially completed email or SMS form.

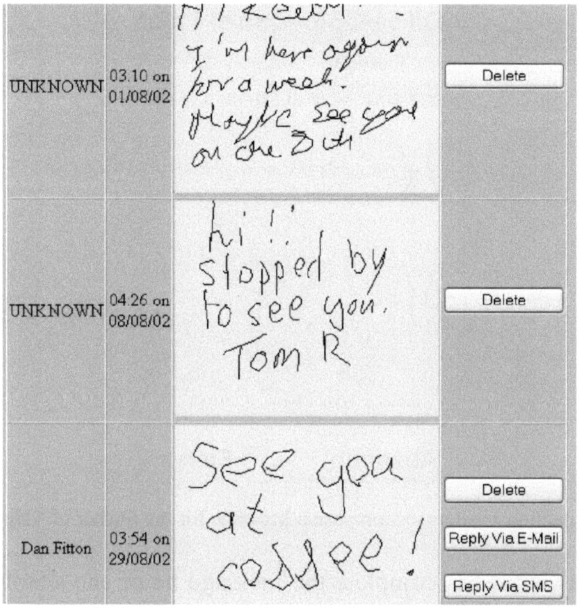

Figure 6-5. Example of a Hermes Web Page showing messages for the Owner.

2.1.6 Functionality Available to the Visitor

We designed Hermes so that any visitor to a Hermes display would not be able to read messages left by other visitors for the owner of that display. In this respect, the system clearly reduces the public nature of visitor's messages over that afforded by the traditional post-it note. One reason behind this design decision was that we were interested to observe, over a prolonged period of evaluation, the extent to which different users react positively or negatively to this feature.

Another restriction that we placed on the functionality available to visitors was the constraint that a visitor must be collocated with a Hermes display in order to leave a message. We implemented this constraint following discussions with potential users of the system and also based the decision on our own personal preferences.

In order to leave a message on a Hermes display, the visitor simply has to tap on a 'leave note' button on the Hermes display (as shown in the bottom left of figure 6-4). Tapping on this button results in the screen shown in figure 6-6 being displayed which enables a message to be 'scribbled' on the touch sensitive display.

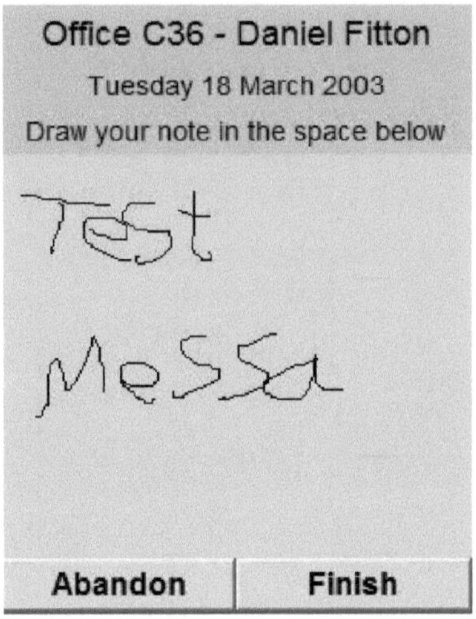

Figure 6-6. Enabling Visitors to Compose a Message for the Owner of a Hermes Display.

When the visitor has complete the message he of she simply taps on the 'Finish' button and the display on the unit is updated to reflect the fact that the owner has an additional message waiting to be read.

2.1.7 *Analysis*

An oversight in this earlier version of the system enabled visitors to walk away from the unit with the screen still showing their message/drawing (by simply not pressing the 'Finish' button). This situation posed significant problems. The fact that the visitor's message could remain on the screen broke our aim that the messages left by visitors should not be public. Another consequence of this situation was that the owner's message would not be publicly visible while the visitor's message remained on the screen. However, the most important consequence of this situation was the adverse effect on the owner's confidence in the integrity and security of the system. Unfortunately, this damage to confidence arose as a result of an anonymous prankster that would leave 'inappropriate' messages on Hermes displays.

One interesting problem that only became apparent when the first units were deployed was the problem of severe network signal degradation that occurs when multiple people stand in front of a wireless Hermes display. In such circumstances, the visitors can actually absorb sufficient 802.11 signals to break network connectivity between the Hermes display and the central server. This has a severe impact on functionality with the affected Hermes display being unable to properly handle the display of new messages created by the owner or a visitor. The severity of this situation is exacerbated by the fact that no appropriate visual feedback is displayed to indicate the reduced functionality. The design of appropriate mechanisms to handle failures in network connectivity is an area of current work.

It soon became apparent during this early development phase that the Hermes display owners (at this stage two of the system developers) were not making use of the private message facility. The main reason for this was that the developers were aware (from observing usage logs) that visitors were not authenticating themselves with Hermes displays but rather using the system anonymously. Consequently, developers realized that without prior authentication no private messages would be read.

One very interesting phenomenon that became apparent during this early stage was that the action of closing the office door when leaving the office often acts as a trigger to remind the user to leave a message. The frustration caused to the owner by having to reenter the office, in order to post a message, suggested the need to extend the ways in which a message can be posted to include posting via a Hermes display directly.

The ability to read messages from remote locations, such as when attending foreign conferences, was clearly very useful. The only problem that arose was that initially it was awkward for owners to remember the appropriate web address; an easy to remember domain name (www.hermesmessenger.co.uk) was registered to help overcome this problem.

It is interesting to consider the trust issue with regard to the posting messages. Initially, the two owners were quite skeptical about trusting that a message posted would actually appear outside respective office doors. This skepticism was justified given that during this early development phase system reliability was fairly poor.

2.2 Phase 2

One of the key aims of phase two was to try to significantly increase system reliability. In addition to code analysis (discovery of memory leaks etc.) we partly tackled the poor network signal problem by modifying the case design to reduce the shielding effect caused by the aluminium housing (see figure 6-7).

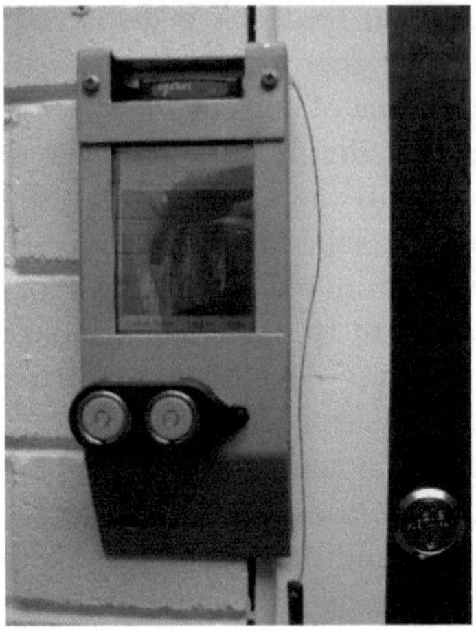

Figure 6-7. The modified case design with iButton reader.

In terms of deployment, during this phase the number of deployed units was increased from 2 to 5 and figure 6-8 shows the deployment of three Hermes displays in close proximity along one corridor.

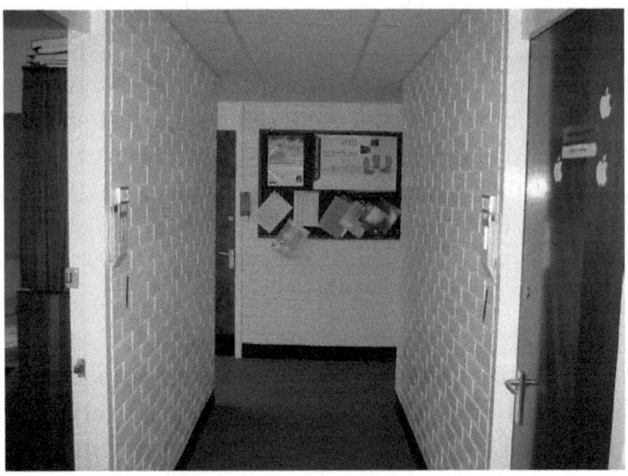

Figure 6-8. Corridor in the main Computing building showing 3 Hermes displays.

Also during this second development phase, a number of fairly straightforward but crucial modifications were made to the client application. One such modification was to introduce an upper time limit on the period that the 'visitor message composition' screen (see figure 6-6) could be displayed. By introducing this time-out, we removed the previous loophole that had enabled anonymous users to leave inappropriate messages on public display.

Another two modifications made during this phase were:

- software for the iButton readers was introduced in order to help reduce the effort required to achieve authentication,
- the client application was modified in order to enable an owner to create and post a message via his or her Hermes display.

Both these modifications are described in the following two sub-sections.

2.2.1 iButton based Authentication

Although the first Hermes display to be deployed was actually equipped with an iButton reader (as shown in figure 6-1) the task of writing the software to support the action of docking an iButton proved troublesome. The appropriate software was only completed during this second phase of development and allowed the authentication process to occur as soon as a user (visitor or owner) docked his or her iButton.

2.2.2 Creating a Message using a Hermes display

In order to enable owners to create and post a message using their Hermes display directly, the client application was modified in order to enable an owner to create a freehand message by using the interface that appears on the Hermes display (see the left hand picture of figure 6-9) once the owner has successfully authenticated themselves.

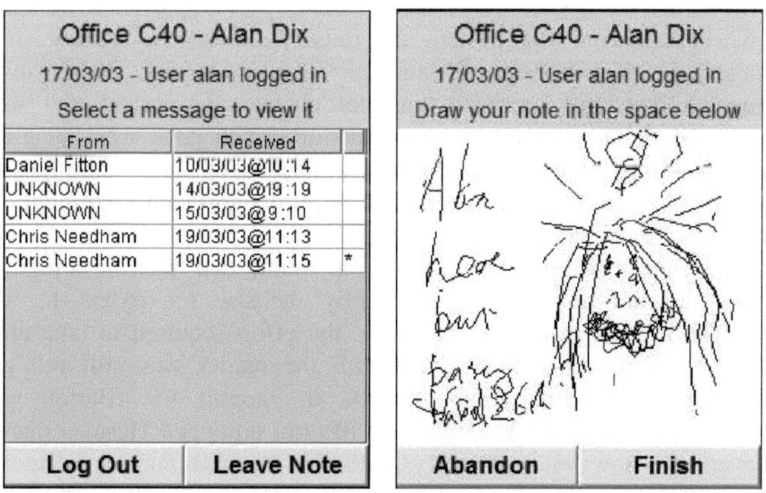

Figure 6-9. Enabling the Hermes Owner to Compose a Freehand Message.

The right hand picture in figure 6-9 shows an example of a freehand message composed by one of our more 'creative' Hermes display owners.

2.2.3 Analysis

Although one of the Hermes display owners does make great use of the freehand message drawing facility, his reason for using this facility is, in part, due to the extra freedom for creativity that freehand drawing permits. However, it should be noted that this user does have a Hermes display that is equipped with an iButton reader.

A number of owners commented that the way in which the system was configured to support the use of public messages did not fit in well with the way in which they wished to post and remove messages. In more detail, the common way in which the system was used is as follows. Owners would set a public message that effectively acted as their default message, e.g. a cute picture or a simple text message like "Adrian's Office". As necessary, owners would change this message to something more transient, e.g. "Gone for coffee". Clearly, an owner would only want this latter kind of message to be displayed temporarily before he or she would wish to revert back to the default public message. However, owners tended to find the action of reverting back to their default public message quite frustrating because they were required to go through the same basic procedure as that used for setting an entirely new public message.

Effectively, the problem encountered during this phase was that the messaging support provided by the system did not match well with the patterns of use being shown by users. As another example of this, a number of owners criticized the system for only enabling the reading of left messages via a web page or another Hermes display. These owners commented that this approach was not always appropriate and simply required too much effort if the corresponding web page was not already open. It was suggested that an alternative mechanism for reading messages should also be available that would not require significant additional effort on the part of the owner.

Unfortunately, during this phase we found that the introduction of iButtons did not appear to significantly increase the extent to which authentication took place. For one user, the effort required to take out his keys in order to dock an iButton with the reader was still too great. Furthermore, the introduction of code to support the iButton reader significantly reduced the reliability of iButton equipped Hermes displays. However, the low rate of acceptability of the iButton as a tool for authentication was not helped by the fact that only two units were equipped with an iButton reader and that not all owners of Hermes displays possessed an iButton.

2.3 Phase 3

During this phase the number of deployed units was increased from 5 to 10 units. Also, during this phase the system was modified to support the emailing of messages and the notion of temporary messages was also introduced.

2.3.1 Emailing Newly Received Messages to the Owner

In order to address the criticism relating to the effort required by an owner to open up a web page in order to read his or her latest messages, we modified the system such that every time a new message was left on an owner's Hermes display, an HTML based email would be sent to the owner containing an image of the message. A sample screen shot example the display of a Hermes email message on a typical email client is shown in figure 6-10.

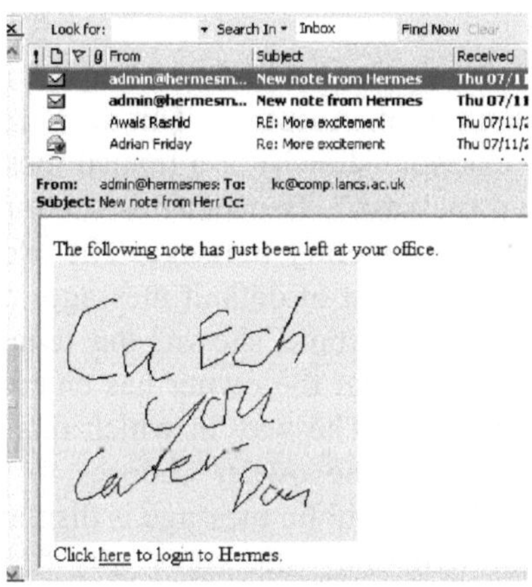

Figure 6-10. Receiving Hermes Messages via Email.

2.3.2 Supporting the Notion of Temporary Messages

We introduced the notion of temporary and default public messages in an attempt to create a simple procedure for enabling an owner to revert back to a default public message when his or her temporary message is no longer appropriate.

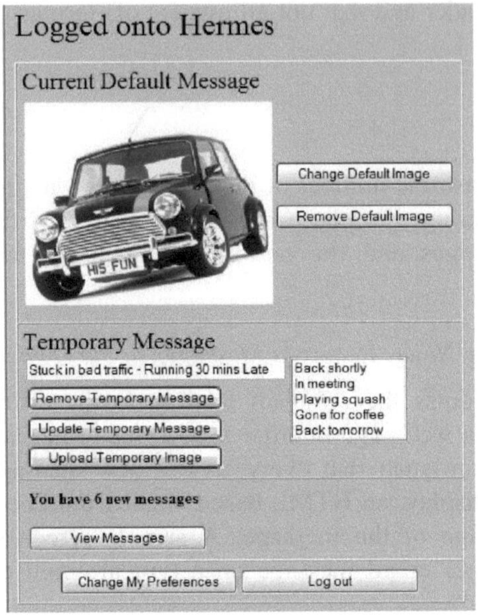

Figure 6-11. The Modified Hermes Web Interface.

As can be seen from figure 6-11, the modified interface enables the owner to specify a default public message. This would usually take the form of a picture (as in the example shown) or a textual message such as "John's Office – Please leave a message". Beneath this section of the interface the owner is able to specify a temporary message. The user still has the choice of selecting a message from a list of default messages or entering a message in a free text field. In the example shown, the temporary message field reflects a temporary message that the owner has entered remotely via SMS but has not yet been removed. The way in which this aspect of the system works is quite simple; when the owner chooses to remove a temporary message then his or her default public message is displayed.

When the notion of temporary messages was first introduced owners commented that the effort required to remove a (temporary) message was still too great. Following discussions, it became apparent that what was required was some very lightweight approach for enabling users to discard temporary messages using the device itself. Consequently, we modified the system to enable owners to dismiss messages by touching the screen for a short period of time (currently set at one second). The implementation of this feature has proved very popular with owners.

We intend to return to exploring the notion of public and private messages when a suitably low effort (for the user) and timely authentication method becomes available.

2.3.3 Analysis

As expected, owners were positive about having the ability to receive a Hermes message as an HTML based email. In addition, owners were also reasonably positive about the notion of default and temporary messages. This changed to being a very positive result when we enabled the removal of temporary messages by simply touching the screen of the Hermes display. The fact that owners were prepared to give visitors the potential to remove a temporary message because it simplified the process of removing messages for themselves demonstrates an interesting instance of the security vs. ease of use trade-off; this tradeoff is considered in greater detail in section 3.3. However, many owners commented that, in addition, they wanted to have a lightweight mechanism for setting temporary messages from their Hermes display.

Unfortunately, the general dependability of the system is still of insufficient quality. Indeed, when a Hermes display fails for some reason, it is up to the owner of the display to notice that the display is not functioning correctly and then to notify the system administrator. This is, of course, entirely the wrong approach. Firstly, it is not always apparent to an owner when his or her display stops functioning correctly. Secondly, staff in the department tend to be extremely busy and (quite rightly) will not always give priority to find time to notify the system administrator when there appears to be a problem with their Hermes display. Thirdly, such dependability problems can greatly reduce the perceived reliability of the system and, consequently, have a detrimental affect on the future use of the system.

2.4 Phase 4: Current Development Phase

The aims of the current development phase are two-fold. Firstly, we are trying to tackle some of the dependability problems that have, to-date, harmed the trust that some users have for the system. Secondly, we are modifying the system in order to enable the owner of a Hermes display to use their display in order to quickly and simply set a temporary message.

2.4.1 *Increasing System Dependability*

In our push to improve system dependability, we are currently modifying the system across various levels in order to detect failures and notify the system administrator(s) as and when these failures are discovered. Hermes displays are now required to send an acknowledgement to the central server on a regular basis (currently set to once every minute) and therefore the discovery time for detecting failure of a Hermes display has a relatively low upper bound.

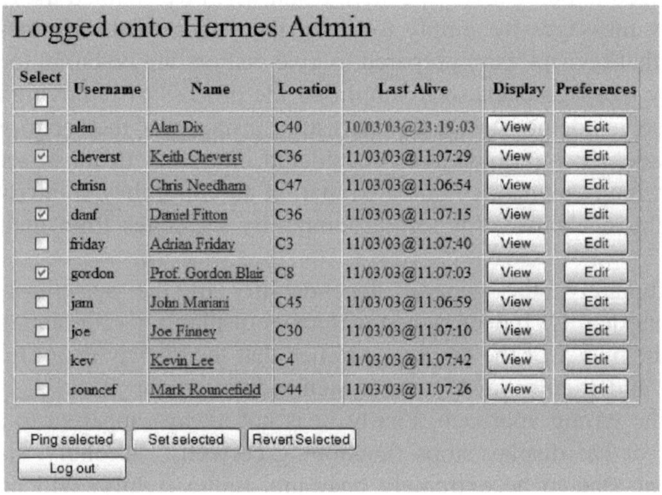

Figure 6-12. The main System Administrator web page.

In addition to providing automatic notification, we are also developing a special web page for system administrator, which, in addition to other features, will present an up-to-date overview of the general state of the system. An illustration of the Administrator web page is shown in figure 6-12.

2.4.2 *Enabling Messages To Be Left Via a Hermes Display*

We are currently considering ways of addressing the criticism raised by some owners that it is still too cumbersome to set a temporary message from the Hermes display itself. Our chosen solution is to enable owners to set temporary messages by using an interface similar to the examples shown in figure 6-13. The different labeling of buttons depicted in the two screen shots shown in figure 6-13 illustrate how we intend to enable users to select from a set of default temporary messages or to select from a set of temporary messages of their own choosing.

When considering this solution, we faced an interesting conundrum involving a security vs. ease of use trade-off. Elaborating on this, in order to make the task of leaving a temporary message as simple as possible, we did not wish to force owners to authenticate themselves with their own Hermes display as a precursor to leaving a temporary message. We believed (and this was validated through discussions with owners) that a more suitable approach would be to make the default behaviour of the system one that did not require authentication for leaving temporary messages but enabling users to change this default behaviour as part of their personal preferences. By prescribing the choice of temporary messages that may be left on public display by an unauthenticated user (as opposed to allowing the display of freehand messages) we hope to have addressed the concerns of owners (described in section 2.1.7) by reducing the likelihood of 'inappropriate' or 'prank' content being left on public display by (unauthenticated) individuals.

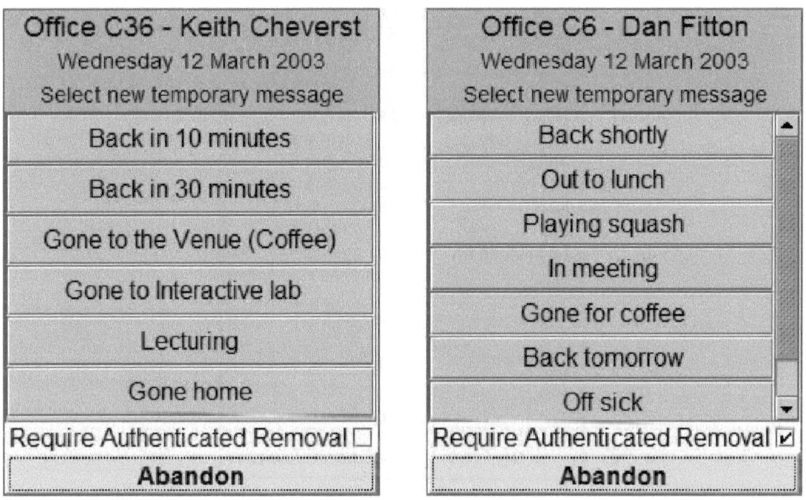

Figure 6-13. Possible GUIs for enabling Owners to Set Temporary Messages from their Hermes Displays.

3. Issues

This section discusses in detail the most significant issues that we have been able to explore (and/or plan to explore further) through our work with the Hermes system.

3.1 Appropriation

As designers, we are keen to explore further the notion of appropriation of publicly situated devices. Currently, following authentication, owners are able to appropriate the displays of other Hermes owners in order to view their own messages. Figure 6-14 illustrates how Alan is able to view his messages from Keith's Hermes display after successful authentication. Working with the example shown in Figure 6-14: if Alan selects the 'Leave Note' option then the message that he composes will appear on the Hermes display outside his own office.

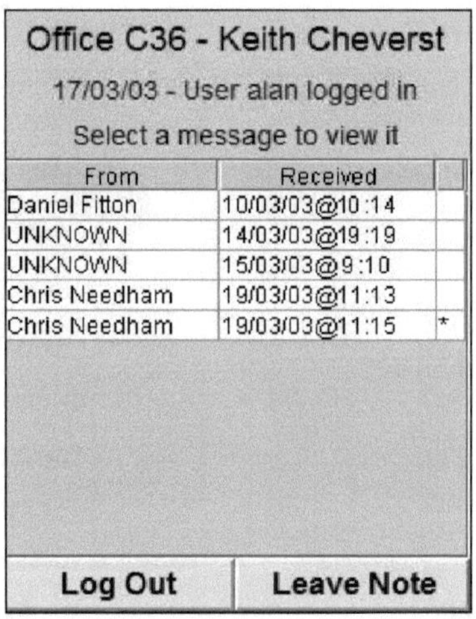

Figure 6-14. Example of Appropriation; Alan viewing his messages from Keith's Display.

One idea for further developing this notion of authentication is to develop some form of distributed game that can effectively run across multiple Hermes displays. Our current plan is to base the game on the Atari classic 'Asteroids'. Effectively, each display will represent one segment of the game's canvas and consequently the action that takes place on one Hermes display (i.e. the shooting of asteroids) will directly affect the action that occurs on other Hermes displays. It will be interesting to observe whether (and under what conditions) the owners of Hermes displays will be prepared to let 'visitors' appropriate the use of their display for the purpose of playing such a game.

Another area that we plan to explore is the notion of allowing administrators (or other users) to display announcements through Hermes displays. A typical example of such an announcement would be "Staff meeting in C29 at 3 pm" which the departmental secretary could issue a short time before the planned start of the meeting. Again, this will hopefully provide some useful insights into the extent to which the owners of Hermes displays are prepared to 'share' their public displays. Initial discussions suggest that owners will be prepared to forsake some control provided they have the ability to specify when it is not acceptable to have one of their public messages overwritten. Another potential way of exploiting the set of Hermes displays is for navigation purposes. Ideally, the number of deployed Hermes displays would be increased such that units are located at various navigation points throughout the department. A system could then be written which would effectively place all Hermes displays in a location model which could then be processed in order to direct visitors to a given office by, for example, displaying appropriate direction icons on selected Hermes displays.

3.2 Sharing Personal Context

Part of the motivation behind the Hermes work was a desire to explore one particular form of support for sharing personal context. In particular, we wished to move away from the current trend of automatically capturing the personal context of users (e.g. through the use of an active badge (Spreitzer, and Theimer, 1993) or sensor-rich coffee mug (Gellersen *et al.*, 1999)) and then making this context available to a wide collection of users. The problems associated with incorporating such approaches in the workspace environment are well documented (e.g. Spreitzer, and Theimer, 1993).

In the Hermes work, we wanted to support coordination through the sharing of personal context but we wanted to give the users of the system a strong degree of control over the context that is shared and also the ability to restrict the visibility of this context based on location.

As far as temporary messages are concerned, the majority displayed tend to share some personal context, e.g. "Gone for Coffee – back soon" or "On bus – in shortly".

In the future, we may modify the system in order to support some kind of automatic context capture, e.g. through permitted access to the owner's calendar, but we would anticipate that some users would stipulate that messages containing such personal context could only be visible to a restricted set of authenticated users.

3.3 Security vs. Ease of Use

One issue that has arisen numerous times throughout development is the trade-off between security and ease-of-use. When we were first started considering the design of the Hermes system it seemed like the issue of security was one area where we could demonstrate clear advantages over traditional approaches, such as post-it notes. In particular, it appeared that we could offer staff at the university a means for leaving messages on public display outside their offices which could not then be tampered with.

In part, the tradeoff between security and ease-of-use arises because of the effort required for an owner or a visitor to authenticate him or herself with a Hermes display. Consequently, if an immediate and very low effort method for achieving authentication was available then this tradeoff would probably become far less significant to the Hermes system.

Owners were first required to consider this tradeoff when deciding upon an acceptable process for removing temporary messages from their Hermes display. It was interesting to discuss with owners the notion of effectively allowing anyone to remove a temporary message. Many owners were clearly concerned about forsaking control in this way but these concerns were outweighed by the promise of being able to remove a message with a single and simple action.

Similar considerations also arose when considering with owners potential solutions for selecting a temporary message using their Hermes display. Again, owners were concerned about the security issues of enabling unauthenticated users to tamper with temporary messages but owners were adamant about having the facility to select a temporary message on their Hermes display without having to go through the effort of authentication. The solution described in section 2.4.2. was felt to offer a good compromise between security (i.e. only a message from the owner's default set of messages could be selected) and ease-of-use (i.e. no authentication process was required; selecting a temporary message only requires two taps on the screen of a Hermes display).

3.4 Personalisation and Tailorability

Currently, tailorability is supported at the level of enabling owners to control what appears on their display, e.g. an animated GIF, a freehand scribble, a simple text message etc. However, following discussions with owners it is clear that for some there is a desire to have greater control over certain attributes of the system. In more detail, the following list represents items to be considered for tailorability:

a) Changing the default set of temporary messages (see sections 2.1.5.1 and 2.4.2),
b) Specifying whether or not the removal of temporary messages requires authentication
c) Controlling how long it is necessary to touch the screen of a Hermes display before a temporary message is removed (if no authentication option is active)
d) Controlling whether temporary messages can be set via the Hermes display without authentication

In terms of personalisation, we intend to explore the use of machine learning techniques in order to support a 'most likely message' feature. A hypothetical example showing the way in which this feature could affect the web interface for selecting a temporary message is show in figure 6-15.

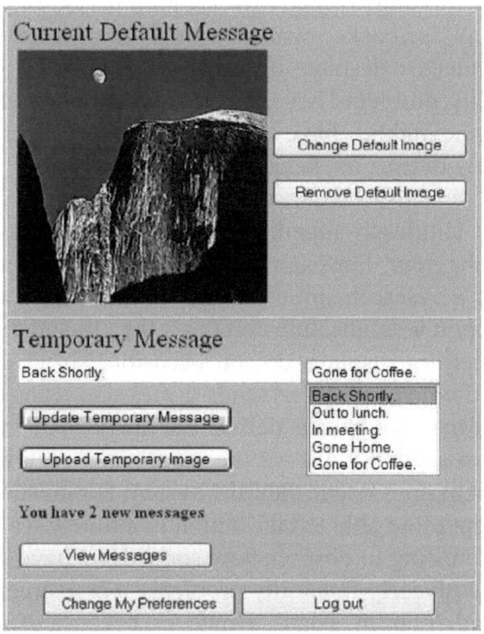

Figure 6-15. A Potential use of Personalization: 'Most Likely Message'.

In the example shown, we presume a scenario in which based on the context history (which would hold previous messages selected by the user tagged with context including time and day of the week) the system has leant that the most likely message that the user will wish to leave given the current context is the message "Gone for Coffee". In the scenario shown, the user has actually chosen to override the 'most likely message' with the message "Back Shortly".

3.5 Dependability

Unless users have a strong degree of trust in the reliability of the Hermes system then it is extremely unlikely that it will become a tool that is used on a regular basis. For example, if someone wishing to leave a message for the owner of Hermes display doubts whether a message left on the display will actually reach the owner then he or she will simply use a post-it note instead. Confidence in the system is then reduced still further as passers-by notice the post-it note next to the Hermes display and naturally start to wonder why it is there.

Of course, in order to encourage users to trust the system, users need to see the system functioning correctly over a long period of time and we have encountered many setbacks while trying to achieve this level of dependability. Indeed, despite our phased approach to deployment, numerous reliability problems have arisen and unfortunately such problems will, somewhat inevitably, have had an adverse effect on the future willingness of users to trust the behaviour of the system.

In the ideal scenario, we would develop a system in which all components work faultlessly together. However, it has not been possible to guarantee such behaviour. For example, the wireless network utilised by our system is part of a research initiative by another research project and so cannot be relied upon with absolute certainty, the OS and the version of Java running on the Hermes displays do, on occasion, suffer apparent memory leak problems and when an owner sends a message using the SMS service the GSM provider may not always deliver the message in a timely manner.

As described in section 2.4.1 we are currently modifying the system so that when a problem does occur then the system administrator is notified of the problem and therefore able to take action in a timely way.

It has been interesting to observe how some users have developed coping strategies to deal with early reliability problems. For example, Alan once left a message that read "I am in! Alan". However, because of a system crash on his Hermes display his message stayed visible for the week that he was away at a conference; he thought he had successfully removed the message via the web. He received several emails saying "your door said you were in, but I couldn't find you". Following this incident, Alan has developed his own coping strategy for overcoming such potential problems by including an explicit date with such messages, e.g. "Alan in all day today, Thurs 13th" (see example notes in figures 6-9 and 6-16).

The door display is situated in space giving it a context, but it is also situated in time. Furthermore the electronic display implicitly says "I am live, up-to-date information". So naturally people read the message "I am in! Alan" as if it was current. The explicit mentioning of dates in the message allows people to assess the currency of the message.

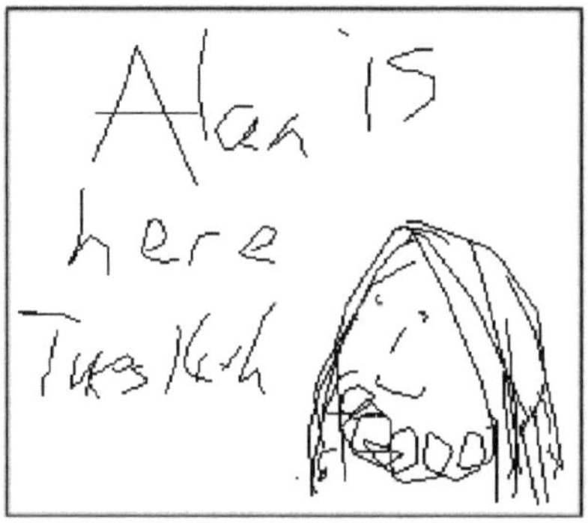

Figure 6-16. A Freehand Message including an Explicit Date.

The danger with the original unreliability was that it could have led to a downward spiral of disuse: visitors would have lost confidence in the messages, then Alan knowing this would have less reason to keep it up to date, leading to further distrust. Of course the incident has led us to consider technical solutions, but the system was successful in that its openness allowed a user-driven and user-controlled solution. The flexibility and informality of the notes allowed Alan to create a solution of his own.

3.6 Participatory Design

Throughout development, one issue that has arisen time and again is the need as a designer to be sympathetic to user's patterns of use. For example, during the early phases of development, we forced owners to interact with their Hermes displays through a web browser. This caused a problem for two reasons. Firstly, it was often inconvenient for users to open a web page and enter their user name in order to set or read a message. Secondly, and perhaps more importantly, the approach did not fit in with the way in which many users seem to process the task of leaving a message. It was only as we involved users in the design of this aspect of the system that we came up with approaches that fitted in well with their existing patterns of work. For example, it was only through discussions with owners that we came to realise the value of emailing Hermes messages to owners.

4. Concluding remarks

This chapter has described our exploration into the use of situated office door displays. Our goal for this system was not to stop at the development of a laboratory prototype but to harness the principles of participatory design in order to experience the evolution of a system that gets used on a day to day basis and provides genuine utility to members of staff in the Computing department where the collection of Hermes displays have been deployed.

To date, a wide and varied range of issues have already arisen from the development process and we are confident that further issues will unfold as the system continues to evolve in the years to come.

Acknowledgements

The work described in this chapter has been conducted through the auspices of the CASCO project that is funded by the UK Engineering and Physical Sciences Research Council. We would also like to acknowledge the help and tolerance of members of Lancaster University's computing department.

References

Burrell J., Gay G. E-graffiti: Evaluating Real-World Use of a Context-Aware System. Interacting with Computers, 2002; 14: 301-312.

CrEme home page: http://www.nsicom.com/

Dourish P., Bly S. Portholes: Supporting Awareness in a Distributed Work Group. Proceedings of CHI '92 Conference on Human Factors in Computing Systems, 1992; Monterey, California, New York: ACM Press: 541-547.

Espinoza F., Persson P., Sandin A., Nyström H., Cacciatore E. Bylund M. GeoNotes: Social and Navigational Aspects of Location-Based Information Systems. Proceedings of the International Conference on Ubiquitous Computing 2001, Atlanta, Georgia: Springer; 2-17; 2001.

Finney J., Davies N. FLUMP: The FLexible Ubiquitous Monitor Project. Proceedings of the 3rd Communication Networks Symposium; 8-9 July; Manchester, U.K.: 68-71, 1996.

Gellersen H., Beigl M., Krull H. The MediaCup: Awareness Technology embedded in an Everyday Object", Proceedings of the 1st International Symposium on Handheld and Ubiquitous Computing (HUC99); September; Karlsruhe, Germany: 308-310, 1999.

iButton home page: http://www.ibutton.com/

McCarthy J. F., Costa T. J., Liongosari E. S. UNICAST, OUTCAST & GROUPCAST: Three Steps toward Ubiquitous Peripheral Displays. Proceedings of the International Conference on Ubiquitous Computing 2001, Atlanta, Georgia: Springer; 332-345. 2001.

Nguyen D., Tullio J, Drewes T., Mynatt E.D. Dynamic Door Displays. Georgia Tech, Unpublished technical report.
(Online version: http://quixotic.cc.gt.atl.ga.us/~dnguyen/writings/DynDoorDisplays.pdf)

Nichols, J., Wobbrock J. Gergle D. Forlizzi J. Mediator and Medium: Doors as Interruption Gateways and Aesthetic Displays Proceedings of the ACM Conference on Designing Interactive Systems; 2002 June 25-28; London, UK: 379-386, 2002.

Schneiderman, Ben., Leonardo's laptop: Human Needs and the New Computing Technologies: MIT Press, 2002.

Spreitzer, M. Theimer M. Providing Location Information in a Ubiquitous Computing Environment', Proceedings of the 14th Symposium on Operating System Principles; 1993 Dec 5-8; Asheville, NC; 270-283: ACM Press, 1993.

Weiser M. The Computer for the 21st Century. Scientific American, 265(3): 66-75, 1991

Chapter 7

THE SOCIAL CONSTRUCTION OF DISPLAYS

Coordinate Displays and Ecologically Distributed Networks

Andy Crabtree, Terry Hemmings and Tom Rodden
University of Nottingham

Abstract: We employ ethnography to consider the nature of existing non-electronic 'displays' in the home. The word display is placed in scare quotes to draw attention to the *act of displaying*. Seen from the point of view of action it is evident that displays are socially constructed by people in their routine interactions with the material technologies available in the settings where their actions are situated. Through the use of a setting's material technologies to construct mutually intelligible displays for one another people come to coordinate their actions. Our ethnographic studies show that these 'coordinate displays' are distributed across a variety of locations within a setting. Taken together these displays articulate an ecologically distributed network elaborating the unique needs of particular environments and requirements for the development of computer support for cooperative work. We elaborate this point of view through an ethnographic study of the coordinate displays implicated in mail use in the home environment.

Key words: Ethnography, home, mail, coordinate displays.

1. Introduction

When we consider the topic of technological displays we find ourselves confronted by that familiar and perennial topic in systems design concerning the essential nature of the interface. Accordingly, a display might initially be thought of as *a site* where interaction and communication are effected and articulated (Grudin 1990). Grudin's classic article 'interface' highlighted the paucity of early cognitive conceptualisations of the interface, which focused on the computer's relationship to the user, rather than the user's relationship

K. O'Hara et al. (eds.), Public and Situated Displays: Social and Interactional Aspects of Shared Display Technologies, 170–190.

to the computer. The distinction drew attention to an ignored and revolutionary phenomenon:

> "Consider the two faces to the user-computer interface. Is the user's interface to a computer the mirror image of the computer's interface to the user? It may seem that it should be, but on reflection it is not, unless one defines 'interface' extremely narrowly. The user's interface to the computer may centre on the software-controlled dialogue, but it also includes any documentation and training that are part of using the computer. It includes colleagues, consultants, systems administrators, customer support and field service representatives, when they are available. These artefacts, processes, and people are so significant in shaping our interactions with a computer that it is myopic not to see them as part of a user's interface to the computer." (Grudin 1990)

The ignored phenomena, then, was this: the organizational context of use and with that, the *social shaping* of the interface. Seen from this point of view it was and is inappropriate to construe of 'users' as information processors. Rather, they are competent practitioners or 'doers of activities' situated in their work with other competent practitioners in real world settings. 'The user' is embedded, then, in concrete constellations and arrangements of collaboration and cooperation and it is in these arrangements of *work* that the user comes to interface with the computer.

Grudin turned design's concern with the interface inside out. Drawing attention to the social shaping or construction of the interface, a more comprehensive model was offered that instructed design to attend to the wider social environment in which the interface is situated and where interaction and communication are effected and articulated in real time. Bowers and Rodden (1993) moved the concern with social construction of the interface further on, 'exploding' a unitary conceptual entity into many fragmentary sites where users construct interfaces out of the material technologies to-hand in the course of their cooperative work. Bowers and Rodden radically reconceptualised the interface as a heterogeneous body of situationally constructed work sites where the workaday trajectories of a setting's staff 'collide' or intersect and interfacing goes on to provide for the coordination of their activities within the organizational division of labour. This point of view was arrived at by suspending 'received wisdom' and consulting the work of a central government department in the UK, where a new computer network had been installed. As a result it was found that *in practice*, rather than in theory, no single interface to the computer exists for an organization's members but rather, that there are a number of *heterogeneous sites* where interfacing goes on (the number being contingent on the organization in question and its workaday activities). The multiplicity of different interfaces dispenses with the conceptual fiction that there is one boundary between users and the computer, namely *the* interface. Instead, a variety of interfaces to the computer are constructed by users at sites where workaday trajectories intersect and where work gets 'articulated' or coordinated (Schmidt and Bannon 1992).

When addressing the topic of displays we adopt a similar position. That is to say, we consider displays as heterogeneous collections of fragmentary sites constructed where workaday trajectories collide and where *displaying goes on* to provide for the articulation of practical action. Accordingly, we to wish consider a number of issues that we believe radically effect technical considerations of situated displays. These issues include addressing:

- What displays already exist in a setting?
- Where are displays currently located?
- How are displays situated in a setting?
- Why or for what purposes are displays constructed?

When addressing these issues we caution against employing restrictive technical concepts that reify the notion of a display. Instead we are concerned with the skilful, craftful or competent ways in which the inhabitants of a setting address the above issues in their working practices. It might be said that instead of employing some conceptual formulation to address these issues we are concerned to establish where the participants in a setting's work see displays as residing? What *they* treat them as being? With what material technologies to-hand? Having what properties? And to what ends are they employed? We consider the use of mail in the home environment in order to explicate these issues and our orientation to the study of situated displays more generally. We do not expect this study to furnish some generic definition of a unitary conceptual entity, however - like the interface before us, that is a myth we would explode. Instead we recognise that the word 'display' is a verb rather than a noun and so refers to a diverse array of practical accomplishments, to a multiplicity of things *done*. Accordingly, our orientation draws design's attention to situated acts of displaying in a setting and thereby makes it visible that multiple technological displayers (screens, interfaces, etc.) will be required to support the ecologically distributed network of displays constructed by participants *in situ* to articulate their work.

2. Making the Social Construction of Situated Displays Visible

We have suggested that displays are essentially social constructions and more specifically, that they are constructed 1) in organizational arrangements of collaboration and cooperation at 2) a diverse array of sites by 3) people in their working practices with 4) the material technologies to-hand. This is not a definition of what makes something a display but rather, an analytic sensibility that furnishes us with an orientation to the study of situated displays from *within* a setting and in terms of that setting's work. Such studies will be 'system-specific' then, which is to say that they will be tied to the particular types of setting that they elaborate and make no claims to further generality. Thus analytic emphasis is placed on attending to the particular and unique needs of a setting in order that design might be responsive to those needs and that solutions might resonate with and support the work that goes on there (Crabtree 2003).

The study of the social construction of situated displays may be undertaken through ethnographic investigation. Ethnography has become a staple feature of research in Computer Supported Cooperative Work (CSCW), where it was initially configured as a 'method' of requirements analysis (COMIC D2.1). In its home disciplines of anthropology and sociology, by way of contrast, the term denotes little more than a distinction between quantative and qualitative research. Here ethnography is construed of as a naturalistic approach to social research. In a design context, the 'naturalism' of the matter often consists of a fieldworker documenting the work that goes on in a setting from the point of view of its *performance*. Attention is paid to the ways in which work is observably and reportably carried out and *ordered* by participants, and to the material technologies (whether computer-based or not) employed in the ordering of the work (Suchman 1983). Documenting the performative, technologically mediated ordering of a setting's work is often achieved today through video recording (Suchman 1991) and the materials gathered are then subject to more detached assessment or 'analysis'. Ethnography may, as such, be put to the service of virtually any school of thought and analysis is more often than not carried out through the use of general anthropological and sociological theories, which cast analysis in terms of an *a priori* ensemble of universal constructs. The setting becomes, as such, yet another site where the workings of the theory are played out, "regardless of what the actual order is, perhaps independently of what the actual order is, and even without the investigator having detected the actual order" (Garfinkel 1967).

An alternate approach to the analysis of ethnographic materials, and one that has enjoyed considerable success in CSCW by providing rich descriptions of work-in-context (Kensing and Simonsen 1996) is provided by ethnomethodology (Garfinkel 2002). As Shapiro (1994) puts it:

> "... ethnomethodology sets for itself a strict agenda which separates it in certain ways from most mainstream social science. It insists on a rigorously

> descriptive rather than theoretical program, or an explanatory one (in the sense that most social sciences would understand it). This lends it its strength in producing rich descriptions of work-in-context."

Ethnomethodology is 'indifferent' to theory (Lynch 1993), which is to say that it suspends the use of theories to analyse ethnographic materials and elects instead to examine those materials in their own terms for their orderly or socially organized properties as made visible by participants in their technologically mediated performance of work (Suchman 1995). The concern with orderliness, to be explicit, is this: ethnomethodology assumes, with evidence in hand (Garfinkel 1991), that the orderly ways in which participants perform work are *identical* to the ways in which they construct work. It follows, then, that observing and analysing the orderly ways in which work is performed by participants will illuminate the system-specific ways in which situated displays are socially constructed by participants in various settings in the course of and for the purposes of their work.

3. The Social Construction of Situated Displays in the Home

The home is not usually thought of as an organized work setting, indeed even with the emergence of mobile computing and more flexible labour patterns 'home' and 'work' are often contrasted and seen to be in competition. We caution against what the later Wittgenstein called a 'one-sided diet of examples' however, which in this case construes of work as paid labour. By invoking the notion of work we are not asking design to recognise such topics as "women's work" in the home either. Ours is not a political or moral use of the word, however laudable those uses may be. Rather, what we have in mind when talking about work in the home - and any other setting beyond the workplace – is a fundamental phenomenon from which there is no time out or possibility of evasion. We illuminate the phenomenon by example. In order to get to work in a morning many people set an alarm clock. When the alarm sounds they turn it off. They get up, wash, dress, feed themselves and others and to do that they move around the home, go from room to room and use a variety of material technologies to get up and get ready for work, to get the kids to school, and get themselves to the workplace. Insofar as people do such things then they 'must' – i.e., they have no other choice than to – *work to accomplish* these and the other everyday activities they engage in, no matter how ordinary, repetitive and routine those activities may be (Blumer 1967). When we invoke the notion of work, then, we do so not in a political sense of the word or a financial sense but in a practical sense. There is no time out from *practical action*, and the practical actions that take place in a setting constitute its organized 'work', paid or not (Venkatesh 1985, 1996). When addressing the social construction of situated displays in the home we will do so then in terms of the observable work of the home.

To this we would add that the work of the home and other settings consists of the use of material technologies. By this we do not refer to computing technologies, although they may be included in the category. By material technologies we mean the range of artefacts that people use in their work to get that work done. Material technologies range from the pen and paper, to everyday objects like tables and desktops, to electronic and computing systems. As design moves out of the workplace and into new domains it is important that the material technologies 'at work' in a setting are taken note of. As Venkatesh and Nicosia (1997) put it with respect to the home, and the same applies elsewhere,

> "... in order to understand the adoption / use issues of computers, one must view the total technological space of the household ... very little insights will be gained by looking at computers alone."

This perspective recognises that computing *has yet to reach out* into the home and a great many other domains other than in the most preliminary of ways which see workplace technologies transplanted wholesale into settings they were never designed for. Consequently 'user' needs are poorly met in these novel domains (Hindus 1999) and there is, then, much for design to learn from the use of existing material technologies in the home and other settings (Tolmie *et al.* 2002).

3.1 Learning from the Use of Existing Material Technologies: Mail Use in the Home

Long-term ethnographic research in 22 family homes in the UK shows that mail handling is a routine activity not only of relevance to individuals but central to the coordination of domestic affairs. Mail occasions such crucial actions as the timely paying of household bills, attending health checks or school meetings, taking the children to parties, and a host of contingent yet commonplace events that vary from household to household in accordance with the home's human composition and inhabitants ages and interests. This is not to say that there are no commonalities in the collaborative handling of mail across households. The following empirical instance allows us to explicate the socially organized work involved in the collaborative use of mail across the range of households in our study. We provide only one instance as space constrains what can be shown and because one instance suffices to make the socially organized work involved in the collaborative use of mail visible and available to design reasoning. Further instances add nothing to the *visibility of the phenomenon* (Sacks 1984). Accordingly, the instance makes it visible that the coordinate accomplishment of a host of contingent and divergent activities occasioned by the arrival of mail relies upon a taken for granted orderliness of action and material technology usage in which displaying is essential.

Mail is typically collected from some central point, whether that point is located at the front door (see figure 7-1), in the grounds outside a house, or from a post box located elsewhere in an apartment block. Depending on the contingencies of location, the collection point for mail is one at which displaying may go on. The displaying simply consists of this: seeing that mail has arrived. Mail may be collected by any household member - in some homes the same person might do the job all the time, whereas in others it simply depends on who gets up first or who is home first. The point to note here is that the collection of mail by household members is not coordinated through the nomination of a 'collector' but through the public availability of a shared and known in common collection point and, contingently, on the visibility of mail. Any household or group member can collect the mail (not anyone can open it, however).

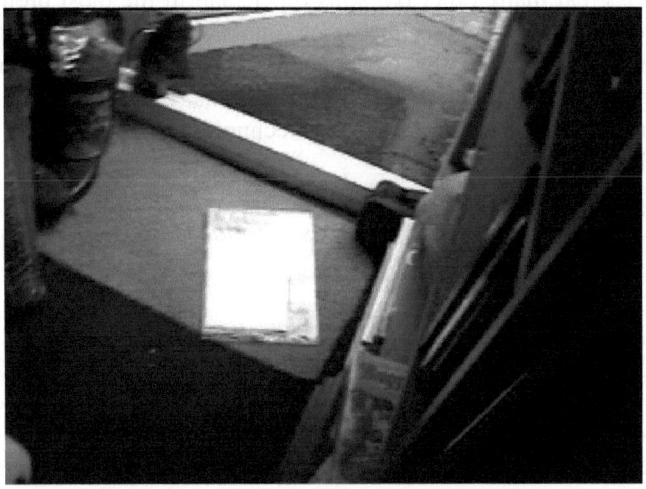

Figure 7-1. The porch: a shared and known in common collection point.

Having collected the mail, it must be sorted (even one single piece of mail requires sorting). The person acting as collector has certain taken for granted rights and expectations attached to their position. It is assumed by members that persons acting as collectors who are also 'householders' (i.e. persons who are responsible for the running of the household) have the right to open mail concerning the maintenance of the home (e.g. bills) and formal matters concerning junior household members (e.g. letters from school concerning children). The opening of mail is not necessarily ordered by recipient name on an envelope, then, but by entitlement to open such mail. The point here is that there is often a visibility to mail that displays and so announces its practical character: what it is about, who it is from, and who may thus be an appropriate recipient and so be entitled to open it (see figure 7-2). This is often conveyed by a logo, organisational stamp, postmark, or the printing of the sender's name on the outside of the envelope.

Figure 7-2. Displaying and announcing the practical character of mail (phone bill arrives).

The visibility of the practical character of mail allows the collector to make judgements as to the relevance of mail to the home and to household members. It is in this respect that members come to categorise certain mail as 'junk', to do so at-a-glance, and to respond to the categorisation by throwing the designated mail away. Junk mail is not always so easily spotted however, as categorisation is a matter of judgement rather than being given in advance. Consequently, the collector may open mail and browse through it to establish its relevancy status.

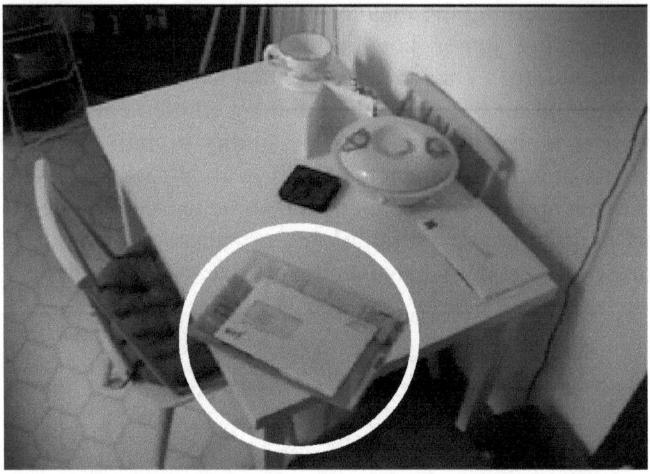

Figure 7-3. Placing mail of relevance to others in general (corner of kitchen table).

Mail that is deemed relevant to other household members is organized in a variety of unique ways. The recipient may decide that the mail received might be of interest to other household members. The relevance of mail to other household members is organized through particular assemblages of display, with each assemblage articulating particular relevancy statuses. Mail which a recipient deems to be of relevance to others in general is displayed in a public location, again shared and known in common, where it is plainly visible (see figure 7-3, for example). The precise location for such displays varies from household to household, as display is contingent upon the particular material arrangements of domestic space. Common places include mantelpieces, bureaus, or tables, but other places may be used as the contingent arrangements of domestic space allow.

Mail that is deemed to be of relevance to a particular household member is often displayed in a different location that is relevant to the member in question: e.g. at the place he or she usually sits when relaxing, at his or her place at the kitchen table, or even outside a bedroom door (see figure 7-4). The recipient designed and accountable character of mail displays enable members to see at-a-glance that mail has arrived that requires their attention and action.

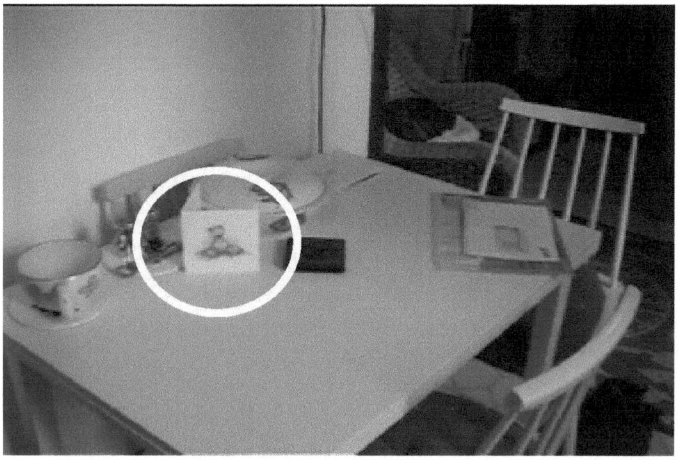

Figure 7-4. Displaying mail of relevance to a particular household member (recipient's seat at kitchen table).

Opened mail that has been viewed is also displayed according to its relevance to practical action. The display of opened and viewed mail is ordered by the temporal flow of sorting work and the organization of mail into discrete groupings that reflect the actions required at-a-glance. Again, these displays are contingent on the material arrangements of domestic space. Mail for external use, such as they payment of bills for example, is placed in a location that reflects the need for external action: e.g. on a desk in the hallway, at the front of the kitchen table (see figure 7-5), or next to a bag that is routinely taken along when a person leaves the house. Postcards, birthday cards and the like may, in contrast, be placed on the mantelpiece or windowsill (see figure 7-6).

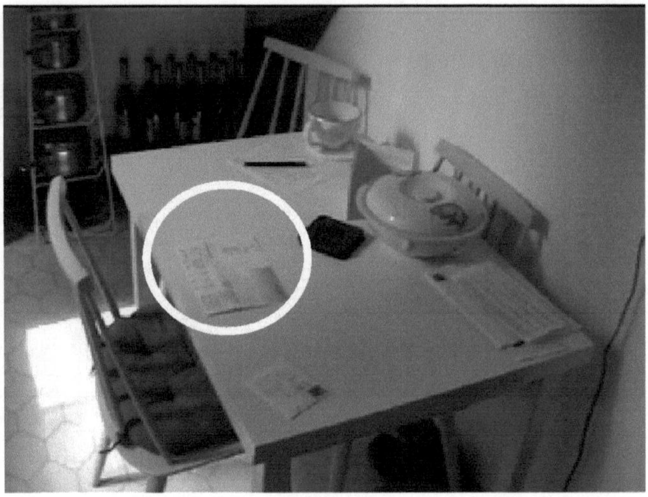

Figure 7-5. Displaying mail for external use.

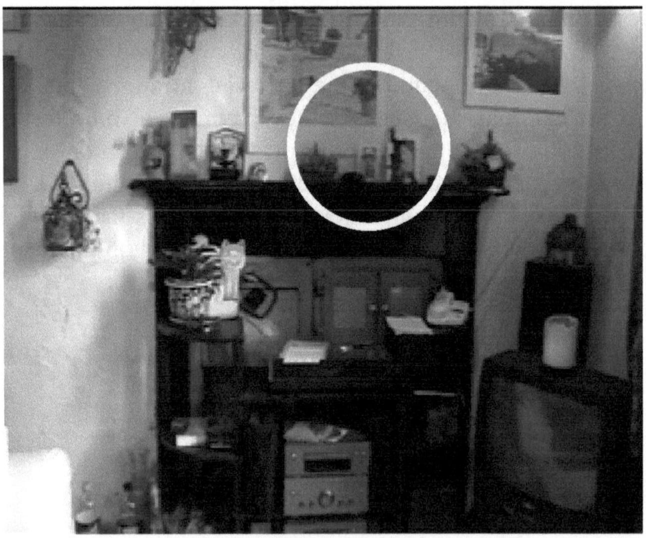

Figure 7-6. Displaying cards.

Mail for internal use is displayed in an alternate location: e.g. on top of the stereo, on top of the bureau, or at the back of the kitchen table. While particular locations vary from home to home, this latter arrangement is effectively a 'pending pile' (see figure 7-7). It may contain mail for external use if it is not of immediate relevance. When sorting through the pending pile it may also transpire that particular items are no longer relevant and so they may be thrown away.

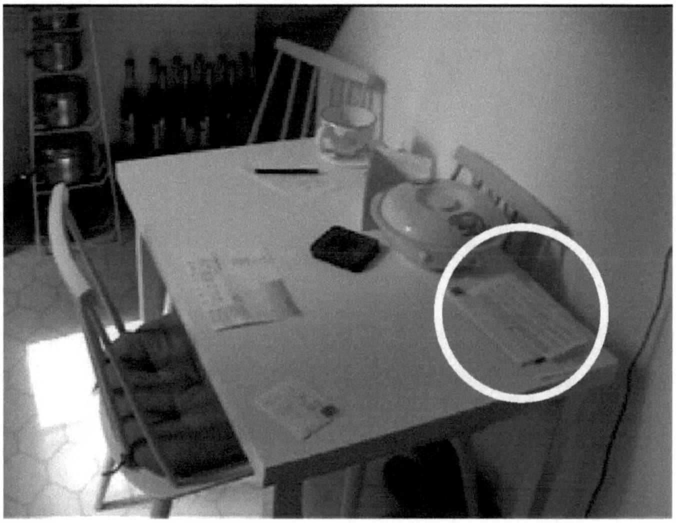

Figure 7-7. Placing mail pending further action.

Opened mail may accrue in the pending pile until it is felt that some further action should be taken. Further action may lead to the display or movement of mail to other discrete locations that are tied to the projected relevance of mail. Accordingly, mail may be displayed on a noticeboard (which may be nothing more than a designated space on a wall). Noticeboards are used as a place to display mail of short-term relevance: things like invoices, concert tickets, appointment cards and invitations, and longer-term information that is frequently consulted, such as school term dates, restaurant menus, etc (see figure 7-8). Mail of longer-term relevance, such as mortgage statements, legal paperwork, financial affairs, etc., is filed away in dedicated location organized for storage and retrieval: e.g. in a bureau, drawer, or filing cabinet.

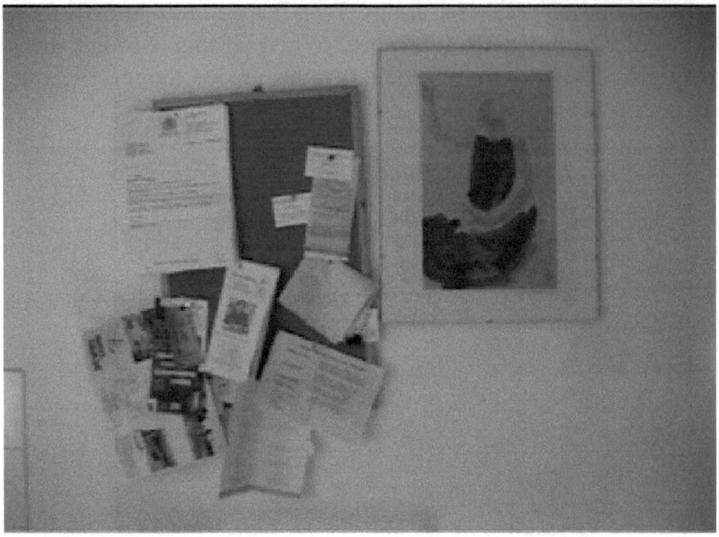

Figure 7-8. Placing mail of short-term relevance.

4. The Emergence of Coordinate Displays and Distributed Ecological Networks

The instance makes it visible that household members construct a series of discrete yet interrelated situated displays at various sites around the home: at various positions on the kitchen table, on the mantelpiece in the living room, and on the noticeboard on the kitchen wall, *for example*. Not all displays have the same properties. The construction of display sites on the mantelpiece is qualitatively and purposefully different to those constructed on the kitchen table and noticeboard in this particular household. Here the mantelpiece is used only as a display site – no work is done there. Displays constructed at the kitchen table and noticeboard are, in contrast, designed by household members to *support collaboration*. Thus, and for example, on walking into the kitchen a member can see at-a-glance whether or not mail has arrived that requires their particular attention and action by its placement by another at particular sites – on the corner of the kitchen table, for example, or at the recipient's seat. Items placed on noticeboards may facilitate collaboration in subtler ways – invitations, invoices, concert tickets, and the rest are kept there and may be drawn upon as and when the occasion demands. However, and more importantly, like pending piles on tables, the contents of noticeboards articulate a *schedule of tasks* yet to be completed and the visible presence of those contents maintains members concerted *awareness* of that fact. We think there is a distinct class of situated display in the home then (and we speculate in other settings too) that are designed by members to support collaboration. We call this class of displays **'coordinate displays'**, a category intended to convey the design and use of situated displays in and for the express purposes of collaborative action.

The instance also allows us to make the following observation about coordinate displays:

(1) They are *ecologically distributed* or distributed at various physical and architectural sites around the home – in porches, on kitchen tables and walls, in living rooms on mantelpieces, etc.

(2) These sites are interconnected and form in their connectedness discrete *networks* of coordinate displays, as can be seen in Figure 7-9.

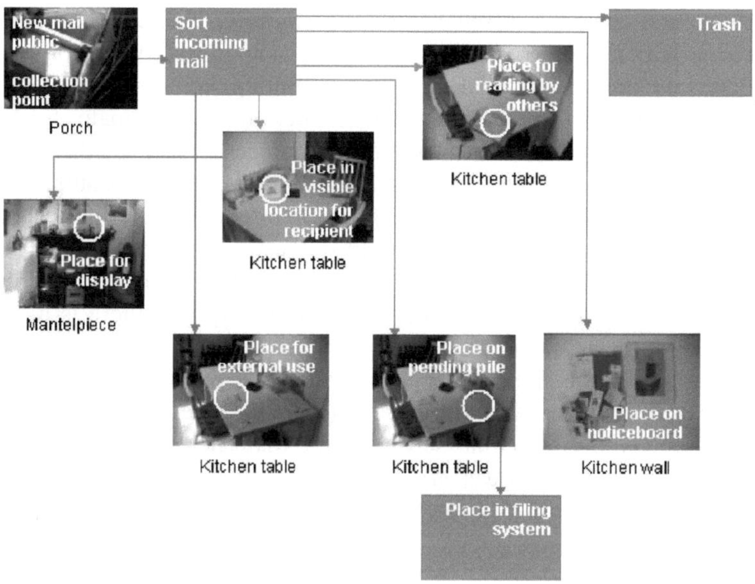

Figure 7-9. Coordinate displays and the emergence of an ecologically distributed network.

There is, then, a distinct phenomenon underpinning mail use in the home. It is one that we find across the homes in our studies that sees household members coordinate their activities amongst themselves and with others through the manipulation of the physical fabric of the home. This recognition complements and moves us beyond existing research on the spatial and temporal distribution of technology in the home (O'Brien *et al.*

1999) to draw our attention to a range of interconnected sites where displaying is done to support coordination. The distribution of mail across a variety of distinct display sites, each reflecting the *action status* of mail, provides for *awareness* amongst household members and the *timely coordination* of activities. Items do not simply come into the environment and 'reside' at a particular site, but instead *move around* the environment from coordinate display to coordinate display according to an item's place in an unfolding order or *schedule of work*. Thus, and for example, a household bill may move from the porch to the bill payer's seat at the kitchen table to the front of the table from where it will subsequently be taken out of the environment and paid.

(3) The instance offers a further observation too. The social construction of coordinate displays is invariably subject to the dual contingencies of *architecture* and *aesthetics*. Even in age of increasing standardization, the architectural character of homes varies immensely. Add to that the particular ways in which people exercise their tastes and furnish their homes and the differences are exponential. The dual contingencies of architecture and aesthetics result in the contingent construction of coordinate displays. We cannot say, then, just where or in just what places coordinate displays will be manifest in domestic settings generally, though over the course of time it may transpire that certain places such as the kitchen table or noticeboards are of reoccurring significance. We would suggest, however, that such a level of generality is not the issue. People do not live in homes in general but in their own particular environments and, as in the workplace, there is a need then for design to be responsive the particular needs of particular settings. Explication of the *locally organized* sites where coordinate displays are constructed through ethnographic study enables design to respond to the unique needs of particular settings and may help designers to identify candidate application 'areas' for design – i.e., to find *places* where new and future technologies might be best situated to meet local needs.

5. Contigency and Design

Although we cannot generalise specific local arrangements of coordinate display as a result of the dual contingences of architecture and aesthetics, we can nevertheless offer some broader insights informing the design of future technologies on the basis of the general existence of ecologically distributed networks of coordinate displays. In other words while we cannot generalise specific instantiations of the phenomenon as a result of the local contingencies to which it is invariably subject, that the phenomenon is generally available allows us to make some broad recommendations. In the context of home-oriented design, which our studies have been concerned with, the construction of coordinate displays articulates potential application areas for design that *transcend* the individual and idiosyncratic arrangements occasioned by the dual contingencies of architecture and aesthetics. While sites for the construction and distribution of specific displays may change from home to home as a result of architectural and aesthetic differences, the actual construction of coordinate displays *is not so plastic*. Regardless of architectural and aesthetic contingencies members routinely construct coordinate displays to organize their activities (e.g. the paying of bills, attending school meetings or a party, etc.). It might be said that the coordination of action is conducted through the 'methodic' construction of coordinate displays, where the method of the matter is understood to refer to the routine construction of coordinate displays in such ways that regardless of architectural and aesthetic contingencies members can see, and see at-a-glance, that items so displayed (e.g. on the mantelpiece, stereo, or that part of table) are items for others in general, particular others, for internal use, and external use, etc. The methodic construction of coordinate displays is an essential feature of mail handling's orderly character and transcends the idiosyncratic and individual, illuminating the different and often subtle *types* of coordinate display (e.g. noticeboards and positional displays on tables) that are constructed by members to order particular *types* of activity (e.g. handling mail) in particular *types* of system-specific setting (e.g. a family home) and in such detail serve to articulate potential application areas for design.

Consider the development of electronic mail for domestic settings, for example, where existing displays are largely confined to a single screen situated in a fixed location in a corner or some other outpost of a room where the computer, transplanted wholesale from the workplace, often lives. Clearly, such interfaces ignore the spatial and temporal construction of coordinate mail displays across a variety of ecologically distributed sites in the domestic space. Projected arrangements of email utilising 3rd Generation mobile technologies promise to support recipient designed displays but, in being personally rather than ecologically situated, such displays do not support the collaboration afforded by the construction of publicly visible coordinate displays. In short, existing and projected displays of electronic mail are inadequate when faced with deployment in the home and they are inadequate as they fail to appreciate and respond to the orderly ways in which mail-based communications enter home life and are practically managed therein.

It is not fair to say that designers are unaware of the spatial and temporal properties of mail use when it comes to the design of email applications. In one of the earliest studies of email use, Mackay (1988) highlighted three essential functions of mail use: information management, task management, and time management. The study made the point that these functions are essential features of mail-based communication and the spatially and temporally distributed construction of coordinate displays instructs us that the same applies to paper-based mail in the home. Attending to the temporal attributes of email use, Gwizdka (2000) also observes that emails are used to organize people's external memories, "they are 'knowledge in the world' and, thus, they should be designed to reflect the *actual life-cycle* of information in different tasks". Harper *et al.* (2000) concur and elaborate the essential nature of the 'actual life-cycle' in considering the implications of paper-based mail use for the design of electronic alternatives:

> "… a letter in the geography of the home is a marker of what point a job-to-do has reached. Email might support this if the screens are located in places that equate to locations within the domestic workflow."

Members construct mail displays so that they can see at-a-glance where-they-are-now and what-needs-to-be-done-next in the *overall flow* of some job of work in an ethnomethodological sense of the word (e.g. receiving and paying bills, receiving and replying to a letter from a family friend, receiving tickets to and attending a concert, receiving legal letters and storing them for later use, etc.). The need to support workflow has already been recognised by researchers in the field (Venolia *et al.* 2001). However, this line of research construes of the user's primary 'habitat' (Duchenaut and Bellotti 2001) as the existing computer interface and seeks to implement solutions through the design of more sophisticated applications that support workflow at that interface. Our studies suggest that support is required in the wider environment - in the habitat *concretely*, not metaphorically, to augment the existing ways in which coordinate displays are constructed by members to handle mail and to get their work done.

What we are suggesting is that the development of computer support for the cooperative work implicated in mail use in domestic settings requires designers to move beyond the desktop and the monolithic interface to consider the design of ecologically distributed networks of interfaces that may be situated in a variety of places within the physical environment of the home to meet local needs. Figure 1, for example, has elaborated the main elements of an ecologically distributed network of interfaces constructed by household members to handle their mail-based communications. The network instructs us that workflow is ecologically distributed across the domestic space through the social construction of visible displays that reflect the current coordinates of a range of ongoing tasks in an unfolding schedule of work. Explication of the network raises the issue of developing a range of ecologically distributed interfaces exploiting both static and mobile displays that may be situated in various contingent locations to support the spatial and temporal ordering of the flow of work in the home.

6. Conclusion

We have suggested that the topic of situated displays might best be appreciated in the context of the historical evolution of the interface. Accordingly, cognitive notions of the interface have been 'exploded' or respecified: from a site at which communication and interaction are articulated through the software control dialogue, to a multiplicity of socially constructed sites where workaday trajectories collide and where the act of interfacing or displaying goes on to provide for the coordination of work. These fragmentary sites are assembled by the members of a setting, who are embedded in concrete arrangements of cooperation and collaboration, through their working practices with the material technologies to-hand. Seen from the point of view of the act of displaying, a number of study questions that are foundational to CSCW research have presented themselves. These include establishing

- What displays already exist in a setting?
- Where are displays currently located?
- How are displays situated in a setting?
- Why or for what purposes are displays constructed?

We have suggested that these issues may be explicated through ethnographic study. That is, through the immersion of a fieldworker in the work of a setting and through ethnomethodological analysis of that work, where theorising is suspended and replaced with a concern to understand work in its own terms and in the orderly details of its material accomplishment.

Such studies are 'system-specific'. Tied to the settings they elaborate, they articulate the various types of display (e.g. noticeboards, positional displays on tables, mantelpiece displays, etc.) that are constructed by members to order particular types of activity (e.g. handling mail) in particular types of setting (e.g. a family home, in contrast to an old peoples' home). The system-specific character of situated displays illuminates potential application areas for design, as we have demonstrated through a consideration of future developments of email in the home environment. Furthermore, by attending to the act of displaying and the socially constructed ways in which that gets done, such studies draw our attention to a distinct class of situated display constructed by members to support collaboration and enable us to furnish answers to the foundational questions of CSCW research posed above.

- *The what of the matter*: This consists of a variety of different displays constructed by members to coordinate the work of a setting. Coordinate displays are constructed out of the specific material technologies to-hand in a setting.
- *The where of the matter*: Just where coordinate displays are constructed in a setting depends upon the dual contingencies architecture and aesthetics the setting is physically composed.
- *The how of the matter:* The coordination of a setting's work is made possible by the distribution of coordinate displays across the ecology of the setting to form a distinct network.
- *The why of the matter:* Ecologically distributed networks of coordinate displays are constructed to enable the collaborative management of work in, and flow of work through, a setting.

We emphasise these issues as they provide an orientation to the study of and design for situated displays. They also allow us to address the contemporary research agenda, which is concerned to transcend the monolithic interface in order to merge the digital with the physical. The ecologically distributed and networked character of coordinate displays draws attention to the physicality of settings and draws our attention to important features of cooperative work in novel domains. Explicating or making the social construction of coordinate displays visible opens up a fruitful avenue of research then, where design may explore technical ways in which digital technologies can augment, be embedded in, and otherwise support the orderly ways in which a wide variety of displays are constructed by members to coordinate their activities in a wide variety of practical settings beyond the workplace.

Acknowledgements

This research was funded by the Equator IRC (EPSRC GR/N15986/01) and the EU Disappearing Computer Initiative ACCORD (IST-2000-26364).

References

Blumer, H. *Symbolic Interactionism: Perspective and Method.* Berkeley: University of California Press, 1969.

Bowers, J. and Rodden, T. Exploding the interface. Proceedings of the ACM INTERCHI '93 Conference on Human Factors in Computing Systems, 1993; Amsterdam, The Netherlands; 255-262. Amsterdam: ACM Press.

COMIC Deliverable 2.1 *Informing CSCW Requirements*, Esprit Basic Research Project 6225; 1994; Lancaster University: Computing Department. ftp://ftp.comp.lancs.ac.uk/pub/comic/

Crabtree, A. *Designing Collaborative Systems: A Practical Guide to Ethnography*, London: Springer-Verlag, 2003.

Duchenaut, N. and Bellotti, V. Email as habitat. Interactions 2001; 8(5): 30-38.

Garfinkel, H. *Studies in Ethnomethodology*, Englewood Cliffs, New Jersey: Prentice-Hall, 1967.

Garfinkel, H. "Respecification: evidence for locally produced, naturally accountable phenomena of order." In *Ethnomethodology and the Human Sciences*, Graham Button, ed, Cambridge: Cambridge University Press, 1991.

Garfinkel, H. *Working Out Durkheim's Aphorism: Ethnomethodology's Program* (ed. Rawls, A.), Lanham, Maryland: Rowman and Littlefield, 2001.

Grudin, J. Interface. Proceedings of the CSCW '90 Conference on Computer Supported Cooperative Work; 1990; Los Angeles, California; 269-278, ACM Press.

Gwizdka, J. Timely reminders: a case study of temporal guidance in PIM and email tools usage. Proceedings of the CHI '00 Conference on Human Factors in Computing Systems; 2000; Amsterdam, The Netherlands; 163-164, ACM Press.

Harper, R., Evergeti, V., Hamill, L. and Strain, J. Paper-mail in the home of the 21st Century: an analysis of the future of paper mail and implications for the design of electronic alternatives; 2000; Digital World Research Centre, The University of Surrey. www.surrey.ac.uk/dwrc/papers/okios.pdf

Hindus, D. The importance of homes in technology research. Proceedings of the 2nd International Workshop on Cooperative Buildings; 1999; Pittsburg, PA, USA; 199-207; Pittsburgh: Springer.

Kensing, F. and Simonsen, J. Using ethnography in contextual design. Communications of the ACM 1997; 40 (7): 82-88.

Lynch, M. *Scientific Practice and Ordinary Action*, Cambridge: Cambridge University Press, 1993.

Mackay, W. More than just a communication system: diversity in the use of electronic mail. ACM Transactions on Information Systems 1988; 6 (4): 380-397.

O'Brien, J., Rodden, T., Rouncefield, M. and Hughes, J.A. At home with the technology. ACM Transactions on Computer-Human Interaction 1999; 6 (3): 282-308.

Sacks, H. "Notes on methodology." In *Structures of Social Action: Studies in Conversation Analysis*, Maxwell, J.M. and Heritage, J., eds. Cambridge: Cambridge University Press, 1984.

Schmidt, K. and Bannon, L. Taking CSCW seriously: supporting articulation work. Computer Supported Cooperative Work: An International Journal 1992; 1 (1): 7-40.

Shapiro, D. The limits of ethnography: combining social sciences for CSCW. Proceedings of CSCW '94 Conference on Computer Supported Cooperative Work; 1994; Chapel Hill, North Carolina; 417- 428, ACM Press.

Suchman, L. Office procedures as practical action: models of work and system design. ACM Transactions on Office Information Systems, 1983; 1 (4): 320-328.

Suchman, L. and Trigg, R. "Understanding practice: video as a medium for reflection and design." In *Design at Work: Cooperative Design of Computer Systems,* Greenbaum, J. and Kyng, M., eds. Hillsdale, New Jersey: Lawrence Erlbaum Associates, 1991.

Suchman, L. Making work visible. Communications of the ACM 1995; 38 (9): 56-64.
Tolmie, P., Pycock, J., Diggins, T., Maclean, A. and Karsenty, A. Unremarkable computing, Proceedings of the CHI '02 Conference on Human Factors in Computing Systems; 2002; Minneapolis, MN, USA; 399-406, ACM Press
Venkatesh, A. A conceptualization of the household/technology interaction. Advances in Consumer Research 1985; 12: 189-194.
Venkatesh, A. Computers and other interactive technologies for the home. Communications of the ACM 1996; 39 (12): 47-54.
Venkatesh, A. and Nicosia, F. New technologies for the home. Advances in Consumer Research, 1997; 24: 522-528.
Venolia, G.D., Dabbish, L., Cadiz, J.J. and Anoop, G. Supporting email workflow, 2001; Microsoft Research, Report MSR-TR-2001-88, http://research.microsoft.com/scripts/pubs/view.asp?TR_ID=MSR-TR-2001-88

Chapter 8

WHEN A BED IS NOT A BED:

The situated display of knowledge on a hospital ward

Karen Clarke, John Hughes, Mark Rouncefield
Lancaster University

Terry Hemmings
University of Nottingham

Abstract: In this chapter we present an instance of how organisational knowledge is constructed, collected and used in the setting of a large hospital trust in the North of England. Our main concern here is to focus upon how representational artefacts of organisational activities and 'states of play' are oriented to in the everyday work of hospital staff – mainly a directorate manager and a ward sister. Here we are specifically focusing on the situated character of the representational artefact – a 'beds board'- and the system of calculability that it affords in the hospital setting. Our view is that such representations must be understood as embedded within the practicalities of the setting, and that any assumed benefits of replacing existing systems must be carefully considered.

Key words: Ethnography, information systems, representation, organisational knowledge

1. Introduction

This paper presents preliminary findings from the Dependability Interdisciplinary Research Collaboration (DIRC) project, a collaborative six-year research project examining issues of dependability in a number of organisational settings. We are in the process of ethnographic fieldwork at three hospitals in the North-West of England, examining managerial work at

K. O'Hara et al. (eds.), Public and Situated Displays: Social and Interactional Aspects of Shared Display Technologies, 191–209.

each of these three sites. The fieldwork has involved shadowing the clinical and directorate managers of various departments, clinics and wards in order to explore the managerial work that they do. The focus of the DIRC project is on trust in technology and the data from our empirical studies are being used to look at trust as a process embedded in the daily work practice of the clinicians, managers and other staff involved in a given area. With this project focus in mind, this chapter examines the use of computerized and paper-based information systems on a particular day, and how a dependable or 'trusted' state of affairs is established in a 'crisis' situation. Here we pay attention to one aspect of this managerial work, namely 'bed management': how the availability of beds is managed on a day-to-day basis.

This research has been carried out within the context of a large organisation undergoing a shift in its approach to record keeping. The hospitals where we have carried out our fieldwork, as part of a national policy process, are using information technology more and more for record-keeping purposes, replacing and supporting previous paper-based systems. This policy process is one whose aim is standardisation of work practice along with assumed improvements in the delivery of healthcare. The UK National Health Service (NHS) is experiencing enormous growth in the deployment of information and communications technologies (ICTs). Extensive use of technology serves to 'reconfigure the organisation' through its application in data analysis, communication and decision support. Recent policy shifts in healthcare in the UK have been towards an evidence-based healthcare approach and clinical governance, approaches that have emphasised the need for standardisation of professional practice in healthcare settings. An increased role for new technology is at the heart of these policy shifts, with increased use of, for example, computerised information systems as the purported route to a more effective healthcare service (Berg, 1997; Bloor and Maynard, 1997; Department of Health, 1997). Standardisation and computerisation are seen as the solutions to the 'health problem', and in this way it is argued that information systems in healthcare will become more trustworthy. Fitzpatrick (2000) argues that that all technology design for healthcare settings "should start with the question 'how do we support clinical practice', which requires that we understand more about the realities of that practice". This policy approach is central to the issues in this chapter.

Shared information displays in Healthcare settings are intended to provide major benefits in support of the co-ordination of patient care; in organising and locating clinical information; in coordinating and managing patient healthcare; and in organisational integration. Providing IT support for contingent managerial work however requires that systems necessarily pay attention to the occasioned character of activities. We propose to discuss issues surrounding the affordances of an existing non-digital display and the ways in which features such as calculation and calculability, and annotation are taken for granted by users and often ignored by designers.

Findings from the ethnographic studies bring to the fore issues regarding the production and utilisation of information in everyday managerial work. The factors relevant to information use in managerial working practices point to issues which must be addressed in the design of digital displays This chapter will examine the use of an existing non-digital display – the 'beds board' – and its use in the management of patient care. The beds board is used within a management process that also uses a computerised Management Information System (MIS) in the provision of bed information. As the use of the 'beds board' indicates, the task of supporting complex, collaborative work is not a matter of simply automating existing records or procedures.

For practical purposes we propose to introduce examples that allow us to focus on everyday managerial work in a hospital trust, namely 'bed management', how the availability of beds is managed on a day-to-day basis. We will deal with some of the complexities involved in the use of technology in the provision of information, the production and utilisation of that information in everyday managerial work, and the factors relevant to information use in managerial working practices. On the DIRC project (http://www.dirc.org.uk) we deployed ethnographic research techniques that have increasingly been utilised in studies of technologies in use (Bowers *et al.*, 1995; Button and Sharrock, 1997; Hughes *et al.*, 1993; Hughes *et al.*, 1994; Hughes *et al.*, 2002). The advantage of this approach lies in the 'sensitising' it promotes to the real world character and practical context of activities. Concrete examples will be incorporated that provide 'live' insight into activities surrounding a 'beds crisis' on a particular day with a specific Directorate Manager (DM), and the use of a non-digital beds board within the management of the crisis.

2. Good Reasons for Bad Records: Representing the Work

Historically, notions of the information age assume a major role for technology in the shaping of work and its day-to-day organisation (Robins and Webster, 1999). Complex organisations most obviously display forms of organisational knowledge in the Weberian sense (Weber, 1978): simply put, information formally collected, collated and archived about the organisation and its activities. The focus here is on what may loosely be termed 'management information'. What is meant by the term 'management information' differs in different contexts. Other ethnographic studies have looked at the production of representations of managerial work (see Hughes *et al.*, 2002 for example) that are used by managers to account for their working activity. Here, we shift in emphasis away from management information used to account for the work of managers themselves, to the use of management information used alongside other sources of local knowledge in the everyday routines of managerial work. The main 'other source' examined in this chapter is the 'beds board' – a notice board consisting of a representation of the occupancy of beds on a ward area. Here we see the 'representation' of the bed occupancy on the ward as a practical, situated activity within the 'real world, real time' work within the hospital. The representation involves the use of the local skills and knowledge of those involved in its production and use. In this way, our interest is in the interactional work involved in the use and monitoring of management information. Through our examination of a 'beds crisis' we will highlight issues regarding the mooted benefits and affordances of public displays. As Button and Sharrock recommend (Bowers *et al.*, 1995; Button and Sharrock, 1997) the key to 'optimal use' of the new communications infrastructures is the appropriate development of systems to support work co-ordination. We also want to keep in mind the cautionary note about displays that:

> "What anyone can find them to say or to mean will depend on interpretation of the displays. Running your eye down the print-out, whizzing through the file returns, tells you very little unless you know what to look for and where" (Anderson *et al.*, 1989)

Garfinkel (in: Turner, 1975) reported on the 'normal, natural troubles' that may be encountered by the researcher in attempting to utilise clinic records for research purposes. The title of Garfinkel's paper – 'Good' Organizational Reasons for 'Bad' Clinic Records' – refers to the context of seemingly 'bad' records as seen by the researcher:

> "Any investigator who has attempted a study with the use of clinic records, almost wherever such records are found, has a litany of troubles to recite. Moreover, hospital and clinic administrators frequently are as knowledgeable and concerned about these 'shortcomings' as are the investigators themselves ... the term 'normal, natural' is used in a conventional sociological sense to mean in accord with prevailing rules of practice". (1975: 114)

Developed from Garfinkel's notion of 'normal, natural troubles', we examine the ways in which a 'beds crisis' is managed on a particular morning in one of these hospitals. Before we look at the specific events relevant to this paper, perhaps a brief outline of the idea of 'normal, natural troubles' would be useful here.

For Garfinkel, 'normal, natural troubles' refers to the troubles that were encountered by the researcher in trying to collect information from clinic records. The paper goes on to explore the moral and practical organisational rationale for its mode of record-keeping, such that there can be seen to be 'good' reasons for what may appear as 'bad' records on first examination. For example, for Garfinkel a 'reason' for bad records is the idea of the "marginal utility of added information" (ibid: 115) – personnel may not understand the purpose of certain forms of information collection or may be suspicious of them, seeing them as ranging from "benign, to irrelevant to ominous". Such records, in terms of both the idea of the records from an organisational perspective and in the member's use of the records from the clinic context fit with the "prevailing rules of practice" of the clinic, and clinic personnel "as self-reporters, actively seek to act in compliance with rules of the clinic's operating procedures that *for them and from their point of view are more or less taken for granted as right ways of doing things...* [they] are integral features of the usual ways of getting each day's work done." (ibid: 114).

We wish to extend this idea of 'normal natural troubles' from the use for research purposes of clinic records to examine how apparently 'bad' records are utilised and also how 'workarounds' are used by a manager in a particular situation where the 'official record' is flawed. Without a detailed understanding of the practices in the setting of the hospital, we cannot get a nuanced view of what may first appear to be simply bad records. In this way we will look at the 'prevailing rules of practice' that should be taken into account prior to the design and implementation of computer-based display systems. Here we are not looking at the use of patients' clinic records or medical files, but at other forms of record keeping. Although we started off thinking abut good reasons for bad records as in Garfinkel's work, this led us to look at other forms of record keeping and the ways in which such records are incorporated into daily work practice. Specifically here we examine bed management practice in the form of:

1. The use of the information available on the computer-based Management Information System (MIS) at the hospital, a system beset by its own problems of apparently 'bad' records
2. The use of a 'state of play' noticeboard on a surgical ward, and

3. The managerial work involved in coming to an 'acceptable' account of the situation for the purposes of the manager involved.

We will argue, as does Garfinkel, that the "least interesting thing that one can say about them [the records] is that they are 'carelessly kept' " (ibid: 114).

Related to the notion of apparently 'bad' records, is the idea of records and displays as 'representing work'. How best to represent the work of an organisation, or group of workers within an organisation, is central to the design of display artefacts to support everyday work. In this chapter we also explore the practical ways in which 'representations' and 'information' are produced and utilised as part of routine and ongoing managerial work. Whilst hospital work cannot be wholly categorised as information work, the increased use of new information and communication technologies (ICT's) to allow more flexible and mobile patterns of working is relevant to the health sector. The directorate managers in the NHS Trust study, for example, have responsibilities and work 'domains' across three geographically separate hospitals and may have discrete ward and clinic areas under their jurisdiction within each hospital. They will also have regular working patterns with human resources departments, other directorate managers, waiting list sections and so on. Thus much of their work is about the exchange and flow of information, in the form of accounts, policy initiatives, waiting list figures, and bed availability to name but a few.

3. The Abiding Concerns of the Organisation: Bed Management

It is important to note here that although we are examining here the events on one day in a particular hospital, these events have a wider relevance. Bed management is an abiding concern, common throughout the National Health Service (NHS). Thus there are generic issues that can be explicated through the use of ethnographic study. For example, bed management can be seen as the broad 'problem', but contained within it are more specific issues e.g. 'winter planning', when the hospitals try to plan for 'known' seasonal problems. Hospital waiting lists and the availability of hospital beds is a highly charged political issue. At the time of the observations detailed here (November 2000) a great deal of concern was given to 'winter planning' which was related to national press reports, from the previous year, of hospitals being full and effectively closed to new patients. As one manager commented; "... it came down from on high that this year there would not be a Winter crisis … and I mean from On High."

This concern over ‘winter planning’ was reflected not just in a daily managerial focus on bed numbers but also related statistics connected to waiting time on trolleys and the 'escalation policy'. Again this was linked to national press reports of patients spending enormous amounts of time on hospitals trolleys as they waited for beds to become available. The 'escalation policy' was linked to a government requirement that no patient should be kept on a trolley for more than 12 hours. Trolley waiting times were closely monitored and the Trust had contingency plans to open up a day-case theatre to accommodate more beds and patients. Bed management was associated with a system of alerts that instigated various managerial responses: " to go to red (alert) the Directorate Manager has to go and count… if the position is that we (the Hospital) are... closed to admissions the Directorate Manager has to come in and physically count the beds … Ward Sisters can be naughty... if they know they have five admissions coming in tomorrow… you can understand where they're coming from... (not clear at this stage why this last part is relevant) ". The managerial focus on bed management was supported by the collation of a weekly site report circulated by email, for example:

> "Weekly site rep attached for your information. Large volume of medical sleepouts at both main sites. Current position:
>
> XXX: no available beds now although position will change. Some elective admissions for today being cancelled and admissions for next 2 days under review with relevant clinical directorates..
>
> ZZZ contacted by GGG last night to take medicine emergencies from south of GGG area… some patients at ZZZ still waiting for beds at DDD to become available"
>
> (Letters indicate areas covered by the hospitals)

The availability of hospital beds across the two sites is coordinated by the Bed Manager (BM). The BM is based at H1, with no dedicated office accommodation at H2 or H3. The ‘bed availability’ data as available on the Management Information System (MIS) may be seen as a ‘bad’ record for a number of reasons to do with the lack of a standardised approach to information collection, time lag between information collection and its appearance in the MIS database. The role of the BM is to constantly monitor and maintain the process of bed management in such a way as to avoid a situation where no beds are available. At a more local level, the directorate managers and ward managers monitor bed management. Here we explore the actions of the directorate manager of orthopaedics (henceforth the DMO) as she deals with a scenario of being "minus nine beds". We will examine what she calls "the usual rituals" used to manage the crisis, and the ways in which the 'bad' record from the Management Information System is used in conjunction with the 'rituals' of ward rounds.

3.1 'Activity' monitoring

Patient treatment, (and in particular the number of patients treated) is referred to by hospital management as 'activity', and frequent discussions were had assessing whether or not enough 'activity' was going on in the directorate. At the time of the fieldwork there were several policy strategies going on which aimed to increase 'activity' through better record-keeping e.g. the production of process maps was being used to potentially identify what are known as "bottlenecks" which delay "knife to skin" time, i.e. those parts in the 'processing' of patients which cause delays to or cancellation of treatment for a variety of reasons e.g. pre-op assessments not being done e.g. trying to standardise practice of record-keeping especially with regard to the Accident and Emergency department, who "don't care" about anything other than the patient, and therefore don't always fill out the required documentation. This shows the highly contingent nature of the hospital work, or, as one manager put it, "It's always crisis management in the NHS". This then feeds into concerns over attempts to standardise practice, for example, the soon to be implemented Electronic Patient Records (EPRs), for which standardisation seems to be a pre-requisite. The electronic record will not afford the kind of flexibility offered by a paper-based system. We write about these issues elsewhere, but point them out to demonstrate that there are many areas of record-keeping which may contribute to a representation of 'good' or 'bad' records.

Bed management and the bed management figures impact on other aspects of managerial activity and reporting - most notably in managerial calculations of activity, bed occupancy and patient turnover, all of which are relevant in national calculations and audit of performance. A great deal of managerial work is consequently devoted to untangling, interpreting and re-calculating the statistics on activity and patient turnover to take into account the process of bed management. It is not that the case that the statistics are not trusted They are not regarded as 'just any old numbers', but their limitations are recognised and related to how there are collected and collated. For example, although activity figures are provided on a Ward basis, this is affected by factors such as 'sleepouts'. An example of this would be when a 'stroke' patient is given a bed on a 'geriatric' ward. The Manager needs to extract 'her patients' and 'her doctors' from the figures in order to gain an accurate account of occupancy and length of stay to generate any performance indicators.

4. 'Minus Nine Beds'

Observations of the ways staff orient to existing shared displays illuminate the complexity of managerial work with the figures produced by the MIS needing to mesh with more local, changeable and situated information. The following example illustrates this with reference to the previously mentioned 'beds board' (see Fig. 7-1) On arrival one morning at one hospital (in a three hospital trust) the Directorate Manager of Orthopaedics' (DMO) first words were "We're minus nine beds". Some kind of 'bed crisis' was happening - assumed to be caused by a road traffic accident by the staff present - and the DMO would be taking some action to determine the position of her directorate. The DMO had received an 'end of day report', produced daily by the MIS, and this had alerted her to the potential shortfall in bed availability. The reference to 'minus nine beds' was to the state of play across all three sites, not only within the orthopaedic directorate. Although the 'minus nine' was referred to as being the "state of play", it actually referred to the future situation if all patients were admitted as expected for that day. The MIS 'end of day report' shows the figure for 8 November, surgical as minus six (see fig. 7-2). The DMO said that she needed to go to the orthopaedic wards to assess the situation, adding, "we go through our usual rituals for situations like these". She explained that it was essential to physically survey the wards rather than trying to get information another way for example, by telephone. She said that this was a process of "chivvying people up". Exactly what this meant became apparent once we arrived on the wards.

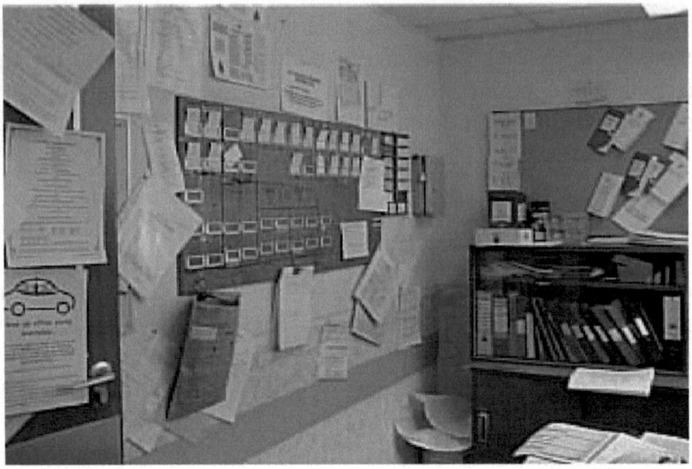

Figure 8-1. The Bed Board

First, the DMO walked around the floor of orthopaedic wards and did a count of seemingly empty beds. She then went to the nurses' station where there is a beds board (see Fig. 7-1) that represents the bed situation. The beds board represented the total ward area, with each ward 'bay' (usually comprising six beds) marked separately. Each bed is indicated by a metal slot where a card, with the patient's details, can be placed. Cards that have been placed straight into the slots represent existing in-patients. Cards placed diagonally in the slots represent patients due to be discharged, pending a visit by social services, a consultant, the physiotherapist etc.

END OF DAY REPORT

	NOV 6 6.30PM	NOV 7 6pm	NOV 8 7pm	NOV 9 4.30pm	NOV 10
PRESTON-BEDS AVAILABLE					
MEDICAL	5	7	2	9	
SURGICAL	0	0	-6	0	
ORTHOPAEDIC	0	2	0	1	
BURNS/PLASTIC	2	2	0	2	
NEUROSURGERY	1	1	0	4	
NEUROLOGY	1	3	2	4	
ONCOLOGY	0	3	1	0	
HDU	1	1	1	2	
RENAL	0	2	2	0	
OPHTHALMOLOGY	0	1	0	0	
ENT	2	0	2	2	
TOTALS	12	22	4	24	0
ITU	1	1	2	1	
GYNAE SGH	6	5	6	12	
SLEEPOUTS-RPH					
MEDICAL	16	12	15	14	
ORTHOPAEDIC	0	0	0	1	
SURGICAL	5	3	10	6	
NEURO	0	0	0	0	
RENAL	2	3	1	0	
ONCOLOGY	1	0	0	0	
BURNS & PLASTIC	0	0	0	1	
TOTALS	24	18	26	22	0
EMERGENCY ADMS-RPH					
CANCELLED OPS-RPH (NO BEDS)	0	0	0	0	
COMMENTS	[illegible] surg very busy	[illegible] sites remain very	[illegible] unable to sustain	[illegible] Surg take remains	
CHORLEY BEDS AVAILABLE					
MEDICAL	3	5	7	8	
SURGICAL	5	4	4	7	
HDU	0	0	1	0	
ORTHOPAEDIC	3	4	4	7	
GYNAE	6	5	4	3	
TOTALS	17	18	20	25	0
ITU	1	3	2	4	
SLEEPOUTS-CDH					
MEDICAL	16	19	20	18	
ORTHOPAEDIC	0	0	0	1	
SURGICAL	2	1	2	1	
TOTALS	17	20	22	20	0
EMERGENCY ADMS- CDH					

Figure 8-10. End of Day Report

The presence of diagonally-placed cards forced an immediate re-count for the DMO, as her count was based on a 'head-count' of patients present. The DMO then discussed available beds with the ward sister, who explained the expected time/date of discharge for the 'diagonals'. The ward sister also pointed to two slanted cards for existing in-patients and explained that they were acutely, terminally ill but said that she *"couldn't guarantee a day or time for them"*. The DMO then left the nurses' station and went to speak to the physiotherapist to ascertain whether there were any other patients who were fit for discharge or who were likely to become so that day. Through these processes, the DMO established that there were enough beds to see them through the 'crisis'. On leaving the ward area, the DMO said that establishing the availability of beds is *"a very physical thing"*.

5. Calculation and Calculability

The observations reveal how apparent solidity and objectivity of managerial information can thus continually be challenged as new data come to the fore, for example, where supposedly 'occupied' beds become available. Understanding of the data is facilitated through reconstructing the available information; that Ward Sisters were 'being naughty' or that some of the beds are occupied by 'walking wounded'. Thus readings of the bed management data are 'defeasible', capable of being re-interpreted to fit with new items of information and presented to different audiences.

What we observe in the work of bed management is that the process is difficult and eventually what emerge are a few 'quick and dirty' figures on which to make a judgement .The bed management figures and the bed management board are then the end product of a series of procedures. These procedures make up a system of calculation and are designed to give a picture, a representation, of the 'bed position' of each ward. But this picture is neither clear nor unambiguous since the figures are embedded in a nest of interactional, organisational and operational contingencies and gets its meaning from them.

Any explication of the work of managing the bed management system has to address what, for specific occasions, constitutes correctness, allowable error and so on. The practical monitoring of the bed availability situation is thus a system of calculability. Whenever there is a 'crisis' - an accident, political pressure, demands on targets or whatever - the figures are subject to reinterpretation and the calculations are subject to change. Such a finding has some repercussions in terms of the extent to which existing systems can be automated or computerised. The knowledge, which anyone working within the system possesses and uses, is a locally organised corpus and is unavailable to analytic reconstruction as a collection of abstracted cases and idealised procedures. There is no authoritative list of what personnel know about the bed management system in any particular medical ward and their peculiarities, nor when this knowledge is to be relevantly applied as a set of general guidelines. At best all that can be achieved is to attempt to apply the system of calculation as consistently as possible. However, any application of the public display system must allow others to follow it to see how the result - in the form of discharging walking wounded, setting up extra beds and so on - was arrived at.

What clearly emerges from our observations of managerial work is its complexity. Much of the 'organisational knowledge' regularly utilised in the managerial work of co-ordination and decision-making is not of a kind that is immediately visible in procedures or simply facilitated by reference to the record. Providing IT support for such contingent work requires that display systems necessarily pay attention to the occasioned character of activities. If the aim is to embed knowledge properties in management information systems then it needs to be captured, managed and displayed in a way that will make it accurate, available, accessible, effective and usable. Such a task is hardly a matter of simply digitalising existing records. These accounts of everyday managerial work would merely be a series of interesting stories were it not for the implications such accounts have for the design of new technologies and the support of working around shared displays. Our research highlights a need to attend to some of the everyday realities of organisational life. As designers attempt to accommodate some of the complexities of organisational working, so the challenges facing systems display designers necessarily increase. These new challenges involve attending to the lived reality of organisational groups - much as we have described it here - in order to design effective systems.

The use of such noticeboards for calculation and planning purposes is written about elsewhere. For example, Button and Sharrock (1997) have written extensively about a fieldwork study carried out in a sector of the print industry. Here too the organisation concerned was about to undergo a change in the nature of calculation and planning through the utilisation of new technology. In this study Button and Sharrock focus on the use of, what is referred to as, a 'forward-loading-board' which "is an organisational artefact that is used to work up the daily array of jobs into a rational production order and by means of which the AM [Administration Manager] is able to perform his necessary calculations" (1997:5). In terms of our study, similar calculation work is being done. Whilst we are careful not to 'see things that aren't there' (Coulter & Sharrock, 1998), it is evident from the fieldwork that calculation relevant to the 'activity' of the hospital is done through the use of artefacts such as the beds-board and through information available via the MIS.

5.1 The Practical Value of Numbers

The specific nature of print jobs and hospital treatment may differ, but calculation is nevertheless done with regard to similar salient features – in the previous scenario – how many beds do we have available? However, the calculation work of the manager may be directed at many other aspects of her managerial work – how much time have we got? What equipment is available? Which staff is available? Will this earn enough money? The direction of the calculation work towards such a range of questions can be seen in the following fieldwork extract and the way in which different categories of orthopaedic surgery are brought into play to meet certain ends. On the morning before the apparent 'beds crisis', the DMO had a meeting with the financial advisor for the Trust where a financial shortfall for that month was discussed. The financial advisor asked, "Have we started that big back yet?" This was referring to a potential earning source of £15K against the monthly shortfall. At a meeting later on in the same day, the DMO had a meeting to discuss the management of waiting lists, the hospital policy of 13 weeks maximum waiting time being under threat, where strategy was discussed to do "more fingers, then joints, then spines", fingers being the quickest to treat and spines the slowest, thus addressing the excessive waiting list figures. The point to be made here is that the categories of patient or of surgical need/status are brought into play when calculations for different ends are required i.e. for bed management, financial or policy purposes.

In the everyday work of the Hospital Trust patients and their representations become the focus for calculation and accounting work. The bed management figures are only one such locus for calculation work and they are interlinked with other sets of figures and calculations. Such accounting work is socially organised in a number of ways.

1. Calculation and calculability is a members problem i.e. it is achieved through the practical action of those involved. It takes the form of the achievement and display of 'proper' calculation. We are interested in the examination of the routine work which goes into making such a system of calculability operate.
2. Our interest in 'calculability' arises in relation to the variety of ways in which calculative rationalities interweave with other rationalities in the context of negotiations over 'beds' - and thus patients, operations, resources, targets.
3. As in other forms of distributed working, calculation work within the hospital - in this case in terms of 'beds' - is calculation within a division of labour. In this fashion calculation work and organisation work are harmonised in and through competent practical action. Related to what Anderson *et al.* (1989) refer to as the 'lore of numbers' - "capacity to play off the requirements for representing a set of activities through a system of calculation against the practicalities and obligations involved in performing those activities effectively and efficiently" (1989: 104)

Of course the calculation process is difficult and subject to rules of thumb and so on, and eventually what emerges is a few 'quick and dirty' figures on which to make a judgement. This is what can be seen in the 'beds crisis' example. Our interest is not in the premise of calculability but the work which medical personnel do to make their activities fit with what might be characterised as 'accountants' terms. "This work involves grappling with the sheer practical difficulties of determining which figures are wanted, pulling them out, and then knowing how to manipulate them and assess their product." (105-6) The idea of 'accountability' that emerges from this is not merely in terms of members' accounts but as a specific form of member's account - that conforms to particular 'rules' etc.

Explicating this work is not simply a question of medical staff seeing what is 'in the bed management figures' and then automatically working out what should be done. 'What is in the figures' is itself something that has to be worked out, and working it out involves balancing operational and organisational objectives and priorities. The bed management figures and the beds board are the end product of a series of procedures. These procedures make up a system of calculation and are designed to give a picture, a representation, of the 'bed position' of each ward. But this picture is neither clear nor unambiguous since the figures are embedded in a nest of interactional, organisational and operational contingencies and get their meaning from them.

Any explication of the work of managing the bed management system, of making a system of calculability work has to address what, for some specific occasion, constitutes correctness, allowable error, the margins of probability and calculability. Whenever there is a 'crisis' – an accident, political pressure, demands on targets or whatever – the figures are subject to reinterpretation and the calculations are subject to change. Essentially, the work involved in 'bed management' consists in a system of rules and their application in contexts – that is it is a system of calculability. The bed management figures and the bed management board are themselves the products of socially organised accounting work. They are 'displays' (Lynch in: Hughes *et al.*, 2002) of the methods used to produce them – what anyone can find them to say or to mean will depend on interpretation of the displays.

If we examine the bed management system as an empirically observable set of activities, as the operation of a system of calculability, we note that the knowledge which anyone working within the system possesses and uses is a locally organised corpus (Polner, 1987). It is a body of knowledge which makes itself available to those who know how to do *these calculations* with *these materials* in *this ward.* As a corpus it is unavailable to analytic reconstruction as a collection of abstracted cases and idealised procedures. There is no authoritative list of what personnel know about the bed management system in any particular medical ward and their peculiarities, nor when this knowledge is to be relevantly applied as a set of general guidelines. At best all that can be achieved is to attempt to apply the system of calculation as consistently as possible. However, any application of the system must allow others to follow it to see how the result – in the form of discharging walking wounded, setting up extra beds etc. was arrived at – the sytematicity of the procedures is both an achievement and a resource.

5.2 The 'At-a-Glance' Visibility of Order

This calculation work also has some resonance in the idea of the 'at-a-glance' visibility of order. In their case study of the print industry Button and Sharrock (1997) look at the use of a 'forward-loading-board' in the day to day management of print jobs and discuss the board as a public display of the order of production available to those who need to see it. The forward-loading-board is:

> "an organisational artefact that is used to work up the daily array of jobs into a rational production order and by means of which the AM [Administration Manager] is able to perform his necessary calculations" (ibid)

The forward-loading-board has a vertical axis and a horizontal axis – the former showing print machines and weeks and the latter showing the number of hours in a week to a maximum of a hundred. In brief, it is used by the Administration manager to project, review, consider different production orders, fine tune the production order and organise timings from origination to finishing. The board may be on the desk of the Administration Manager, but it is still publicly available to others such as the Production Manager (PM). In the same way, the beds board, although sited next to the ward sister's desk, is publicly available to other nursing staff, physiotherapists, occupational therapists, consultants, and in our example, the DMO. This public display allows for the re-calculation outlined above in our beds crisis scenario.

Although the nature of the work being undertaken in the hospital differs from the print centre, the beds board is used in similar ways by 'organisational toolsmiths' (Bittner: in Turner, 1975) in the day to day running of the hospital ward such as the ward sister or the DMO. However, their use of the board is oriented to different priorities. For the DMO, there is the at-a glance visibility of order afforded by the beds board and the public nature of it as an artefact. She can use and recognise the order shown by the beds board and all its features – empty slots, slanted cards and so on. The beds board helps the DMO to make bed management and, in this case, crisis management, a calculable phenomenon. The DMO has a range of organisational responsibilities – some oriented to the priorities of the Trust as a whole in the form of Trust policies, and some oriented to her domain – the orthopaedics directorate – and its staff and patients. In the case shown here, although there is an apparent beds crisis across the three hospital sites, the DMO is concerned to establish an acceptable state of affairs in her local domain rather than attending to the broader concerns of the Trust.

From the starting point of the MIS figures that indicated a crisis, the DMO establishes what is 'behind the numbers' in a local sense. The beds board makes the status in the ward "available to others in a format that they can work with" (Hughes, *et al.*, 2002). Where other studies have looked at the use of 'management information' in the sense of information used only for managerial purposes on one level, we have explored the way in which management information is used alongside other local knowledge in the everyday routines of bed management. The MIS figures are not used here as accounting devices for managers to demonstrate some kind of performance indicators for the Trust management board (although they are required to do this at specific times), but are an alert to a potential problem which the DMO then deals with via her 'usual rituals'. The DMO has established an acceptable situation in her own directorate, and the broader bed availability crisis is something that she "can let pass for now" (ibid).

6. Cautionary Tales for the Design of Situated and Public Displays

The strength of the ethnographic approach is in that it uncovers the mundane and taken for granted routines in the everyday management of the hospital. Although the daily working practices of those in the orthopaedics directorate may be reasonably described as mundane and taken for granted, this should not be read in a way that belies the skills and experience of the staff involved. The hospital staff routinely avoid serious, sometimes life-threatening, crises, and, as a design community, we must make ourselves aware of factors to be considered before the implementation of new forms of public display. We would suggest that designers revisit their unexplicated assumptions regarding the uses of new ICTs. The nature of the organisation involved is key here. For example, many studies of the use of new forms of situated and public displays, including some in this volume, explore the use of large whiteboards for distributed workers and they have been installed and evaluated in a quite 'experimental' fashion. This is inappropriate a for a safety critical setting such as a hospital, where 'failure' of the technology can have serious results.

The calculation work in the 'minus nine beds' situation detailed above is directed at a number of ends all related to 'activity' in the hospital. Garfinkel's notion of 'normal, natural troubles' led us to think about record-keeping practices as displays that are the result of socially organised accounting work and which are or may be re-interpreted according to the contingent matters of the moment. It is not the case that representations and displays here are 'trusted' or 'not trusted'. They are used within known limitations and in conjunction with other artefacts and local knowledge. Information is, as Pettersson *et al.* (2002: 287) put it, "*made* reliable by this complex amalgam of artefacts and practices".

Although we have said that the DMO established an 'acceptable' situation within her domain, this was still dependant to a certain extent on the ward sister's interpretation of the 'story' told by the beds board. It may be suggested, for example, that there could be a digital version of the beds board that the DMO could access from her office. However, when bed availability is not a problem she would not need to look at it, and when bed availability is a potential problem, she is still dependant on the local knowledge of the ward sister (and others) to give her a more precise information e.g. that certain beds currently indicated as slanted cards will be vacated that day or the next. Some benefits may be seen in the introduction of a digital beds board accessible on the hospital network e.g. such that the DMO could monitor the situation from any of the three hospital sites. However, in the same way that Bowers, Button and Sharrock (1995 & 1997) warned that the design community should develop 'measures of value' for proposed systems for organisations, we suggest that it should not be assumed that a digital display would bring enough benefits to warrant its design and implementation. The affordances of the current displays, practices and 'usual rituals' carried out by the DMO indicate that such a measure of value is not immediately apparent.

In considering some new form of beds board display, other issues that need careful consideration. The existing beds board is situated in the ward sister's office and as such its 'public' character is limited to those deemed appropriate members to view it i.e. hospital staff. It would not be suitable, for example, to place the beds board in an area of the wards where patients and their friends and family could view it – they might start to ask why a certain 'card' was slanted. In this way, any computerised display should also not be on 'public' view'. The location of the board has also evolved as the 'appropriate' location for other pieces of information relevant to the ward (see Fig. 7-1). Thus, policy change announcements, memos and other documents are routinely pinned to the edges of the board because it is known that staff will see them there. For the hospital staff, much work has already gone into placing the appropriate artefacts in the place of optimal use. This is not to say that there could not be some kind of digital display which may benefit the hospital staff, but that this should not be assumed.

7. References

Anderson, R, Hughes, J, and Sharrock, W. Working For Profit; the social organisation of Calculation in an Entrepreneurial Firm. Aldershot: Avebury, 1989

Bannon, L. & Bodker, S. Constructing Common Information Spaces. Proceedings of ECSCW'97 5th European Conference on Computer Supported Cooperative Work; 1997; Lancaster, UK; 81-96.

Berg, M. *Rationalising Medical Work: Decision Support techniques and Medical Practices.* Cambridge: MIT Press 1997.

Bloor, K. and Maynard, A. *Clinical Governance: Clinician Heal Thyself.* Institute of Health Services Management, 1997.

Bowers, J., Button, G. & Sharrock, W. Workflow from Within and Without: Technology and Cooperative Work on the Print Industry Shopfloor. Proceedings of ECSCW'95 4th European Conference on Computer Supported Cooperative Work; 1995; Stockholm, Sweden; 51-66.

Button, G. & Sharrock, W. 'The Production of Order and the Order of Production: Possibilities for Distributed Organisations, Work and Technology in the Print Industry Proceedings of ECSCW'97 5th European Conference on Computer Supported Cooperative Work; 1997; Lancaster, UK; 1-16.

Coulter, J & Sharrock, W. On What We Can See. Theory And Psychology, 1998; 8(2).

Department of Health *The New NHS: Modern, Dependable*, The Stationery Office, London, December 1997, ISBN 0 10 138072 0.

DIRC see http://www.dirc.org.uk/

Fitzpatrick, G. Understanding the Paper Record in Practice: Implications for EHRs. In Proceedings of HIC '2000

Hughes, J.A, King, V., Randall, D., Sharrock, W. Ethnography for system design: a guide. COMIC Working Paper; 1993; Computing Department, Lancaster University, UK

Hughes, J., King, V., Rodden, T., Andersen, H. (1994). 'Moving out of the control room: ethnography in system design', in Proceedings of CSCW'94 (Chapel Hill NC), ACM Press, pp. 429-438

Hughes, J., Rouncefield, M., & Tolmie, P. 'Representing Knowledge. The British Journal of Sociology 2002; 53(2): 221-238.

Petterson, M., Randall, D. & Helgeson, B. 'Ambiguities, Awareness and Economy: A Study of Emergency Service Work' in CSCW2002: Proceedings of ACM 2002 Conference on Computer Supported Cooperative Work; 2002; New Orleans, LO, USA; 286-295

Pollner, M. *Mundane Reason: Reality in Everyday and Sociological Discourse.* Cambridge: Cambridge University Press, 1987.

Robins, K. & Webster, F. *Times of the Technoculture: From the Information Society to the Virtual Life.* London: Routledge, 1999.

Turner, R. (ed) *Ethnomethodology.* Penguin, 1975.

Weber, M. *Economy and Society, Vols 1 and 2.* Berkeley, CA: University of California Press, 1978.

Chapter 9

FROM CONCEPTION TO DESIGN

A practical guide to designing ambient displays

Jennifer Mankoff[1] & Anind K. Dey[1,2]
[1]*UC Berkeley,* [2]*Intel Research Berkeley*

Abstract: This chapter discusses displays that sit on the periphery of a user's attention. Many public displays of information that we encounter are in this category the majority of the time, including clocks, posters, and windows. Computationally enhanced variations on this theme are called *peripheral displays*. Our work focuses on *ambient displays*, a subset of peripheral displays that continuously display information to be monitored. Peripheral (and ambient) displays have the peculiar property that they are *not* meant to be the focus of the user's attention. Contrast this with desktop applications, which require a user's attention. In this chapter, we present a case study of two public ambient displays that we developed and evaluated. We present some lessons learned about the design of ambient displays, and conclude with a practical guide to using a modified version of heuristic evaluation that we developed as a result of designing these displays.

Key words: ambient displays, peripheral displays, heuristic evaluation, attention, iterative design

1. Introduction

Many of the public displays of information that we encounter sit on the periphery of a user's attention the majority of the time, including clocks, posters, and windows. Computationally enhanced variations on this theme are called *peripheral displays*. This chapter is concerned with *ambient displays*, a subset of peripheral displays that continuously display information that can be monitored by the user without requiring her focused attention. For example, one of the first such displays, created by an artist and technologist in collaboration, was a "dangling string" attached to a motor

K. O'Hara et al. (eds.), Public and Situated Displays: Social and Interactional Aspects of Shared Display Technologies, 210–230.

(Weiser and Brown, 1996). The string spun around at different speeds depending on network load (See Figure 9-1). Contrast this with a discrete display of information such as an alarm, an *alerting display* that only rings when the network load reaches a certain threshold.

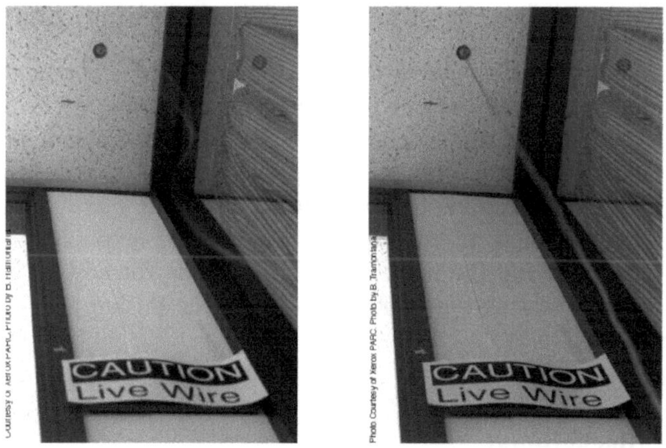

Figure 9-1. "The 'Dangling String' is an 8 foot piece of plastic spaghetti that hangs from a small electric motor hanging in the ceiling.... A very busy network causes a madly whirling string with a characteristic noise [left]; a quiet network causes only a small twitch every few seconds [right]. Placed in an unused corner of a hallway, the long string is visible and audible from many offices without being obtrusive" (Weiser and Brown, 1996). Courtesy of the Palo Alto Research Center (PARC). Photos by B. Tramontana.

Peripheral displays have the peculiar property that they are *not* meant to be the focus of a user's attention. They can be broken into two categories: *Ambient displays*, are a subclass of peripheral displays that present information in such a way so as to allow people to monitor a data source while not being distracted from their main task. *Alerting displays* alert a user through more direct means about salient information. This chapter will focus in particular on ambient displays. However, many alerting displays include an ambient component when they are not actively alerting the user about something, and thus alerting display designers may benefit from some of the material in this chapter. Similarly, an ambient display may at times alert a user about something.

One of the biggest challenges facing the developers of ambient displays is the lack of information about what constitutes a *good* design, and which ambient display designs will succeed or fail. Considering the literature regarding ambient displays, there have been few in-depth evaluations, and even fewer examples of design iteration (exceptions are the evaluation work of Mamyinka *et al.* (2001), and the design iterations of Mynatt *et al.* (2001)). Far more evaluations of alerting displays exist (including Cutrell *et al.* (2001); Dumais and Czerwinski (2001); Ho-Ching *et al.* (2003); Horvitz *et al.* (1999); Maglio and Campbell (2000); Tiernan, *et al.* (2001) and van Dantzich *et al.* (2002)). In these cases, as in the ambient display case, discount evaluation techniques[4], useful in the early stages of design, do not exist.

The goal of this chapter is to provide a guide to ambient display design and evaluation. After reviewing relevant literature, we present our experiences with the design and evaluation of two ambient displays. We present metrics for successful ambient display design (changes in *awareness* or *behaviour*), and describe lessons learned designing our displays. We then present an evaluation technique that we adapted explicitly for ambient display design, giving the reader a practical guide for how to apply it. We conclude with a discussion of future work in the design and evaluation of ambient displays.

2. Background

2.1 Peripheral Displays

Peripheral displays are devices that usually reside in the *periphery*, but show information relevant to a user (Examples may be found in: Dumais and Czerwinski, 2001; Mamyinka *et al.*, 2001; McCrickard *et al.*, 2001; McCrickard *et al.*, 2002; Mynatt *et al.*, 1998; Mynatt *et al.*, 2001). By definition, in today's world of ubiquitous devices, the majority of applications must reside in the user's periphery – a person can only interact closely with one or two things at a time. As Weiser states in his seminal article on Ubiquitous Computing "Most of the computers… will be invisible in fact as well as metaphor (Weiser, 1991)" – not at the center of a user's task or attention. Treismann's theory of feature integration states that singular focused attention (or spotlight) is a necessity when interacting with complex information (Treismann and Gelade, 1980). In addition, other studies have shown that recognizing a change in a visual environment does not require this spotlight, although knowing what the change is does require it (Sagi and Julesz, 1985). Good design is crucial for applications, or

[4] Discount evaluation techniques are techniques that have a reduced cost. They typically require less time and/or money, may involve fewer participants, and less extravagant equipment (Nielsen, 1994).

displays of information, that reside in the periphery to succeed without representing a constant distraction, or further overloading users who are already overwhelmed by information in today's world.

Peripheral displays may be public or personal displays of information, and may show ambient information, or may show alerts. An example of a personal, alerting display is Yahoo's Instant Messenger program. We classify it as an *alerting display* because it moves from the periphery to the focus of the user's attention to notify the user that someone wishes to communicate a message to her. Another example in this category is the mobile phone, which grabs the user's attention when it rings. In contrast Mamyinka *et al.* (2001) designed a personal, ambient display that indicates to a presenter using PowerPoint™ how much time is left in his presentation. We classify this as an *ambient display* because it presents information continuously to the presenter without interrupting the presentation in any way. An example of a public, ambient display is the Dangling String, described in the introduction and shown in Figure 9-1 (Weiser and Brown, 1996). Both of these ambient displays are abstract (one represents time as a color bar, the other represents network load as the rotation speed of a string. This is typical of computer-based ambient displays. A focus on aesthetics is also typical: The Dangling String is a piece of artwork, created to explore the idea of embodied information.

In summary, work in peripheral displays, whether personal or public, falls into two classes – ambient displays and alerting displays. Ambient displays are peripheral displays that do not attempt to move into the foreground of a user's attention. They are *continuous* displays of information, and are often abstract, aesthetic, and non-disruptive. In contrast to ambient displays, alerting displays show information at *discrete* intervals, and are defined by their attempts to move into the foreground of a user's attention. It should be noted that in practice, many peripheral displays include components of both ambient displays and alerting displays. The focus of this chapter is on continuous displays of information, ambient displays, although some of our displays may include alerting features.

2.2 Ambient Displays

Many ambient displays have been built over the years, and those presented here are only a sample. Ambient displays have become an increasingly important focus for artists, designers, and technologists since the introduction of the Dangling String. For example, the Oxygen Flute (Chafe and Niemeyer, 2002) was an art piece designed to reflect the amount of oxygen available in an enclosed space depending on the presence and breathing patterns of human participants. Traditional user interface design had little relevance to this provocative exhibit.

In contrast, Hallnäs and Redström's (2001) work with slow technology was a deliberate exploration of the uses of slowly changing physical artifacts such as moving curtains, wind-blown leaves, and drawers, to show (write) and sense (read) information. As well as being aesthetic and compelling, this work also begins to explore ideas that might guide future design.

Researchers approaching the problem from a human-computer interaction perspective have performed studies of detection, distraction, and other factors that can inform ambient display design. For example, Bartram *et al.* (2001) found that motion is an effective way to notify a user of information, while color change is less effective. McCrickard *et al.* (2003) studied a variety of different styles of animation and their impact in terms of interruption and comprehension. The result of their studies was a table recommending different types of notifications[5] depending on system design goals. Czerwinski *et al.* (2000) investigated the impact of interruptions caused by Instant Messaging on different types of primary tasks, showing generally harmful effects on overall task time. In related work, the same authors found that Instant Messaging interruptions can cause a user to forget what they were scanning for in a visual scan task (Cutrell *et al.,* 2001). Intille (2002) demonstrated techniques for supporting change blindness, changing visual information in ways that make the changes difficult to detect, and reduces interruption/distraction. Hudson *et al.* studied predictors for the interruptibility of administrative assistants, and developed sensing technology that can accurately predict appropriate times to display peripheral information, based on sensors as simple as a noise-detecting microphone. Other work, including our own, has led to an understanding of how different evaluation methods can be adapted to support the evaluation of peripheral and ambient displays (Mankoff *et al.*, 2003; Chewar and McCrickard, 2002).

Finally, technologists such as Ishii *et al.* (1998) and Pederson and Sokolor (1997) have developed tools and techniques for constructing tangible, sensing-based ambient displays. Both sets of authors used their tools to gain experience with ambient display design. Ishii *et al.* particularly mention the importance of choosing an appropriate modality to display data ("mapping"). They also discuss the importance of understanding when data will transition into a user's foreground, and the existence of learning effects. Pederson and Sokolor discuss the connection between learning effects and levels of

[5] Note that the peripheral display community has not entirely settled on a terminology yet. The term "notification systems" has been used in the past to refer to alerting displays, but McCrickard uses it more broadly and includes ambient displays in his definition.

abstraction. Long-term use showed them the importance of aesthetics as they became "tired of the abstract displays" they had created. Finally, they suggest that because a user is not constantly attending to a display, information cannot change too quickly, and some sort of memory or history must be provided.

One important question to ask about the evaluation of ambient displays is: "What are the characteristics of a successful ambient display?" In other words, what high-level outcomes should we expect from a good display? Our answer to this question is that a successful ambient display should modify someone's awareness of certain information and potentially change one's behaviour with respect to that information. The next section presents our design process for two ambient displays, from conception to an evaluation intended to measure successful changes in awareness and behaviour.

3. Our design process

Our design process typically involves three main steps: (1) We conduct interviews and/or surveys of the people using the area where the display will be located to determine which information sources are of interest to them, and how they currently monitor that information. (2) We select an appropriate information source based on that data and design an ambient display that shows that information. (3) We conduct a summative evaluation of the display. Our general approach has been to test awareness and behaviour of the information displayed twice – once before and once after the deployment. Next, we give an example of this design process for two recent displays built in our lab, the Bus Mobile and the Daylight Display.

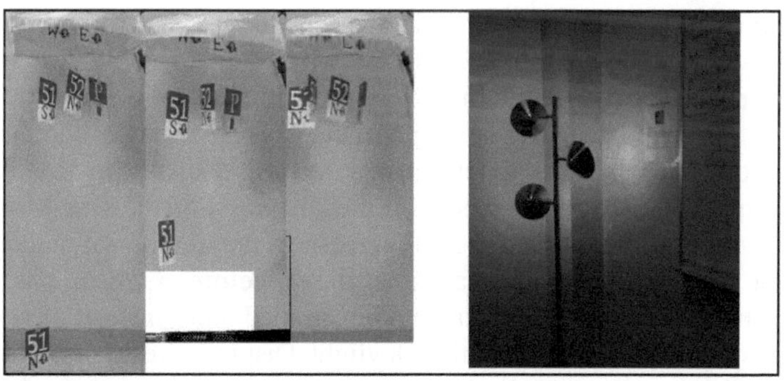

Figure 9-2. Two displays that were placed at the front of an underground student computing laboratory. **Bus Mobile** (left): The three images show a token for bus 51 moving upwards,

indicating that the bus is approaching the bus stop. **Daylight Display** (right): The light dims as sunset approaches, and brightens as dawn approaches.

3.1.1 Bus Mobile and Daylight Display

Both the Bus Mobile and the Daylight Display were built to address the needs of undergraduate computer science students working in underground laboratories in our building. We designed them to provide a service to the users of two computer labs that do not have windows.

To determine what kinds of information would be useful to users, we conducted a preliminary survey, asking participants to rank in order information they would like to see in an ambient display. Some of the choices included how dark it is outside (leaving the lab before dark is important to many students for safety reasons), the weather, the population of the computer labs, the network load on the login servers, when a bus was next scheduled to arrive, and sports statistics. The survey also queried the lab users with questions such as which bus lines they used frequently and which sports teams they followed. Some of the highest ranking information included how full the labs were and which servers had the most traffic. However, it was decided that these data sources would not make effective ambient displays, because the information only need be obtained once before entering the lab, and continual awareness of the information is not needed while one is working. Instead, we chose the highest ranked information sources that included dynamic change (and thus were amenable to an ambient display approach). The two most popular information sources that fit this requirement were bus schedules and the amount of daylight remaining. Students typically memorize bus schedules, or look them up online. Daylight is estimated by checking the time. As students are usually engrossed in their projects, it is very easy for them to lose track of time and more importantly, when their buses arrive or when it gets dark.

Once we completed our analysis of what data to show, we built the displays and deployed them in the aforementioned labs for a two week period. It was expected that having the displays in the two computer labs would allow the lab users to make an informed decision to leave the lab within a specific time frame based on their needs. For the Bus Mobile, we hypothesized that there would be an increase in the number of students who leave the lab within an optimal time frame before a given bus arrival, because students would like to catch a bus immediately instead of waiting at the stop for one to arrive. For the Daylight Display, we hypothesized that there would be an increase in the number of students leaving the lab in the time leading up to sunset.

Bus Mobile: The Bus Mobile, shown in Figure 9-2 (left), was designed to provide information about how soon local buses would arrive at nearby bus stops. It was constructed using six computer-controlled motors attached to aluminum rods. Around the base of the display hangs a curtain that is approximately six inches long, behind which the icons, attached to each of the motors with a wire, can be hidden from view. Bus numbers painted on wooden plaques for the six most popular bus lines mentioned on the pre-survey were hung from the motors.

The display was designed so that the six bus numbers hang at depths corresponding to how many minutes are left before the relevant bus is scheduled to arrive at the stop closest to the building where the labs are located. For example, in Figure 9-2 (left), Bus 51N is further from the bus stop than Bus 51S. For each inch the number hangs below the bottom edge of the skirt, there is one minute remaining before the bus arrives, with a maximum range of twenty-five minutes. If no bus is scheduled to arrive within twenty-five minutes, the bus number moves to its minimum depth and is hidden from view behind the curtain. The display is updated every minute, and the icons move up one inch per minute. After the bus has passed, the bus number is lowered the appropriate number of inches based upon the next scheduled arrival of the same bus line. As mentioned above, we queried students to determine the most popular bus lines to display with the Bus Mobile.

Daylight Display: The second display, shown in Figure 9-2 (right), was designed to provide information about whether it was dusky, light, or dark outside. This was of interest to students for safety reasons (*i.e.* some students are uncomfortable walking home alone after dark) and also as an approximate indicator of time of day. The display consists of a regular floor lamp with an X10 controller, a common home automation device. The display controls the brightness of a lamp by adjusting how much power is supplied to the lamp.

The Daylight Display was designed to adjust its brightness according to the recorded sunrise and sunset times. A number of sunrises and sunsets were observed to determine when it actually begins to get light and dark, so that the display could more accurately show the light level outside. It was determined that during the summer months in Berkeley in 2002, the sun began to set about forty-five minutes before the listed sunset time (taken from a website with weather information), and it was completely dark about thirty minutes after the listed sunset time. For the sunrise, it began to get light thirty minutes before the listed sunrise time, and it was completely light about forty-five minutes after the listed sunrise time. The display was designed to alert a user of the lab that it is beginning to get dark or light outside by flickering the lamp a few times, then beginning the cycle of brightening or dimming the lamp, depending on the time of day. The X10 controller allowed for twenty-two brightness levels from off to on, which meant that the light adjusted its brightness approximately every 3.5 minutes.

3.1.2 Study Method

The study was conducted in three phases. The first phase occurred in the week before the displays were deployed in the labs, when a questionnaire was distributed to the users of three labs, which they could fill out at their own leisure. Two of the labs were ones where the displays would be located, and the third lab was one that would have no display and would be used as a control. The questions on the survey covered various topics that could give us an indication of whether or not information about bus arrivals and outdoor light levels affected a subject's behaviour.

Phase 2 of the project started about a week and a half after the surveys were first made available. It began with the installation of the two displays in two different labs. The Bus Mobile was suspended from the ceiling on one side of the room in a location where most users in the lab could see it when they looked up from their desktop computers. The Daylight Display was set up in a corner of the other lab where it would be the most noticeable. We hung a sign by each of the displays, explaining how to use them and where a user could go for more information. As soon as the displays were deployed, we removed the Phase 1 surveys from the labs.

Phase 2 lasted for two and a half weeks. The first week of deployment allowed the users of the lab comfortable with using the ambient displays, so that when the next survey became available, the novelty of the displays would have worn off. Surveys with different questions were made available to the users of the labs, this time with questions pertaining to how they use the display and whether or not it was useful to them. Users had the opportunity to complete surveys posted on the door, using an online form with the web address advertised in the labs, or completing the survey after being recruited in the hallway after leaving.

Phase 3 started when the Bus Mobile and Daylight Display were removed, along with the surveys from the second phase. Surveys were again distributed to the labs in the same manner as the surveys from the second round. The objective of this questionnaire was to find data on the impact of the removal of the displays and whether or not the users of the labs missed having them.

In addition to the data collected from the surveys, we monitored the labs for ten minutes a day at random times for approximately two weeks, spread over phases 1 and 2. The observations made during the monitoring sessions consisted of how many people were in the lab initially, how many people entered or left the lab during the time period, how many users were there in the end, and then any observations that could be made about people using the displays, discussing them, or filling out the surveys. Our last source of data was a system log that listed all of the students' account login and logout times. This data was retrieved in each of the phases.

3.1.3 Study Results

Qualitative feedback indicated that students preferred the Bus Mobile to the Daylight Display. For example, one student wrote "bus mobile -> ultra cool. makes life easier [sic]" about the Bus Mobile. Written comments criticized the Daylight Display for being too bright, or indicated that a respondent had not noticed it or thought it was broken.

We surveyed a total of 60 students during the study period. Of those, 6 respondents were interested in the bus schedules and 10 were interested in awareness of light (based on a Likert scale response of 4 or 5 out of 5). There was a strong correlation (Spearman's rho=.618, p<.01) between those who reported interest in the daylight information and those who reported finding the daylight display useful. There was a very strong correlation (rho=.808, p<.01) between interest in the bus schedules and the usefulness of the Bus Mobile, while there was a moderate correlation (rho=.595, p<.01) between interest in the bus schedules and respondents who missed it after it was removed. Although 83% of the respondents who were interested in the Bus Mobile found it useful, only 30% interested in the daylight found it useful.

As stated above, we observed the lab each day for ten minutes over the course of two weeks. During these observations, very few people left or entered the lab, and students did not attend to the displays in noticeable ways or discuss them with each other. Instead, they remained focused on their lab work during the entire observation period.

Lastly, we analyzed the login and logout data for the Bus Mobile. We removed certain data to make our results resemble the typical use of the lab. This included removing the entry of any user who was logged in for 5 minutes or less. This was to reduce the amount of data that might skew the results due to a user merely logging in to check mail or logging into a machine, then immediately deciding to use another one. Another set of confounding factors that could alter the results were the times that lab sessions were scheduled to meet in the rooms with the displays. All logout times just before, during, and just after all lab sessions were removed from the data set.

We then calculated a "logout delta" for each data point. The logout delta measured the time from a logout event to the most likely trigger for that event. To calculate the logout delta, we subtracted each logout time from the nearest bus arrival time.

To check for a statistical significance of the Bus Mobile on logout times, we ran a t-test across the three phases of the project. Our analysis was not able to show a statistically significant change in user logout behaviour.

The above results, even without the additional login time data factored in, give some qualitative insight into whether or not the hypotheses were correct. For the prediction that the Bus Mobile and Daylight Display would impact people's decisions to leave the lab at a certain time, it can be said that the Bus Mobile was definitely effective for the people interested in the data, although not for as many people as originally expected. Some subjects had very positive comments about the Bus Mobile, saying they chose to work in the lab where it was displayed because they found it so convenient.

For the Daylight Display, the survey results show the display was only effective for about 30% of the subjects interested in the daylight schedule, which did not meet our expectations. There are several possible explanations for why this might be the case, using the comments from the surveys as an indication. For one, the design of the Daylight Display might not have been appealing. Many people saw it as just a lamp in the corner of the room and may not have noticed there was anything special about it unless they got closer to it and read the sign. Also, some subjects mentioned they never noticed the display working, which could mean a display that changes more frequently than two 75 minute long periods each day is more useful. One subject complained that the lamp was too bright and painful to the eyes, which would also make it less appealing. These are all things to take into consideration in our next iteration of the Daylight Display.

In summary, we used a user-centered design process to build two ambient displays and gain feedback on their usefulness and some of the problems with their design. Our analysis showed that these displays are useful to users interested in the information they display.

3.2 Lessons Learned

From a design perspective, we learned several things about ambient displays. First, we learned that it is crucial to pick the right sort of information source. Information that changes very rarely (such as whether it is light or dark out) is not appropriate for an ambient display, because it is difficult for the user to notice changes in the display. Users may get out of the habit of attending to it, since there is little change, and may receive little benefit from having the display. This issue interacts with the noticeability of the cue. For example, a window might succeed at the same goal because eventually a user will notice that he is having difficulty reading due to the fading of natural light.

Second, we learned that, since most of the people viewing a public ambient display may care nothing about the information it is displaying, a good design must be able to stand on its aesthetic merits alone. In other words, a display may be a purely decorative object to the majority of its "users." There may be some tension between this decorative role and the additional goal of displaying information, and this creates additional challenges for the display designer. It is also difficult to evaluate the aesthetic goals of a display, although examples of such evaluations exist (See Höök *et al.*, 2003).

Third, since those users who are interested in the data source still may not attend to a display much of the time, it must be able to smoothly transition from a background, peripheral object to the main focus of a user's attention. This transition may be difficult to manage, since the display cannot easily sense a user's interruptibility, or other aspects of her cognitive state. Although sensors may help with this issue (see, for example, the work of Hudson *et al.,* 2003), it also creates challenges for the designer. For example, a display may attempt to attract attention, demand attention, or simply allow a user to interact once it has a user's attention. Each of these possibilities brings about different sorts of design and interactivity challenges.

In retrospect, we felt that our designs would have benefited from more iteration before the actual deployment. As a result, we adapted a popular discount evaluation technique, *Heuristic Evaluation*, to the domain of ambient displays (Mankoff *et al.*, 2003). Heuristic evaluation does not require a working interface and thus can be used at the early stages of design. Additionally, it can be done by designers rather than end users, making it an inexpensive solution for supporting multiple design iterations. This is important since reports of development time for a single design iteration can be as high as a year (Heiner *et al.*, 1999). Below, we describe how our modified version of Heuristic Evaluation can be used to evaluate an ambient display.

4. Using Heuristic Evaluation to Develop Ambient Displays

Heuristic evaluation involves recruiting evaluators, who may be novices, to critique an interface (usually represented with pictures and a textual description)[6]. Evaluators look for problems in an interface's compliance with heuristics that encode important usability guidelines. Nielsen found that 3-5 novice evaluators find 40-60% of known issues when applying heuristic evaluation to desktop interfaces (Nielsen and Molich, 1990). The canonical list of heuristics as defined by Nielsen (2002) is: (1) Visibility of system status; (2) Match between system and the real world; (3) User control and freedom; (4) Consistency and standards; (5) Error prevention; (6) Recognition rather than recall; (7) Flexibility and efficiency of use; (8) Aesthetic and minimalist design; (9) Help users recognize, diagnose and recover from errors; (10) Help and documentation.

We believe heuristic evaluation is important to ambient display designers because of its potential to provide quick, inexpensive feedback about the possible issues with a specific display (Nielsen, 1990). Heuristic evaluation, because of its informal nature and low cost, was rated as one of the top techniques currently in use in a survey of usability practitioners (Vredenburg *et al.* 2002). Among discount evaluation techniques, only "informal expert review" ranked higher than heuristic evaluation. However, heuristic evaluation was considered to be more effective than informal expert reviews by the survey participants. Also, it was believed to be low cost, fast, and easy to apply. Cost and speed were both highly ranked factors in choosing an evaluation methodology.

The major difference between evaluating ambient displays and evaluating traditional displays comes from the way users interact with the interface. Ambient display users are passive in obtaining information from a display. Users do not *use* a display as they would use a computer; they *perceive* a display. Consequently, some of Nielsen's original heuristics (those associated with interactivity and productivity) do not apply to ambient displays. Furthermore, since ambient displays are passive, more responsibility lies with the designer to ensure that the displays are conveying a sufficient amount of information, and that the information is being conveyed unobtrusively. We were particularly concerned with how Nielsen's heuristics were defined, not only how they were named, as the definitions made assumptions about the goals of the interface being evaluated. For example, two heuristics explicitly refer to a "dialog" with which the user interacts, something that is central to conventional interfaces, but rare in ambient displays. Our conclusion was that the methodology of heuristic evaluation could be applied to ambient displays if the heuristics used were modified.

[6] Note that heuristic evaluation is most effective when performed by trained usability evaluators and does not help to identify which of the identified issues are real problems that will have a measurable impact on usability (Gray and Salzman, 1998).

We adapted heuristic evaluation for use with ambient displays (Mankoff *et al.* 2003). With the help of ambient display designers, we defined and tested a modified set of heuristics. Next, we give a practical guide to conducting a heuristic evaluation of an ambient display using our modified heuristics.

4.1 How it Works

We begin by presenting the basic methodology, which we did not change from Nielsen and Molich's (1990) original description[7]. The participants in a heuristic evaluation are generally designers. They may or may not be domain experts. They should not be the same people who developed the original display. Three to five evaluators generally conduct a heuristic evaluation. Five evaluators are typically cited as sufficient to find 80% of issues when conducting a heuristic evaluation (Nielsen and Landauer 1993). However, Woolrych and Cockton (2002) criticize the claim that five users is sufficient on the basis that problems may not be evenly distributed by severity, and users may not consistently find 30% of problems (an assumption of Nielsen and Landauer's (1993) original claim). These criticisms are directed not at the technique itself, simply at the number of users necessary to conduct an effective evaluation.

4.1.1 Method

Each evaluator is given a description of the user interface to be evaluated, a list of the heuristics to be used, and a form in which she or he can enter problems as they are found. For each problem found, a description of the problem is written down and a severity is assigned to the problem. Evaluators work independently to generate problems.

Once each evaluator has generated a list of problems, the designer of the ambient display must organize the results. One or more designers work together to group problems that are similar. Cox and Greenberg (2000) have developed a method for doing this systematically using *results synthesis*. Designers may also reassign severity levels at this point.

Heuristic evaluation is a qualitative technique, since it cannot be used to measure how well an interface meets numerical metrics. Once the problems found by the participants have been coded, no further analysis need be done. At this point, most designers work through the interface addressing each problem in turn.

[7] We refine some details of this methodology that are underspecified, particularly in how to analyze the results produced by evaluators.

The heuristics given below are based on our previous work (Mankoff *et al.*, 2003), but have been modified slightly as follows: Originally we determined that complete problem coverage would require all but one of the heuristics we had derived, as well as five of Nielsen's original heuristics (Match between system and real world, Visibility of system status, User control and freedom, Error Prevention, and Flexibility and efficiency of use). However, Nielsen's heuristics, although effective, are not entirely appropriate for ambient displays. Thus, we combined "User control and freedom" and "Error prevention", because our evaluators used them both to capture problems with identifying the occurrence of an error. Additionally, we deleted the least relevant heuristic, "Flexibility and efficiency of use", because it would be difficult or impossible to tailor a public display to the needs of specific, individual users. Table 9-1 has the full set of heuristics.

Table 9-1. Heuristics for use when conducting a Heuristic Evaluation of Ambient Displays. Heuristic (7) is a direct quote from Nielsen (2002)

#	**Heuristic and definition**
1.	**Sufficient information design:** The display should be designed to convey "just enough" information. Too much information cramps the display, and too little makes the display less useful.
2.	**Consistent and intuitive mapping:** Ambient displays should add minimal cognitive load. Cognitive load may be higher when users must remember what states or changes in the display mean. The display should be intuitive.
3.	**Match between system and real world:** The system should speak the user's language, with words, phrases, and concepts familiar to the user. Follow real-world conventions, making information appear in a natural and logical order.
4.	**Visibility of state:** An ambient display should make the states of the system noticeable. The transition from one state to another should be easily perceptible
5.	**Aesthetic and pleasing design:** The display should be pleasing when it is placed in the intended setting.
6.	**Useful and relevant information:** The information should be useful and relevant to the users in the intended setting.
7.	**Visibility of system status:** The system should always keep users informed about what is going on, through appropriate feedback, within reasonable time.
8.	**Easy transition to more in-depth information:** If the display offers multi-leveled information, the display should make it easy and quick for users to find out more detailed information.
9.	**"Peripherality" of display:** The display should be unobtrusive and remain so unless it requires the user's attention. Users should be able to easily monitor the display.
10.	**Error prevention and user control:** Users should be able to distinguish between a inactive display and a broken display. When a display enters an error state, or a state that a user does not want, users must have a way to reset it.

4.1.2 Special considerations for ambient displays

As stated above, our major modification to the heuristic evaluation technique was to generate and validate a new list of heuristics appropriate for ambient displays. We validated our heuristics by comparing their performance to Nielsen's heuristics on the two ambient displays described in Section 3. Evaluators using our heuristics found more, severe problems than evaluators using Nielsen's heuristics. Additionally, when using our heuristics, 3-5 evaluators were able to identify 40-60% of known usability issues. This implies that heuristic evaluation is an effective technique for identifying usability issues with ambient displays, given our modified set of heuristics.

Our modified heuristics are given in Table 9-1, with definitions. Our work showed that even people with little experience designing ambient displays could be useful evaluators given our list of heuristics. We recommend selecting people with general design experience, however. One other detail is necessary for successful evaluation of an ambient display using heuristic evaluation: it is important to set the scene in which the ambient display is operating. A description of its location in a public space, information about what tasks might be co-occurring with the display, and so on, are all helpful to the evaluator. We are still working to determine what the necessary elements of such a description might be, but the high-level important message is that an ambient display cannot be understood in isolation, but must be contextualized for the evaluator. As an example, here is a description of the Bus Mobile, used in our validation of the new heuristics.

> "The Bus Mobile is a mobile that hangs from the ceiling and has six bus numbers hanging from it, each representing a distinct route, which adjust their height according to the closeness of a bus. It is designed to show when the next bus for various bus lines is scheduled to stop at the location closest to Soda Hall. The Bus Mobile is located in Soda Hall Instructional Lab 273. It is pretty much the typical computer lab setting with desks, chairs and computers. The Bus Mobile is hung from the ceiling in the front of the lab, near the left side of the whiteboard. All the desks and chairs are lined up facing the whiteboard. It is important to note that there are no windows to the outside in the lab. When a bus for a particular bus line is 25 minutes from the bus stop, its icon drops to its maximum depth. For each minute that passes, moving closer to the bus arrival time, the icon moves up towards the white skirt [which is visible at the top of Figure 9-2]. When the bus is not scheduled to arrive, the icon moves completely under the white skirt, disappearing from view and stays out of sight until 25 minutes before it is scheduled to arrive again. If

buses for a particular bus line are scheduled to arrive less than 25 minutes apart, the icon's height represents the bus that will arrive next."

We also provided the evaluators with four time-delayed pictures of the 51N bus token in motion upwards towards the white skirt of the display.

4.2 *Summary of Heuristic Evaluation*

As stated above, we believe that heuristic evaluation is a viable design tool for constructing ambient displays. Our own studies proved that our modified heuristics were effective for evaluating ambient displays (Mankoff *et al.*, 2003). The technique is simple and low-cost, and can help ambient display designers to improve their designs before running a more costly, longer-term evaluation.

5. Conclusions and Future Work

In conclusion, this chapter focuses on the design and early-stage evaluation of ambient displays, a subset of peripheral displays that help a user to maintain awareness of information by continuously displaying information in a way that can easily be monitored without requiring focused attention. In this chapter, we contrast ambient displays with alerting displays, which typically display information at discrete intervals, when it is important to gain a user's attention. In practice, peripheral displays may include properties of both.

As discussed in Section 2, a mixture of artists and technologists has built a variety of interesting ambient displays over the years since Jerimijenko, Weiser, and Brown first presented the Dangling String (Figure 9-1). However, much less is known about what makes a particular display succeed or fail, or how, exactly, to design for specific attentional issues.

We described a study of two such displays that we built, the Bus Mobile and Daylight Display, in Section 3. Although time consuming, the study lead to a set of lessons about ambient display design. In particular, we learned that the rate of information change, and the noticeability of change, are crucial to display success. We also learned that public displays create a tension between aesthetics and information content. This is because they will have many groups of users with varying interests. Third, we learned that a good design must carefully mediate between the importance of the information being displayed (which may change over time), and the amount of attention required. This is a design challenge. Last, we learned how important iterative design and early feedback are to display success.

In Section 4, we showed how a particular technique, Heuristic Evaluation, can be used to study ambient displays. This technique is ideal for early-stage iteration because it does not require a working display to succeed. Using the heuristics presented in this paper, around 5 evaluators can find many potential problems without the overhead of an extensive study such as that described in Section 3.

Evaluation of ambient displays is clearly difficult. However, we believe this is due in part to a lack of evaluation techniques that are appropriate to use during the early stages of design of ambient and peripheral displays. Our modifications to heuristic evaluation have resulted in a practical, effective technique to use during these early stages.

Ideally, a designer should have a choice of more than one early stage technique, and our current and future efforts are focused on expanding the repertoire of techniques available. In particular, we are looking at the role of paper-based prototyping in ambient and peripheral display design.

We are also interested in exploring the usefulness of our heuristics in helping to develop design guidelines. However, we believe that peripheral display design requires more than qualitative information such as that encoded in our heuristics. We are currently investigating the literature on attention in cognitive science in the hopes of establishing a scientific basis for deciding between different manifestations of information.

Lastly, we are working to create a tool that can support rapid prototyping of peripheral displays. Such a tool should allow designers to easily experiment with different levels of noticeability and different types of transitions indicating changes in information. This would allow a display designer to focus on aesthetics while handling the underlying tasks necessary to a display changing computational information over time.

References

Bartram, L., Ware, C., and Calvert, T. Moving icons: Detection and distraction. Proceedings of Human-Computer Interaction—Interact; 2001, July; Tokyo, Japan. IOS Press, IFIP.

Chafe, C., and Niemeyer, G. Oxygen flute. Installation by Artists, San Jose Museum of Art, October 13, 2001–June, 2002.

Chewar, C., and McCrickard, D. S. (2002). Adapting UEMs for notification systems. Design and evaluation of notification interfaces for ubiquitous computing, Ubicomp 2002: workshop 9; 2002, September 29-October 1; Göteborg, Sweden.

Cox, D. and Greenberg, S. Supporting collaborative interpretation in distributed groupwear. Proceedings of the CSCW 2000 Conference Computer Supported Collaborative Work; 2000, December 2-6; Philadelphia, PA. ACM Press. pp. 289–298.

Cutrell, E., Czerwinski, M. & Horvitz, E. Notification, disruption and memory: Effects of messaging interruptions on memory and performance. Proceedings of Human-Computer Interaction—Interact; 2001, July; Tokyo, Japan. IOS Press, IFIP. pp. 263-269.

Czerwinski, M., Cutrell, E. & Horvitz, E. Instant Messaging and Interruption: Influence of Task Type on Performance. Proceedings of OZCHI 2000 Conference; 2000, December 4-8; Sydney, Australia. pp. 356-361.

Dumais, S. and Czerwinski, M.. Building bridges from theory to practice. Proceedings of HCI International 2001, 9th Conference on Human-Computer Interaction. 2001, August 5-10; New Orleans, LA, USA. Lawrence Erlbaum Associates. pp. 1358-1362.

Gray, W. D., and Salzman, M. C. Damaged merchandise? A review of experiments that compare usability evaluation methods. Human-Computer Interaction 1998; 13(3): 203–261.

Hallnas, L., and Redstrom, J. Slow technology; designing for reflection. Personal and Ubiquitous Computing 2001; 5(3): 201–212.

Heiner, J. M., Hudson, S. E., and Tanaka, K. The information percolator: Ambient information display in a decorative object. Proceedings of the UIST 1999 Symposium on User Interface Software and Technology. 1999, November 7-10; Asheville, NC, USA. ACM Press. pp. 141–148.

Ho-Ching, W. L., Mankoff, J., and Landay, J. From data to display: the design and evaluation of a peripheral sound display for the deaf. Proceedings of the CHI 2003 Conference on Human Factors in Computing Systems. 2003, April 05-10; Ft. Lauderdale, CA, USA. ACM Press. pp. 161-168.

Höök, K., Sengers, P. and Andersson, G. Sense and sensibility: Evaluation and interactive art. Proceedings of the CHI 2003 Conference on Human Factors in Computing Systems. 2003, April 05-10; Ft. Lauderdale, CA, USA. ACM Press. pp. 241-248.

Horvitz, E., Jacobs, A., and Hovel, D. Attention-sensitive alerting. Proceedings of the UAI 1999 Conference on Uncertainty and Artificial Intelligence (UAI 99). 1999, July 30-Aug 1; San Francisco, CA, USA. Morgan Kaufmann. pp. 305-313.

Hudson, S.E., Fogarty, J., Atkeson, C.G., Forlizzi, J., Kielser, S., Lee, J.C., and Yang, J (2003). Predicting human interruptibility with sensors: A Wizard of Oz feasibility study. Proceedings of the CHI 2003 Conference on Human Factors in Computing Systems. 2003, April 05-10; Ft. Lauderdale, CA, USA. ACM Press. pp. 257-264.

Intille, S. S. Change blind information display for ubiquitous computing environments. Proceedings of Ubicomp 2002, LCNS 2498. 2002, September 29-October 1; Göteborg, Sweden. Springer-Verlag. pp. 91-106.

Ishii, H., Wisneski, C., Brave, S., Dahley, A., Gorbet, M., Ullmer, B., and Yarin, P. Ambient displays: Turning architectural space into an interface between people and digital information. Proceedings of the CoBuild 1998 First International Workshop on Cooperative Buildings, LCNS 1370. 1998, February; Darmstadt, Germany. Springer-Verlag. pp. 22-32.

Maglio, P.P. & Campbell, C.S. Tradeoffs in displaying peripheral information. Proceedings of the CHI 2000 Conference on Human Factors in Computing Systems. 2000, April 1-6; The Hague, The Netherlands. ACM Press. pp. 241-248.

Mamykina, O., Mynatt, E.D., and Terry, M. Time aura: Interfaces for pacing. Proceedings of the CHI 2001 Conference on Human Factors in Computing Systems. 2001, March 31-April 5; Seattle, WA, USA. ACM Press. pp. 144-151.

Mankoff, J., Dey, A., Hsieh, G., Kientz, J., Lederer, S., and Ames, M. Heuristic evaluation of ambient displays. Proceedings of the CHI 2003 Conference on Human Factors in Computing Systems. 2003, April 05-10; Ft. Lauderdale, CA, USA. ACM Press. pp. 169-176.

McCrickard, D. S., Catrambone, R. and Stasko, J. T. Evaluating animation in the periphery as a mechanism for maintaining awareness. Proceedings of Human-Computer Interaction—Interact; 2001, July; Tokyo, Japan. IOS Press, IFIP. pp. 148-156.

McCrickard, D. S., Catrambone, R., Chewar, C. M. and Stasko, J. T. Establishing tradeoffs that leverage attention for utility: Empirically evaluating information display in notification systems. International Journal of Human-Computer Studies 2003; 8(5):547-582.

McCrickard, D.S., Wrighton, D., and Bussert, D. Supporting the construction of real world interfaces. Proceedings of the 2000 IEEE Symposia on Human Centric Computing Languages and Environments. 2002, September 03-06; Arlington, VA, USA. IEEE Press. pp. 54-56.

Mynatt, E., Back, M., Want, R., Baer, M., and Ellis, J. B. Designing Audio Aura. Proceedings of the CHI 1998 Conference on Human Factors in Computing Systems 1998, April 18-23; Los Angeles, CA. ACM Press. pp. 566-573.

Mynatt, E., Rowan, J., Craighill, S., and Jacobs, A. (2001). Digital family portraits: Providing peace of mind for extended family members. Proceedings of the CHI 2001 Conference on Human Factors in Computing Systems. 2001, March 31-April 5; Seattle, WA, USA. ACM Press. pp. 333–340.

Nielsen, J. "Guerrilla HCI: Using discount usability engineering to penetrate the intimidation barrier." In Cost-Justifying Usability, R. G. Bias and D. J. Mayhew, ed., Academic Press, 1994. pp. 245-272.

(Online Version: http://www.useit.com/papers/guerrilla_hci.html)

Nielsen, J. Ten usability heuristics. Retrieved August, 2002 from: http://www.useit.com/papers/heuristic/heuristic_list.html

Nielsen, J. and Landauer, T. K. A mathematical model of the finding of usability problems. Proceedings of the INTERCHI 1993 Conference on Human Factors in Computing Systems. 1993, April 24-29; Amsterdam, The Netherlands. ACM Press. pp. 206-213.

Nielsen, J., and Molich, R. Heuristic evaluation of user interfaces. Proceedings of the CHI 1990 Conference on Human Factors in Computing Systems. 1990, April 1-5; Seattle, WA, USA. ACM Press. pp. 249–256.

Pederson, E.R. and Sokoler, T. Aroma: abstract representation of presence supporting mutual awareness. Proceedings of the CHI 1997 Conference on Human Factors in Computing Systems. 1997, March 22-27; Atlanta, GA. ACM Press. pp. 51-58.

Sagi, D., and Julesz, B. "Where" and "what" in vision. Science 1985; 228:1217-1219.

Tiernan, S. L., Cutrell, E., and Czerwinski, M. Effective notification systems depend on user trust. Proceedings of Human-Computer Interaction—Interact; 2001, July; Tokyo, Japan. IOS Press, IFIP. pp. 684-685.

Treismann, A., and Gelade, G. A feature integration theory of attention. Cognitive Psychology 1980; 12:97-136.

van Dantzich, M., Robbins, D., Horvitz, E., and Czerwinski, M. Scope: Providing awareness of multiple notifications at a glance. Proceedings of the AVI 2002 6th International Working Conference on Advanced Visual Interfaces. 2002, May 22-24; Trento, Italy. ACM Press.

Vredenburg, K., Mao, J.-Y., Smith, P. W., and Carey, T. A survey of user-centered design practice. Proceedings of the CHI 2002 Conference on Human Factors in Computing Systems. 2002, April 20-25; Minneapolis, MN, USA. ACM Press. pp. 471–478.

Weiser, M. (1991). The computer for the 21st century. Scientific American 1991; 265(3):94–104.

Weiser, M., and Brown, J. S. Designing calm technology. PowerGrid Journal. 1996; 1(1). (Online Version: http://www.ubiq.com/weiser/calmtech/calmtech.htm).

PART III:

COMMUNITY AND SOCIAL CONNECTEDNESS

Chapter 10

THE PLASMA POSTER NETWORK

Social Hypermedia on Public Display

Elizabeth Churchill, Les Nelson, Laurent Denoue, Paul Murphy, Jonathan Helfman
FX Palo Alto Laboratory

Abstract: The sharing of digital materials within online communities has increased significantly in recent years. Our work focuses on promoting community information sharing in public spaces using large screen, interactive, digital poster boards called the Plasma Posters. In this chapter we first describe our fieldwork-led, iterative design process, and elaborate a number of design guidelines that resulted. Following this, the design and development of the Plasma Posters themselves and the underlying network infrastructure is discussed. Finally, we present results from qualitative and quantitative evaluations over the course of a ten-month deployment of three Plasma Posters within our own organization, a software research community made up of technologists and designers. We conclude with observations regarding ergonomic, social and other factors that were raised during the design and deployment and offer reflections on factors in the success of this deployment.

Key words: community information sharing, interactive public displays, social networking, collaborative browsing

1. Introduction

Developments in networking and display technologies have resulted in the placement of many large-screen, digital displays in public places for advertising and information distribution. Recent examples include AdSpace Network's CoolSign, which "utilizes multimedia displays to offer advertisers a vehicle with the impact of print, the pull of television, and the immediacy of the web" and the London-based Progress Bar public display

K. O'Hara et al. (eds.), Public and Situated Displays: Social and Interactional Aspects of Shared Display Technologies, 233–260.

onto which patrons can post images snapped with camera phones via the Meshbox wi-fi and Bluetooth access point[8].

Within the workplace, large screen, public displays are being used as memory aids (e.g. Fass *et al.*, 2002), and to offer awareness of colleagues' activities within small working groups (e.g. Greenberg and Rounding, 2001). Pushing further into the domain of focused, collaborative work a number of public displays also capitalize on touch-screen interaction capabilities allowing collocated collaborators to manipulate digital content (Guimbretiere *et al.*, 2001; Klemmer *et al.*, 2001; Pederson *et al.*, 1993; Russell *et al.*, 2002; Streitz *et al.*, 1999).

In this paper we describe our work on the design and deployment of the Plasma Poster Network, digital bulletin boards that display community-generated interactive, multi-media content as a mechanism for low-effort, collaborative browsing and informal networking. This work sits within the same design space as work by Snowdon and Grasso on the 'Community Wall' (CWall; Snowdon and Grasso, 2001; Grasso *et al.*, Chapter 11 this volume) and work by Houde *et al.* on the Newslens community display (Houde *et al.*, 1998).

These research efforts aim to situate displays in public places as a means of promoting information sharing, encouraging social participation and strengthening weak social ties (see Wellman, 1999; Wellman and Giulia, 1999 on the computer mediated communication and the creation and maintenance of social ties), and thus promote cross-fertilization of ideas and interests across groups. These goals are in keeping with those of many online community technologies (Schuler, 1996; Virnoche and Marx, 1997). However, while online community spaces do not assume physical proximity, but rather assume focused, solitary readers who are connected only in the "virtual" space (Calhoun, 1998), the XRCE's CWall, Apple's Newslens display and our Plasma Posters are inspired by the use of physical poster boards in social spaces (see Figure 10-1), and are designed for people who, at least on occasion, occupy or move through the same geographical location. Our aim is to blur the notional "boundary" between content sharing in the virtual and physical domains, by encouraging offline, face-to-face interactions around content that is generated online.

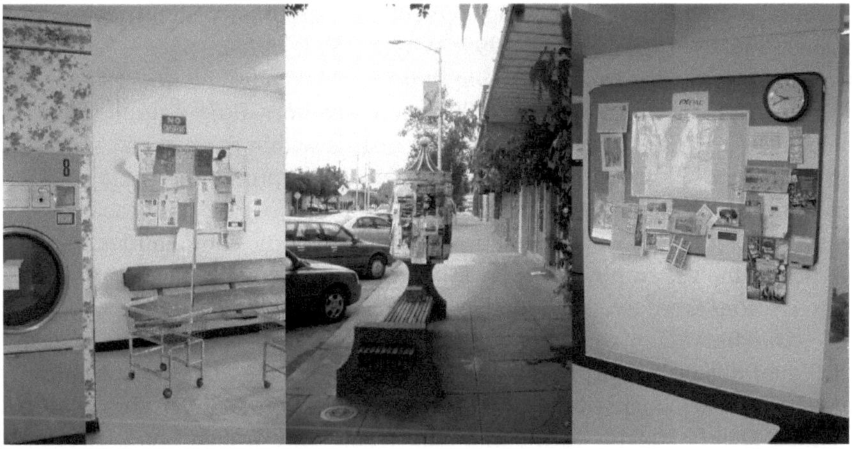

Figure 10-1: Community poster boards: in the launderette; on the street; in the workplace

In the next sections, we present results from our fieldwork on the use of informal poster boards within several different communities, and within our own organization. Following this, we describe the design of the Plasma Poster Network and its deployment in our building. We conclude with reflections on some of the socio-technical challenges in the design and deployment of community bulletin boards, and some comments about the potential for distributing community content in public places.

2. Information Sharing with Public Displays and Environmental Annotations

Street gang graffiti (see Castleman, 1982; Phillips, 1999) and billboard advertising are instances of textual and graphical annotation of the physical environment. They play a strong role in asserting the identity of a place, and more specifically reflecting the habitation of that place. Similarly, posted paper fliers are a form of asynchronous communication that utilise the physical environment as their canvas or stage. They take advantage of the movement of people through social spaces, and are thus part of "the interplay of human activity with the physical place" (Jacobs, 1999, page 6). Such poster boards are part of the fabric but not the infrastructure of a space; in Brand's terms poster boards are part of the malleable "space plan", with the posted fliers part of the "stuff" that "twitches around daily to monthly" (Brand, 1994, p13). However, while there has been much written about billboard advertising (and the design of the physical environment to encourage interaction, social engagement and community identification (e.g. *streets*: Jacobs, 1961; Jacobs, 1999; Whyte, 1971; *public spaces, bus stands, waiting rooms, interior gathering places*: Alexander *et al.*, 1977; *work places*: Albrecht and Broikos, 2000), there has been little written about the placement and use of community poster boards within these social spaces, or on the effect of such community poster boards in promoting social ties and encouraging community identification[9]. Therefore, our design process began with consideration of information sharing within communities, and in particular the use of physical poster boards in such communication practices. Observations from two field studies are presented below.

Our first study was intended to elaborate a design space for the design of digital poster boards, based on consideration of the placement and use of physical, poster boards in public settings. For the purposes of this study we defined "public" to be on a continuum from "unrestricted" (e.g. streets) to "restricted" (e.g. small group, closed workplaces). The second study focused on our own workplace, the site of our first technology deployment. Observations from this study were aimed at generating specific design instances as appropriate for our use community, but also to establish whether there was a 'natural' role for public poster boards as a content sharing technology within our lab; that is, if there was a potentially good "match" between the technology and communication styles within our lab (Bly and Churchill, 1999; see also Harper and Carter (1994) for an instance of a bad "match" between a social milieu and technology features).

2.1 Study 1: Community Bulletin Boards in Public Spaces

We investigated the use of poster boards in unrestricted, "open", public spaces (e.g. cafes, sports clubs and streets) in three local areas (Palo Alto, and two districts of San Francisco), and interviewed six local community members about their use of and views regarding public poster boards. In addition, we observed the use of public poster boards within three workplaces as instances of the content sharing in public places in more restricted settings (a research center, a technology sales office and a technology start-up). Our observations focused on: (1) location and access; (2) content analysis of posted material; (3) usage; and (4) people's perceptions of poster boards.

Observations: Poster boards are located in waiting areas (waiting rooms, stations, bus stops), where people are relaxing (cafes) and in community spaces where people go to seek community information (local and neighbourhood libraries, community centres).

Content analysis of local community poster boards and interviews with local residents indicated that they provide an important communication function within communities, providing a means for people to seek and advertise viewpoints (e.g. support ecological initiatives), activities (e.g. join our band), events (e.g. come to the local Arts and Wine Fair) and services (e.g. babysitter wanted, carpool partners sought). Community members felt these boards provided an important function in demonstrating the vitality of their neighbourhoods. Loosely speaking, the boards provide a sense of the community "personality", reflecting the preferred activities and the needs of the local inhabitants; poster boards in the Mission District of San Francisco advertised dance and cooking classes, English lessons and political meetings, while nearby Noe Valley poster boards sought and advertised babysitters, hiking partners, lost pets and yoga classes.

A major dimension on which boards varied could be characterized mapped well to online electronic bulletin board systems: from *formal and moderated* (items can only be posted by asking a "gatekeeper's" permission; someone regularly "garbage collects"; items tend to be in prescribed formats) at one end of the scale, to *reviewed and informally monitored* (checked over regularly; sometimes cleared by various people), to *open* (anyone can post anything, in any format, anytime; old posters seldom cleared off). Posted items in the latter two cases tended to demonstrate by far the greatest variety. However, posting genres were visible: 'accommodation wanted' ads tended to be on small cards; announcements for events tended to be larger and on colored paper; items for sale were often accompanied by tear-off tags with phone numbers and email addresses; lost pet fliers were usually accompanied by a photograph.

Informal poster boards within three local organizations (two research laboratories and one technology start-up) varied in much the same way, lying between moderated and open. Content was less varied, and tended to be related to competitors' activities, conferences, upcoming events, and recent news articles. Surprisingly, even in small organizations, people seldom had any idea of who had posted informal content. Within organizations, people were less uniformly enthusiastic about the presence of poster boards than the "external" community members we interviewed.

2.2 *Study 2: Information Sharing Within FXPAL*

FX Palo Alto Laboratory (FXPAL) is a software research company based in California, and is a subsidiary of Fuji Xerox, Japan. At the time of our study, 34 full-time employees worked at FXPAL. Of these, 25 were full-time researchers drawn from diverse disciplines (e.g. computer science, psychology, engineering, linguistics), 6 were administrative staff and 3 were technical support staff. In addition to the full time staff, there were 14 contractors/consultants currently working on projects, in full and part-time capacities. Student interns and visiting scientists are present during Summer months. Researchers tend to work in separate project groups; currently there are 7 such groups with little overlap in membership. The lab is located on the first floor of a two-storey building. All full time researchers have their own offices; contractors/consultants have offices or individual booths and interns have either booths or desk space within a large, shared room.

Our study was in three parts. First, we mapped the lab space using floor layout charts, and observed/photographed activities in public areas and people's movement through the building. Following this we engaged 17 people in a photograph and text diary study with subsequent interviews about their online and offline information sharing practices within the organization, and about the presence and use of community bulletin boards within their home communities. Photographs and fliers people brought to the interview session were used as props to drive interview questions. We interviewed 2 administrative staff, 2 summer interns, 2 contractors/ consultants, 3 support staff and 8 researchers. Interviews were semi-structured and lasted between 30 and 90 minutes.

Observations: In accord with other studies, our observations confirmed that people are not always at their desks, but are often locally mobile, moving physically around the building (Bellotti and Bly, 1996), and engaging in "water cooler", informal conversations (Whittaker *et al.*, 1994).

Given our interest in content sharing in public spaces, we analyzed the use of *corkboards and paper postings*. There are 7 corkboards in the building; most are in corridors, one is located in the kitchen area and another in the mailroom area. As with the external community boards, each poster board has a different "personality"; one is dedicated to the display of items that are legally required to be on view (located in the mailroom), one is dedicated to newspaper clippings of interest (e.g. from the Nikkei Weekly), one is dedicated to conference and journal announcements, and the others are more informal, displaying jokes, ticket reductions for local events, and lunch menus.

Observations indicated that people's interest *is* piqued by others' postings in the physical environment. Most of our interviewees thought they were a valuable resource and that the environment would be "sterile" without them. Boards that changed frequently were deemed to be most interesting and eye-catching, and that posted content was considered to reflect the "identity" and "milieu" of the lab. Events, such as presentations and visitors, and items posted on corkboards occasionally spark *in situ* conversations. People said they were sometimes pleasantly surprised to discover mutual interests with other colleagues when such conversations took place. The most read corkboards were those in areas where people were waiting or engaged in low concentration tasks such as waiting for printouts or coffee to brew, although hallway corkboards were also glanced at and sometimes referred to as people moved about the building. The 3 that are posted to and read most frequently are the conference announcement board, the newspaper clipping board and the kitchen-based, informal board. Four perceived problems with corkboards were expressed: (1) the presence of out-of-date materials – it is sometimes hard to tell what was still relevant; (2) interesting content sometimes "disappears" before it has been read; (3) it is hard to tell who posted material, so follow-up conversations are difficult to initiate; and (4) information on corkboards is not easy to copy and/or easily access digitally for later follow-up (e.g. URLs). This comment clearly reflected the fact that most information sharing occurs via computer. Therefore, to provide context for the use of poster boards as an information sharing resource we also interviewed people about other methods for information sharing.

As suspected, online sharing is common and, being seen as low overhead, given most people are working at their computers most of the time ("it doesn't take much effort to forward a link"). However, such online sharing tends to occur between members of *established* project and social groups. Little social mingling occurs through electronic media, and few opportunities arise for serendipitously discovering shared interests. *Email* is by far the most frequently used means of communication, although some people complained about email overload (cf. Whittaker and Sidner, 1996). Email is used for coordination, to share formal and informal information (e.g. jokes), send announcements, and share ideas and interests. Most emails are sent to small sub-groups and targeted individuals. When interviewees were asked about sending company-wide emails on things that may be of general interest, a reticence was apparent. Email is perceived to be socially risky and a potential intrusion into people's personal digital space, so people err on the side of caution. As one person phrased it, "I don't want to fill other people's email boxes up with things that may be of peripheral interest to them. People get irritated". *Intranet web pages* are used for general administrative purposes and within projects for recording activities and research results. People seldom browse the intranet to learn about projects and colleagues' interests (one new person to the organization reported doing so). Use of the intranet tends to be for directed information access. *Presentations, seminars and reading groups* are used to share ideas about research areas and research results. On occasion, supporting materials are disseminated. Presentations tend to be company-wide, while participants in seminars and reading groups tend to be members of established teams. *Chats* in the hallways are a means of hearing about formal and informal information. These take place where people are waiting (e.g. the kitchen area, by printers), passing time (e.g. by the magazine racks) or doing low concentration tasks in public areas (e.g. photocopying, checking mailboxes) (Whittaker *et al.*, 1994).

2.3 Summary and Design Requirements

Communication and content sharing with colleagues outside project and social groups is seen as valuable within our organization, but does not occur as frequently as is desired. We posited that digital poster boards could represent a new genre of informal, "lightweight" communication medium within FXPAL, leveraging the existing bias for electronic communications but providing a less intrusive method (not direct to others' InBoxes) for sharing content. The following more specific requirements were generated:

- Place digital community bulletin boards in high traffic areas and in spaces where people are waiting, "idling" or passing by.
- Consider ease of (physical) access to boards for reading (make sure people can reach interactive content)
- Design for low effort sociability; allow community members easy access to poster boards (make posting low effort by using tools for content sharing that are already familiar, such as email and the Web, see also comments by Houde *et al.*, 1998)
- Create attractive, inviting interfaces where content changes regularly
- Associate content clearly with people who have authored/sent that content
- Provide an easy way to get overviews of what has been posted
- Allow duration of posting to be manually specified if desired
- Provide a means whereby postings of interest can be easily printed or forwarded (to others or to oneself)
- Provide a community repository or memory of postings that may be browsed after public showing of the content has expired
- Design appropriate content moderation policies
- Support easy administration and garbage collection of posted content, both for system developers, and for community members

3. The Plasma Poster Network

Plasma Posters are plasma displays with interactive overlays that enable direct touch interaction. We placed three Plasma Posters in our lab, one in the kitchen area, one in a foyer and one in a hallway (see Figure 10-2). Inspired by the aspect ratio and layout of paper posters (Timmers, 1998),

Plasma Posters are oriented in portrait format, distinguishing them from other plasma displays. Underlying the Plasma Posters is the Plasma Poster Network, a content storage and distribution infrastructure that posts content to all registered Plasma Posters. We first describe the interfaces that have been iteratively designed over the last year to suit the needs of our local community members, then offer a brief overview of the underlying infrastructure.

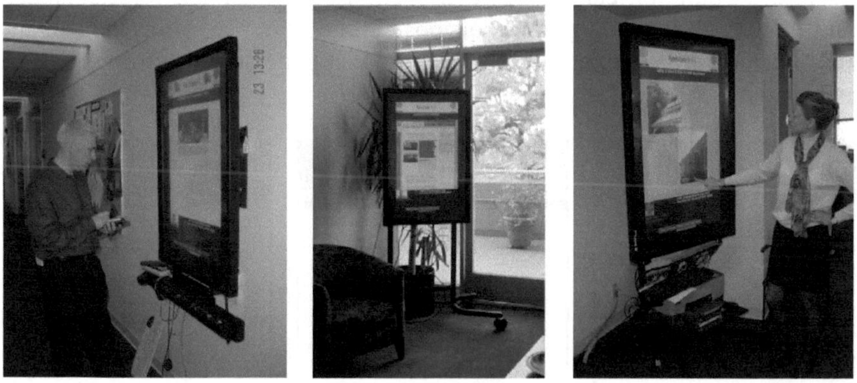

Figure 10-2: Plasma Posters are located in a corridor (left), a foyer (middle) and the kitchen (right)

3.1 *Content, Interfaces and Reading Practices*

Posting Content: The Plasma Poster Network stands in contrast to the deployment of advertising bulletin boards and digital poster boards, where non-interactive content is centrally authored and/or moderated, broadcast and displayed for an audience of consumers in public spaces. Rather, content that is displayed on the Plasma Posters is generated from two sources: content that is explicitly posted by individuals, and content that is automatically retrieved from selected intranet Web pages (e.g. announcements of new technical reports, announcements of upcoming meetings). To support the former case, we have implemented applications that allow authenticated community members to email items as attachments (text, URLs, images, digital movie clips) or post items from a Web. In designing applications that leverage existing information sharing tools and practices, our intention has been to minimize effort and expertise requirements on the past of our community members; the requirement of such effort would, we believe, prove a barrier to use.

Displaying Content: Figure 10-3 shows the current "PosterShow" interface. The image on the left is a posting from a traveling colleague who has emailed images and some accompanying text as commentary. Any number of images can be posted; once displayed they can be zoomed, reduced and dragged. The image in the middle is posted text that has been formatted by the author. The image on the right is of a URL. Content can be scrolled and all links are live. Postings are by default removed after 2 weeks, but posting duration can be manually set. All postings and relevant meta-data (e.g. date of posting, duration posted and comments) are kept in the user's personal profile, accessible from a Web page so old postings can be reviewed and reposted.

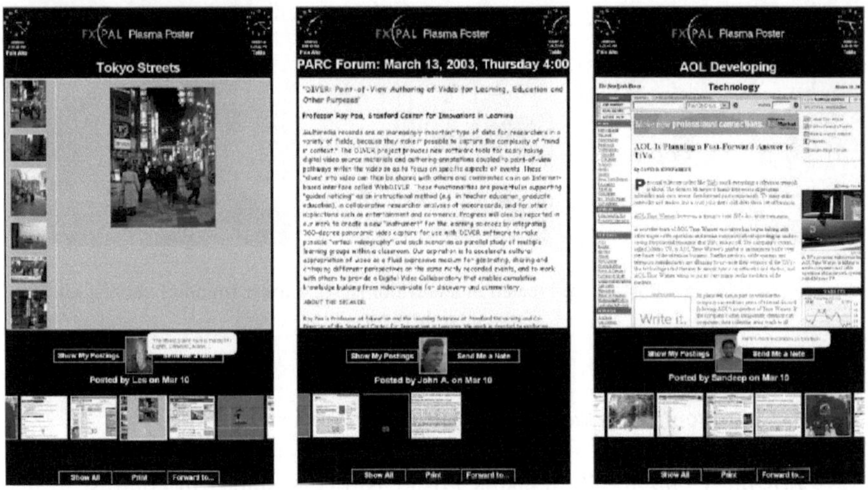

Figure 10-3: Examples from the "PosterShow" Interface showing posted images, text and a URL. Author comments appear in the speech bubbles by their photographs. Upcoming and recently shown content appears as thumbnails below the currently displayed 'main' posting. Buttons along the bottom bring up the overview of all content, print current content and support the forwarding to others of the currently displayed main content.

Reading content: Interactive, multi-media content on large displays in (relatively) public spaces is a different form of *reader engagement with text* than reading personal content from paper (O'Hara, 1996; Adler *et al.*, 1998) or from a personal computer screen (Schilit *et al.*, 1998). However, analytic categories discussed in these contexts map fairly well to interaction with content on physical public poster boards (e.g. goal or task driven: skimming and active reading; undirected: browsing).

Therefore, we have designed for the following forms of engagement with content:

Peripheral noticing. Public displays are a form of peripheral technology – *until something catches one's eye* when attention becomes focused and cognitive engagement with the text ensues. In the design of the Plasma Posters, effort has been expended in designing content to be visually attractive and to invite observation and interaction. To achieve this we have designed to display colors that stand out in the local lighting conditions, designed animation and movement in the interface, and used fonts that are large enough to give some gist of the content from a distance. Rather than recreating the clutter of many physical bulletin boards, we have taken advantage of the dynamic properties of a digital posting board, and postings are cycled through automatically one at a time and displayed for 60 seconds. Given our focus on the social aspects of information sharing and our belief that an initial attractor for information is *who* posted it, all postings are augmented with contact information of the person who posted the content, the date/time of posting, and any additional audio or text commentary.

(Inter)active reading People manipulate posted pages on physical poster boards to be able to read content (lifting, moving aside). On the Plasma Posters, content that is displayed can be *paused*, *scrolled* and *printed.* Touching the display (e.g. when scrolling) or selecting the pause button reinitiates the 60-second timer. Given digital content is hypertextual, we support the following of live Web links. In physically embodied contexts, people remove postings; digital content on the Plasma Posters can be printed.

Browsing and searching. People remove physical postings to see what lies beneath. When they have noticed something previously, they sometimes come back to explicitly look for it. On the Plasma Posters, buttons are available for manually moving *forward* and *backward* through upcoming and previously displayed content. Browsing and navigating all items in the current list of postings is possible using with the *overviews* (Figure 10-4).

Messaging. People tear off tags and note down phone numbers, URLs and email addresses from physical postings for later follow-up. Items displayed on the Plasma Posters can be *forwarded* to others who may be interested. The author can also be emailed with comments.

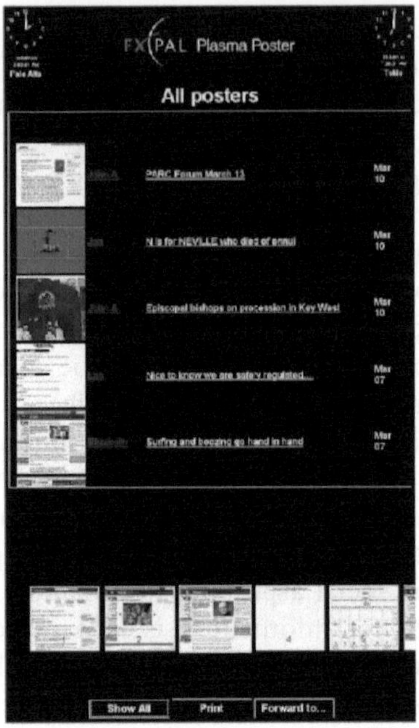

Figure 10-4: Scrollable content overviews by person, by posting date and by content help readers at the Plasma Posters browse posted content

3.2 *Implementation: Parsing, Storing and Distributing Content*

The Plasma Poster Network is a client-server system (Figure 10-5) designed for the collection, management, and publishing of community content. Server components provide an infrastructure for sharing multimedia content within a user community. Client components provide a variety of reading and writing interfaces for displaying and interacting with content, as described above.

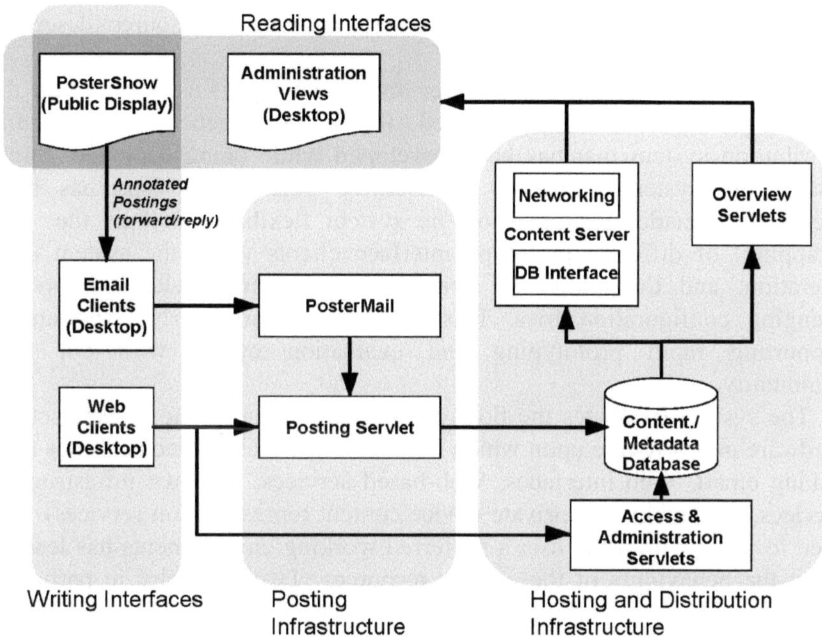

Figure 10-5: The Plasma Poster is a client-server system that supports community knowledge sharing

The Plasma Poster Network infrastructure consists of the following server components: a number of Java servlets that run in a standard Web server (e.g., Tomcat from the Apache Software Foundation) that manage the flow of posted content and user data into the system; a relational database for content and user data and metadata (e.g., MySQL from MySQL AB); a Content Server Java application program that controls access to the database using standard interfaces (JDBC from Sun Microsystems) and provides a remote Networking interface (implemented as a Java object and includes monitor and callbacks for pushing information updates to clients); and a number of parameterized Java servlets that extract content and metadata based on the needs of different client types (e.g., overview suitable for public displays such as interactive plasma display).

Reading and writing client interfaces have been incorporated into the system as standalone Visual Basic applications, Web-based programs implemented as Java applets, and dynamic Web pages using Javascript.

These access community content through the server resource described above.

This standards-based, client-server implementation is used to provide the scalability and flexibility required for a heterogeneous information distribution system that has been developed while being deployed. Stress testing the system with 400 consecutive postings/deletions has been successfully made. Examples of the system flexibility include the 'hot-swapping' of different prototype interface clients while the system is in operation, and the ability to switch database and servlet software by changing configuration files. This has proven particularly important in supporting rapid prototyping and evaluation cycles with our user community.

The system facilitates the flow of information across the diverse sets of hardware and software upon which users conduct their online activities (i.e., linking email, Web interfaces, Web-based services, our own infrastructure services, and public and private device content representation services). The need to work within the user's preferred working environments has lead us adapt the behaviours of these other resources. Two examples in particular highlight this approach for *repurposing*. The PosterMail servlet parses incoming email messages that users spend minimal time formatting (e.g., drag, drop, send). Different content types (e.g., texts, movies, URLs, and collections of photographs) are detected and the content is appropriately arranged for presentation on the Plasma Posters (e.g., single frame, linked frames, or collages of content, with titles and commentary attached). Another repurposing is found in our PosterShow application that displays posted content on large screen, interactive, publicly situated displays. Posted content is rendered by a Web browser, but for public display we do not want the display to behave interactively in the same manner as a desktop browser. For example, many people post specific Web pages for further discussion; however, these Web pages may in turn be navigated, thereby leading to some confusion about what content is posted and what subsequently browsed. Our solution is to re-host the browser (in this case Internet Explorer) inside another application (our own Visual Basic program) and to trap and reprocess all user input events. In this way we can represent posted and browsed pages as distinguishable kinds of reading (e.g., showing all browsed pages in a separate overlaid frame).

We are currently using our infrastructure to develop and evaluate a larger range of reading and writing interfaces, including awareness and overview representations suitable for display on PDAs and other personal and desktop devices.

3.3 *Use and Impact of the Plasma Posters*

Data from 10 months' use of the Plasma Poster Network were collected (see Churchill *et al.* 2003 for evaluations after 6 months' usage). In addition, qualitative evaluations have been carried out to document people's experiences, responses, and reasons for posting/non-posting; these were three interview-based evaluations (with 7, 10 and 8 interviewees respectively) and an email survey (with 23 respondents of which 13 had never or only once posted content to the Plasma Poster Network). Another interview-based evaluation is currently being planned. These evaluations have provided us with ongoing user feedback regarding interface design and system features. In addition, the evaluation data are pertinent to our broader research questions regarding the potential in fostering social interactions for large screen, digital, community bulletin boards. For the purposes of the data analysis, we posed the following sets of questions:

1. **Technology use:** posting and interaction with content: Will people *post items* to share with others in physical spaces? Will people *read digital content* in public spaces? Do people *engage with content* on the Plasma Posters, and if so, are there *patterns of interaction by location and time*? What are *patterns of posting*?
2. **Technology reception and impact:** Are the Plasma Posters perceived by members of the community (posters and non-posters) to be a valuable addition to existing methods of content sharing? That is, is content projected into the local physical environment seen as a *valuable addition* to existing environmental and desktop methods of content sharing (for example corkboards, email and Web pages)? What are the most *popular forms of content*? What are *reasons for posting and non-posting*? Does content in the physical environment *cue conversations* between colleagues?

3.3.1 *Posting content*

Eight hundred and fifty-nine postings have been sent to the Plasma Poster Network, with an average of 85.9 posted per month (sd = 28.7; min = 45.0; max = 137.0; median = 91.5)[i]. Figure 10-6 shows the mean postings by month, and clearly indicates an upward trend for posting.

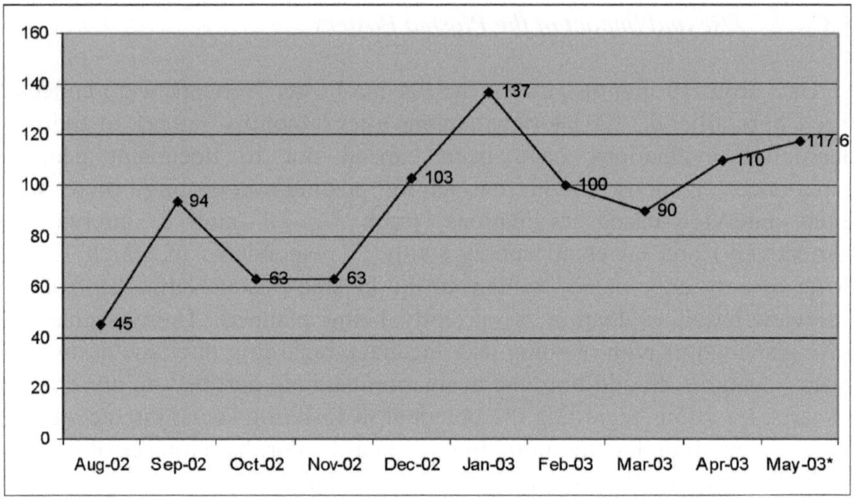

Figure 10-6: Number of postings by month over 10-month deployment period

Most postings are during the working week (Monday-Friday; mean = 167.8; sd = 18.2), rather than the weekend (mean = 10; sd = 3.0). There are no significant differences between the days of the working week in terms of number of postings. Content has been emailed to the Plasma Poster Network from traveling colleagues; interview comments suggest these postings are very popular; authors and viewers feel a presence within the community is maintained by these postings.

Content has varied from work-related to hobbies, and from general interest to company specific, including announcements of product releases and upcoming events, visitors, lunch menus and images from company events; 79% of the postings have been text or URLs, 21% have been images and <1% have been short movie clips. URLs largely consist of announcements for local and external events (e.g. conferences, movies, plays, sports), news items (unsurprisingly especially concerned with technology innovations), unusual examples of technology related products or designs, political commentary, interactive surveys (these range from comical, e.g. "Which Simpson are you?"; Edward Gorey's GashlyCrumb Tinies; to discussion documents, e.g., National Geographic's "Why Does Geography Matter?"), items of cultural or personal significance to the posting community member (e.g., favorite Web cams, unusual language use or customs), book reviews, and poetry. Jokes and satirical commentary are also popular; sometimes items indirectly refer to ongoing work or related work, and to previous conversations. Barsoux (1993) has noted the role of humor in organizations, stating humans use humor "to criticize without alienating, to defuse tension or anxiety, to introduce new ideas, to bond teams, ease relationships and elicit cooperation". The Plasma Posters offer a non-intrusive, socially lightweight, informal way to tease others and to share funny and satirical items as a stimulus for and/or reaction to conversations.

As can be seen from the above list, posted content tends to be for low urgency information sharing, and few items that explicitly invite transactions or interactions are posted (e.g. items for sale, requests for carpools). Interview comments revealed that queries regarding specific projects are still are sent via email to targeted individuals. Content that is posted also tends to be ephemeral; although people can explicitly extend the length of time something in available on the posters by setting expiry dates and/or can repost items, almost all items posted are left with the default setting and expire after 2 weeks.

Interview and survey data revealed that content sent to the Plasma Posters would "probably not be emailed" to the lab-wide email alias, as people felt they wouldn't want to "fill up others' mailboxes" with things that may be of peripheral interest. These comments suggest to us the Plasma Posters do indeed provide a complementary mechanism for content sharing within our lab. InBox cluttering from bulk email has been a common complaint in the organization even with work specific (e.g., technology innovation) or company sanctioned (e.g., product and organisational information) contents. This is not a complaint with the Posters.

The most common reason for not posting was that people felt they didn't think others would be interested in their content ("I'm not sure what to post, my sense of humor is pretty different"; "my topics would be too boring"). Some people expressed that they tended to share content with smaller groups; lab-wide visibility was not something they were comfortable with ("with most things I would want to share with only a select group"; "I haven't come up with anything that would be of interest lab-wide yet").

3.3.2 Interacting with Content

We have logged 58,878 user interaction events from the three Plasma Posters during the past months. The mean interaction events per month is 5887.8 (sd = 4191.4; min = 380; max = 15685; median = 5360.5). We evaluated activity by the analytic categories outlined above, (inter)*active reading* accounts for 73% of all activity (scrolling content and following links; pausing content and printing); *navigation and browsing* for 25% (show all postings; resuming content cycling by pressing "Play"; show previous posting; show next posting) and *messaging* for 2% of activity (replying to content authors; forwarding content to others).

3.3.3 *Interacting with Content by Location and Time*

Location makes a big difference to interaction. 75.4% of all activity occurred at the kitchen Plasma Poster, 17.0% at the hallway poster and 7.7% at the foyer poster. Table 10-1 shows the mean number of interactions per day broken down by the different Plasma Posters, and by reading, navigating and messaging activities. People interacted with content that was on display on the Plasma Posters, but did not forward content or reply to content authors, although in interview people were intrigued by the potential of these features.

Table 10-1: mean and percentage interactions per day by poster and reading activity

Category	Foyer *(Clicks per day)*		Hallway *(Clicks per day)*		Kitchen *(Clicks per day)*		Total *(Clicks per day)*	
Active Reading	32.2	75.5%	122.0	79.4%	148.5	72.0%	201.3	73.5%
Messaging	0.7	1.7%	6.0	3.9%	3.3	1.6%	5.5	2.0%
Navigating	9.7	22.8%	25.7	16.7%	54.6	26.4%	67.1	24.5%
Total	42.6		153.7		206.3		273.9	

Figure 10-7 illustrates that interactions at all posters has increased over time, with the kitchen poster being the most used. Again, this was in accord with our interview and survey findings. Few people reported reading content on the foyer poster or the hallway Plasma Poster. When asked why not, people said the foyer poster was “out of the way”, and the hallway poster was “too close to people’s offices”, where “it feels odd to stand outside someone’s office door and read stuff”.

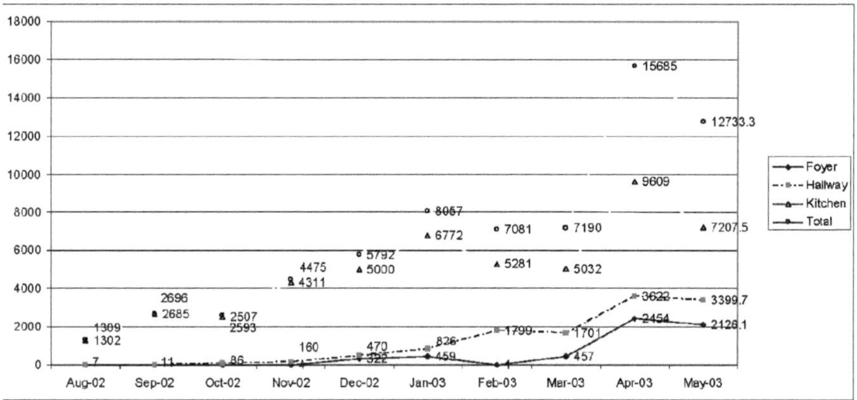

Figure 10-7: Total interaction events by Plasma Poster by month

Activity data reflect the working rhythms of the lab. Weekday interactions account for 99% of the data logged. Interview and survey data suggested people read content early in the morning and at coffee breaks, and this was reflected in our activity logs; activity peaks are at 10 am, 3 pm and 4 pm, and activity tails off around 6 pm (not surprisingly, as most people leave the building between 5 pm and 6 pm).

The category that is not reflected in our activity logs is *peripheral noticing*, as no touch interaction occurs when people are not (inter)actively reading, messaging or browsing. Observational studies are currently being carried out to measure the extent of peripheral noticing and distant reading (e.g., analyzing basic motion near a poster along with the interaction events), by content and poster location. Initial results show the kitchen area is the most traveled and populated of the three areas. It is also where people tend to "hang out". While people glance at all the Plasma Posters, only glances at the kitchen Plasma Poster regularly lead to touch screen interactions.

Observations and logged data suggest that current affairs articles, technology news items, images and movies draw the most attention. Popularity of content is also driven in part by sender; content (especially images) posted by regular posters of "quirky content" and by absent colleagues is very popular. Not all content starts in digital format; several postings have been scans of paper materials.

3.3.4 Perceived Impact

Surveys with follow-up interviews conducted when the Plasma Poster had been deployed for 6 months revealed a positive attitude towards the posters; preliminary results from more recent discussions suggest this is still the case. At 6 months, survey respondents said they had read items posted to the Plasma Poster, and 19 of the 23 said they had conversed with people about posted content. Many said conversations occurred when they were with others in front of the Plasma Posters, but 13 said they also conversed with others later about content they had seen on the displays. One respondent said "I often talk about stuff I see on the Plasma Posters, more usually with friends outside of work in fact". Two people said they had posted content to the Plasma Poster Network as part of an ongoing discussion. Although we cannot measure whether the Plasma Posters have increased informal interactions in the lab, we took reportage of these "conversational threads" as support for our assertion that the Plasma Posters spark conversations.

People commented that they liked finding out about others' interests. As one person phrased it, "I like seeing other people's interests and foibles, plus there is often quite a lot of interesting and relevant information in there". Another said, "I like coming across things I would not see otherwise". People also liked getting postings from absent and remote colleagues ("it is nice to find out what they are thinking about or doing"; "it is great to see their face on the display").

Survey respondents were asked to comment on whether they saw value in having the Plasma Posters and if they would miss them were they to be taken away. All but three of our 23 survey respondents saw value in having the Plasma Posters, and were in favor of retaining them. Comments included: "I would especially miss the pictures posted by people who are away and I like seeing pictures of things people have attended, like conferences"; "I would miss having topics to talk about when it goes quiet at lunchtimes"; "I would miss interacting with people on topics posted on the poster"; and finally, "I would miss tidbits and insights into people's personalities and what interests them". By contrast, one person (a non-poster) said they would not miss the Plasma Posters because they felt the posters actually *detracted* from spontaneous conversational topics arising over coffee breaks and lunch because conversational topics naturally drifted to what was being shown on the Plasma Posters.

The Plasma Posters were not valued equally. While 20 of our survey respondents stated they would miss the kitchen Plasma Poster, only 4 said they would miss the hallway Plasma Poster. Three people said they would miss the foyer Plasma Poster, and 3 others said they thought it is good for visitors. It has taken time for the technology to be accepted, and for people to want to use it. One regular poster said although they had been unsure what to post at first, once they had started doing so "it was addictive". Recent informal conversations suggest the interest in the Plasma Posters continues to grow.

More recent comments have been offered in preliminary conversations to another interview-based survey. Our users feel like the Plasma Poster is a "direct" community content sharing tool, and contrast this to technologies where content is only automatically selected from selected Web sites and content repositories. Our users appreciate the diversity of content that is displayed, and indicate that finding out about interesting *sources* of information is as useful as the specific content that is posted. Many postings contain games and artful demonstrations that feed into the already existing appetite for jokes, games and whimsical multimedia amongst company members. Finally people appreciate the display itself and the fact that it is large and not "owned" by any one group. This is in accord with Bellamy *et al.* (1998), who state their display made sharing "... not feel like 'work' " but feel "lightweight and fun". Comments we received included "the posters are in open territory, it's no one's turf, so you don't feel like you're interrupting to share or talk about something."

3.4 Summary

Observations have made it clear that the Plasma Posters have become an everyday part of life within FXPAL, and have increased social interaction between members of the lab.

Discovery of overlapping interests has been reported and posting 'chains' (posting in response to others' postings) have been observed. Content that in the past has been sent to small friendship and project groups has been posted to the Plasma Posters. Of course, previously popular means of content sharing (i.e. email) continue to be used. However, interview data suggested that some content sent to the Plasma Posters might not have been posted at all, suggesting we have created a space and means for sharing *new* kinds of content between lab members. In this regard the Plasma Posters are a new communication genre within our lab (Yates and Orlikowski, 1992).

Members of our community are active readers, following links and scrolling through postings; at present forwarding content, printing, messaging and replying to content authors is rare, although people are positive about the potential for these features.

Location is a big factor affecting the ways people interact with content on the boards. There are more consumers than producers of content within our organization; some people post regularly, while others have sent no postings despite liking the technology. This finding is in keeping with others' observations of online community participation (Nonnecke and Preece, 2003).

4. Discussion

Before drawing general conclusions we would like to reflect on broader design issues that have arisen during the deployment of this public space, community technology with regard to the *ergonomic factors* (physical, behavioural and cognitive ergonomic factors), *technical factors* (both the prototype requirements and the supporting technical infrastructure of the deployment location, i.e. are there power sockets available?), and *social factors* (knowledge, expertise, relationship dynamics, broader civic/organization context).

In terms of the ergonomic issues explored for the current deployment, we have made efforts to ensure the Plasma Posters are *effective* interactive, public displays. We have addressed issues of screen height, lighting and glare, font and button size, and color saturation on the display. Sensitivity to visual pollution has been essential; certain animations and dynamic screen changes have proven disturbing to some viewers. Sound pollution has also been addressed; initially all Plasma Posters had speakers, but these have been inactivated at the request of our users. Interface design has proceeded with consideration of how to effectively signal functionality and invite interaction, without implying features that are not supported. Given we have a highly technical community, it has been a challenge to restrict interaction to our design intent without incurring frustration; on occasions members of our user community have wanted to appropriate the plasma displays as collaborative, digital workspaces, or as large screen interfaces to personal computers. On the other hand, as is always the case in design, there are tradeoffs; just as these behaviours derive from their comfort with technologies, their expertise has also meant they are tolerant of prototype failures, vocal with feedback and helpful with debugging.

While these considerations pertain to the design of interfaces, or the "public face" or "skin" of the technology, it is also clear that the technical infrastructure of the lab has been crucial in the success of the technology. Without the ability to easily access power sockets, utilize existing mail servers, take benefit from our high-speed intranet, draw on the expertise of our technical support team and so on, the integration with existing tools and practices far more difficult. The impact of this foundational infrastructure has already become apparent as we design for an upcoming external deployment.

Although deploying within our organisational setting has meant maintaining a sense of corporate professionalism that may not be so important in other settings, it is clear that the restricted physical setting and the relative informality of our workplace have been central to the success of the technology. We have a minimal content moderation policy, relying on social accountability to ensure appropriate content is posted. This works solely because of a shared sense of content appropriateness; in other situations this shared understanding may well not exist and stricter guidelines and posting policies would need to be enforced. Having said that, our workplace has permeable boundaries, and, on occasions (3), we have been asked to remove material to avoid possible offense to visitors, or because company sensitive material was alluded to in a posting. Interestingly, when problematic content was posted, it was seen by some of our users as a problem caused by the existence of the *technology itself* and not an issue to be raised with person who posted the content.

In considering the issue of appropriate content, as we move toward distribution of content to remote (and possibly culturally very different) locations, content moderation becomes more important. In our current deployment situation there is enormous overlap between online and offline community membership and all members are familiar with the social and physical locale. People's ability to envision the audience for their content when they are distant from the physical location of its appearance is limited. Thus, by making it easy to post without going to the physical space, we are also making it easy for people to be inadvertently (or intentionally) socially inappropriate.

Finally, we would like to speculate on reasons for the successful adoption of the Plasma Posters in our organization. There has been much work done to tease out factors that lead to successful adoption of information technologies, and groupware in particular, within organizations (e.g. Cockburn and Jones, 1995; Ehrlich, 1987; Grudin, 1988; Steves and Knutilla, 1999; Steves, 2001). Steves and Knutilla (1999) outline major factors to be (1) management backing; (2) grassroots champions who are also users; (3) conducive group dynamics; (4) corporate mentality that is conducive to cooperative or collaborative work; (5) non-threatening technology, especially in terms of job security; and (6) support for tasks and processes. Ehrlich (1987) also highlights the importance of ongoing attentiveness to user reactions and to system problems, suggesting teams should provide adequate "follow-through to encourage system use" and make sure they are "troubleshooting system problems quickly to avoid premature rejection".

Although the Plasma Poster Network represents an *informal,* social technology that is not concerned with task accomplishment, unlike the foci of these acceptance and adoption studies, many of these factors have also been important in the success of our deployment. Steves and Knutilla's sixth factor is therefore not as relevant for our deployment, although we would argue that information sharing is a fundamental process and of great value in our organization. We have identified the following individual, group and organizational levels as being important:

- Corresponding to Steves and Knutilla's first and fifth factors, the Plasma Poster Network has organizational endorsement, including a relaxed attitudes to content that is not directly work-related or corporately vetted. Further the organization is supportive of collaborative and cooperative work, and sees social intercourse and cross-fertilization of ideas wrought by informal sharing to be of value.
- Corresponding to the third factor, there are conducive group dynamics for the presence of a lightweight social technology. In addition to the group dynamics, individuals also have skills that make them comfortable sharing digital media in this way, and have an appetite for information. Recent comments supplement those above: "people wanted to talk to each other already, and now the posters are there, the content breaks the ice" and "there is no stigma here associated with forwarding bad jokes as long as it doesn't fill up mailboxes".
- Corresponding to Ehrlich's points and to Steves and Knutilla's second factor, the physical presence of the design and development team creates a "buzz" and excitement around the technology that may not be present if we were remote. In some sense, the evident engagement and enthusiasm of the team provides an advertising function for the technology itself, even though intentional solicitation for participation is minimal. In addition, the physical presence of our team means bugs and problems can quickly be noted and rectified.
- In addition to the points above, the social and physical characteristics of the place in which our Plasma Posters are located are important, including the presence of open, shared spaces within a restricted-access building. This allows people to notice things while moving through the building or "hanging out" but also there is a sense of comfort when posting content, as people know who is likely to see what is posted. The characteristics of the physical space is less clearly important when considering "invisible", online groupware systems and applications. Finally, the capacity of the Plasma Posters to contribute directly to more subtle social aspects like trust, enjoyment and playfulness are central factors in the success of the technology.

5. Conclusions and Future Work

In this chapter we have described the design and deployment of the Plasma Poster Network within our lab, focusing on the large screen, interactive displays that represent the public "face" of the network. Quantitative and qualitative data and informal observation testify to the success of this deployment.

While our current implementation is well received, we have plans for further development work that will allow us to explore more deeply people's practices around content sharing with personal and/or public displays. Based on user feedback and further analysis of field data on the use of physical community poster boards, we are currently modifying our content distribution services, content management applications and content authoring tools. In particular, we are designing: a content distribution manager to allow users to direct content to specific Plasma Posters; applications for accessing community content from personal desktops and from mobile devices; and content authoring and presentation tools that allow people expressive freedom in creating the look and feel of their postings.

We are encouraged by our initial explorations within this area. As a new genre of community communication, technologies like the Plasma Poster Network move interactions with and over hypermedia content off personal technologies and into public arenas.

Notes

1. Reported by the BBC, http://news.bbc.co.uk/2/hi/technology/2861749.stm
2. However, much has been said about the vital role of community print media in the form of local newspapers (that include classified ads, which in many instances are the print version of community bulletin board content) in this regard (e.g. Janowitz, 1952; Stamm and Fortini-Campbell, 1983; Tripp, 1994).
3. At present, no authentication procedure is required at the board; members of the local community are trusted to identify themselves manually. However, implementing a badge-in mechanism or pin entry would be trivial.
4. Note that occasional host machine crashes meant that at times, not all of the three Plasma Posters were available.
5. Data for May are partial and have been extrapolated.

References

AdSpace Networks http://www.casinovendors.com/VendorPage.cfm/79183.html

Adler, A., Gujar, A., Harrison, B. L., OHara, K., & Sellen, A. (1998). A Diary Study of Work-Related Reading: Design Implications for Digital Reading Devices. In Proceedings of CHI'98 Conference on Human Factors in Computing Systems; 1998; Los Angeles, CA, USA. New York: ACM Press: 241-248.

Albrecht, D. and Broikos, C.B. (Eds). *On the Job: Design and the American Office.* New York and Washington. D.C. Princeton Architectural Press and National Building Museum, 2000.

Alexander, C., Ishikawa, S., Silverstein, M., Jacobson, M., Fiksdahl-King, I. and Angel, S. A Pattern Language. Towns, Buildings, Construction. New York: Oxford University Press, 1977.

Barsoux, J.L. Funny Business. Humor Management and Business Culture. Cassell, New York, USA, 1993.

Bellotti, V. and Bly, S. Walking away from the desktop computer: distributed collaboration and mobility in a product design team. Proceedings of CSCW '96 Conference on Computer Supported Cooperative Work; 1996; Boston, MA, USA.

Bly, S. and Churchill, E.F. Design Through Matchmaking: Technology in Search of Users. Interactions 1999; 6(2): 23-31.

Brand, S. *How Buildings Learn. What Happens After They Are Built.* New York: Penguin Books, 1994.

Calhoun, C. Community without propinquity revisited: communications technology and the transformation of the urban public sphere. Sociological Inquiry 1998; 68 (3): 373-397.

Castleman, C. *Getting Up: Subway Graffiti in New York. New York.* New York: The Massachusetts Institute of Technology, 1982.

Churchill, E.F., Nelson, L., Denoue, L. and Girgensohn, A. The Plasma Poster Network: Posting Multimedia Content in Public Places. In Proceedings of Interact' 03; 2003; Zurich, Switzerland.

Cockburn, A. and Jones. S. Four Principles for Groupware Design. Interacting with Computers: The Interdisciplinary Journal of Human-Computer Interaction 1995; 7(2): 195-210.

Ehrlich, S. F. Strategies for Encouraging Successful Adoption of Office Communication Systems. ACM Transactions on Office Information Systems, 1987; 5(4).

Fass, A.M., Forlizzi, J. & Pausch, R. MessyDesk and MessyBoard: Two designs inspired by the goal of improving human memory. Proceedings of DIS '02 Conference on Designing Interactive Systems: processes, practices, methods, and techniques; 2002; London, UK. New York: ACM Press: 303-311.

Greenberg, S. and Rounding, M., The Notification Collage: Posting Information to Public and Personal Displays. In Proceedings of CHI '01 Conference on Human Factors in Computing Systems, 2001; Seattle, WA, USA.

Guimbretiere, F., Stone, M. and Winograd, T. Fluid Interaction with High Resolution, Wall–sized Displays. In Proceedings of UIST 2001 14th Annual ACM Symposium On User Interface Software and Technology; 2001; Orlando, FL, USA; ACM Press,.

O'Hara, K., Towards a Typology of Reading Goals, Xerox Technical Report EPC-1996-107, 1996.

Harper, R. and Carter, K. Keeping People Apart. A Research Note. In Computer Supporter Cooperative Work (CSCW) 1994; 2:199-207.

Houde, S., Bellamy, R., Leahy, L. In search of design principles for Tools and Practices to Support Communication within a Learning Community, SIGCHI Bulletin, 1998; 30(2).

Jacobs, A.B. *Great Streets*. MIT Press, 1999.

Jacobs, J. *The Death and Life of Great American Cities*, New York: Vintage Books, 1961.

Janowitz, M. *The community press in an urban setting: The social elements of urbanism (2d ed.).* Chicago: The University of Chicago Press, 1952.

Klemmer, S.R., M.W. Newman, R. Farrell, M. Bilezikjian, J.A. Landay, The Designers' Outpost: A Tangible Interface for Collaborative Web Site Design. In Proc. UIST2001, CHI Letters, 2001; 3(2): 1-10.

Lupton, E. "Graphic Design in the Urban Landscape." In *Design and Feminism, Re-visioning spaces, places and everyday things*, Rothschild, J., ed. Rutgers University Press, 1999.

McCarthy, J., Costa, T.J., Huang, E.M. and Tullio, J. Defragmenting the organization: Disseminating Community Knowledge Through Peripheral Displays. ECSCW 2001 Workshop on Community Knowledge; 2001; Bonn, Germany.

Nonnecke, B. & Preece, J. "Silent Participants: Getting to Know Lurkers Better." In *From Usenet to CoWebs: Interacting with Social Information Spaces*, C. Leug & D. Fisher, eds. Springer-Verlag: Amsterdam, Holland, 2003.

Pedersen, E. McCall, K., Moran, T., Halasz, F., Tivoli: An Electronic Whiteboard for Informal Workgroup Meetings. Proceedings of InterCHI '93 Conference on Human Factors in Computing Systems; 1993 Amsterdam, The Netherlands: 391-398.

Russell, D., Trimble, J. and Wales, R. Two paths from the same place: Task driven and human centered evolution of a group information source. IBM Make it Easy Conference, June 2002. www.ibm.com/ibm/easy/eou_ext.nsf/Publish/2778.

Schilit, B., Golovchinsky, G., Price, M., Beyond Paper: Supporting Active Reading with Free Form Digital Ink Annotations. Proceedings of CHI'98 Conference on Human Factors in Computing Systems; 1998; Los Angeles, CA, USA. New York: ACM Press: 249-256.

Schuler, D. *New community networks: Wired for change*. ACM Press, New York, 1996.

Snowden, D. and Grasso, A. Diffusing Information in Organisational Settings: Learning from Experience. In Proceedings of CHI'02 Conference on Human Factors in Computing Systems; 2002; Minneapolis, MA, USA. New York: ACM Press: 331-338

Stamm, K.R., and Fortini-Campbell, L. The relationship of community ties to newspaper use. Journalism Monographs, 1983; 84.

Steves, M. and Knutilla, A. Collaboration Technologies for Global Manufacturing. Proceedings of the ASME International Mechanical Engineering Congress and Exposition (IMECE): Symposium on Manufacturing Logistics in a Global Economy (Nashville, TN, November 1999), 541-555.

Steves, M., Knutilla, A. and Wierba, E. A Manufacturing Collaboratory Case Study - Companion Document, NISTIR 6809, National Institution of Standards and Technology, Gaithersburg, MD, 2001.

Streitz, N., J. Geißler, T. Holmer, S. Konomi, C. Müller-Tomfelde, W. Reischl, P. Rexroth, P. Seitz, R. Steinmetz i-LAND: An interactive Landscape for Creativity and Innovation. In: Proceedings of CHI '99 Conference on Human Factors in Computing Systems; 1999 Pittsburgh, PA USA: 120-127.

Timmers, M. (Ed) *The Power of the Poster*. London, UK: V&A Publications, 1998.

Tripp, B.E. "The media and community cohesiveness." In *The significance of the media in American history*, J.D. Startt & W. D. Sloan, eds, Northport, AL: Vision Press, 1994.

Virnoche, M. E., & Marx, G. T. "Only connect" - E.M. Foster in an age of electronic communication: Computer-mediated association and community networks. Sociological Inquiry 1997; 67 (1): 85-100.

Wellman, B. Living Networked in a Wired World. IEEE Intelligent Systems 1999; 14(1): 15-17.

Wellman, Barry and Milena Gulia. "Net Surfers Don't Ride Alone." In *Networks in the Global Village*, Barry Wellman, ed.; Boulder, Colorado: Westview Press, 1999.

Whittaker, S., Frohlich, D. and Daly-Jones, O. Informal workplace communication: what is it like and how might we support it? In Proceedings of CHI'94 Conference on Human

Factors in Computing Systems; 1994; Boston, MA, USA. New York: ACM Press: 130-137.

Whittaker, S. and Sidner, C. E-mail overload: Exploring personal information management of e-mail. In Proc. CHI'96, Conference on Human Factors in Computing Systems; 1996; Vancouver, Canada; ACM Press.

Whyte, W. H. *The Social Life of Small Urban Spaces*. New York: Anchor Books, 1971.

Yates, J. and Orlikowski, W.J. Genres of Organizational Communication: A Structurational approach to studying communication and media, Academy of Management Review 1992; 17: 299-326.

Chapter 11

SUPPORTING COMMUNITIES OF PRACTICE WITH LARGE SCREEN DISPLAYS

Antonietta Grasso, Martin Muehlenbrock, Frederic Roulland, Dave Snowdon
Xerox Research Centre Europe

Abstract: In the foreseeable future large screen displays will be affordable and consequently widely available in work organisations. Several projects have started to investigate what kinds of information are most usefully presented by large screen displays and in which ways. This research is part of a larger effort concerning Ambient Displays, but here we focus on the visual presentation of information in work settings. Starting from communication needs in work organisations, we identify Communities of Practice as a relevant organisational group to address, and present a system for supporting them. On the basis of our experience and experience found in the literature we analyse design choices that can alleviate the cost of using these systems. Furthermore, context-sensitiveness may provide additional ways of improving the cost/benefit ratio.

Key words: Communities of practice, large screen displays, ubiquitous computing, contextual computing

1. Introduction

A decade ago, Mark Weiser identified a new trend in the development of information technology, which he called Ubiquitous Computing (UC) and identified as the third computing wave after mainframe and personal computing: "The third wave of computing is that of ubiquitous computing, whose cross-over point with personal computing will be around 2005-2020. The 'UC' era will have lots of computers sharing each of us. Some of these computers will be the hundreds we may access in the course of a few minutes of Internet browsing. Others will be embedded in walls, chairs,

K. O'Hara et al. (eds.), Public and Situated Displays: Social and Interactional Aspects of Shared Display Technologies, 261–282.

clothing, light switches, cars, in everything." (Weiser and Brown, 1995). Given such a scenario it is appropriate to wonder how one might interact with such a complex ecosystem of connected devices. Obviously, we do not want each device to be as demanding of our attention as current desktop computers and devices such as mobile phones and PDAs otherwise we will quickly become overwhelmed. It was for this reason that the concept of calm computing (Weiser and Brown, 1995) was developed to allow information to be presented in such a way that it exploited people's peripheral awareness without constant demands on foreground attention.

In this vein, Ishii and colleagues have started to look at the architectural space as a suitable interface between people and digital information (Ishii *et al.*, 1998; Dahley *et al.*, 1998; Wisneski *et al.*, 1998). This enlargement of the traditional GUI to the whole space surrounding the user has been termed *Ambient Displays* information (Ishii *et al.*, 1998; Dahley *et al.*, 1998; Heiner *et al.*, 1999; Wisneski *et al.*, 1998). Of particular relevance to this concept is the fact that "Ambient Displays are well suited as a means to keep users aware of people or general states of large systems" and "can be used to create a persistent, yet non-intrusive connection between loved ones, bringing people a sense of community through shared awareness" (Ishii *et al.*, 1998).

In recent years a number of research groups have been investigating the use of large screen displays to provide peripheral awareness of the activities of a group of users. In this chapter we will focus on these types of display and will analyse the design requirements they pose. Some examples of these systems are:

- The CommunityWall – or CWall for short – an interactive large-screen display prototype at XRCE using documents or news and peoples' opinions on them as a trigger (Snowden and Grasso, 2002).
- GroupCast is part of a group of systems meant to provide peripheral awareness in physical spaces representing different working contexts (McCarthy *et al.*, 2001)
- Like the CWall, the Notification Collage uses the metaphor of a bulletin board, which can simultaneously display several randomly placed items (Greenberg and Rounding, 2000).
- The final system in our review is the Apple Newspaper, which was designed to improve communication among a group of researchers at Apple research (Houde *et al.*, 1998).

2. Communities of Practice

In our own experience and in some of the cases reported so far, there has been a lot of emphasis on the support of *casual interaction* (Isaacs *et al.*, 1997), but without enough understanding of the mechanisms that trigger it, either collocated or remote. While we do agree that informal communication is the actual glue that supports the accomplishment of work and also more long term organisational functions, such as innovation and the sense of a shared organisational objective, we believe that a deeper understanding of the modalities that trigger the communication exchange are needed.

2.1 Communication Patterns in Workplaces

Let's start with the different types of workgroups and the communication patterns they have. After having observed work in several organisations, Isaacs *et al.* have proposed a clear typology of workgroups (Isaacs *et al.*, 1997). Four main categories have been identified, which could be useful to revisit here:

- **Project workgroup.** A group of people typically collocated. A major characteristic of this category is to be officially acknowledged by the organisations. In workgroups, communication is frequent and its main characteristic is task-orientation, and having a lot of shared context that is not retrieved and recalled at each exchange. Communication can be very long, typically in formal meetings, but also very short.
- **Cross-functional.** In this case the group supports the work of several other groups (e.g. in human resources). The work and the communication tend to be more structured and organised around formal processes. Informal communication happens anyway and tends to be document-centric.
- **External.** In this case communication is with external partners and a major part of it tends to be formal (typically inside meetings). Informal communication includes meeting arrangements, tracking and task-focused exchange.
- **Community of practice** (originally "peer" in (Isaacs *et al.*, 1997]). In this case communication is longer and less task oriented. It is more spontaneous and driven by the common work-related interests and practices. This category has been labelled peer in the original taxonomy of Isaacs *et al.*, and it has very similar attributes with the community of practice concept (Lave and Wenger, 1991). This category of users has been widely studied recently, because it is quite challenging to support and it is based on spontaneous efforts. Usually, it cannot be found in any

organisational chart. However, communities of practice include project workgroups.

Among these workgroups, the latter has got our attention, because of the challenges that it poses to the support of informal communication, while being a very important structure of the organisation. It is important to distinguish a community of practice from a project team or task force. Project teams and task forces are formed for a specific assignment and normally disband after this assignment is complete. In addition such teams are often composed of members with different roles. In contrast, a community of practice is not formed for a specific assignment and its members usually have the same role. Wenger (1999) identifies several key aspects of a community of practice: joint enterprise (the members have some kind of work in common), mutual engagement (they interact to clarify their work, not just to get it done) and shared repertoire (they have common tools, techniques and terminology).

In the following two sections we explain in more detail why this structure is an important one to support and what are the benefits that the usage of large public displays can bring in supporting informal exchange in communities.

2.2 The Benefits of Ambient Displays for Communities

The understanding of how innovation gets fostered in organisations has been of paramount interest in the past decades because of the increasing need to stay competitive in a very fast changing economy. Some light on this complex question has been shed by two complementary sets of concepts that have been developed in the early nineties: the concept of community of practice (Lave and Wenger, 1991) and the concept of *ba* as an enabling environment for the community itself (Nonaka and Takeuchi, 1995). In the former, Lave and Wenger rethink the whole learning process by re-conceptualising how it happens. In their conceptualisation, learning occurs not because of the consumption of some "knowledge" coming from the external world to us, but through mechanisms that are inherently social. They propose that learning is supported by the participation in a community of practice, at first legitimately peripheral and then gradually increasing in engagement and complexity.

In the work of Nonaka, the *ba* has been proposed as an enabling environment that can support aspects of peripheral participation and interaction. In a *ba* the role of technology for community support is that of an enabler that facilitates and maybe reinforces mechanisms and interactions already in place in the organisation. In a survey of existing technology done recently (Snowden and Grasso, 2002), several dimensions have been identified as relevant in support of communities of practice. In Table 11-1 there is a comprehensive list of aspects that have to be supported during the life of a community; for each of these, technology can provide some support. The usage of ambient displays can complement such support, even if it cannot be the sole one. In table 11-1 we list all of them and mark the ones where the usage of ambient displays can be of assistance.

Table 11-1. The benefit of Ambient Displays in support of communities of practice

Community need	**Function**	**Example of support by Ambient Displays**
Presence and visibility	Providing visibility of the community to its members	The public display is a reminder of the community activity that is encountered while doing other activities in the workspace.
Rhythm	Supporting periodic events	
Knowledge-generating interactions	Supporting interaction	Interaction can be both collocated and with remote members and is triggered by the information on the display
Efficiency of involvement	Making it easy to participate	Easy access to system via display in public space.
Short-term value	Making expertise available	
Long-term value	Support for projects that are related to the practice	
Connections to the world	Relevant news from the external world	Provision of news that is contextualized to a community.
Personal identities	Support of personal reputation	Making public what the individual contributions are
Communal identity	About providing a sense of "place"	Community information is visible where both members and non-members have other activities.
Belonging and relationships	Support for communication	Triggering face-to-face interactions
Complex boundaries	Support for different levels of visibility	
Evolution: maturation and integration	Flexibility in integrating new functionality	
Active community building	Management of community evolution	

2.3 *Types of Organisational Public Spaces*

In addition to the understanding of the different communication patterns and work structures, it is important to consider the locations in which the public screens are used (Churchill *et al.*, Chapter 10 this volume). While we are still at the beginning of this understanding, we believe it useful to recall a first characterisation that we have found in our own experience as designers of these systems. We found that at least three types of public spaces can be recognised in an organisational space, and they are the following:

Dedicated – a room specifically designed to host formal meetings. Formal meetings are meetings that happen in a scheduled way, where an agenda is sent in advance and potentially involve participants from remote sites. These meetings are usually present in *project* and *external* workgroups.

Service – a room used to provide a common service to several people. Typical service rooms provide a printing/faxing area. The usage of these rooms is not booked in advance, and their resources are used as needed. Other service rooms could be a cafeteria or a library. Confidential information flows in these areas to a degree, both in the form of documents and discussions, because they are shielded from external visibility.

Entrance – is the area in a building that provides an interface to external people. Usually, everyone in the building uses these areas at least for entering and leaving. They convey an organisational brand message to the visitor; however they are not suited to for the display of confidential information or work in progress.

With respect to the affordances that these spaces offer to the use of large displays to promote informal communication inside communities, we have found it useful - in our experience as designers of large public displays - to concentrate on the features of the *service* and *entrance* spaces. These places have been chosen because most people working on the site pass by at least once during a day. Furthermore, in these places the behavioural patterns are of a form that the peripheral awareness through large screens can take place, e.g. in a service room while waiting for a print job or collecting it. See also O'Hara *et al.*, (Chapter 5 this volume) for further discussion on the different types of space and their usage.

3. Community Wall

The Community Wall (or CWall for short) is an interactive large screen display prototype at the Xerox Research Centre Europe. Its purpose is to support information discovery in and across communities of practice and create an environment that fosters social encounters (conversations) using documents or news and peoples' opinions on them as triggers. The CWall provides a focus for social activity in a similar way to notice boards, which display notices concerning current community activities (ranging from formal printed notices to hand written scraps of paper). Originally intended as a stand-alone system, the CWall is now one of the user interfaces of a recommender system, Knowledge Pump (Glance *et al.*, 1999) that was originally designed for Web-only use. Knowledge Pump was extended by adding additional user interfaces created for the CWall (the CWall display itself, email, paper and PDA) in order to make it as easy as possible to enter information and counter criticism that the web interface was too time consuming. From a CWall perspective Knowledge Pump is just an invisible (to the user) storage mechanism that users do not need to know about. However, Knowledge Pump users can also use the CWall to access the same content as they find via Knowledge Pump's web interface.

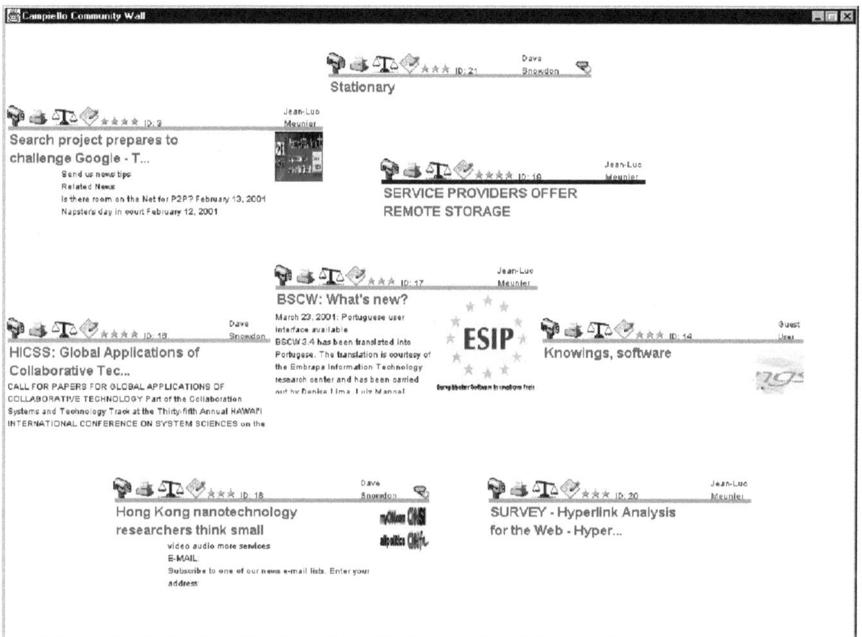

Figure 11-1. CWall screen.

The CWall consists of a large screen display that everyone would see several times in the course of a normal working day. Everyone can post information to the CWall. The information can be plain text or web pages that include images. We wanted to avoid a standard desktop look & feel and so items are placed randomly on the screen to give a more "organic" feeling. However, in order to increase readability items are not permitted to overlap (see figure 11-1). The large screen is touch-sensitive and people can interact with it using their fingers. Content can be submitted to the CWall via email,

Flowport™ forms, web bookmarklets, Knowledge Pump and Palm PDAs. The following sections will describe submission and display of content in more detail.

In Figure 11-2, a common scheme for describing ambient displays in a conceptual way is presented, which is comprised of four general modules:

- **Collection.** Monitors one or more information sources.
- **Processing.** Decides which among all the information passed by the collection module to process and how. This is where specific ambient information is taken into account to decide how to prioritise.
- **Presentation.** Maps the information to the possibilities of the chosen output.
- **User interaction.** Not all ambient displays are interactive. However, interactivity could appear at every level, from data source choice to deciding how to process and display the information. Finally interaction could be with the system or with other users through the mediation of it.

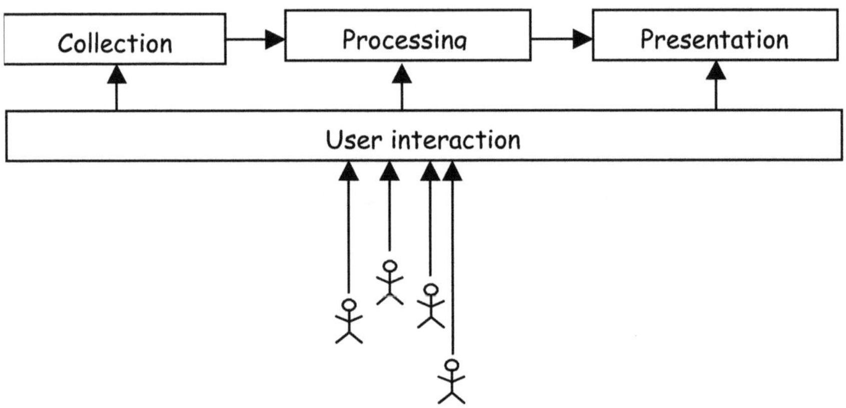

Figure 11-2. Overview of an Ambient Display.

3.1 Collection: Integration with the Working Environment

There are different ways of improving the integration with the working environment. One possible way is realised in the Notification Collage (Greenberg and Rounding, 2000). The system is designed to be used on a large public display as well as on personal displays. It is reported that in practice the NC quickly found its way to almost permanent display on everyone's desktop, even if those people were in the same room as the public display (Greenberg and Rounding, 2000). Users were observed to say that they felt that having an instance of the NC on their own machine made them more aware of changes, and they were better able to respond to particular events. However, there might be a trade-off in designing a (single) system that is adequate for large displays as well personal displays.

Another way to integrate with the working environment is to make the large display interoperable with the tools that are usually be used in a workgroup. In order to reduce the cost of submitting information the CWall provides several additional user interfaces that can be used to submit information to the system:

- **Email.** Many hi-tech organisations have a strong email culture (Houde *et al.*, 1998) and hence the CWall allows people to submit new items by email. This means that documents such as call for papers, which are often received by email, can be forwarded to the CWall using any mail program. Also the CWall can be put in copy of messages sent to others.
- **Web bookmarklets.** In order not to disrupt browsing by forcing users to go to a particular page in order to submit an item (as in Knowledge Pump) we created bookmarklets[10] that would capture the current page URL and title, and pop up a window allowing the user to confirm the selection and optionally add more information such as a numeric rating or comment. Cookies are used to prevent the user from needing to login after the first time the system is used. This proved to be the most popular way of submitting content to the CWall.
- **Paper.** Using Xerox's Flowport(tm) software it is possible to submit hardcopy documents. Using a combined printer/scanner/copier next to the large screen users can place a specialised cover sheet on top of the document and press the start button on the copier. The cover sheet is recognised as introducing a new document, the document is scanned, OCR'd and then the keywords in the OCR'd document are analysed to decide which community it is best suited to.
- **PDA.** Since many people now have PDAs such as the Palm Pilot(tm) these could become a sort of personal interface to the system. A prototypical Palm application has been implemented in CWall that uses infrared communication to retrieve a list of items currently on display on the screen. Users can read the items, to read comments and ratings on the items submitted by other users, rate and comment on items, print the items and email the items to them-selves or others. It is also possible to create new items that could be submitted to the CWall via infrared.

[10] Small JavaScript programs that can be stored as bookmarks and which are activated when they are selected by the user.

3.2 Processing: System Smartness

Given the information available a system can either automate the selection and placement of content, rely entirely on users to select content and placement or use some combination of both automatic and manual selection and placement. Manual selection has the advantage of more reliably choosing interesting and relevant content but suffers from the increased housekeeping demands made upon the user community in order to remove old and no-longer relevant items from the display.

With respect to this aspect, the systems that we have reviewed have chosen approaches, which are on the two extremes of the scale. Some of them are completely controllable by the users, both in terms of deciding what to have on the screen and in deciding where and how to position it; this is the case of the Apple Newspaper (Houde *et al.*, 1998) and of the Notification Collage (Greenberg and Rounding, 2000). Some others have a degree of system autonomy, ranging from trying to guess what is appropriate for the people sharing a certain space, arriving to being able to recognise the identity of the group of people currently in front and tune the content exactly to them; this is the case of the CWall and of the GroupCast (McCarthy *et al.* 2001).

Questions related to system smartness are:

- Which type of information can best support an informal conversation, is it completely new information or information particularly selected according to one person's interests?
- Which type of information should appear?
- Is it required to have identity recognition in place, or can the system rely on a profile description capturing the global interest of the people using the space?
- And more precisely, is it necessary that the system knows and matches the detailed interests of the people in front it or should the content be new to one or more of them?

In the case of the CWall, since only about 10-15 items can fit on the display at one time, we implemented a mechanism for automatically selecting items from the database. Items can be classified into a number of types (sticky note, paper, meeting, conference announcement, etc) and each type can be associated with a rule that is responsible for assigning a priority to items of that type. For example, the relevance of a scientific paper might be linked to its numeric rating and the number of comments it has received, whereas a meeting announcement might rise in priority shortly before the time of the meeting and then fall to zero afterwards. We implemented a "toolbox" of simple rules and the means to compose them hierarchically to form compound rules. Administrators of a display can create compound rules using a simple text configuration format and rules from the toolbox without having to understand how to program. At intervals (currently every 10 minutes) the system reapplies the rules to any active items (those that have been created, rated, commented on or interacted with in the recent past) and selects those with the highest priority for display. This means that the display changes often enough that people who pass by several times in a day should see different items. It also allows the system to give priorities to different types of item at different times of day.

The implemented collection of rules includes a rule that adds a small amount of random noise and a rule that decreases the priority of items according to how much time they have already spent on the display in order to prevent a few items from monopolising the display and to ensure that users see a variety of items if they pass by the display several times in one day.

3.3 Presentation: Familiar Look and Feel

This dimension is about how to present the information and it is probably the one in which progress is most needed. Approaches so far have included projecting a web site, just making it larger, but without specifically designing it for the public large display [Houde *et al.*, 1998] and creating digital versions bulletin boards which rely on users manually arranging the space (Denoue *et al.*, 2003, Fass *et al.*, 2002). At least one system, AttrActive Windows (Denoue *et al.*, 2003), has gone so far as to use a physics-based model incorporating gravity and the properties of cloth in order to allow users to lift the corners of items to see what is beneath, manipulate the placement and orientation of items using virtual pushpins and allow effects such as items rippling in a simulated breeze.

However these systems are by definition in the periphery of the activities carried on in the public spaces where they are installed and should fully take into account issues like what kind of presentation is more likely to attract and sustain attention.

Questions related to these dimensions are:

- Which metaphor is most adapted to convey heterogeneous community information where not only the information but also the people related to it are relevant?
- Which kind of appearance should the information have to convey information like novelty, relevance and topic?
- How should information be presented in order to be eye-catching to people who are far away as well as those who are close by?

In the design of the CWall the choice has been the metaphor of a bulletin board to which anyone can post information. The information can be plain text or web pages that include images (including animated GIFs). This choice was motivated by the attempt to avoid a standard desktop look & feel and have items that are placed randomly on the screen to give a more "organic" feeling. However, in order to increase readability items are not permitted to overlap. However in other systems like the Notification Collage, information items can overlap to convey information about age and novelty. In both cases the large screen is touch sensitive and people can interact with it using their fingers.

On the CWall, each item displayed on the screen shows at least a title, a number of stars indicating the average numeric rating, (i.e. the average evaluation of the community about its relevancy), an icon indicating the number of comments on this item, the name of the person who submitted the item and some icons allowing the user to perform specific actions on the item. Items which the system decides are more relevant at a given moment may also have images selected from the web page displayed, the first few lines of text from the page and a display of any comments submitted by other users. An example item representation is shown in Figure 11-3.

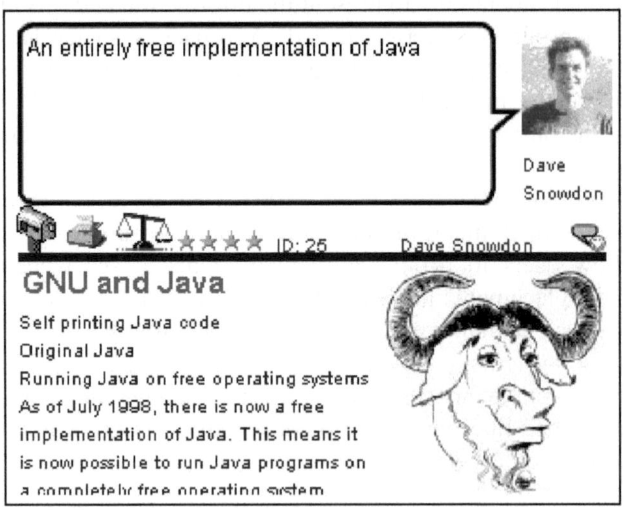

Figure 11-3. Close up on an item displayed on the CWall showing a comment, the picture and name of the person who submitted the comment, some images from the page, the rating (4 stars) and the first few lines of text.

Interaction with the system is deliberately simple, users can:

- Touch the item anywhere except for the four action icons to cause the system to expand the amount of space given to the item (up to the limit of about 30 lines of text) in order to find out more about an item.
- Touch the mailbox icon to email the item to himself or herself or someone else (a palette of faces is displayed and the user selects the face of the recipient).
- Touch the printer icon to print the document at a nearby printer.
- Touch the balance item to record a numeric rating (the user is asked to identify themselves by selecting their image).
- Touch the pen and paper icon to write a comment on the screen. We use software delivered with the SMARTBoard to convert the handwriting to text.

One point to note is that we make no attempt to display the full text of a document on the large screen – the CWall was designed on the assumption that a public space was probably not the ideal location to read possibly long documents and we wanted to keep interaction quick and simple and avoid more difficult interactions require active content navigation.

4. A Context-Sensitive Community Wall

By providing applications with more information about users and their context, systems will able to be more responsive, the information presented more pertinent, and user-machine dialogue a lot less laborious. We believe that context awareness will introduce new possibilities in the improvement of the cost/benefit ratio. The GroupCast project has done some investigation on the capability to react to the precise identities of the people in front of the screen (McCarthy, 2001). In a first stage the system, comprising an active badge infrastructure, had been designed in such a way to contain a global profile in which each user would specify their interests. The group of users detected in front of the display is used to compute the intersection of their interests in the global profile and then show something that each of them could talk about in order to sustain the conversation. However, they quickly noticed that such a profile could be very large, therefore a bit impractical and very rarely filled in. It did not help that its usage was specific to GroupCast. Subsequent to this a new version of the system used personal profiles and displayed content that was of interest to at least one of the people in front.

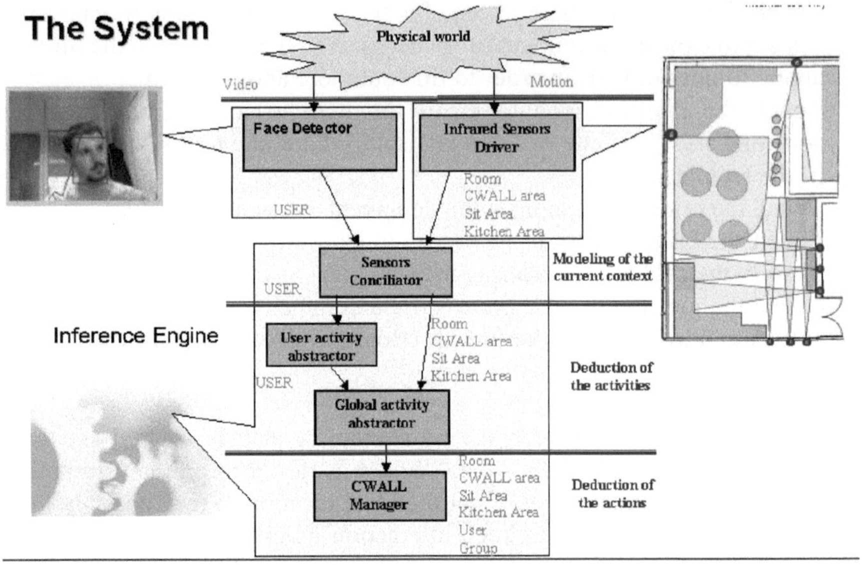

Figure 11-4. The architecture of the context-sensitive presentation layer.

In the case of the CWall we decided to see if we could improve the utility of the display by differentiating between people passing by and people standing in front of the display actively reading the content. In this way we hoped to address two criticisms of the existing interface. Namely, that

1. It was too hard to work out if something interesting was displayed with a passing glance from a distance - people had to approach the display in order to read the titles.
2. The display often changed while people were reading it. This occurred when the internal timer caused a refresh and people were reading the contents but not interacting with the display. Since it detected no active usage of its user interface the CWall had no way of telling that there were people reading the items on display.

For passers-by, the information on the screen should be presented in an eye-catching manner and change frequently, whereas the information shown to an interested reader could be more detailed and stable.

We did not want to force people to carry additional devices such as active badges and so we experimented with two sensing techniques that don't require people to be specially equipped - a grid of infrared movement sensors and face detection using real-time analysis of a video image from a camera mounted on the CWall display. The architecture of the resulting system is shown in figure 11-4.

The face detection sensor is built mixing two image processing techniques that complement each other weaknesses: motion detection and colour detection. The motion detector allows the rapid detection of faces whatever their skin colour and at a wide range of distances. However it works only indoors, it cannot detect and follow people moving too fast, and finally it cannot distinguish between a face and the back of a head. The skin colour detector is very sensitive to lighting conditions and can produce false detections for background colours similar to skin. However if applied to the areas already detected by the motion detector, it can be used to refine the results of the motion technique.

We also implemented a module devoted to building high-level description of context from the basic sensed characteristics. The decision part of the system is basic (user attentiveness to the screen, and activity of groups in the room) but it provides a very strong structure to extend it. We have a working component-based architecture with an embedded inference engine. Rules can be added and tuned easily loading new scripts files through the user interface. The resulting system has the following behaviour:

- Uses bigger titles to attract people attention when people are in the room but far from the CWall (figure 11-5).
- Freezes the content of the board when a user is detected to be reading, and communicate the transition to the user. At the same time, move from a presentation where only headlines are displayed to one where people can read more contents about the topics (figure 11-6).

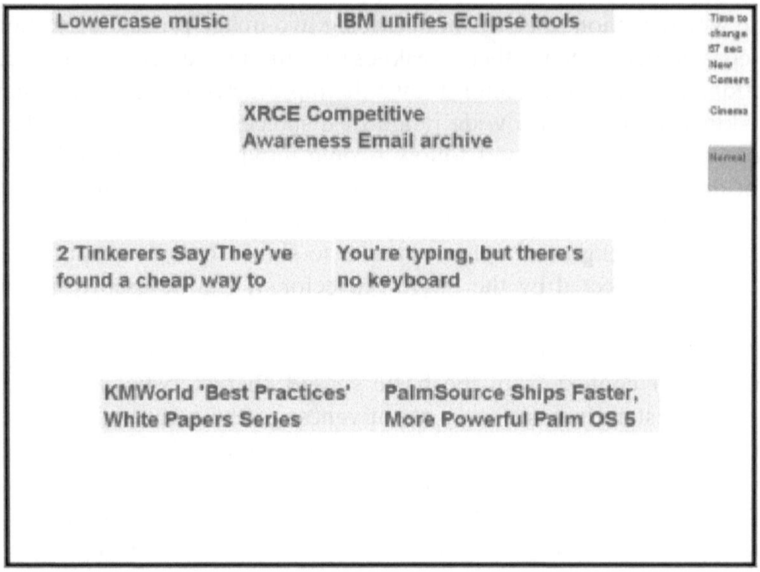

Figure 11-5.. No one standing in front of the CWall looking at it.

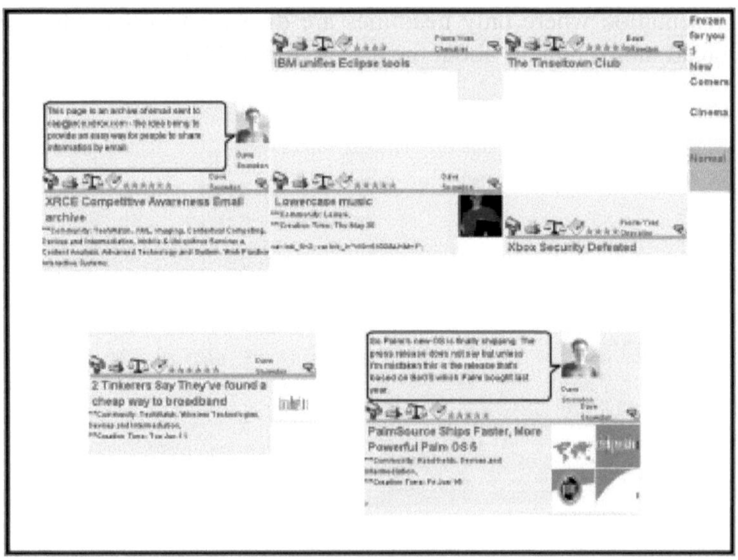

Figure 11-6. Someone looking at the screen (text in upper right corner says "frozen for you").

5. Evaluation

We currently have two CWall displays running at our site one in the cafeteria and one in an entrance foyer. On an average day two documents are printed and users send two more to themselves by email. We estimate that we have 20 regular users and a few other occasional users. In 2001, after the system had been in use for about a year, we performed an analysis of the CWall log files and asked both users and non-users to fill in a questionnaire designed to understand why people did and did not use the system, the results of which are presented in a detailed way in (Snowden and Grasso, 2002).

When we first installed the CWall it met with initial scepticism and many people were not sure that it would be of any use. However, after the CWall had been stable for some weeks we began to receive positive feedback from group members who had found interesting information on the screen. In addition, the person charged with XRCE communications used the CWall as a means of distributing information. In reaction to comments from users we made minor changes such as improving the printed output and improving the feedback when a user prints or emails a document.

After two months of use there were 443 items in the CWall database of which 223 have been interacted with by users - in other words users have either visited them (clicked on an item to expand the level of detail), printed them or emailed them. This is quite encouraging as it shows that at least 50% of the information is interesting to the CWall community and has reached someone who found it interesting. The CWall has had 1024 visit requests, 151 email requests and 123 print requests. In other words the average interaction rate is over 2 documents printed per day and two emails sent per day. Given the fact that this took place during the summer holiday period (for several weeks the group has been at less than half strength) and that the work group at full strength comprised 12 people this indicates a reasonable level of use. Nor is the interaction random, the usage logs show that some items are definitely more interesting that others.

Figures 11-7 to 11-10 show the number of items that received a particular type of interaction (visit/selection, print item, and email to user). As can be seen while many items received only a single request many items attracted interest from several users (assuming that one user did not print or email the same item several times). We take this to be an encouraging sign that much of the information displayed is read by several group members.

We also further analysed the logs to get an idea of how many people were actively using the CWall. Print and visit requests do not require user identification so we cannot use these. When users rate or comment on an item they are identified but since ratings and comments can come from multiple sources (such as via the wrapped recommender Knowledge Pump) it's hard to identify those that took place at the display itself. For these reasons we based this analysis on email requests alone. Figure 11-10 shows how many users made a given number of email requests. From this we can see that 20 people have sent email messages and therefore other lab members are using the system, not just the workgroup (which consists of 12 people) whose offices are located nearest to where the screen is located. We can also see that 3 people use the system relatively heavily (16, 29 and 44 email requests) whereas most users have submitted 10 or fewer requests.

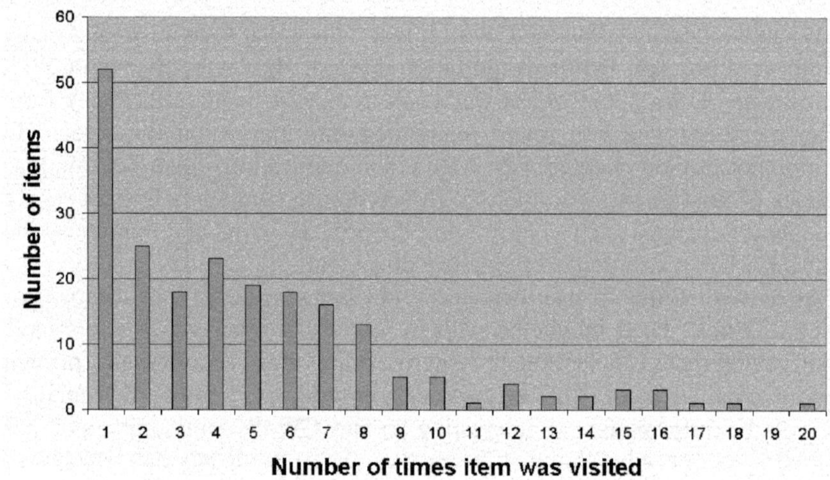

Figure 11-7. Number of items receiving a given number of visits.

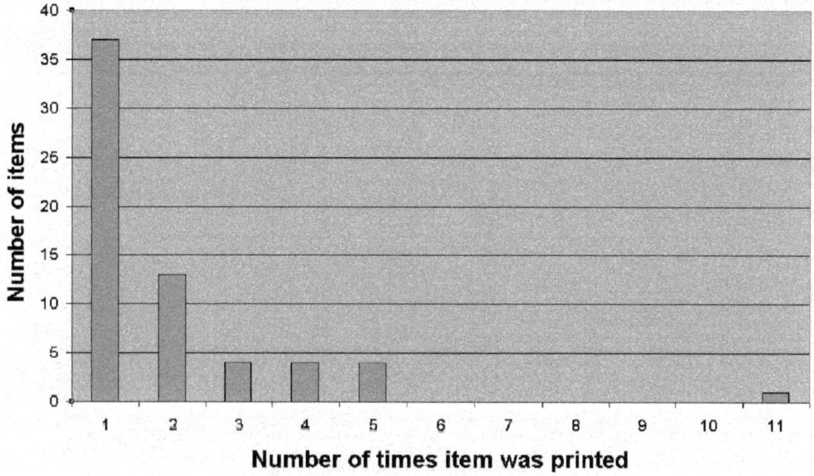

Figure 11-8. Number of items that have been printed a given number of times.

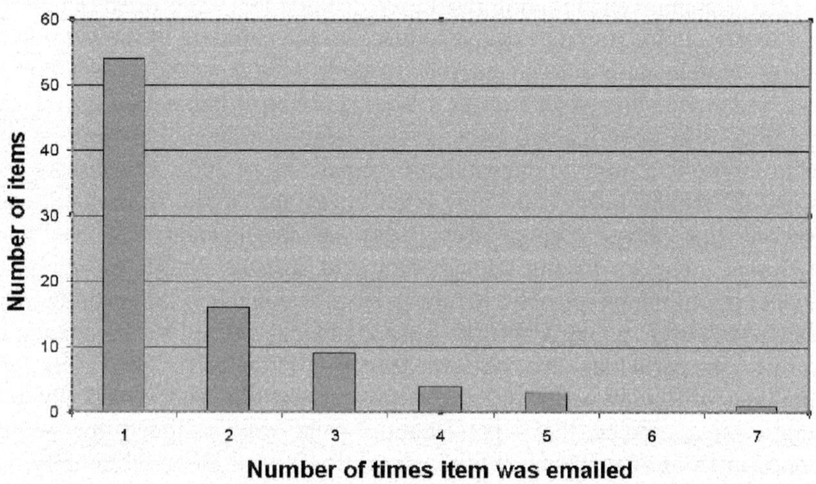

Figure 11-9. Number of items that have been emailed a given number of times.

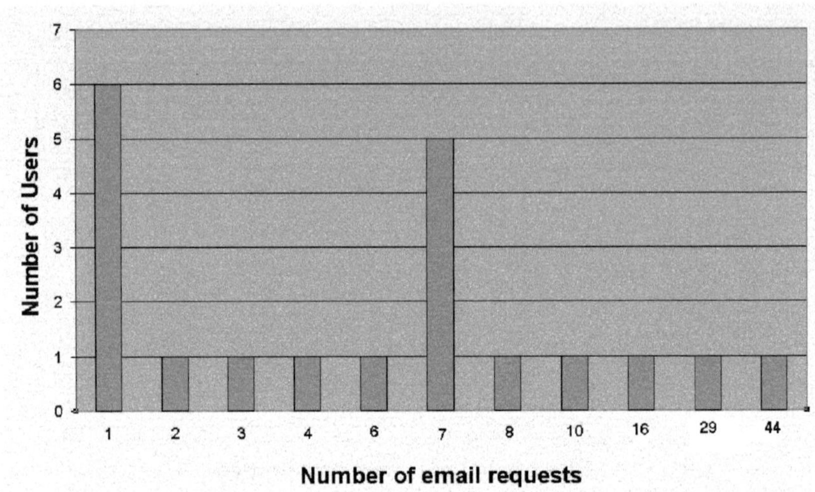

Figure 11-10. Number of users who made a given number of email requests.

After this quite encouraging result, we decided that we wanted to enlarge the user population and moved the screen into the cafeteria of the laboratory thereby guaranteeing a large number of people near to the screen during lunch and coffee breaks as well as a large number of passers-by during the day. Since this move we had on an average day two documents printed and users sending two more to themselves by email. As of 2002 we estimate that we had 20 regular users and a few other occasional users. In particular we observed that those regular users were in the category of the ones "interested", but not having enough time and sharing attitude to belong to the category of the people who regularly entered items into the recommender system. However, we also noticed some problems, related to the change of location. In particular, we noticed that in the cafeteria the users had completely different peripheral awareness bandwidth, and would not pay attention to a screen that's presentation style was designed for people stopped in front of it such as while waiting for a print job. Additionally, we noticed that the sense of trust and ownership changed, and it became a truly shared device belonging to everyone and therefore to no one. The system was more like a common good (Hardin, 1968) - people were happy to make use of it but less happy to devote effort to submitting useful content. We started to receive submissions that were not trustworthy and comments that were junk. We believe this to be due to people wishing to play with the system or experiment with the handwriting recognition rather from any deliberate bad intent. This behaviour was possible because the system had no identification mechanism, and people were required to choose their identity from a palette of users. The same mechanism that worked well when the device was shared by a workgroup in a service area did not work anymore in a more public place

6. Summary

Ambient Displays are an emerging topic of research motivated on one side by technology advances in areas like devices, displays and sensors and on the other from the intuition that they can be used to surround people with information that gracefully stays in the periphery to move in the centre when needed. In this chapter we have first presented an overview of the types of workgroups and communication needs in organisations and then argued that a specific workgroup type, the community of practice, can particularly benefit from this kind of system. However, because the community participation is usually not the primary focus of work for the community members, it is of paramount important for these systems to be designed in such a way to minimise the costs associated with their usage. For better understanding what these design possibilities are we have presented our own system, the CWall and highlighted some of its features explaining the benefit they can bring in reducing the cost of usage. We described a version of the CWall that reacts in a simple way to its context. Finally, we presented a simple evaluation of the usage of the system so far. We are currently working on a re-implementation of the CWall based on Macromedia Flash which we hope will provide a richer and more interesting user experience.

7. References

Dahley, A., Wisneski, C., and Ishii, H. Water Lamp and Pinwheels: Ambient Projection of Digital Information into Architectural Space. In Summary of CHI '98, 1998, pp. 269-270.

Denoue, L., Nelson, L. and Churchill, E., AttrActive Windows: Dynamic Windows for Digital Bulletin Boards, in ACM CHI 2003.

Fass, A.m., Forlizzi, J., Pausch, R., MessyDesk and MessyBoard: Two Designs Inspired By the Goal of Improving Human Memory; in Proceedings of Designing Interactive Systems (DIS), 2002, Pages 303 - 311.

Glance, N., Arregui, D., Dardenne, M. (1998), Knowledge Pump: Supporting the Flow and Use of Knowledge in Networked Organizations, Information Technology for Knowledge Management, Eds. Borghoff and Pareschi, Springer, 1998.

Glance, N.S., Arregui, D., Dardenne, M. Making Recommender Systems Work for Organizations. Proceedings of PAAM'99 (London UK, April 1999).

Greenberg, S. and Rounding, M. The Notification Collage: Posting Information to Public and Personal Displays. Yellow Series Report 2000-667-19, Department of Computer Science,

University of Calgary, Albert, Canada, 2000. http://www.cpsc.ucalgary.ca/grouplab/papers/index.htm

Hardin, G.: The tragedy of the Commons. In Science, 162, 1968, 1243-1248.

Heiner, J.M., Hudson, S.E., and Tanaka, K. The Information Percolator: Ambient Information Display in a Decorative Object. In Proceedings of the 12th annual ACM Symposium on User Interface Software and Technology, 1999, pp. 141-148.

Houde, S., Bellamy, R., and Leahy, L., In Search of Design Principles for Tools and Practices to Support Communication within a learning Community, SIGCHI Bulletin, 30(2), April 1998. http://www.acm.org/sigchi/bulletin/1998.2/houde.html

Isaacs, E., Whittaker, S., Frohlich, D., and O'Conaill, B., Informal Communication re-examined: New functions for video in supporting opportunistic encounters, Video-Mediated Communication, Finn, K. E., Sellen, A. J., and Wilbur, S. B. (eds.), New Jersey: Laurence Erlbaum, 1997, pp. 459-485.

Ishii, H., Wisneski, C., Brave, S., Dahley, A., Gorbet, M., Ullmer, B., and Yarin, P. ambientROOM: Integrating Ambient Media with Architectural Space. In Summary of CHI '98, 1998, pp. 173-174.

Lave J. and Wenger E., Situated Learning. Legitimate Peripheral Participation, Cambridge University Press, 1991.

McCarthy, J., Costa, T. J., and Liongorasi, E. S. UniCast, OutCast & GroupCast: Three steps toward ubiquitous, peripheral displays, UBICOMP-2001.

Nonaka, I. and Takeuchi, H. The Knowledge Creating Company, Oxford University Press, 1995.

Snowdon D. and Grasso A., Diffusing Information in Organizational Settings: Learning from Experience, Proceedings of CHI 2002, ACM.

Weiser, M. and Brown, J.S., Designing Calm Technology, 1995. http://www.ubiq.com/hypertext/weiser/calmtech/calmtech.htm

Wenger, E., Communities of Practice: Learning, Meaning, and Identity, Cambridge University Press; December 1999

Wenger E., Supporting communities of practice: a survey of community-oriented technology, 2001, shareware on the site www.wenger.org.

Wisneski, C., Ishii, H., Dahley, A., Gorbet, M., Brave, S., Ullmer, B., and Yarin, P. Ambient displays: Turning architectural space into an interface between people and information. In N. A. Streitz, S. Konomi and H.-J. Burkhardt (Eds.) Cooperative Buildings - Integrating Information, Organization and Architecture. Proceedings of the First International Workshop on Cooperative Buildings (CoBuild '98), Darmstadt, Germany. Lecture Notes in Computer Science, Vol. 1370. Springer, Heidelberg, pp. 22-32, 1998.

Chapter 12

PROMOTING A SENSE OF COMMUNITY WITH UBIQUITOUS PERIPHERAL DISPLAYS

Joseph F. McCarthy
Intel Research, Seattle

Abstract: Computer display and sensor technologies have advanced to the point where it is increasingly possible to deploy displays in public places that can sense and respond to the people in their vicinities. Several research initiatives are exploring how displays can be used in the *foreground* to support *highly focused* collaborative activities. We are exploring how displays can be used in the *background* or *periphery* to enrich *casual* interactions of the people nearby, creating greater mutual awareness of the interests and activities of people in a workplace community. Three applications are described in this chapter: GROUPCAST uses profiles of people's interests in conjunction with an infrared personnel badge system to select content of mutual interest to those passing nearby a large, public display in a common area; UNICAST runs on a peripheral display in one's individual workspace, cycling through interesting, non-urgent, visual content specified in a profile created by each individual user; OUTCAST runs on a display outside an individual office, acting as a virtual proxy by showing content about the occupant that is specifically selected to represent the occupant's public face. The chapter concludes with a broader discussion of issues common to any application seeking to enhance the experience of people gathered near a public display.

Key words: Situated computing, ubiquitous computing, proactive computing, CSCW, human-computer interaction, public displays, proactive displays, social issues.

1. Introduction

We often hear predictions of a technology-rich future in which our environments will be filled with artifacts that can sense and respond to us in new ways – a world filled with cameras, microphones, visual displays and

K. O'Hara et al. (eds.), Public and Situated Displays: Social and Interactional Aspects of Shared Display Technologies, 283–308.

audio speakers, to name but a few. Although such a world may seem threatening or menacing in some depictions, it is possible that such developments will lead to more accommodating environments, encouraging more frequent and beneficial interactions, and creating a stronger sense of community among the inhabitants of such spaces.

A physical space that can sense the people within it, and has knowledge of their interests, can use this information to create new informal interaction opportunities for these people. For example, a shared public display in a workplace, combined with a tracking system, can display information of mutual interest to the people passing by the display, providing "tickets" to talk (Sacks, 1992; p. 365). People may choose to take advantage of this information to initiate a conversation with someone about whom they may know very little, helping to increase the social capital (see Putnam, 2000) within an organization.

These conversation opportunities may be particularly useful in the workplace, where a number of trends are leading to increased fragmentation within organizations. Contributing factors include: the globalization of the economy and workforce, leading to colleagues being increasingly distributed across geographical locales; the dynamic nature of project-oriented workgroups, leading to the formation and dissolution of teams with relatively short durations; and flexible work arrangements such as telecommuting that permit people to work outside of the office on a regular basis. As a consequence of these trends, more people are spending less time collocated with a core group of colleagues for extended periods of time, and are becoming less aware of what kinds of activities other people in their group are involved in. This reduced awareness results in missed opportunities for collaboration, referrals and sharing of relevant knowledge, as well as leading to a diminished sense of community among the group members (see Deutsch, 1995; Naylor, *et al.*, 1996).

We have built a suite of applications to overcome some of these problems and promote greater awareness and a stronger sense of community within the workplace, using displays in a variety of workplace contexts. We call these *peripheral* displays because they are intended to exist on the periphery of users' attention: noticeable, but not the primary object of focus[11]. Although they are not truly *ubiquitous* [yet], by experimenting with the use of these displays in different contexts, we hope to open up new vistas for their effective deployment.

[11] *Ambient* displays (Weiser & Brown, 1997; Wisnewski, *et al.*, 1998; Redström, *et al.*, 2000; Mankoff, *et al.*, 2003) are also designed for the periphery of attention but tend to focus on abstract representations of non-urgent information.

The first application, GROUPCAST, runs on a computer with a large display situated in a casual group setting, such as a break area, where the content is selected based on the combined interest profiles of the group assembled (or walking by) the display at any given time. An infrared personnel badge system is used to detect who is in proximity to the display, and the interest profiles are borrowed from our UNICAST application.

UNICAST runs on a peripheral display within an individual workspace, cycling through content that is of interest – but not of particularly great importance or urgency – to the occupant of that workspace. Since this application provides an ongoing benefit throughout the day to its users, they are generally more willing to customize an interest profile for this application than they would be solely for the use by GROUPCAST, which they encounter only intermittently.

Finally, OUTCAST runs on a peripheral display on the outside of an individual workspace, presenting content that is intended to represent the work and/or public persona of the occupant of the workspace while he or she is away.

The chapter concludes with a broader discussion of issues that arose in the design, implementation and deployment of these applications; issues that must be addressed in some fashion by any public display application that is intended to sense and respond appropriately to the people and activities taking place in its vicinity.

2. GroupCast

Many employees of large organizations, especially those who work in large facilities, appear as nameless faces, or faceless names, to one another: familiar strangers (Milgram, 1992) who happen to work in the same place. Given the law of large numbers, it is likely that many of them share common goals, interests and/or experiences, but they are unlikely to discover these commonalities in their ordinary encounters with – or passing by – one another. Some organizations sponsor special community-building events to provide opportunities for special encounters, but we believe that technology can be of service in creating such opportunities on a more regular basis.

GROUPCAST is an application that seeks to increase the sense of community by displaying content on a large display in an open area of a workplace that may create opportunities for informal interactions. Using a network of infrared badges and sensors throughout the workplace[12], the system is aware of who is near the display, and can use profile information about those people to identify potential shared interests and display content that may provide opportunities for those people to start a conversation.

Other researchers have investigated how to create greater awareness among people who are electronically connected but not physically collocated (Zhao & Stasko, 2000; Sawhney, *et al.*, 2001; Greenberg & Rounding; 2001). Our focus has been how to create greater awareness of each other when people are gathered together – or passing each other – in the same physical space. We also want to distinguish our work from other work using large public displays in the foreground to support the performance of primary work activities (e.g., Streitz, *et al.*, 1999, Russell & Gossweiler, 2001, Guimbretière, *et al.*, 2001); although GROUPCAST uses a large public display, it is intended to be more of a background or peripheral display, and we believe that the content is more likely to spark informal conversations if it is not directly related to work activities.

GROUPCAST is intended to be more of a background or peripheral display, and we believe that the content is more likely to spark informal conversations if it is not directly related to work activities. Other examples of prototypes that seek to provide peripheral awareness in a work setting include the CWall (Snowdon & Grasso, 2002) and the Plasma Poster (Churchill, *et al.*, 2003).

Our goal is to explore how content that is responsive to the people near these displays can spark conversations (cf. O'Hara & Brown, 2001) and increase the sense of community among the passers-by, who often share more in common then they realize.

[12] See McCarthy & Meidel (1999) for more information on the ArialView infrared badge and sensor system.

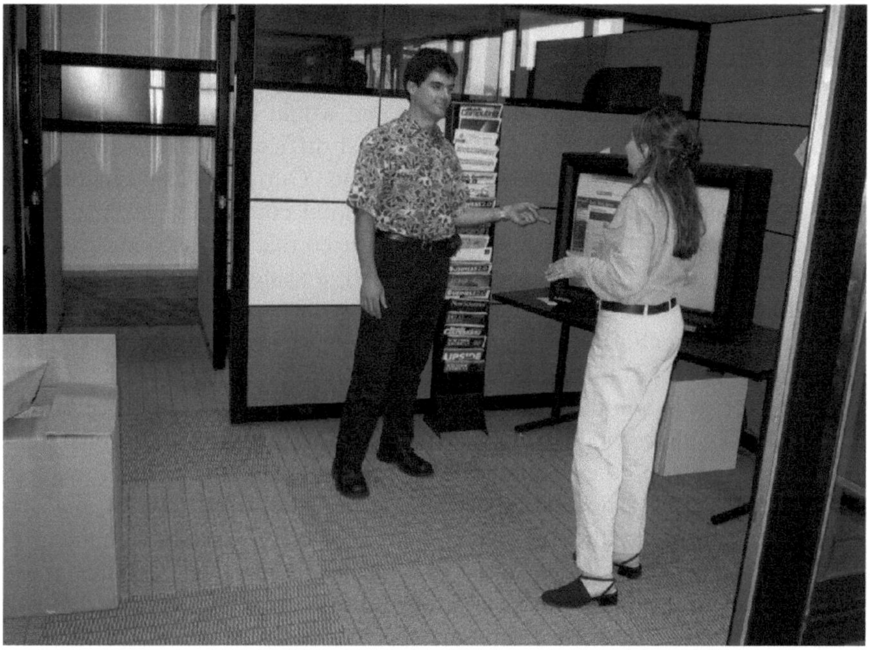

Figure 12-11. An example of GROUPCAST in context of use.

Figure 12-1 depicts an example scenario, in which Joe and Teresa pass each other regularly but do not know each other very well. However, their shared passion for wine is mutually revealed when the "Wine of the Day" web site pops up as they both pass by the GROUPCAST display, leading to a spontaneous and serendipitous discussion about the merits of old-vine zinfandels. After the discussion, they go their separate ways, knowing a little more about each other, and are more likely to have conversations – about wine and other matters – in the future.

GROUPCAST is an example of a *peripheral* display: a display placed in a physical location that is outside the primary visual focus of people as they engage in their typical work activities throughout the day. The goal is to strike a balance between presenting content that may spark a conversation and preserving some sort of *plausible deniability* – or perhaps *plausible ignoreability* – so that people need not feel compelled to respond to the conversation opportunity presented to them.

The following sections describe GROUPCAST in more detail, focusing on the interest profiles, content selection process and interaction model.

2.1 Interest Profiles for GroupCast

One of the stumbling blocks we encountered in the initial design of GroupCast was how to acquire content that would be of mutual interest – indeed, content acquisition is one of the most difficult problems to address when designing any responsive public displays. Our first design included a large web-based form describing items of digital content that people could rate with respect to their interest levels. We used this approach successfully for MusicFX (McCarthy & Anagnost, 1998), a system that selected music to best suit the preferences of people working out in a fitness center at any given time – essentially, adapting aural aspects of the workout place rather than visual aspects of the workplace.

However, we soon discovered we had conflicting goals: having a profile representation that would be broad enough to include visual content of potential interest to a large number of people, and yet still be small enough so that we could reasonably expect people to specify that content, e.g., by filling out a form. By the time we had amassed enough potential content in our profile form, we were fairly confident that no one (besides those working on the project) would take the time to fill it out. For MusicFX, people were generally willing to spend approximately 10 minutes to fill out a form specifying their preferences – on a scale of 1 to 5 – for 91 genres of music; however, these people were exposed to the music selected by the system for an average of 90 minutes per day, 5 days per week. Exposure to the visual content selected by GroupCast may be for as little as a few seconds at a time, and so people could hardly be expected to invest much time developing a comprehensive profile of interests.

Our solution was to take advantage of another application (and display setting): UniCast, an application driving a peripheral display in an individual's office that can cycle through a wide range of interesting—but not extremely urgent or important—content that a person may not actively seek out on his or her primary computer workstation, e.g., events of interest, artwork, cartoons, and a range of X-of-the-day web sites whose content changes daily.

The content for UniCast—and thus, GroupCast—includes the "usual suspects" (headlines, stocks, weather, and traffic) as well as many other types of content, including digital photographs, live feeds from local webcams throughout the workplace, and any arbitrary web page (a full list of content sources can be found in Section 3).

Using the UniCast profile, we can rely on people's own self-interest in customizing content that they will see regularly (in their office), rather than struggling with the somewhat less rewarding task of specifying content that is available only when they are in a public area.

2.2 *Content Selection in GROUPCAST*

The initial design of GROUPCAST specified that the selection content would be based on the *intersection* of interests of people in proximity to the public display, where the interests of individual people are represented by their UNICAST profiles and their proximity is detected via their infrared personnel badges. Our motivation was to find mutually interesting content to display, in order to spark conversation, and selecting content based on the intersection of interests seemed the best way to find such content. Unfortunately, we soon discovered that the intersection of any pair of people's interest profiles was very small (often null). Adding more people into the mix only diminished the size of the candidate set of prospective content.

We therefore decided to use the *union* of interest profiles for those people near the GROUPCAST display to identify potential content items, and then randomly cycled through items in this set (by default, every 15 seconds) for as long as those people were within range of the infrared sensor above the display unit. Although that content is likely not match the profile of the *all* the people, it is still of interest to at least one person near the display, and the revelation of even one person's interest still has the potential to generate the desired conversation between the passersby.

2.3 *Interaction with GROUPCAST*

As stated earlier, GROUPCAST was originally intended as an example of a *peripheral* display, one that can be conveniently ignored if the passersby do not wish to engage in conversation. However, after deploying the application, many of the users complained that soon after a particular item of mutually interesting content had drawn them into a conversation, it was replaced by another item (randomly chosen from the union of their interest profiles), disrupting their conversation.

In order to better support the continuation of conversations based on displayed content, we added finger-sized button controls to *pause* or *resume* the cycling, and to go *back* to the most recently displayed page. It should be noted that as soon as content displayed by GROUPCAST became the primary focus of attention, it ceased to be a purely peripheral display; however, it is not clear whether it is possible to design a display that is always peripheral and yet still useful in some way. In effect, there exists a *continuum* of peripherality for all public displays, which engage people's attention at different levels at different times.

2.4 The Awareness Module

GROUPCAST was originally intended to create conversation opportunities and promote awareness of mutual interests outside of the work context (e.g., hobbies and other personal interests). A user study conducted a year after its initial deployment revealed growing concern over people's diminished awareness of work activities. To address this problem, we added a new content module – and new interaction model – to GROUPCAST: the Awareness Module (Huang, *et al.*, 2002).

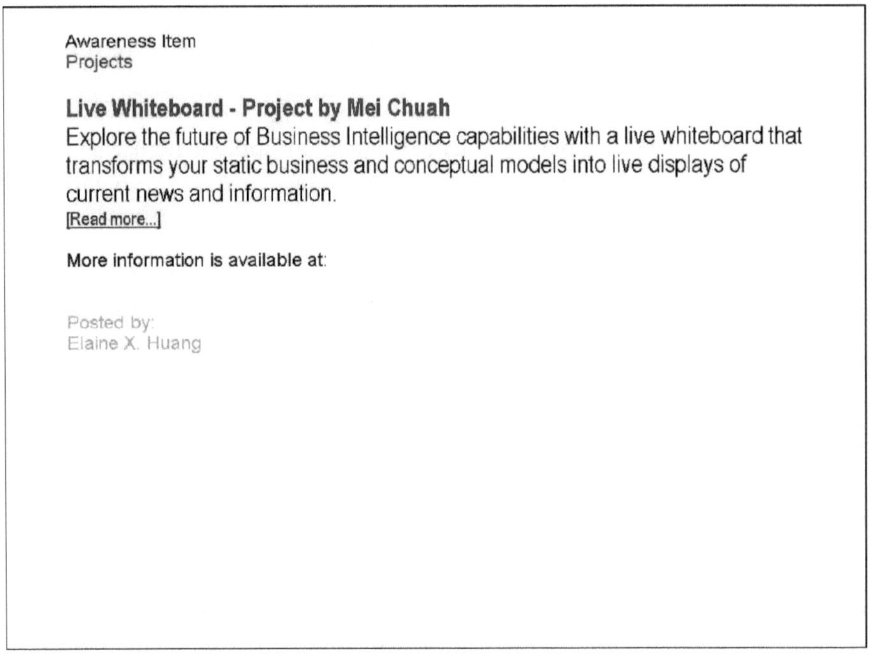

Figure 12-12. Example of Awareness Module content.

Content for the Awareness Module is generated by individual users via a web-based form accessed through the UNICAST homepage. The form provides fields for a title, short description (one paragraph), and URL (for more information), to provide a brief overview of milestones or other noteworthy activities or accomplishments of colleagues: in effect, an abbreviated status report. The name and email address of the person who filled out the information is automatically added to the form. An example of a screenshot for GROUPCAST with Awareness Module content is shown in Figure 12-2.

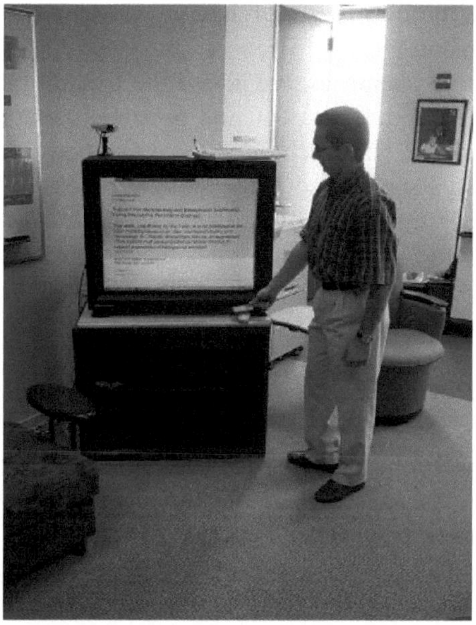

Figure 12-13. Example of interaction with Awareness Module content

We also added a new interaction model for the Awareness Module, providing a proximity badge reader (similar to those used throughout the workplace for access-controlled entry points) that people could use to swipe their badges to indicate interest in an item. Upon a badge swipe (see Figure 12-3), an awareness module content item would be automatically mailed to the owner of the badge, allowing the person to follow up and learn more about a colleague's activity at their primary workstation at a later time.

We had several interesting instances of use of the new tool. Several people noted that they became aware of a new project in the Palo Alto lab through an awareness item; people typically don't learn of projects in other labs until project leads present them in weekly videoconferences, which often does not occur until a project is fairly mature. Another item concerned a person who had changed jobs within the firm, which had not been known to most of the other members of the lab prior to its display on the public monitor. Another unexpected use was to post messages such as "I need to leave early today. If you need me, find me by 3:00" posted by a support person. All of these items might have been circulated via email, but people reported that the delivery via public display was preferable. This preference was due, in part, to the higher signal-to-nose ratio of Awareness Module content compared with the overall content of their email inbox, as well as the novelty (and thus, noticeability) of having content displayed on a large screen in a public place.

Given the positive responses, we added the capability to include content from the Awareness Module to UNICAST profiles (using the Announcement feature – see below). The early deployment required the GROUPCAST display to operate in a special mode for the Awareness Module. Future work includes better integration of the Awareness Module with other content used in GROUPCAST, and to enable other types of content to be emailed back to users through the badge reader.

3. UniCast

UNICAST is an application that allows users to specify content they would like to see on peripheral displays located within their primary workspaces. In some respects, UNICAST represents an extension of the functionality provided by the PointCast system (cf. Franklin & Zdonik, 1998), which allows people to specify news topics and stock symbols about which they would like to stay informed while their desktop computer is in screensaver mode. However, UNICAST is different in several key aspects: it runs continuously on a dedicated, peripheral display; it allows for a broader selection of content; it reacts to the location of its "owner" via an infrared badge system; and it is tied into and makes use of content belonging to other UNICAST user profiles. Figure 12-4 shows an example of UNICAST in one office context: the rightmost monitor is used for UNICAST content, the laptop in the middle is used as the primary workstation.[13]

[13] The monitor on the left is running ACTIVEMAP (McCarthy & Meidel, 1999), a blueprint style map of the workplace with images of people superimposed over the places they – or rather, their infrared badges – were last seen. In this particular office context, ACTIVEMAP is being used primarily as a peripheral display

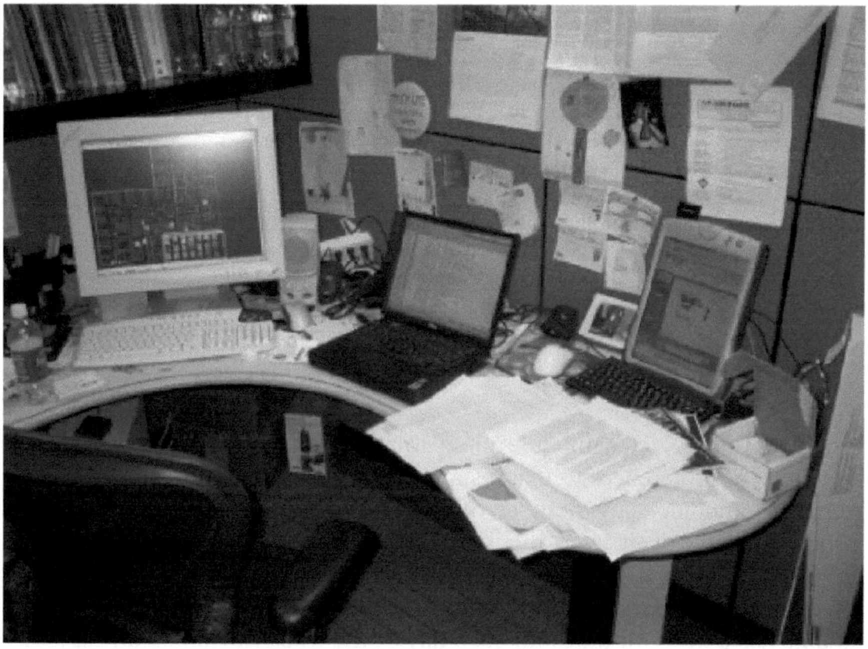

Figure 12-14. An example of UNICAST in context.

3.1 Interest Profiles in UNICAST

The content for UNICAST includes the kinds of information found in many general awareness applications – headlines, weather and stock information – as well as many other more specialized types of content. The current implementation includes user-configurable modules of fifteen different classes, named and briefly described in Table 12-1 (see McCarthy, *et al.*, 2001 for more detailed descriptions).

Table 12-1. UNICAST Modules

Module Name	**Description**
Headlines	273 channels in 16 categories
Stocks	Quotes from Yahoo! Finance
Weather	Forecast for any US zip code
Traffic	Chicagoland Expressway Congestion map
Horoscopes	From Yahoo! Astrology
Web pages	Any URL

Module Name	Description
InfoShare	A local, shared "What's Cool?" repository[14]
Announcements	Title, body & expiration date
Reminders	Regularly scheduled group-wide events
WebCams	Local feeds from workplace webcams
In/Out List	Based on infrared badge system[15]
Factoids	363 factoids across 8 categories
Flashcards	Short questions & answers (w/ delay)
Artwork	1000 images across 10 categories
Pictures	Digital images uploaded by user

3.2 Content Selection in UNICAST

Users first select a module class to install and then add personalized selections or preferences to that instance of the module. For example: for the web page module, any number of URLs can be specified (and different instances of the web page module can have different sets of URLs); for headlines, there is a form with checkboxes for listing news categories; and for weather, the user enters one or more U.S. zip codes. Every instance of a module has a range of times for each day of the week (including an easy way to specify all day and/or every day), and a priority level from 1 (lowest) to 5 (highest).

Each user's modules and preferences are stored in their UNICAST profile (see Figure 12-4). UNICAST randomly cycles through modules in the profile, generating content that is delivered to the user's UNICAST display for a fixed period of time (the default is 15 seconds, but this can be modified by the user) before moving on to the next module. Priorities are implemented using a vector scheme wherein copies of module instances are placed in the vector – one copy for each level of priority (e.g., 5 copies for the highest priority items) – and then vector items are randomly selected for display.

[14] See McCarthy (1998) for more information on this shared repository.

[15] See McCarthy & Meidel (1999) for more information on the badge system (and other associated applications).

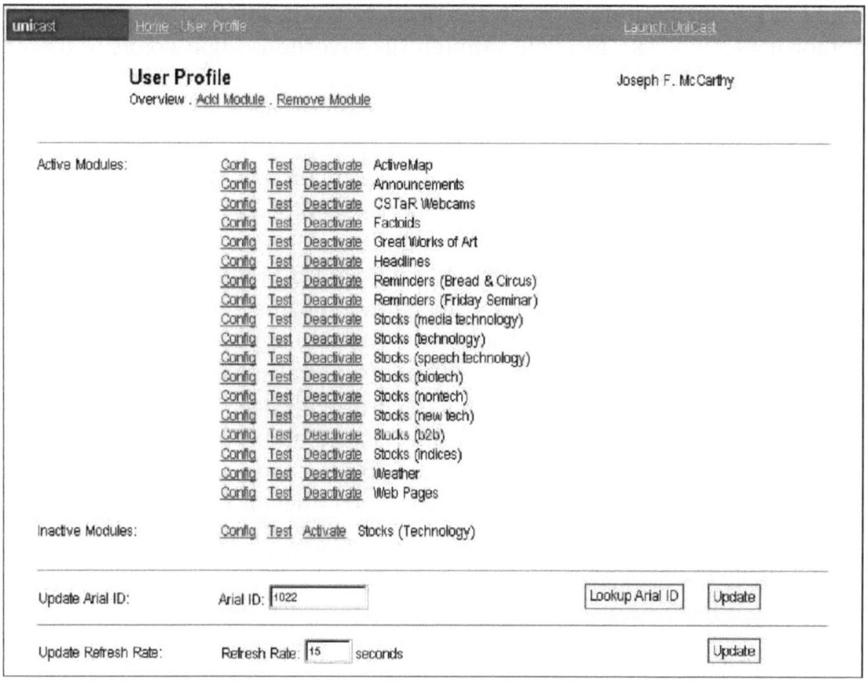

Figure 12-15. Example of a UNICAST profile.

Adding modules and editing module preferences in the UNICAST Profile is done using a web browser, usually on the user's primary workstation (but optionally on the UNICAST display). As the profile is modified, changes are instantly reflected in the content being delivered to the user's UNICAST display. This enables UNICAST content to be displayed all the time on a device other than the user's primary workstation. In addition to increasing UNICAST's usage and utility (initial UNICAST observations indicated that usage and utility was greatly diminished when it was used on a primary workstation), it also provides the ability to maintain the simplicity of the device (eliminate a keyboard and mouse) while providing users with a richer environment when detailed customization is desired.

3.3 *Interacting with UNICAST*

UNICAST is intended to run on a peripheral display rather than the primary workstation display used for supporting a user's primary work tasks. Our belief is that content on a peripheral display should be interesting, but not terribly important or urgent, since important or urgent information is (or could be) sought out directly on the primary workstation. For example, the author uses UNICAST to cycle through his favorite on-line comics (among other types of content) which help to brighten his day, but are rather peripheral to his work, and which he therefore rarely seeks out on his primary workstation.

UNICAST content is viewed on a variety of flat-panel displays we have installed in individual offices throughout our workplace (see Figure 12-5 for an example of a UNICAST display screen). Each UNICAST video display unit is connected to the local network and, although it is intended to mostly be used as a passive display, each unit includes a touch-screen and/or keyboard and mouse. We found that users wanted to be able to pause and occasionally go back to a page displayed on UNICAST (especially pages that had a high density of text). The Java-based interface provides the user with minimal control of the display using a set of finger-sized button controls to *pause* or *resume* the cycling, to go *back* to the most recently displayed page. An additional *send* button to allow users to transfer content from their peripheral displays to a browser on their primary workstations for further exploration is currently under development.

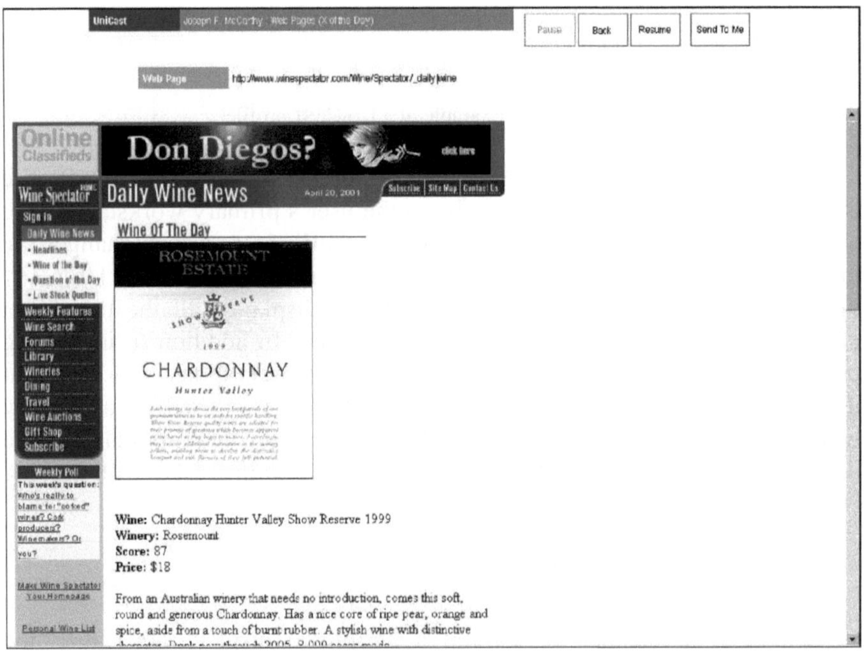

Figure 12-16. An example of UNICAST content.

The behavior of UNICAST is tied into the infrared badge infrastructure in our office environment. By sensing the owner's location, the UNICAST display toggles between two modes: home and away. When the user is in his or her office (*home* mode), UNICAST displays content as described above. When the user leaves his or her office, the UNICAST display switches to an *away* mode that either displays the user's current location in the office (using the infrared badge system) or a message predetermined by the user.

4. OutCast

OUTCAST is another variation on the peripheral display theme. Whereas GROUPCAST is directed toward groups of people in shared spaces, and UNICAST is directed toward an individual user (occupant) within his or her own office space, OUTCAST is directed toward co-workers outside the occupant's individual office space (see Figure 12-6). Rather than display information intended to spark conversation, or that is only of interest to the owner, OUTCAST displays information about the owner that is specifically intended for others to view. In many ways, OUTCAST reflects a behavior that is pervasive throughout the office environment – the posting of articles, cartoons, photographs, and other paraphernalia on office doors. OUTCAST picks up on this behavior and moves it into the electronic realm, enhancing it where possible.

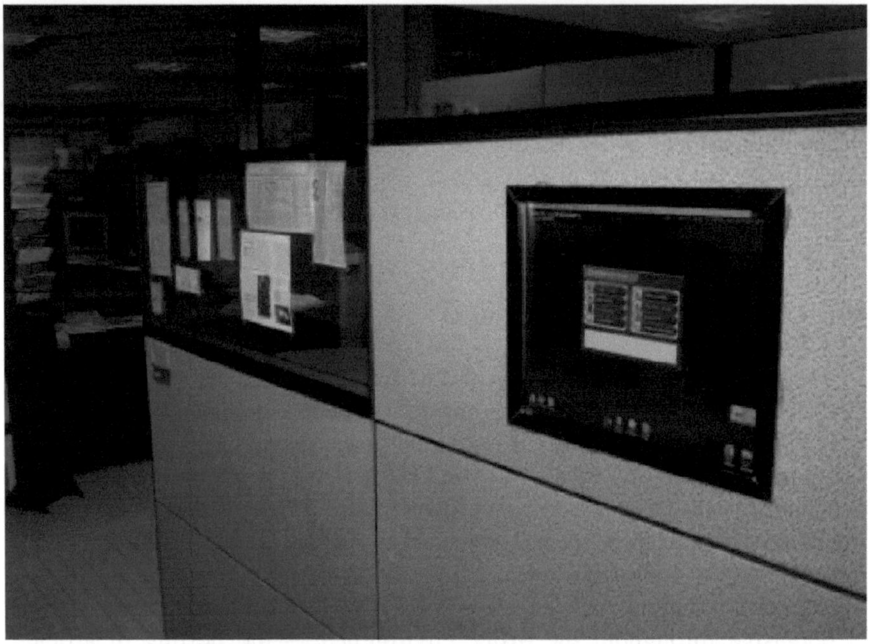

Figure 12-17. An example of OUTCAST in context.

4.1 *Profiles in OUTCAST*

OUTCAST runs in a web browser, and is displayed on an NEC 2010 flat-panel monitor augmented by a MicroTouch touch-screen, embedded in a cubicle wall and connected to a Pentium II computer. Visitors to this office can access any of the types of content shown in Table 12-2 (in which "owner" refers to the occupant of the office).

Table 12-2. OUTCAST Modules

Module Name	Description
Biography	Info from owner's personal web page (see Figure 12-7)
Calendar	Entries from owner's Outlook Calendar (non-private)
Location	Owner's location (based on infrared badge system)
Projects	Brief descriptions of owner's past and current research projects
Demonstrations	Online demonstrations of these projects (where applicable)
Favorites	List of favorite web pages
Text Message	Messages to owner left by visitors

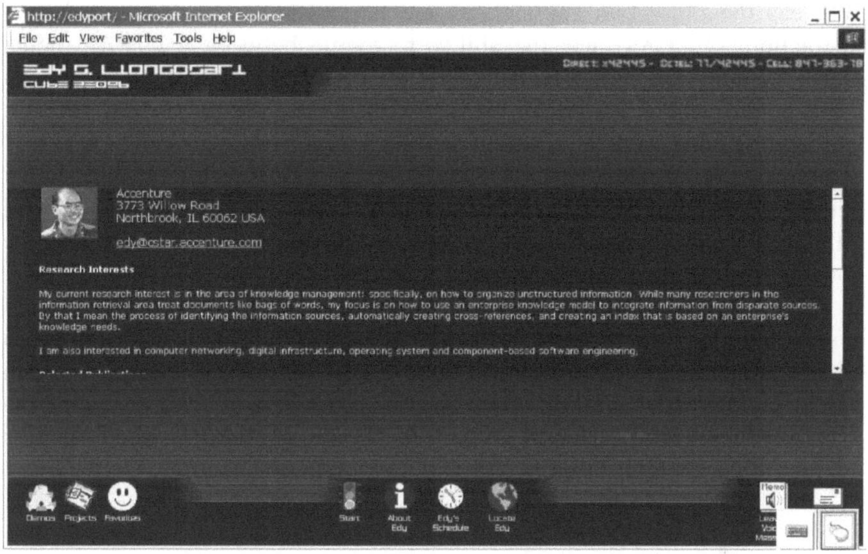

Figure 12-18. An example of OUTCAST content.

One capability in OUTCAST that is not yet incorporated into UNICAST is the ability to tie into existing enterprise applications and database resources. For example, calendar information can be pulled from the centralized calendaring system for the office, and project and biography information can be pulled from their corresponding web pages or databases.

4.2 *Content Selection in OUTCAST*

Content selection in OUTCAST is largely user-driven, where users directly specify the content they want to read – or write (in the case of text messages). However, it can also operate in a more ambient mode, randomly selecting content from a special folder to display. The current version of OUTCAST restricts the ambient content to digital images; in the future, we intend to make the broader collection of UNICAST profile content available for OUTCAST displays, with the capability for occupants to specify which content is appropriate for display on the *outside* of their offices.

4.3 *Interacting with OUTCAST*

Although we consider OUTCAST to be an example of a peripheral display, in that it is not used as a primary workstation, OUTCAST employs a distinctly different interaction paradigm from UNICAST and GROUPCAST.

Whereas the other two applications are largely passive, offering minimal interaction, OUTCAST has the ability to toggle between a *passive* mode, where content randomly cycles much as UNICAST content does, and an *active* mode, where a user can interact with the display to navigate through and explore each module's content or leave a text message for the OUTCAST display owner. While UNICAST and GROUPCAST offer the capabilities for pausing, resuming, going back and jumping forward in the cycle of content, OUTCAST provides much more control to the user to navigate among the content provided through the display.

OUTCAST provides the capability for visitors to leave text messages (via a soft keyboard on the touchscreen). We are exploring ways add video and/or audio capture capabilities to the display – or, rather, the wall – which would enable video and/or audio messages to be left, and to adapt the displayed content to different visitors or classes of visitors, where visitors are identified via their infrared badges.

5. User Experience

GROUPCAST, UNICAST and OUTCAST have been in use – though also under continuous development – for several months. We have collected qualitative and quantitative data about the use of UNICAST from a variety of users; however, due to the small number of installations of OUTCAST and GROUPCAST (one each), we are not yet in a position to provide much data on these applications. The qualitative data presented in this section is based on interviews conducted with four UNICAST users; the quantitative data is based on analysis of the profiles of all eighteen users.

All UNICAST users run the application on a display that is peripheral to their primary workstation display. Most users have a separate computer to run the application, however one runs it on a second monitor attached to a workstation, though that workstation itself is not this user's primary workstation, providing this user with two peripheral displays (the other display is used for two purposes -- a browser window which has the MyYahoo portal and an instance of AOL's Instant Messenger).[16]

Of the fifteen classes of content modules available in UNICAST, the most popular modules among the users we interviewed were the Web Pages

[16] See Grudin (2001) for a more extensive study on the use of multiple monitor ("multimon") usage. We concur with his assertion that there is generally poor software support of such use, particularly among laptop computers. Since most of our colleagues use laptops as their primary workstations, we provide [older] desktop computers & laptops to power the UniCast displays.

modules, allowing people to add any arbitrary web site to the stream of content that cycles through their UNICAST display. Other popular modules cited include Weather, Factoids, WebCams and the infrared badge-based In/Out List. These last two are particularly interesting, since they raise a number of privacy issues among some people. Our group appears to have a high tolerance for [perceived] privacy intrusion, since more than 90% of the group wear their badges regularly, and only one person ever complained about the web cameras (and even that person appears to have grown used to them).

The least popular modules that were cited by interviewees are those for Traffic and Reminders. In the case of the former, we believe that this is due to the fact that several people have commuting patterns not covered by the Chicagoland Expressway Congestion Map. In the case of the latter, we believe this may be due to an ineffective design of the reminders (particularly with respect to the audio component of reminders, which some people find annoying).

We also have some information as to how people are customizing their UNICAST profiles (see Table 12-3). The first column lists the module class name. The second column shows the average number of selections per module class, e.g., the average number of stocks or average number of headline channels a person is monitoring through UNICAST. The third column shows the minimum number of selections per module class and the fourth column shows the maximum number of selections per module class. Note that there may be more than one module instance per class (which is why one person has 13 webcam selections when there are only 11 webcams).

Table 12-3. Numbers of instances and selections of UNICAST modules

Module Name	# of users who created a module instance	Average selections / module	Minimum selections / module	Maximum selections / module
Internal Webcams	18	9.1	1	13
Weather	17	2.4	1	4
Headlines	16	22.2	4	58
Stocks	15	16.4	4	74
Web Pages	13	12.5	2	42
Factoids	12	5.8	4	8
Artwork	12	6.0	2	10
In/Out List	11	13.7	12	16
Announcements	10	3.0	3	3
Horoscopes	8	1.4	1	2
Pictures	8	9.0	3	39
Reminders	8	3.8	2	6
Flashcards	6	25.5	1	50

Module Name	# of users who created a module instance	Average selections / module	Minimum selections / module	Maximum selections / module
Traffic	6	1.0	1	1
InfoShare	5	4.4	1	9

Table 3: Numbers of instances and selections of UNICAST modules

We have also collected some informal feedback from OUTCAST users. Users typically use OUTCAST when the owner (office occupant) is away. The features that people reported liking and using most were the Location Information (to hunt down the owner in real-time, if he is in the office) and Calendar (to identify the next available opening in the owner's schedule). The least liked and used was the Text Message feature, since people were uncertain about the reliability of this function; users still tend to leave text messages using atoms – Post-It® notes – rather than bits (see Cheverst, *et al.*, Chapter 6 this volume) for a more successful deployment of a display that was used for text messages).

6. Future Work

These three applications originated as three separate projects, but as work progresses, it is becoming increasingly apparent that there are many opportunities for sharing content and infrastructure among them. One of our near-term future goals is to come up with a common profile structure for all three applications, with an interface that allows users to easily specify which content is intended for which application (and physical setting).

In UNICAST, we want to continue work on our InfoShare module; it was only recently made available, and we don't have many users who have created instances of the module. We think that increased use of this module can help create a greater sense of community among people in the group (another mechanism for learning about each other's interests, without being physically co-present). We also need to be more diligent about keeping our Announcement information fresh (and well populated – several people have commented that modules with few items get boring quickly).

With GROUPCAST, we'd eventually like to investigate other ways of using the profiles, such as using an intersection of the profiles (returning to the original design) or the set difference between profiles (since that would ensure novelty on at least one person's part). We also want to create multiple installations of GROUPCAST, and have at least one be in a space where there is something that helps attract people and keep them lingering for at least a few seconds (the badges fire every two seconds, and it sometimes takes a few seconds for new content to be displayed). Our current plan is to place a water cooler or coffee maker near one installation. We also want to design an evaluation that would help us assess whether – or how well – GROUPCAST is accomplishing its goal of increasing social capital in the workplace.

OUTCAST is truly an outcast with respect to the other two applications. At present, it shares no content or infrastructure with the other two. In addition to including UNICAST and GROUPCAST content on OUTCAST displays – e.g., to provide content for the screensaver, or list of Favorites – we'd like to be able to incorporate some of the infrastructure from OUTCAST in the others. For example, with access to an enterprise-wide calendar system, we might identify commonalities with respect to locations people have traveled, or will be traveling, to, and use that to bring up travel-related pages when people pass by a GROUPCAST display ... for example, showing a map of Napa Valley vineyards when Joe and Teresa next pass each other.

7. Discussion

Our experience with GROUPCAST, as well as the other peripheral display applications, highlights issues that need to be addressed by any public display that is intended to sense and respond to the people and activities taking place nearby (we might call these *proactive* public displays (Tennenhouse, 2000). These issues include the identification of people (or objects) in the vicinity of the display, the acquisition & maintenance of profiles about people, selecting appropriate content and designing useful interaction models.

7.1 Identifying People or Objects Nearby

Public displays need not identify, nor respond to, the people or objects in their vicinity to be useful, but knowing something about whom or what is nearby provides the potential to enrich the experience with such displays. We have had the luxury of an infrared badge system for the installations described here, but other technologies for identification can be used. Other identification devices and technologies that have been utilized in other research prototypes include radio frequency identification (RFID) tags (Russell & Gossweiler, 2001), RF "beacons" (Carter, *et al.*, 2002), iButtons (Cheverst, *et al.*, Chapter 6 this volume) and Personal Servers (small, mobile devices with BlueTooth communication capabilities, (Pering, *et al.*, Chapter 14 this volume).

A recent example of a public, proactive display is the E-Board, an electronic billboard (Alaris Media Network, Inc.), coupled with the MobilTrak system, which scans the radio stations to which passing cars are tuned, and selects advertisements based on the demographics inferred from those radio stations (Barrows, 2002). Future proactive display applications may be able to tailor content based on the ability to identify clothing that nearby people are wearing, using radio RFID tags embedded in the garments (Chai & Shim, 2003), though early public reactions reveal the need to ensure that privacy concerns are effectively addressed before such applications can be successfully deployed.

7.2 Acquiring Profiles

Detecting or identifying people or objects nearby is the first step, but a proactive public display also needs to know something about them. People often do seem to enjoy revealing certain things about themselves, as can be seen in the variety of content that appears on people's t-shirts, jackets, hats and skin (tattoos), not to mention the cars they drive or the books, CDs and artwork they display in their homes.

However, as we move from the physical toward the digital world, the issue of acquiring profile information – in a way that does not alarm people – becomes more challenging. Although we do see examples of people revealing information about themselves in the digital realm – email signatures, personal web pages and web logs ("blogs") all represent profile information that is often widely accessible – this information is not typically readily available in the physical world, especially not in the proximity of the people who authored the information.

In the present context, it is not clear how much people want to reveal about themselves on a public display, especially outside of a restricted context such as a workplace or campus. Our approach has been to collect and use explicitly specified profile information, an approach shared by other prototypes such as BlueBoard (Russell & Gossweiller, 2001) and MERLBoard (Chen, *et al.*, 2002) but one can imagine a multitude of possible sources of such information that might be collected in the background, e.g., electronic music playlists or electronic auction or purchase histories.

Other sources of profiles that have been tapped for use with public displays include internal web pages and/or a history of postings (Churchill, *et al.*, 2003; Snowdon & Grasso, 2002), and a history of requests for information (Mynatt, *et al.*, Chapter 4 this volume).

7.3 Selecting Content to Display

If something is known about the people and objects near a display, the next challenge is to determine what kind of content may be of interest to those people (for the moment, we'll ignore the issue of how to interest shoes and handbags). It should be noted that, unlike the previous two issues we considered, this one is of more general applicability, in that any electronic display that is situated in a public place needs to select from a variety of content (if content appropriate to the place is relatively static, a paper poster is a much more cost-effective solution).

Content for potential selection might include news (Black, *et al.*, Chapter 15 this volume), electronic post-its (Cheverst, *et al.*, Chapter 6 this volume), web pages (Russell & Gossweiller, 2001) or information that is specifically about activities in the place occupied by the display (O'Hara & Perry, Chapter 5 this volume). Dynamic sources of content are particularly important for public displays that are situated in places that are frequented by the same group of people, so as not to be ignored by passersby.

7.4 Designing the Interaction Model

The final issue to be raised here is what kind of interaction – if any – should be supported by the public display. There was no interaction supported by the original GROUPCAST, but as we added new modules of content, we found that people wanted to bring content "home" to their UNICAST profiles (see Huang, *et al.*, 2002), and have other basic kinds of interaction (e.g., pause, resume) – interactions supported by other systems as well (Russell & Gossweiller, 2001; Black, *et al.*, Chapter 15 this volume; Churchill, *et al.*, 2003). As was mentioned earlier, there is a peripherality continuum on which many public display applications occupy variable positions: an application may start off as being highly peripheral – barely noticed – but move between the background and foreground of users' attention as content on the display and other elements in the physical context change over time.

Other kinds of interaction supported by other systems include sketching (Chen, *et al.*, 2002), moving content around on the display (Chen, *et al.*, 2002; Churchill, *et al.*, 2003) and even commandeering the display (Black, *et al.*, Chapter 15 this volume; Pering, *et al.*, Chapter 14 this volume). Technologies and techniques such as gesture recognition, eye gaze detection and speech recognition may expand the modes of interaction that can be supported by future interactive public displays.

8. Conclusion

We have created three applications that explore the use of peripheral displays in three contexts: within an individual office (UNICAST), outside an individual office (OUTCAST) and in a group setting (GROUPCAST). We believe that proactive public displays, most clearly exemplified by GROUPCAST, have tremendous potential for creating greater awareness and a stronger sense of community among people in the neighborhood of such displays.

Although we are still far from a truly ubiquitous deployment of peripheral displays, we hope that others can learn from our experience and be more inclined to experiment with their own peripheral displays in these, and other, contexts.

Acknowledgements

The author wishes to thank: Tony Costa, for his contributions to the GROUPCAST & UNICAST applications; Edy Liongosari, for contributions to the OUTCAST application; Elaine Huang and Joe Tullio, for their contributions of the Awareness Module; Jeremy Goecks, for his contribution to an earlier version of the GROUPCAST application; Ted Anagnost and Eric Meidel, for their contributions to the ACTIVEMAP and EVENTMANAGER applications (which provide content for the peripheral displays); Barry Brown, for directing me to Sacks' articulation of "tickets" to talk; Eric Paulos, for directing me to Milgram's concept of "familiar strangers"; and Elizabeth Churchill and Kenton O'Hara for their support and encouragement in writing this chapter.

References

Barrows, Matthew. The Signs have Ears: Two Billboards will Scan Car Radios and Tailor Pitches to Match Listening Preferences. Sacramento Bee, 2002, November 24,.

Carter, Scott, Mankoff, J and Goddi, P. 2002. Representing and Supporting Action on Buried Relationships in Smart Environments. In Workshop on Public, Community and Situated Displays, CSCW '02 Conference on Computer Supported Cooperative Work 2002, New Orleans, LO, USA.

Chai, Winston, and Shim, R. Benetton Takes Stock of Chip Plan. CNET (news.com), April 7, 2003.

Churchill, Elizabeth F., Les Nelson and Laurent Denoue. Multimedia Fliers: Information Sharing with Digital Community Bulletin Boards. To appear in Proceedings of the

International Conference on Communities and Technologies; 2003; Amsterdam, The Netherlands.

Deutsch, Claudia H. Commercial Property; Communication in the Workplace; Companies Using Coffee Bars to Get Ideas Brewing. The New York Times, 5 November 1995.

Franklin, Michael, and Stan Zdonik. Data in your Face: Push Technology in Perspective. In Proceedings of SIGMOD '98 Conference on Management of Data; 1998; Seattle, WA, USA: 516-519.

Greenberg, Saul, and Michael Rounding. 2001. The Notification Collage: Posting Information to Public and Personal Displays. In Proceedings of CHI '01 Conference on Human Factors in Computer Systems; 2001; Seattle, WA, USA: 514-521.

Grudin, Jonathan. 2001. Partitioning Digital Worlds: Focal and Peripheral Awareness in Multiple Monitor Use. In Proceedings of CHI '01 Conference on Human Factors in Computer Systems; 2001; Seattle, WA, USA: 458-465.

François Guimbretière, Maureen Stone and Terry Winograd. 2001. Off the Wall: Fluid Interaction with High-Resolution Wall-Size Displays. In Proceedings of UIST' 01, 14th ACM Symposium on User Interface Software and Technology; 2001; Orlando, Fl, USA: 21-30.

Harper, Richard H. R. Looking at Ourselves: An Examination of the Social Organisation of Two Research Laboratories. In Proceedings of CSCW '92 Conference on Computer Supported Cooperative; 1992, Toronto, Canada: 330-337.

Huang, Elaine M., Joe Tullio, Tony J. Costa and Joseph F. McCarthy. Promoting Awareness of Work Activities through Peripheral Displays. In Extended Abstracts of CHI '02 Conference on Human Factors in Computer Systems; 2002; Minneapolis, Minnesota USA: 648-649.

Mankoff, Jennifer, Anind K. Dey, Gary Hsieh, Julie Kientz, Scott Lederer and Morgan Ames. Heurstic Evaluation of Ambient Displays. In Proceedings of CHI '03 Conference on Human Factors in Computer Systems; 2003; Ft Lauderdale, Fl, USA: 169-176.

McCarthy, Joseph F. InfoShare: A System to Support Co-operative Information Seeking in a Real Community of Users. In the Workshop on Collaborative and Cooperative Information Seeking in Digital Information Environments at CSCW '98 Conference on Computer Supported Cooperative Work; 1998; Seattle, WA, USA.

McCarthy, Joseph F., and Theodore D. Anagnost. MusicFX: An Arbiter of Group Preferences for Computer Supported Collaborative Workouts. In Proceedings of CSCW '98 Conference on Computer Supported Cooperative Work; 1998; Seattle, WA, USA: 363-372.

McCarthy, Joseph F., and Theodore D. Anagnost. EventManager: Support for the Peripheral Awareness of Events In Proceedings of HUC '00, 2nd International Symposium on Handheld and Ubiquitous Computing; 2000; Bristol, UK: 227-235.

McCarthy, Joseph F., Tony J. Costa and Edy S. Liongosari.. UNICAST, OUTCAST & GROUPCAST: Three Steps toward Ubiquitous Peripheral Displays. In Proceedings of UbiComp '01 Conference on Ubiquitous Computing; 2001; Atlanta, GA, USA:332-345.

McCarthy, Joseph F., and Eric S. Meidel. 1999. ActiveMap: A Visualization Tool for Location Awareness to Support Informal Interactions. In Proceedings of HUC '99, 1st International Symposium on Handheld and Ubiquitous Computing; 1999; Karlsruhe, Germany: 158-170.

Milgram, Stanley, Sabini, J. and Silver, M. *The Individual in a Social World: Essays and Experiments*. New York: McGraw Hill, 1992.

Naylor, Thomas H., William H. Willimon and Rolf Österberg. The Search for Community in the Workplace. Business and Society Review, 1996; 97:42-47.

Nguyen, David H., and Elizabeth D. Mynatt. Privacy Mirrors: Understanding and Shaping Socio-technical Ubiquitous Computing Systems. Atlanta, GA: Georgia Institute of Technology Technical Report, 2002 (GIT-GVU-02-16).

O'Hara, Kenton, and Barry Brown. 2001. Designing CSCW Technologies to Support Tacit Knowledge Sharing Through Conversation Initiation. Workshop on Managing Tacit Knowledge at ECSCW '01 European Conference on Computer Supported Cooperative Work, Bonn, Germany.

Putnam, Robert. *Bowling Alone: The Collapse and Revival of American Community*. New York: Simon & Schuster, 2000

Redström, Johan, Peter Ljungstrand and Patricija Jaksetic. The ChatterBox: Using Text Manipulation in an Entertaining Information Display. In Proceedings of Graphics Interface '00; 2000; Montréal, Canada.

Russell, Daniel M., and Rich Gossweiler. On the Design of Large Communal and Personal Displays. In . In Proceedings of UbiComp '01 Conference on Ubiquitous Computing; 2001; Atlanta, GA, USA.

Sacks, Harvey. *Lectures on Conversation*. Oxford: Basil Blackwell, 1992.

Sawhney, Nitin, Sean Wheeler and Chris Schmandt. Aware Community Portals: Shared Information Appliances for Transitional Spaces. In Journal of Personal and Ubiquitous Computing, 2001; 5(1): 66-70.

Shen, Chia, Neal B. Lesh, Frederic Vernier, Clifton Forlines and Jeana Frost. Sharing and Building Digital Group Histories. In Proceedings of CSCW '02 Conference on Computer Supported Cooperative Work; 2002; New Orleans, LO, USA: 324 - 333.

Snowdon, Dave, and Antonietta Grasso. Diffusing Information in Organizational Settings: Learning from Experience. In Proceedings of CHI '02 Conference on Human Factors in Computer Systems; 2002; Minneapolis, Minnesota USA: 331-338.

Streitz, Norbert A., Jörg Geißler, Torsten Holmer, Shin'ichi Konomi, Christian Müller-Tomfelde, Wolfgang Reischl, Petra Rexroth, Peter Seitz and Ralf Steinmetz. i-LAND: An Interactive Landscape for Creativity and Innovation. In Proceedings of CHI '99 Conference on Human Factors in Computer Systems; 1999; Pittsburgh, PA, USA: 120-127.

Tennenhouse, David. Proactive Computing. In Communications of the ACM, 2000; 43(5): 43-50.

Weiser, Mark, and John Seely Brown. 1997. "The Coming Age of Calm Technology". In *Beyond Calculation: The Next Fifty Years of Computing*, Denning, P.J. & Metcalfe, R.M., eds. New York: Springer-Verlag, 1997.

Wisneski, Craig, Hiroshi Ishii, Andrew Dahley, Matt Gorbet, Scott Brave, Brygg Ulmer and Paul Yarin. Ambient Displays: Turning Architectural Space into an Interface between People and Information. In Proceedings of CoBuild '98, 1st International Workshop on Cooperative Buildings; 1998; Darmstadt, Germany: 22-32.

Zhao, Qiang Alex, and John T. Stasko. What's Happening? The Community Awareness Application. In Extended Abstracts of CHI '00 Conference on Human Factors in Computer Systems; 2000; The Hague, The Netherlands: 253-254.

Chapter 13

DESIGNING DISPLAYS FOR HUMAN CONNECTEDNESS

Stefan Agamanolis
Media Lab Europe

Abstract: How can we design displays that foster a sense of presence and awareness... that enhance a sense of community and togetherness... that enable human bonds to grow and flourish? Using five prototypes from the Human Connectedness research group at Media Lab Europe as a context for reflection, this chapter attempts to assemble a framework of questions and strategies for designers to consider when working to achieve these kinds of effects. The prototypes discussed include a media space that connects several physical locations in our organization, a video conference system based on the metaphor of a magic mirror, a video installation that displays layers of recorded social interaction, an ambient display for hospital patients in isolation wards, and a "sports over a distance" application with an "exertion" interface.

Key words: displays, presence, awareness, community, togetherness, connectedness, design principles

1. Introduction

Although not the only means of interfacing with digital information, bit-mapped visual displays are certainly one of the most common. Advances in display technology have enabled them to take an increasingly wider variety of forms that depart from that of a general-purpose computer monitor sitting on a desk in an office behind a keyboard and mouse. Displays of radically different shapes and sizes can now be embedded in or projected onto unexpected surfaces in unexpected places, and they can incorporate a variety of new sensing technologies that enable new kinds of interaction. Many of the chapters in this book illustrate the advantages of *situating* displays in particular kinds of configurations and in particular kinds of spaces that might

K. O'Hara et al. (eds.), Public and Situated Displays: Social and Interactional Aspects of Shared Display Technologies, 309–334.

be more appropriate for supporting certain applications, especially those that are focused on background communication or that work to foster enhanced awareness or a sense of community among different groups of people.

What constitutes a good or bad design choice with respect to these kinds of displays? What questions should we be asking during their development? What general rules or guidelines are we operating with, if any? Can these be articulated so they might inform future efforts?

Some insight into these issues is being gained in the Human Connectedness group at Media Lab Europe. This chapter is an attempt to distill some broader design principles that are noticeable across several of the group's endeavors (as well as others in related research programs, past and present). I begin with a short background of the group itself and follow with descriptions of five of our most display-centered prototypes. Using these as a context, I then present an evolving list of design "nuggets" that appear to run across these projects and that could be useful in guiding future undertakings.

2. The Human Connectedness Group

In addition to other basic requirements, humans have a biological need for contact with other humans. Our interactions and relationships with other people form a network that supports us, makes our lives meaningful, and ultimately enables us to survive. Authors like Lewis, Amini, and Lannon (2000) describe in detail the critical regulating effects that social contact and healthy relationships have on human mental and physical well-being, as well as the sometimes devastating consequences that arise from a lack of these necessities. House, Landis, and Umberson (1988) discuss developments that suggest that a lack of social relationships constitutes a risk factor for health that rivals that of other well-established factors such as cigarette smoking, obesity, and lack of physical activity.

A variety of factors threaten our ability to form and attain balance in the kinds of relationships that we want and need to have with others. In addition to unavoidable personal factors, such the need to travel or live in a different place apart from family and friends in order to fulfill work responsibilities, trends that exist at a societal level also have an impact. Putnam (2000) describes how people in American society increasingly lack social interactions, and how this loss of social interconnectedness jeopardizes health on both a physical and civic level. A study undertaken by Carnegie Mellon University suggests the use of computers and the Internet may contribute to social isolation and individual stress levels (Kraut *et al.*, 2002).

The Human Connectedness research group explores the topic of human relationships and how they are mediated by technology, with the ultimate mission of conceiving a new genre of technologies and experiences that combat the effects mentioned above and allow us to build, maintain, and enhance human relationships in new ways. It also aims to enable new kinds of individual bonds and communities that were not possible before but may be beneficial or fun.

Beyond imagining new forms of social interaction, the group explores how new technologies change the way people can *be related* to each other—in the same way that, for example, we feel *related* to people in our families, *attached* to things that are important to us, or *bonded* to friends and loved ones. Some other key research questions for the group as a whole are: How can we convey a sense of presence and togetherness over space and time? How can we promote and support collaboration between different groups of people? How can we achieve greater balance in our relationships with others? How can we share a sense of intimacy and closeness in new ways? How can we enable new forms of cultural exchange?

The group aims to build a technological framework for applications in this domain, taking advantage of the infinite bandwidth and processing-rich computing environments of the future and the opportunity to extend these networked media environments into our physical and architectural surroundings. It is equally interested in forming a design framework that includes an understanding of sociological and psychological factors to help shape these systems in a fashion that reflects the needs and sensibilities of the groups within which they operate.

The group gains inspiration for the development of its prototypes from a variety of channels that include the results of scientific studies, observations of people and how they interact, ongoing dialogues with potential users of new technologies, as well as personal experience in relationships. While we want to project ourselves into the future to the greatest extent possible in imagining new technologies, we place emphasis on building working prototypes, the use of which we can study and learn from.

3. Survey of Projects

The following sections present descriptions of five different research projects underway in the Human Connectedness research group, each of which consists of a significant display component. These projects range in development from an early prototype stage to having undergone a formal evaluation. The purpose of these brief descriptions is to provide a context for a discussion later in the chapter concerning general design strategies for display-based applications in this domain. Additional details and background may be found in the accompanying references.

In addition to these five projects from our laboratory, there are many projects in other organizations that have explored or are exploring different angles on the general theme of forming and sustaining human relationships that the reader may wish to follow up on, such as the interLiving project and their work with "technology probes" for inspiring design for families (Hutchinson *et al.*, 2003), the Digital Family Portraits project at Georgia Tech for supporting cross-generation interaction and awareness (Mynatt, 2001) and the Casablanca work on media space designs for home environments (Hindus *et al.*, 2001). Additional related work is cited in the sections below.

3.1 iCom

A media space, a notion pioneered at Xerox PARC in the late 1980s, could be described as an electronic media environment that supports a shared activity between people who may be physically or temporally distant from each other. The classic PARC media space connected several offices and common areas in multiple geographic settings via audio and video links, enabling awareness, chance encounters, group meetings, and other kinds of functionality (Bly *et al.*, 1993). Many others since then have explored different aspects of the concept of media space. The RAVE system investigated different levels of engagement as well as issues of access and privacy (Mackay, 1999). The Portholes project specifically delved into the topic of awareness [7]. Some, such as Montage (Tang and Rua, 1994) and Piazza (Isaacs *et al.*, 1996) with their "glancing" mechanism, particularly explored the notion of reciprocity.

Building on this past research, iCom explores ways of integrating awareness, conferencing, and community messaging functionalities into a situated architectural media installation. The prototype, which has provided a continuous link between several workspaces at the MIT Media Lab and Media Lab Europe for over two years, has provided a platform for exploring notions of foreground and background and their impact on fostering a sense of presence and community between distributed work colleagues and friends.

The development of iCom was motivated by a desire to maintain a basic sense of awareness and cohesiveness between people at the newly established Media Lab Europe and its parent MIT Media Lab. We wanted some kind of system that would convey an ongoing impression that we were all working together as part of a larger whole, that we were working in one large laboratory and not two different ones separated by thousands of miles.

Bridging physical distance between different areas of just one of the labs was also a part of our thinking. From a foreground communication perspective, we were interested in making ad-hoc meetings between researchers at these two organizations as easy as possible to accomplish, but more importantly we wished to build some kind of electronic venue that would motivate the activity of "hanging out" with people from the other locations, something we felt was not particularly well supported by other communication media.

At each iCom location (of which there are currently 4) there is a large-screen projection and seating area integrated within a larger work space such that the screen is visible from as much of the room as possible (see Figures 13-1 & 13-2). The characteristics of each connected space are similar and the inhabitants of these spaces generally know each other. We tried to design these locations to motivate their use as informal socializing areas, places to take a break and maybe chat with others. Specifically, a sofa and coffee table are placed in front of the screen, and other elements, such as an oriental rug at one location, serve as markers of the station and give it an aesthetic identity different from that of a dedicated work area.

The screen displays several streams of video from each location as well as the subject lines from recent messages and announcements sent via email to community bulletin boards at both laboratories (see Figure 13-3). Listed in chronological order, these subject lines are varied in size based on how old the message is and how many times it has been selected recently. There are two cameras at each station, one mounted above the screen with a view of the surrounding work area, and the other situated on the coffee table. A trackball enables people at the station to rearrange the windows, read the messages, or enable audio connections for meetings or casual interaction with the remote sites. The system addresses some potential privacy issues by synchronizing the screen projections at each site. What you see on the screen is what the other sites see on their screens, and nothing is recorded or displayed in other venues or on the Web. The system is turned on 24 hours a day, which makes it similar to such systems like the Bellcore VideoWindow (Hill and Hollan, 1992), and other more recent experiments, such as that at Microsoft Research (Jancke *et al.*, 2001), which both emphasized connecting public or semi-public spaces in an always-on fashion.

In addition to being a long running example of an Internet-based multi-point media space, iCom experiments with the addition of a community message tracking element as well as connectionless peer-to-peer networking strategies to achieve low latency and enhance stability in congested or problematic network environments. The system conserves bandwidth by reducing frame rates where no activity is detected and by adjusting transmitted resolution to reflect the size of each video window.

It is difficult evaluate whether iCom has been successful in its overall goal of enhancing a sense of community between the connected locations, mainly because there is no way to know how the culture may have developed in the absence of it. Our strategy for studying it thus far has included keeping a written record of observed behaviours, collecting personal accounts from those in contact with the system for various lengths of time, and distributing questionnaires requesting feedback of various sorts. Beyond the types of activities supported in earlier media space experiments, there are some other behaviours we have noticed that may be worth reporting. For one, persons on travel from one lab to the other appear to be drawn to the iCom to a greater extent and spend more time near it than others normally do, at least initially. One such person commented that it made her feel like she wasn't "so far away" from home. A certain amount of flirting between remotely-located persons has been noted as well, the extent of which seems intuitively greater than what might have happened if these persons were collocated, leading us to wonder if perhaps some aspect of the interface or the distance involved made this kind of activity somehow easier to engage in or "safer" than it would have been in person.

In addition, over the course of the project thus far we have engaged in a couple of "tea party" events synchronized between both laboratories to offer an opportunity for new members of either community to get acquainted with each other, with the specific goal of taking early steps to minimize the occasionally-reported discomfort of not knowing who is at the other end possibly peering into one's space. But we have also noticed that many who use the iCom regularly to keep in touch with friends will, on their own, introduce those friends to new researchers inside their own site or others who are standing or passing nearby, which suggests there might be a quorum of regular users with established remote relationships that would support the formation of new acquaintances and a reduction in discomfort in a more organic way.

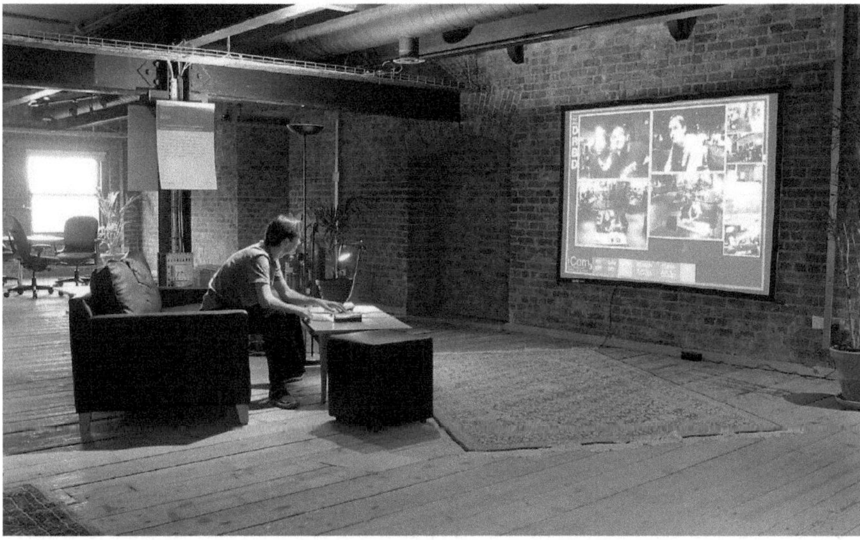

Figure 13-1. An iCom station at Media Lab Europe.

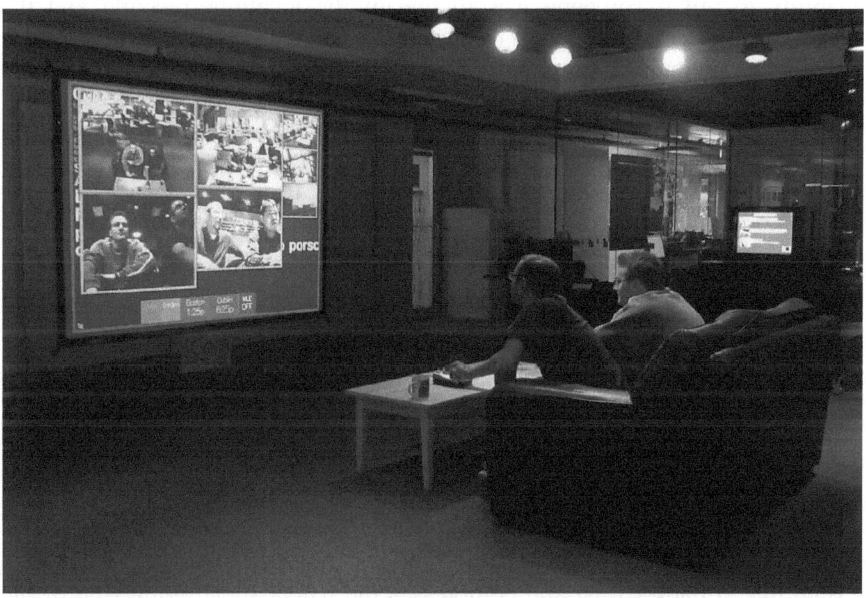

Figure 13-2. An iCom station at the MIT Media Lab.

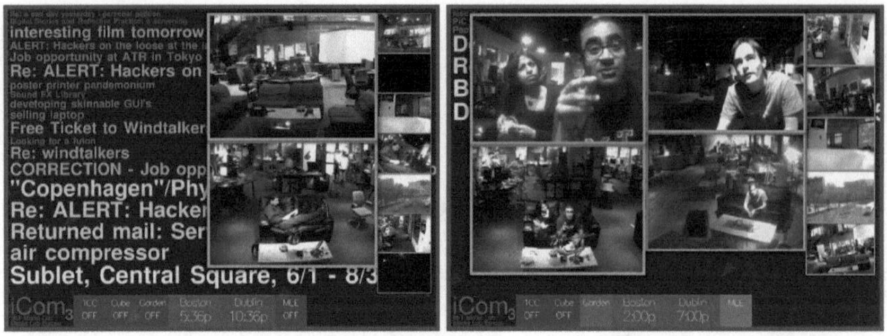

Figure 13-3. Screen shots of iCom showing it in a background state and in use for a live meeting between Media Lab Europe in Dublin and the MIT Media Lab in Boston

3.2 Palimpsest

In contrast to the iCom, which aims to facilitate chance encounters between people at different points in space, Palimpsest tries to enable chance encounters between people at different points in *time*. The project is partly motivated by some shortcomings of iCom in the time domain, such as the inability to tell if someone was in one of the locations recently and the difficulty in conveying a sense of community between locations in different time zones without some kind of recording functionality, around which privacy concerns often arise.

In a manner similar to a real palimpsest (a manuscript consisting of a later writing superimposed upon an original writing), our Palimpsest superimposes layers of recorded video activity and presents them as a single visual as a way of expressing the recent social history of a place. The installation consists of a rear-projection screen and camera aimed across an interaction area, which could be a hallway or passage inside a building, or a special area dedicated to the project. Images of passers-by or participants are extracted from the background and layered into a video loop that repeats itself every few seconds.

Because the video is looped, if passers-by linger in the space, they will see a delayed copy of themselves entering the space from several seconds ago, and even more layers if they remain longer, together with the layers generated by other passers-by from earlier points in time. These layers accrue on the screen over several minutes, hours, even days, creating a visual that collapses time and compresses the recent social goings-on of the given space, allowing the viewer to witness the human crowd that has intersected with it. Even if totally alone in a seemingly quiet and empty space, a passer-by is able to "transcend time" and become a part of this community and to interact with its members, including possibly oneself (see Figures 13-4 & 13-5).

Experience thus far with Palimpsest has included leaving it running for long periods of time in a dedicated space in our laboratory and showing it at a local digital film and art festival. Both resulted in much feedback, including suggestions to vary the loop duration, make the layers fade over a certain interval of time, and to add sound capability. In both instances the installation was arranged so that people could clearly walk around it if they did not wish to be captured. At least one person at the film festival, once he figured out what the system was doing, used it to leave a visual message for someone who he expected to arrive later. On a few occasions passers-by made obscene gestures, and interestingly, after realizing their gestures were repeating themselves in a loop, some of these perpetrators returned to conceal their gestures, while others seemed to gain great enjoyment from trying to fill the screen with as many looping obscene gestures as possible. This playfulness aside, several people became interested in using the Palimpsest for a new form of theater in which a single actor could play all the parts of a short play asynchronously, layering in each performance after the last. This idea sparked a new research project at our lab.

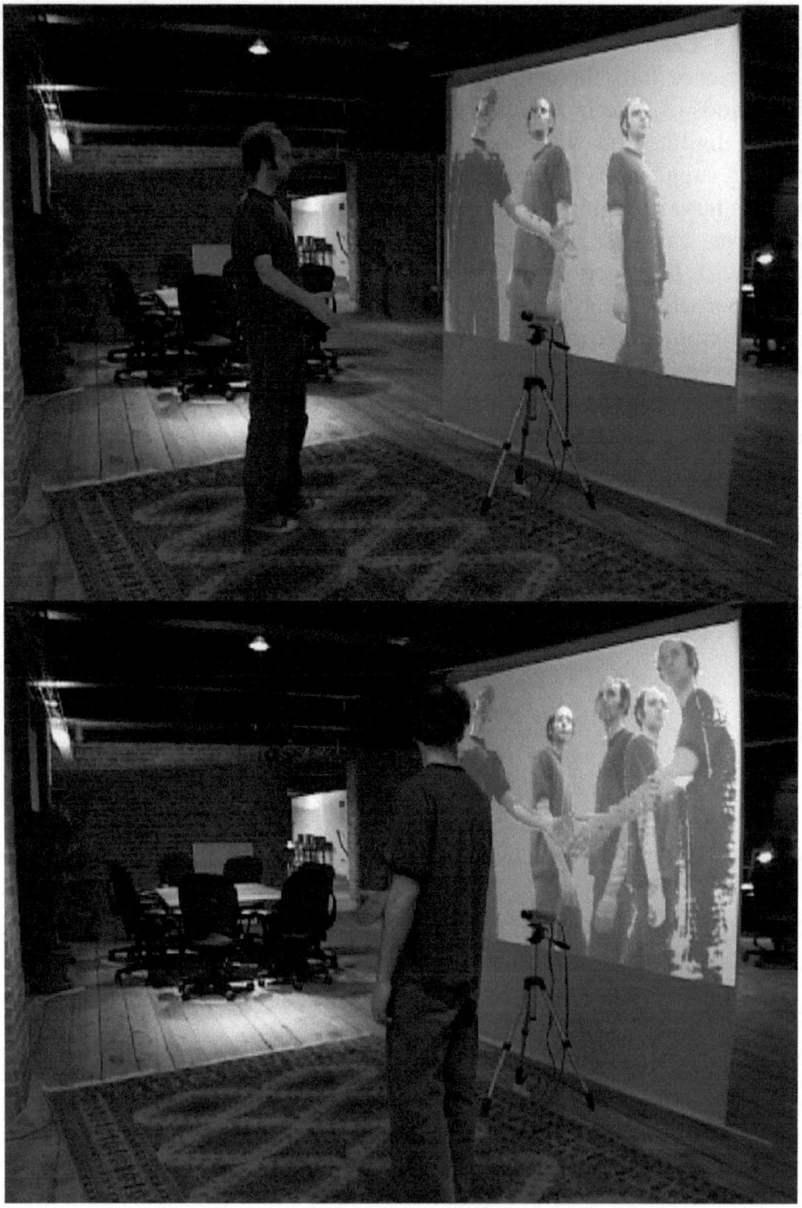

Figure 13-4. A passer-by interacts with himself from an earlier point in time in the Palimpsest space at our lab.

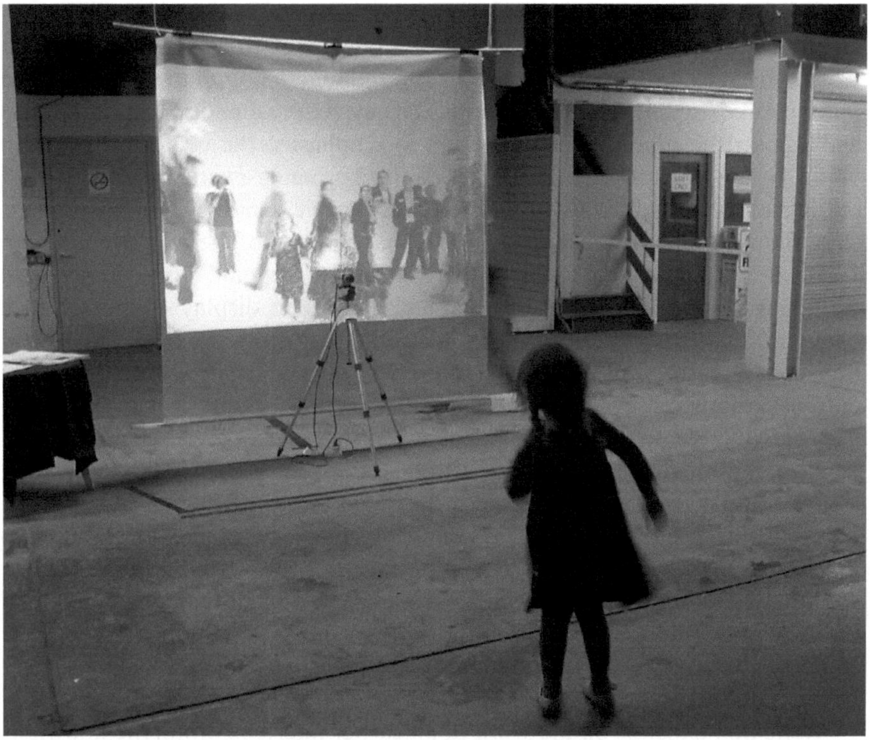

Figure 13-5. A girl dances with delayed copies of herself (and other earlier passers-by) in a public installation of Palimpsest.

3.3 Reflexion

Traditional multi-party video conferencing systems often display participants in separate screens or windows, sometimes using a grid pattern reminiscent of the title sequence of the classic American TV show *The Brady Bunch*. We think the visual separation characteristic of these multi-window designs may introduce a confrontational or divisional dynamic that can have a negative impact on a meeting or interaction even before it begins. In the absence of a multi-window design, some systems employ audio-based camera selection algorithms to switch between views of the active participants. We believe this approach can result in an even greater sense of separation since individual users do not appear on the screen together, and it also limits awareness of the inactive participants.

Reflexion is a multi-point interpersonal communication system that broadly aims to address these issues and create a more intimate dynamic that fosters an enriched sense of togetherness between its users. The system employs an interface design based on the metaphor of a "magic mirror" in which you see a reflection of yourself layered together with the reflections of other participants in remote locations. The system responds to auditory cues and adjusts the graphical composition to emphasize the center of attention while trying to preserve a sense of background awareness among all participants (see Figure 13-6). Participants can view and discuss documents, slide shows, or movies that appear in the background of the mirror.

Each participant, of which there may be several, uses a separate Reflexion station consisting of a camera and video display connected to a computer that extracts an image of the participant from the background and transmits a mirror image of it to the other stations (see Figure 13-7). The current prototype uses a peer-to-peer multicast networking strategy for audio and video transmission to help achieve lower latency. A central server handles control messages that synchronize the screen compositions at each station so that each participant sees the same thing. Active participants, as judged from audio levels, are rendered opaque and in the foreground to emphasize their visual presence while other less-active participants appear slightly faded in the background in a manner that attempts to maintain awareness of their state without drawing undue attention. The system smoothly transitions the layering and appearance of the participants as their interactions continue.

Reflexion expands on the work of an earlier interface prototype known as Reflection of Presence (Agamanolis *et al.*, 1997). Some references to other key related work include: an early system for "voice voting" to determine camera views in a video conference (Edson *et al.*, 1971), the Clearboard system for shared drawing and interpersonal spaces (Ishii *et al.*, 1994), and the HyperMirror system which has experimented with blue screen technology to layer one participant into a scene consisting of another (Morikawa and Maesako, 1998).

Our experience with Reflexion thus far consists mainly of testing it on ourselves and exhibiting it for visitors of our laboratory. A number of first-time users report that seeing themselves on the screen is distracting, and some report becoming overly obsessed with their appearance. However, these effects appear to diminish with continued use. On the other hand, some report liking this feature because of the increased awareness and peace of mind it provides about how one is being portrayed to the remote participants, an awareness that isn't necessarily possible in a regular face-to-face encounter. Some participants also feel it is difficult to use their fingers to point to things in the backdrop because, rather than point to something directly on the screen surface, it is necessary to maneuver a finger in mid-air while watching its reflection in the image to make it point to something in the virtual backdrop. A formal study is planned to compare the effects of Reflexion against more traditional conferencing interfaces for supporting various kinds of activities ranging from focused work tasks to informal social interaction.

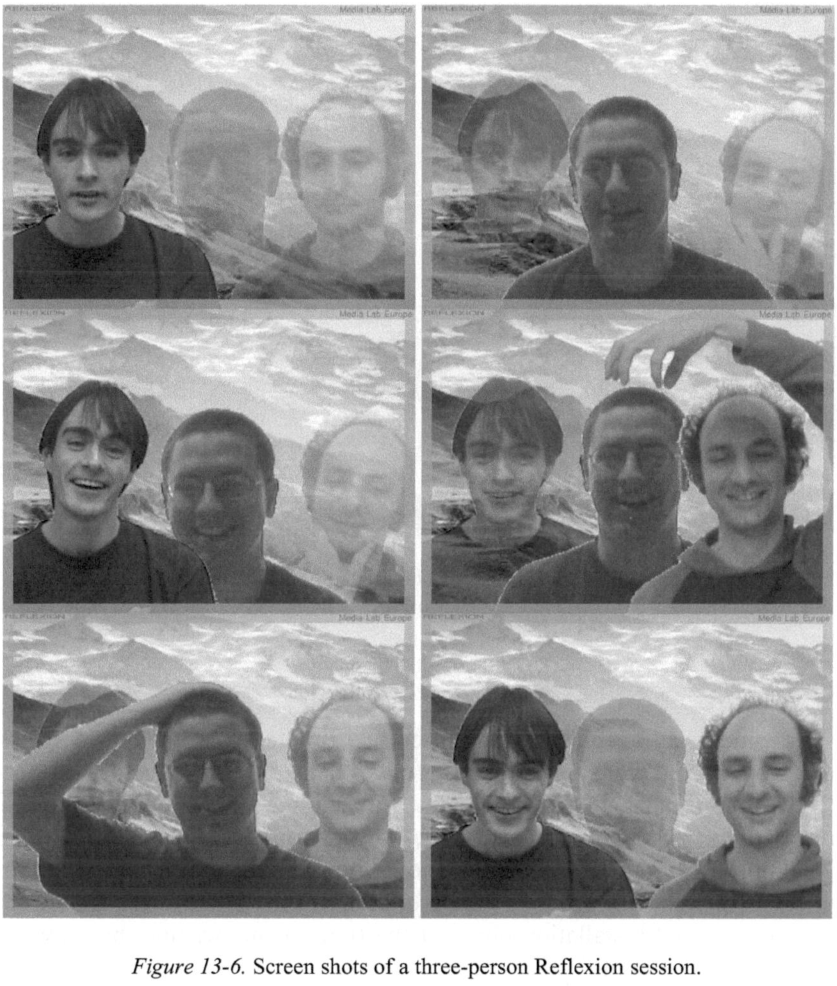

Figure 13-6. Screen shots of a three-person Reflexion session.

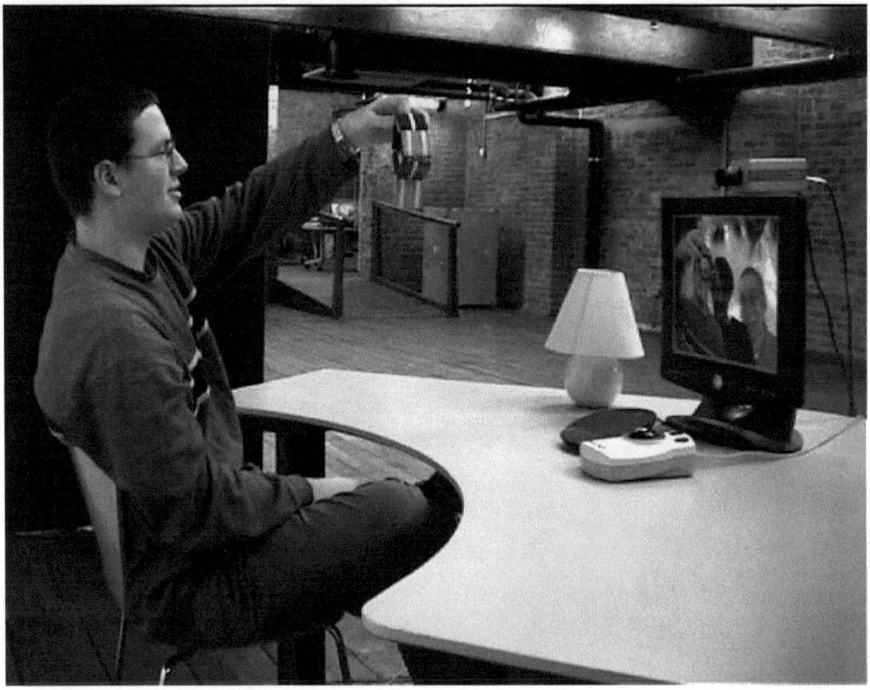

Figure 13-7. Scene of a Reflexion station at our lab, illustrating the mirror effect of the display.

3.4 Wellness Window

Extended-stay hospital patients often feel isolated from the outside world and disconnected from the people that love them, and these factors can lead to depression and a reduced potential for healing. The Wellness Window project aims to counteract these effects by creating an always-on ambient visual portal from the patient's room to a familiar place or environment with which the patient has a strong positive relationship. The project is still in a development and installation phase at the time of this writing, but is worth discussing in this context as a design concept.

A collaboration with a cancer unit at a local hospital, the scenario under consideration involves bone marrow transplant patients who must undergo a difficult chemotherapy program and are allowed only a limited number of visitors for several weeks while their immune systems recuperate. As a first step, interviews were conducted with former patients of this ward, and the characteristics of the ward itself were studied in depth. The rooms the patients inhabit are small and filled with various foreign medical technologies. Most have only a small window with a very limited view of the outside world. The drugs used in the therapy often cause patients to have difficulty focusing on simple foreground mental tasks like reading a book or watching television. All of these factors contribute additional mental strain and feelings of isolation to an experience that is already very physically challenging.

The Wellness Window prototype in development involves creating a projection on a wall of the patient's room that displays a live yet low frame-rate video stream from a place chosen by the patient in advance of treatment, such as a window facing the patient's garden, a room in the patient's house, or a favorite hilltop view. These video images will be captured with high quality web or security camera technologies set up in the desired places. We are aiming for an ambient design that conveys an ongoing impression of the place while not drawing attention to itself and, most importantly, not overwhelming the patient's senses. The patient will see a single moderately static image projection that will update itself once every few seconds or minutes. Instead of a jarring cut, the transition from one image frame to the next will be a slow dissolve over several seconds.

With its focus on ambience, the Wellness Window concept is distinguished from more foreground social technologies for hospital settings, such as HutchWorld (Cheng *et al.*, 2000) and CHESS (Shaw *et al.*, 2000), which incorporate elements like chat rooms and discussion groups as well as access to sources of medical information. It has perhaps more in common with the AROMA project (Pederson and Sokoler, 1997) or the ambientROOM (Ishii *et al.*, 1998), though these ambient media systems dealt more with abstract representations of activity rather than realistic imagery as in our concept.

The hope is that the ongoing presence of this connection will have a positive and strengthening effect on the patient's mental state and healing potential. Our prototype design includes just a one-way connection into the patient's room, because patient interviews revealed they felt relatively less comfortable with the idea of imagery of themselves being conveyed to the outside world, even if it was only to their families or other patients. Given that they have telephones available to them, they speculated just the continuous unidirectional link would be the most helpful.

3.5 Breakout for Two

Traditional sports foster bonding and team spirit through the sharing of a physically taxing competitive activity. This project aims to build the same sense of community over a distance, partly through the use of an *exertion interface* – an interface that deliberately requires intense and potentially exhausting physical effort.

In Breakout For Two, two participants in remote locations compete in a game that is a cross between tennis, soccer, and the classic video game Breakout. Each player has a real soccer ball and must repeatedly aim and kick this ball against a wall consisting of a video projection of virtual "blocks." A live video feed of the other player appears layered behind this wall of virtual targets. The effect is one of a virtual game "court" in which the participants are separated by a boundary over which they may see and talk to each other (see Figures 13-8 & 13-9). The blocks on each player's screen are synchronized—when one player strikes and breaks through a block, the same block disappears from the other player's screen. The player who breaks through the most blocks wins. Games typically last several minutes and can incorporate varying levels of difficulty or multiple players (see Figure 13-10).

Our hypothesis is that augmenting an online sport or gaming environment with exertion will greatly enhance the potential for social bonding, just as playing an exhausting game of squash or tennis with a new acquaintance or co-worker helps to "break the ice" and build friendships. The heightened state of arousal induced by the exertion also potentially makes the interaction more memorable.

We conducted a formal study to test these hypotheses and evaluate the effects of exertion interfaces, and the results were encouraging (Mueller, 2003). In brief, 56 volunteers were recruited, none of whom had any prior experience with the system. These volunteers were matched randomly into pairs. No such pair of participants knew each other prior to participating in the experiment. Each pair of players played one of two different versions of the game for about half an hour—either the real Breakout for Two exertion game, or a alternate form of the game that was as similar as possible to the original (same wall-size video conference and game strategy) except that it employed a traditional non-exertion keyboard interface and a virtual ball and foot. Afterwards, the players completed a questionnaire designed particularly to gain insight into their impressions of and feelings toward the other player. In a nutshell, the results of this questionnaire were that players of the real Breakout for Two game said they got to know each other better, became better friends, felt the other player was more talkative, and were happier with the audio and video conference quality than those who played the non-exertion form of the game. After completing the questionnaire, the pair of players were taken to a room where they met in person for the first time and were interviewed together on video tape so that we could observe the way they interacted after their remote sport experience as well as gain additional thoughts from them on how to improve the prototype.

As more and more people work and live at a distance from colleagues and friends, sports over a distance applications may hold potential in replacing some important types of interpersonal contact that are missed because of this distance. Instead of a traditional gym or sports club, players might go to a "virtual sports club" in their geographic area that consists of several exertion interface environments like the one in our prototype, as well as appropriate post-sport online socializing spaces.

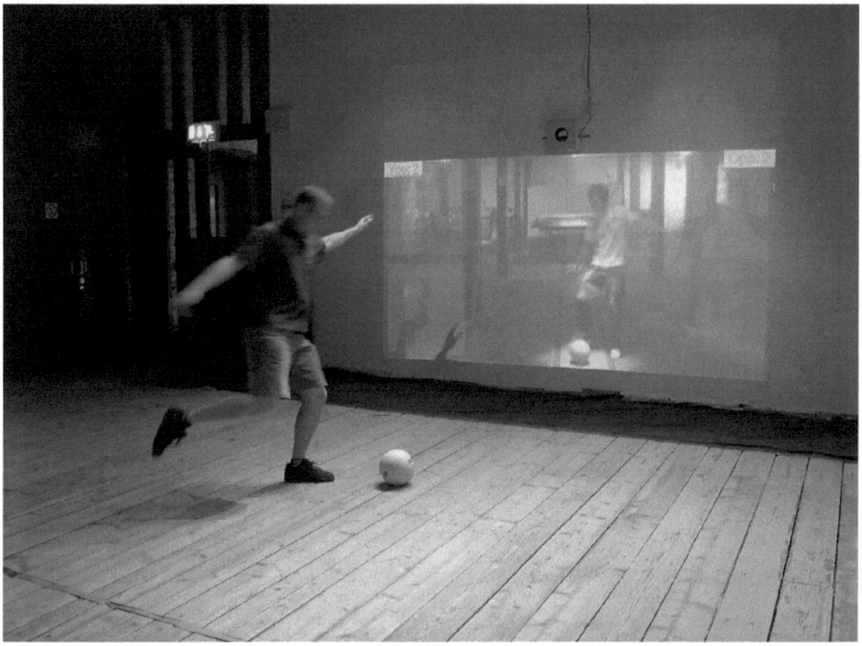

Figure 13-8. Scene of a game of Breakout for Two, illustrating the "playing court" effect of the display design.

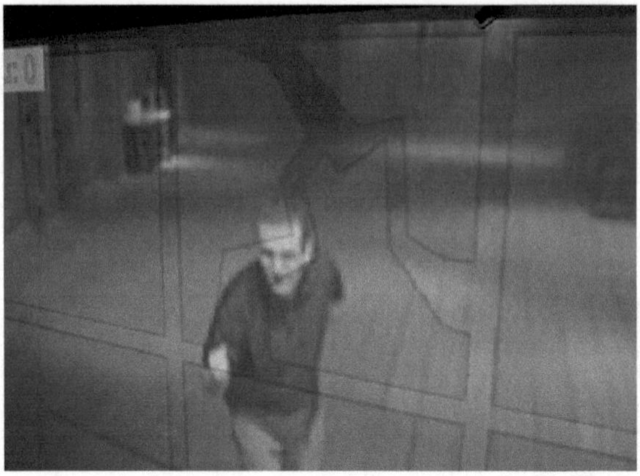

Figure 13-9. Remote participants appear layered together with translucent "blocks" representing the targets that must be struck during the course of a game of Breakout for Two.

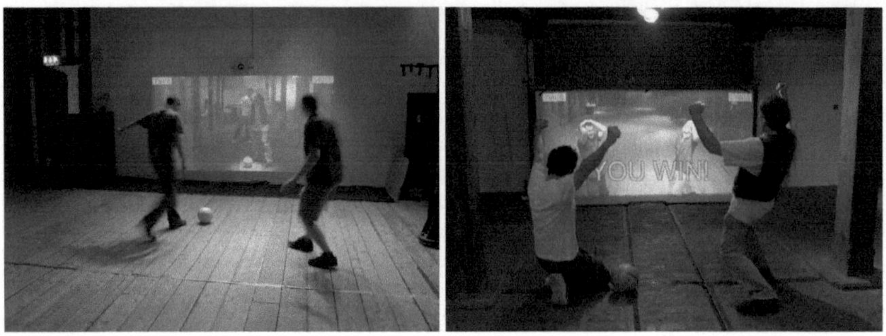

Figure 13-10. Scenes of a four-player Breakout for Two game.

4. Design Nuggets

The experience of developing the specific projects described above (as well as others not mentioned) has highlighted a few general questions and suggested a few general strategies that could be helpful in guiding future undertakings involving public, community, and situated displays for "human connectedness" applications. These are expressed below as a collection of design nuggets, some of which might be more obvious and well-understood than others, and some of which might be applicable more broadly than others. Some have been raised by other authors, and some important issues have probably been missed or have yet to be identified. In any case, these nuggets are not intended to be viewed as verified and established design principles. Rather, they are presented to provoke discussion and further inquiry.

4.1 Think Beyond the Screen

Designing a display includes more than just designing the imagery formed by its pixels. What is the best position, orientation, size, shape, aspect ratio, and so on, to support the application? How does the display integrate with the surrounding space? How does it meld with yet have its own identity within its architectural context? How does it make best use of the constraints presented by the environment within which it is set? In addition, the word "display" must also include a sense of input as well as output. What kind of interaction is desired, if any, and what input devices or sensors would be most effective to achieve that interaction and complement the theme of the display?

All of the prototypes described earlier raise some of these points, but the iCom project in particular highlights the importance of thinking about physical and architectural design as much as graphic and information design. The configurations of each station were developed around (in some cases severe) constraints on the usage of space in each laboratory area, and the challenge was to have the screen visible from as much of the room as possible yet also to create a defined space that would motivate casual gatherings and social interaction. Proximity to natural foot-traffic lanes was also favored to enhance the potential for chance encounters between sites.

4.2 Engage the Periphery

At any moment in time our senses are showered with a variety of different stimuli. Thankfully, our brains filter these stimuli and bring only the bits and pieces that matter the most into the foreground of our consciousness. To avoid perceptual overload, displays, especially those that are intended to be near us all the time, must engage and appropriately manipulate these different levels of attentiveness and our innate ability to seamlessly shift between them as needed.

For example, Reflexion attempts to visually steer our attention toward the person who is speaking while at the same time offering a peripheral awareness of the other less active participants. The Wellness Window scenario is especially interesting since patients are often not capable or desirous of concentrating on a foreground source of stimuli, like a book or television program, for any length of time. Therefore, the real challenge lies in exploiting the background in the most effective way, and possibly responding to passively-sensed cues from the patient to judge what levels of engagement are suitable. Others have explored the theme of ambient and peripheral awareness as well (Dunne and Raby, 1994; Ishii *et al.*, 1998; Pederson and Sokoler, 1997).

4.3 *Instill a Sense of Reciprocity*

If multiple displays are connected in some way, as they often are in awareness or conferencing applications, the design should attempt to instill a sense of reciprocity and equal access. For example, there should be a feeling that participants at one site do not have some special benefit or, alternately, an added risk that those on the other side do not.

iCom and Reflexion address this issue by synchronizing the screen projections at each location to create a sense of shared space, and by providing exactly the same controls over that space at each site. What you see is what the other sites see, and nothing is recorded or displayed in other venues, such as on the Web. Similarly, we deployed iCom in physical spaces that are similar in character and in which the inhabitants generally know each other as research colleagues and friends—we didn't attempt to connect the Director's office or the lobby of the building to the lab areas, for example. The importance of reciprocity was also explored by much of the media space work cited earlier (Bly *et al.*, 1993; Isaacs *et al.*, 1996; Mackay, 1999; Tang and Rua, 1994). Reciprocity is also a significant issue in Breakout for Two, in which players would complain if they believed one side had a competitive advantage, such as more space with fewer obstacles or a larger projection with larger screen targets.

4.4 *Transcend Time*

Good graphic design can merge information gathered over the course of a possibly very long temporal interval and reflect it back in a way that increases awareness of the passage of time and changes that have occurred, an awareness that perhaps isn't possible through simple human recollection. Given their potential for remote control and for making dynamic changes based on complex analyses of real-time input factors and stored data, computationally-mediated display technologies offer opportunities to transcend time in new ways – to express a richer history of use for example, or perhaps to provide a more meaningful temporal context for a collaborative activity.

Palimpsest, for example, gathers layers of video as passers-by walk through its interaction area, slowly building up a visual that reveals a hidden community of the many mobile humans who have intersected with a certain place over an extended period of time. iCom tries to express the recent history of the community as well as a history of interaction through its list of bulletin board messages, the titles of which vary in size depending on the age of the message and how many times it has been selected to be read recently. The Aware Community Portals (Sawney *et al.*, 2001) and Edit Wear/Read Wear (Hill and Hollan, 1992) projects, among others, explore different ways to reflect a history of use that may be of interest.

4.5 Motivate interaction

Half the battle in designing an interactive situated or public display is designing how the display will *invite* that interaction. What makes us glance at a display when we might normally not have? What turns a glance into a more extended gaze? What makes us walk over to it? What makes us want to interact? Going beyond eye-catching graphics and other techniques from the domain of advertising, a useful way of thinking about this problem is through the notion of creating mystery. Can a display entice our natural curiosity to reveal or clarify things that are hidden or ambiguous?

iCom does this in a simplistic way by displaying the often cryptic subject lines from community announcements, attempting to motivate passers-by to click and reveal their full text. Similarly, if there is strange or unusual activity in one of the smaller video windows, a passer-by may be more likely to approach the station and click to enlarge those views to figure out what is going on. In Breakout For Two, the initial motivation to interact is perhaps based on the curiosity of what would happen if the clearly kickable projectile were to strike the targets displayed on the screen. Some other ways of attracting attention, especially with motion, have been explored in projects like AttrActive Windows (Denoue *et al.* 2003].

4.6 Design for Investment and Growth

Once the initial gratification and novelty factors wear off, what makes us want to come back to the display? One hypothesis is that humans will continue to share things if they believe they will gain something in return at some point in the future. How does the system motivate and reflect this long-term investment? People may exhibit greater attachment to a display that knows and respects them—for example, by remembering who they are when they return or by being open to their influence in various ways. How does the display adapt to and grow along with the community within which it is situated?

This nugget partly relates to the notion mentioned earlier of reflecting a history of use, but at another level it is about setting a stage for and tracking the growth of the user and the changing character of the relationships the display may be there to help build and enhance. For example, Breakout for Two demands investment in the form of intense physical exertion, but with the potential reward of having fun, making a new friend, and over the course of multiple encounters, building a richer relationship with one's competitor than might have been possible using other communication technologies. In contrast, having the display *itself* grow with and adapt to the way it is used calls into play techniques from the domain of machine learning.

4.7 Balance Togetherness and Uniqueness

Observation suggests that at the same time we like to feel like we are part of a group (we join clubs, eat meals together, live in communities), we also have a desire to establish and maintain our own identity within those groups (we define and defend territories, purposefully dress and decorate in unique ways, cultivate individual styles). This suggests, in turn, that at the same time displays in connectedness applications aim to enhance awareness and togetherness, they should also enable users and groups to assert their individuality, their desire to be different from the rest. A display that combines the offerings of many people should convey a sense of sharing and of contributing to a larger whole while also preserving a sense of ownership over one's own offering.

For example, iCom displays postings from both Media Lab Europe and the MIT Media Lab together in the same chronological list, which helps to convey a sense of a single larger community, but each side's message titles appear in their own assigned color so that the origin of any contribution is immediately identifiable. Reflexion and iCom aim to build a sense of shared space through the synchronization of each site's display, but at the same time they try to offer each participant their own visual identity or terrain within that space. Competitors in Breakout for Two share a single virtual game court and targets while at the same time possessing their own distinct territory within that court.

4.8 Embrace the Creativity of Your Users

Any display will have to impose constraints of different kinds on its users, for example on the amount of information that can be presented, their physical configuration, the bandwidth and types of transfers possible between connected displays, and so on. Fortunately, humans are creative and often invent ways to triumph over constraints and use them to their advantage, to display more information in less space or to send richer messages than originally imagined. Display makers should encourage and try to provide avenues for this kind of community creativity, as it may result in significant operational improvements or inspire ideas for new applications.

For example, several lab denizens who were intrigued by Palimpsest began co-opting the system occasionally to enact short pantomime plays in which actors would layer their performances into the video scene asynchronously. This strategy also enabled a single actor to play multiple parts and overall suggested a new form of improvisational theater. As another example, for privacy reasons, iCom does not enable recording of the audio and video captured by the system, but its users quickly discovered they could leave humorous decorations in front of its cameras to asynchronously joke around with the inhabitants of the other sites. We also found that, after the introduction of a new iCom station, inhabitants who work near it would gradually reconfigure its physical surroundings to suite preferences and give it a unique personality, and this is a behaviour that we embraced and later tried to encourage. Other media space experiments echo the importance of "affording appropriation" (Bly *et al.*, 1993; Dourish *et al.*, 1996). While this overall nugget is largely about embracing a certain flexibility and open-endedness in design, it also relates to notions of tailorability and openness in software systems as explored by authors like Mackay (1991) and Dourish (1995).

4.9 Be Patient

New behaviours are not created overnight. To really understand if and how a public or situated display will change a community, you need to study it over more than just a few days or even weeks. There must be time for the novelty factor to wear off, for its users to come to terms with its presence, to reject and hate it, to later reflect on how it can benefit them, to take ownership and integrate it into their lives and spaces, to gradually take it for granted.

The timing and duration of academic terms and funding contracts makes long term cultivation and study of this kind more difficult, yet it is essential if we wish to more deeply understand the effects these displays have on us. Our experience specifically with iCom and Palimpsest, as well as accounts from other research programs (Bly *et al.*, 1993; Dourish *et al.*, 1996), confirms this suggestion. After more than two years of continuous operation, we are only beginning to notice certain evolving behaviours related to the iCom system, as well as revisions of previously observed behaviours, especially as new members join the community and others leave.

5. Conclusion

Below is a recap of the design nuggets presented in this chapter:

1. Think beyond the screen
2. Engage the periphery
3. Instill a sense of reciprocity
4. Transcend time
5. Motivate interaction
6. Design for investment and growth
7. Balance togetherness and uniqueness
8. Embrace the creativity of your users
9. Be patient

As discussed earlier, these nuggets are not meant to be considered as recognized and verified design principles. Rather, they are intended to serve as a collection of possible questions to ask and strategies to consider when developing display-centered "human connectedness" applications. Not all of these nuggets will be applicable in all situations all of the time. One can easily imagine, for example, scenarios in which it would be most appropriate for a display to not identify its users, not store a history of its use, or not try to draw attention to itself.

This particular compilation of nuggets is largely inspired by our experience in building the five prototypes described in earlier sections, though they clearly relate to many other projects in other research programs. The list is certainly not complete and will evolve as our collective understanding about this realm grows, but hopefully it can serve as a starting point for helping applications in this domain reach their full potential.

Acknowledgements

Thanks to the members of the Human Connectedness research group for their wonderful ideas and hard work in realizing the prototypes described in this chapter, especially Florian Mueller (Breakout for Two), Cian Cullinan (Reflexion and Wellness Window), and Ben Piper (Palimpsest). Thanks also to Tom Walter, Rosalind Picard, Jim McBride, V. Michael Bove, Jr., Alex Westner, Denis Roche, and the many others who contributed to the development of these projects. This research has been supported by sponsors and partners of Media Lab Europe and the MIT Media Lab.

References

Agamanolis, S., Westner, A., & Bove, V. M., Jr. Reflection of Presence: Toward more natural and responsive telecollaboration. Proceedings SPIE Multimedia Networks; 1997; 3228.

Bly, S. A., Harrison, S. R., & Irwin, S. Media Spaces: Bringing People Together in a Video, Audio, and Computing Environment. Communications of the ACM 1993; 36(1): 28-47.

Cheng, L., Stone, L., Farnham, S., Clark, A. M., & Zaner, M. Hutchworld: Lessons Learned. A Collaborative Project: Fred Hutchinson Cancer Research Center & Microsoft Research Proceedings Virtual Worlds 2000, Springer.

Denoue, L., Nelson, L., & Churchill, E. AttrActive Windows: Dynamic Windows for Digital Bulletin Boards. Extended Abstracts of CHI '03 Conference on Human Factors in Computing Systems; 2003; Ft Lauderdale, FL, USA; ACM Press.

Dourish, P. Developing a Reflective Model of Collaborative Systems. ACM Transactions on Computer-Human Interaction 1995; 2(1) 40-63.

Dourish, P., Adler, A., Bellotti, V., Henderson, A. Your Place or Mine? Learning from Long-Term Use of Audio-Video Communication. Computer-Supported Collaborative Work 1996; 1(5): 33-62.

Dourish, P., & Bly, S. Portholes: Supporting awareness in a distributed work group. Proceedings of the CHI '92 Conference on Human Factors in Computing Systems; 1992; Monterey, CA USA. New York: ACM Press: 541–547.

Dunne, A. & Raby, F. Fields and Thresholds. Presentation at Doors of Perception 2, 1994; Amsterdam, The Netherlands.

Edson, R. C., *et al.*. Video Conference System using Voice-Switched Cameras. U.S. Patent 3,601,530, 1971.

Fish, R. S., Kraut, R. E., & Chalfonte, B. L. The VideoWindow System in Informal Communication. Proceedings of the CSCW '90 Conference on Computer Supported Cooperative Work; 1990; Los Angeles, California; 1-11, ACM Press.

Hill, W. C., & Hollan, J. D.Edit Wear and Read Wear. Proceedings of the CHI '92 Conference on Human Factors in Computing Systems; 1992; Monterey, CA USA. New York: ACM Press.

Hindus, D., Mainwaring, S. D., Leduc, N., Hagström, A. E., & Bayley, O. Casablanca: Designing Social Communication Devices for the Home. Proceedings CHI '01 Conference on Human Factors in Computing Systems; 2001; Seattle, WA, USA. ACM Press.

House, J. S., Landis, K. R., & Umberson, D. Social Relationships and Health. Science 1988; 241(4865): 540-545.

Hutchinson, H., Mackay, W., Westerlund, B., Bederson, B., Druin, A., Plaisant, C., Beaudouin-Lafon, M., Conversy, S., Evans, H., Hansen, H., Roussel, N., Eiderbäck, B., Sinna Lindquist, S., Sundblad, Y. Technology Probes: Inspiring Design for and with Families. Proceedings CHI '03, Conference on Human Factors in Computing Systems; 2003; Ft Lauderdale, FL, USA; 17-24; ACM Press.

Isaacs, E. A., Tang, J. C., & Morris, T. Piazza: A Desktop Environment Supporting Impromptu and Planned Interactions. Proceedings of CSCW '96 Conference on Computer Supported Cooperative Work; 1996, November 2-6; Boston, MA. ACM Press. Cambridge, MA. ACM Press:

Ishii, H., Wisneski, C., Brave, S., Dahley, A., Gorbet, M., Ullmer, B., and Yarin, P. "ambientROOM: integrating ambient media with architectural space. Extended Abstracts of CHI'98 Conference on Human Factors in Computing Systems; 1998; Los Angeles, CA, USA. ACM Press,

Ishii, H., Kobayashi, M., & Arita, K. Iterative Design of Seamless Collaboration Media. Communications of the ACM; 1994; 37(8): 83-97.

Jancke, G., et. al. Linking Public Spaces: Technical and Social Issues. Proceedings of CHI '01 Conference on Human Factors in Computing Systems, 2001; Seattle, WA, USA.

Kraut, R., Kiesler, S., Boneva, B., Cummings, J., Helgeson, V., & Crawford, A. Internet Paradox Revisited. Journal of Social Issues; 2002; 58(1): 49-74.

Lewis, T., Amini, F., & Landon, R. *A General Theory of Love*, Random House, 2000.

Mackay, W. E. Triggers and Barriers to Customizing Software. Proceedings of CHI '91 Conference on Human Factors in Computing Systems, 1991; New Orleans, LA, USA; ACM Press.

Mackay, W. E. "Media Spaces: Environments for Informal Multimedia Interaction," in Beaudouin-Lafon, M., ed., *Computer Supported Cooperative Work*. John Wiley & Sons, 1999.

Morikawa, O., & Maesako, T. HyperMirror: Toward Pleasant-to-use Video Mediated Communication System. Proceedings CSCW '98 Conference on Computer Supported Cooperative Work; 1998, November 2-6; Seattle, WA. ACM Press.

Mueller, F., Agamanolis, S., & Picard R. Exertion Interfaces: Sports over a Distance for Social Bonding and Fun. Proceedings CHI '03, Conference on Human Factors in Computing Systems; 2003; Ft Lauderdale, FL, USA; ACM Press

Mynatt, E. D., Rowan, J., Jacobs, A., & Craighill, S. Digital Family Portraits: Supporting Peace of Mind for Extended Family Members. Proceedings of CHI '01 Conference on Human Factors in Computing Systems, 2001; Seattle, WA, USA; 333-340; ACM Press.

Pederson, E. R., & Sokoler, T. AROMA: abstract representation of presence supporting mutual awareness. Proceedings of CHI '97 Conference on Human Factors in Computing Systems, 1997; Atlanta, GA, USA; 51-58; ACM Press.

Putnam, R. *Bowling Alone: The Collapse and Revival of American Community*. Simon & Schuster, 2000.

Sawney, N., Wheeler, S., & Schmandt, C. Aware Community Portals: Shared Information Appliances for Transitional Spaces. Personal and Ubiquitous Computing 2001; 5(1): 66-70.

Shaw, B. R., McTavish, F., Hawkins, R., Gustafson, D. H., & Pingree, S. Experiences of women with breast cancer: exchanging social support over the CHESS computer network. Journal of Health Communications 2000; 5(2): 135-159.

Tang, J., & Rua, M. Montage: Providing Teleproximity for Distributed Groups. Proceedings of CHI '94 Conference on Human Factors in Computing Systems; 1994; Boston, MA, USA; 37-43; New York: ACM Press.

PART IV:
MOBILITY

Chapter 14

SITUATED MOBILITY

Using situated displays to support mobile activities

Trevor Pering and Michael Kozuch
Intel Research

Abstract: The Personal Server and Internet Suspend/Resume are two technologies that support *situated mobility* – i.e., using situated displays in support of mobile computing. By leveraging advances in high density storage and virtual machines, these systems endeavor to enhance a user's mobility without requiring them to either rely on small-screen displays or impoverished computing platforms. These two emerging proactive computing paradigms lead towards a more complete vision of mobile computing, bridging the gap between the situated and mobile worlds.

Key words: Mobile computing virtual machines, high-density storage, Internet Suspend/Resume, Personal Server, Proactive Computing, and mobile computing

1. Introduction

Most of the other chapters in this book deal with situated displays that are closely related with a particular environment: office conference rooms, mission control room, or a particular user's workplace. In contrast, this chapter considers situated displays in support of *mobility*. In this model, users use fixed displays to support their mobile computing needs, instead of relying on the small displays typically associated with mobile devices. For example, if users were effortlessly able to utilize kiosk displays available in airport lounges (Figure 15-1) to access personal information, such as travel plans or photograph collections, they could enjoy a much richer media experience without being required to carry a bulky display as they travel. The phrase *situated mobility* refers to the capability of mobile users to

K. O'Hara et al. (eds.), Public and Situated Displays: Social and Interactional Aspects of Shared Display Technologies, 337–358.

effectively use situated displays to access personal information and applications.

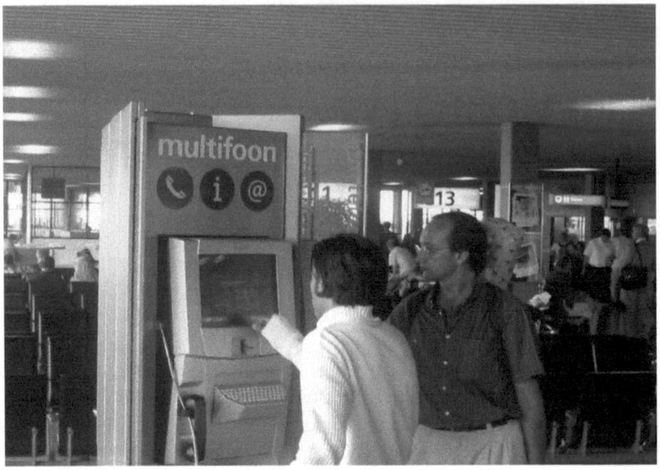

Figure 14-8. Situated display in an airport used for mobile computing.

The richness of a user's computing experience is often highly dependent upon the size and fidelity of human interface devices such as displays, keyboards, and audio speakers. Unfortunately, these devices often impose significant size and power constraints on mobile computing platforms. One way to enhance the experience of mobile users without burdening them with large devices and batteries is to provide technologies that enable users to take advantage of situated displays. Since these displays may be found in many locations (television sets in the home, workstations in the office, or reader boards in public transportation buildings), they represent a powerful means for increasing the utility of mobile computing. Furthermore, the prevalence of public displays is steadily increasing due to technology improvements and cost reductions.

Current web technologies afford a limited form of situated mobility by enabling access to personal information hosted on a remote web server through web-based applications. Web browsers are available on nearly every computer, and are sufficient to support simple applications such as contact list management and email access. By publishing information on web servers, users are able to access that information from nearly any connected access point. However, web technology falls short of seamless situated mobility because it relies on an Internet connection, which provides a variable-speed connection. Furthermore, the local application environment supported by web applications is greatly restricted and does not provide users with a fully customizable computing environment. For example, editing photographs over the web is a daunting task: simple operations such as rotating or sizing an image can be arbitrarily slow. Additionally, the web application is not likely to support the latest plug-ins and customizations that can be important to a serious photographer.

Proactive Computing (Tennenhouse, 2003) is a research initiative designed to facilitate the interaction between humans and the physical world: allowing computing to pervade the environment without requiring the user's constant attention. Two emerging research platforms in proactive computing, the Personal Server and Internet Suspend/Resume, are specifically designed to enable situated mobility. Despite leveraging different technologies, both of these platforms endeavor to support personal mobility while the user moves through unfamiliar environments. With Personal Server technology, a user's data files and applications are housed in a small device carried by the user. This device leverages situated displays, like those found in a store front-window (Figure 15-2), to provide users with access to their data through a short-range wireless link – relieving the reliance on either a "home" network connection or small mobile display. Internet Suspend/Resume technology enables the migration of a user's complete execution environment, including the operating system, applications, data files, and customizations, from one computer to another. This migration supports personal mobility by enabling the user to resume their execution environment on situated displays near the user. Although ostensibly approaching the problem from completely different viewpoints, these two technologies both enable personal mobility through unfamiliar environments and can be combined into a unified model of situated display technologies.

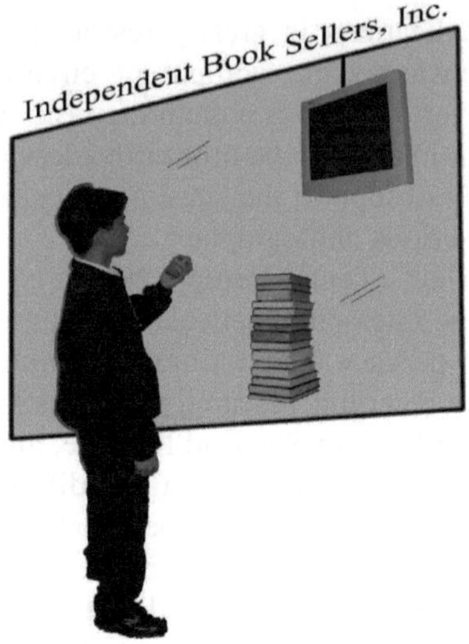

Figure 14-9. Using a display situated behind a storefront window.

In addition to technology and implementation considerations, system designers must bear in mind many usability factors such as how the user will interact with different situated displays? Is the user presented with a display that is tailored to the user (using familiar icons and images, for example) or one that is tailored to the local environment (highlighting items that may be of interest near the location of the display)? Does the user experience performance problems when accessing remote data? Can different users share information easily? Casting emerging technologies into an understanding of the resulting user experience helps clarify the advantages and disadvantages of component technologies, and better focuses the development the entire computing system.

Situated displays are a powerful concept that can be used to support mobile computing. Many challenges facing mobile systems, such as small displays or limited computing environments, can be mitigated by interacting through a full-feature display platform in the environment. The Personal Server focusing on lightweight interaction with mobile data, while Internet Suspend/Resume utilizes a full featured local execution environment. Together, these technologies define a more complete vision of mobile computing that provide the availability of high-density mobile storage, the power of a full-featured local environment, and richness of full-featured display interaction. There has been a long history of separating the display from computing and storage resources, mostly enabling new forms of distributed computing. Situated mobility simply represents the next step in bringing truly effective mobile computing to everyday life.

2. Using Situated Displays to Support Mobility

True mobile computing is primarily concerned with the mobility of people, not computing devices. System designers can help users attain greater mobility: not by providing more and more portable devices, but by enabling users to take advantage of fixed devices that pervade our modern infrastructure. Situated displays are particularly interesting in this context because displays simultaneously determine the richness of many computing applications and impose the greatest power and size constraints on hardware implementations. The ultimate goal of harvesting situated displays is to enable users to move through environments and seamlessly interact with data at will without focusing on the devices and systems supporting this interaction – even enabling systems to proactively adapt to a user's behaviour without their direct interaction.

To date, device-centric approaches to mobility have enjoyed only limited success. Cell phones are the one great success story in the field of mobility providing a focused solution to a specific problem. Most handheld devices enjoy very little success outside narrow niche markets. Personal digital assistants (PDAs), in particular, have failed to become commonplace because they don't sufficiently improve many user's lives. In fact, these media-poor devices employing small screens and limited human-input capability often prove to be more of a distraction to the user than a productivity enhancement.

Situated displays, which in this care are large-screen displays fixed in the environment, offer a compelling counterpoint to device-centric mobility. Although inherently non-mobile, being physically large and often physically attached to the surrounding infrastructure, they provide an attractive interface through which mobile users may access information. So, although the distractions of a mobile environment still abound, the larger-screened situated displays are more engaging than their small-screened counterparts. For example, viewing a map on a situated display, with both a broad view of location and a fine level of detail, would be much more efficient than manipulating it on a small-screen display. Further, large-screen displays enable collaboration between multiple users in ways that are untenable on smaller displays.

Of course, situated displays are not available in all situations. To provide human input/output in such situations, users will still rely on handheld displays. Consequently, mobile system designers should consider augmenting systems with technology enabling those systems to leverage small portable displays in addition to large situated displays. With such hybrid systems, the user may be presented with usability choices: attempt to locate a situated display or employ a limited portable display. The display chosen will depend on the nature of the information and context of use. No single solution will be optimal in all cases – designing for flexibility is extremely important in mobile systems.

One other significant aspect of situated displays is that they often have a fixed purpose in the environment: that is, they are intended to augment a particular locale with some form of digital information. For example, airports often provide large displays showing flight arrival and departure information (Figure 15-3). To use these displays, a traveler must scan through the entire list – although first remembering their particular flight details. In such a case, enabling a single person to control the entire display is not appropriate. Instead, the system designer could enable a new interaction that augments location-specific public information with information specific to users that happen to be nearby. One example, following from the transit situation, would be to highlight specific flights corresponding to people in the vicinity of the display. That way, each nearby user may more easily determine their flight information from a list of many, while still retaining the function of the original display. Although insignificant in itself, remembering flight numbers can be distracting, and having to look them up on your personal cell-phone or PDA would be just "one more thing" you needed to day. This basic concept can be generalized to form a notion of situated displays that spans the rage from personal (single user controlled) to generic (public untailored information). Ideally, situated displays will hide the unnecessary details and proactively respond to a mobile user's presence needs.

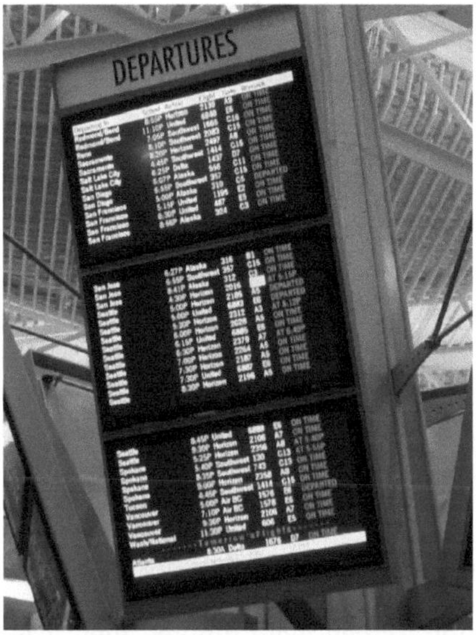

Figure 14-10. Airport display showing public information.

3. Challenges for Existing Approaches to Mobile Computing

Mobile computing already exists in many forms, including a few examples that already leverage situated displays. Typically, the phrase "mobile computing" conveys the notion of mobile hardware devices, such as mobile phones and laptop computers, that people carry with them to support their computing needs (Figure 15-4). As mentioned previously, these devices are often resource-constrained: the displays can be quite small, the battery life is often limited, and familiar input devices such as keyboards are often lacking. Alternatively, people can access web-based resources from anywhere in the world. Both approaches, device-based mobility and web-based mobility, possess strengths and weaknesses. By understanding the tradeoffs associated with each, a system designer may better frame the support needed for efficient mobile computing including the opportunities for situated displays.

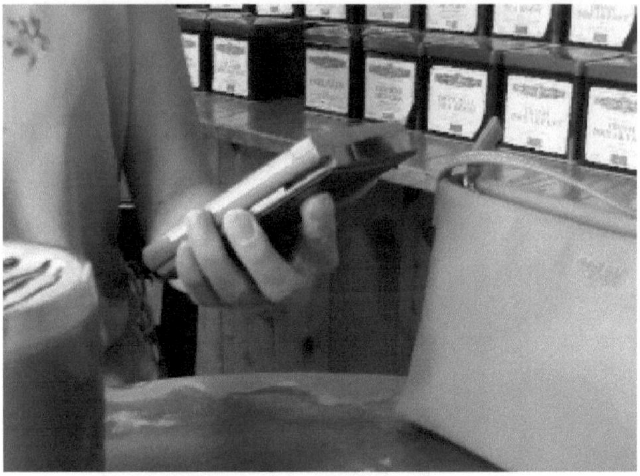

Figure 14-11. Mobile device carried in a hand-bag.

Power consumption, screen glare, limited input capability, and physical frailty are factors that make the use of portable devices difficult in many mobile circumstances. Further, these factors are closely linked with the desire to have an interaction-rich environment in a portable form factor. The LCD backlight found on many mobile devices is a significant source of power consumption, but this feature is often necessary to overcome glare from other light sources. Additionally, LCD displays are very fragile components and prone to breaking when dropped. Screens, which are enhanced with touch-sensitivity, are often also used as the primary input mechanism on portable devices, notably PDAs and tablet PCs, but they are a poor substitute for a full-featured keyboard when the user is engaged in more "high-input" tasks like word processing and extensive email authoring.

Fortunately, the technology used for all these components is constantly improving. In the near future, users may expect low-power displays with high-contrast reflective surfaces, complex projection keyboards or hand-held input devices that do not require a large physical footprint, and more efficient electronics yielding longer battery lifetimes. However, users may also expect that the capabilities of fixed-infrastructure devices will always exceed the capabilities of portable devices. In particular, the human interface of fixed-infrastructure devices is typically much better than portable devices, including larger screens, better keyboards, and high-fidelity audio output. This is a fundamental property that has not changed even as the capabilities of mobile devices have improved.

Ironically, because the user-experience with such devices is often rather poor, much of the "mobile computing" in the world today is actually carried out through fixed-infrastructure devices in the form of *web-based mobility*: the ubiquitous access to personal data by leveraging Internet cafés and other locations that provide workstation-based Internet access. Frequent travelers may quite easily create web-based email accounts, which are accessible through Internet cafés, and communicate with co-workers and friends from many places around the world – without having to carry any device at all. Naturally, more savvy web-users can extend this model to include additional applications: an online diary that chronicles a tourist's voyage is an interesting example for the leisure traveler.

Although web-based mobility has the capability for "large-screen" interaction virtually anywhere a user may travel, the basic web-browser model does not work well with slow or unreliable Internet connections, and presents a very impoverished interaction environment. Many applications, such as image editing, require high-bandwidth channels between the storage, computation, and display components. In many such applications, high network latencies will also degrade the user experience substantially. Web-based, client-side applications, such as those based on Java and other languages, are an attempt to solve some of these problems, but such applications, by their very nature, do not interoperate well and are unable to fully utilize local resources. Further, dependence on the network for data transport can render a user's data completely inaccessible in the case of network outages. Fundamentally, the web-based model is problematic because it separates users from their data, reducing their control over the interaction and putting them at the mercy of network performance and accessibility.

4. Emerging Mobile Computing Research

Two emerging research projects, the *Personal Server* and Internet Suspend/Resume, build further on device- and web-based systems, respectively, to form more robust mobile systems that include additional features for improved user interfaces. Both these systems personalize situated displays, and their associated computing platforms, merging the concepts of situated- and mobile-computing to create "situated mobility." Although two distinct system designs, the basic concepts behind these two systems share a number of common themes and can be combined to form a more complete model of situated mobility that captures strengths of both mobile devices and situated computing infrastructure. Both designs employ aspects of proactive computing and automatically adapt to users' needs as environmental changes occur. As these projects grow to consider an increasing variety of circumstances, proactive operation will become an increasing important cornerstone of the complete system. Eventually, combining automatic management of multiple displays and intelligent presentation of users' data will become crucial to the effective use of situated displays in complex environments.

Both projects attempt to improve the typical mobile experience by providing effective use of displays that a user might find in the environment. Currently, most situated displays serve "thin client" systems that include minimal computing resources. These systems, although often outfitted with high-quality display hardware, are not capable of supporting computationally intensive tasks such as photo editing, a common task for leisure travelers who may chronicle their vacations in a web-journal (see for example the data in Churchill *et al.*, this volume).

However, the plummeting cost of computing hardware makes it possible to imagine a world in which coffee shops, airport lounges, dental and medical offices, and other semi-public spaces provide high-performance network-connected hardware for the benefit of their clientele. The comfortable chairs, table lamps, and magazines that these establishments typically provide suggest that their proprietors might consider also providing computers for the convenience and comfort of their customers. Traveling and waiting are currently often considered "dead time," (Perry *et al.*, 2001) where no useful work can be accomplished; however, users could take advantage of these idle times provided that situated displays, backed by sufficient computational resources, are available.

4.1 The Personal Server

The Personal Server (PS) (Want *et al.*, 2003) is a set of core technologies that enables a user to interact with their personal data and applications, which are stored on a personal mobile device, through the public infrastructure. For example, you could use a situated airport kiosk to edit your personal photo album through your address book while waiting for your flight in an airport. The initial PS prototype (Figure 15-5) is a small portable device that provides short-range wireless connectivity, energy-efficient processing, and high-density storage – everything except a direct human-interface. This design allows exploration of three main areas surrounding the Personal Server concept: user experience, software infrastructure, and hardware platform. By addressing these three levels, the Personal Server project aims to develop a new understanding of mobile interaction.

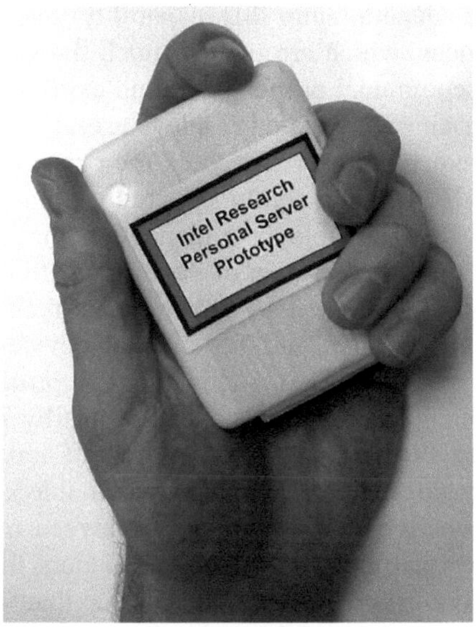

Figure 14-12. Personal Server prototype.

While the current PS prototype is a stand-alone device, future implementations will be integrated with other portable devices, such as a cell-phone, PDA, or laptop. A portable device, such as a cell phone, that has been enhanced with PS technology will enable a user to access a large volume of personal data through interface-rich public displays. As users will both have a mobile display available and be surrounded by situated displays, they can choose which interface to use in a particular situation. To enable interaction with a PS-enabled device, public access points (situated displays) must be augmented with a software layer, similar to a "network neighborhood" that streamlines the connection process. In turn, PS-enabled devices must be designed to support "always on" operation, rather than requiring the user to activate the device explicitly for every use.

The Personal Server enables access to a user's mobile information through the most *convenient* interface available, instead of the one interface provided by a particular device. For example, a user may be able to borrow a PDA from somebody sitting next to them, pull a display tablet out of their bag, or choose to walk over to a nearby information kiosk, rather than use the small display on their cell-phone. Similarly, the PS system enables a telecommuting user to travel between home and office workstations without explicitly managing the migration of files and connections. The Personal Server does not replace existing mobile technologies such as PDAs or cell-phones; instead it augments their operation by providing flexible access to personal resources. Generalizing this capability leads to the notion of "scrap" display devices, which are treated much the same way as pens and scrap paper, i.e., as communal property with no explicit ownership. The key property that will make such situated displays useful is seamless interaction: how long does it take for a user to access their personal data through the intended display? If the interaction is cumbersome, requiring lengthy discovery processes and unwieldy authentication mechanisms, the user is likely to be quite unhappy with overall system and find a more convenient display – even if that display is a four square inch screen on their cell phone.

Together, situated displays and PS-enabled devices form a symbiotic system supporting mobility. The communication protocol of this system must support two main functions: discovery of nearby PS devices and data connections to those devices. Imagine a group of travelers in an airport: Each available flight information display and available kiosk must be able to detect all multiple nearby PSs and arbitrate between multiple devices that request service. For a particular class of information, the system must then decide which displays, if any, are appropriate for that information. Finally, when a match is made between a PS and a display, the proper protocols and communication channels must be coordinated to provide data access.

To provide support for PS-enabled interaction, software on available situated displays should support simple, well-accepted communication mechanisms, such as network file systems and web-browser (HTTP) protocols. For applications, either a standard web-based interaction model, using HTML or applets, or standard software running on the display host can be used to view or edit a user's data. Architecturally, the key piece of system infrastructure necessary to enable the Personal Server model is a thin layer of softwarc called the "Neighborhood Manager" that provides a connection between the low-level radio subsystem and higher-level applications, such as a web browser or photo editor. Although wireless technology has advanced substantially in recent years, system software that streamlines and enables applications to leverage ubiquitous connectivity is still lacking. A major focus of the PS project is the development of the system software, both device-side and display-side, that allows users easy access data on the device easily through conventional applications and mechanisms.

On the portable device, the key hardware challenge is providing enough resources to sufficiently support a mobile user. The wireless subsystem must provide acceptable bandwidth, communicate with low latency, consume little power, and be physically small. Furthermore, it must connect to a wide variety of devices and coexist with other wireless technologies. For many devices, both the overall size of the device and its power consumption are dictated primarily by the display. Because the Personal Server relies primarily on remote display interaction, the radio subsystem radio becomes one of the more power-demanding components in the platform. Removing the need for a feature-rich display also opens the door to novel and interesting industrial design opportunities that would easily allows a PS to be designed into a wristwatch or other wearable component.

The current Personal Server prototype is implemented using an Intel® XScale™ processor, on board flash, built-in Bluetooth radio, and high-capacity storage provided by a removable Compact-Flash card. The platform uses the Linux operating system and runs the standard Apache web-server, supporting both web-page access and network drive mounting. Numerous applications such as media (music and videos) streaming, presentation foil display, and web-browser favorites migration are supported through this basic platform. This platform is intended as a broad research base that can be utilized by internal and external research organizations to gain a better understanding of mobile computing. To lower power consumption without significantly impacting the user experience, the radio and processor subsystems are designed to support "always-on" operation: the device can be contacted externally through the Bluetooth radio without requiring an explicit user action (such as pressing a power button). This capability is important because it enables access through situated displays without either compromising the user experience or physical device size.

Personal Server technology is designed to personalise each user's environment as the user moves through it. This personalisation is not only achieved by enabling access to personal information through situated displays, but also by customizing the presentation of that information on each display without requiring the user's attention. This customization may include the passive collection of information as the user moves through the environment. For example, the device can act as a "mobile data collection" platform that silently records the names, photographs, and location of various restaurants as they are passed (Figure 156). Later on, when a user decides that they are hungry, they can simply use a nearby kiosk to access a list of establishments already seen: helping the user recall a restaurant that looked "interesting" earlier in the day without having to search through faceless records in a simple proximity listing. This application is providing *remembrances*: where users have been and what they have seen. Furthermore, after recalling the restaurant, the user can use the large-screen kiosk display to view a map of its exact location. This kind of interaction highlights the basic vision of the Personal Server: seamless integration of the virtual and physical worlds without requiring the user to juggle many small and inconvenient mobile devices.

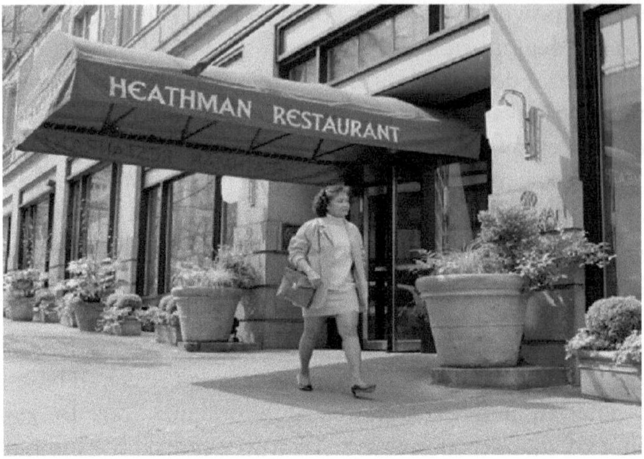

Figure 14-13. Automatically capturing info-beacons from the environment.

4.2 *Internet Suspend/Resume*

Internet Suspend/Resume (ISR) (Kozuch and Satyanarayanan, 2002) technology, like the Personal Server, leverages situated displays to provide unencumbered mobility. The goal of the ISR project is to faithfully reproduce a user's entire computing environment on any situated display. With ISR technology, when a user departs from a particular computing location, he or she *suspends* the computing session in progress. That is, the state of the entire computing environment, including the user's files, applications, customizations, and current windowing session, is captured and stored in the network. When the user arrives at a new computing location, he or she *resumes* the computing session and finds the environment exactly as it was when suspended: the same files are available, the same applications are open, and the cursor is still blinking in the same window location. The user's experience is very similar to suspending and resuming a laptop – except of course, that ISR technology eliminates the need to carry laptop hardware.

ISR technology assumes that situated displays are both resource-rich and globally connected. Consider modern assumptions regarding the availability of electricity and lighting. In modern cities, most people do not carry flashlights with them; they are confident that the lighting infrastructure is sufficiently pervasive and robust. In the future, might computer users not make similar assumptions regarding the availability of situated displays? This model is already relevant today as Internet connections and PCs proliferate in all areas of life, public and private; however, as yet, no common system software exists that enables users to make effective use of these resource-rich situated displays. To date, the ISR project has focused on the development of this enabling system software. This comprises of two main components: virtual machine technology and distributed file system technology.

Virtual machine technology (Figure 15-7) provides a software mechanism (called a *virtual machine monitor*, or VMM) through which computers may be "virtualized." Virtualized computers appear to be similar to system software regardless of differences in the underlying hardware – the details are abstracted away to a common machine view. Because of this property, a user's environment may be migrated between machines that differ substantially. Further, the virtual machine interface provides a natural mechanism for encapsulating the state of the user's environment. This state can be collected by the VMM and stored in network for later retrieval. This encapsulated state may be conveniently stored as a set of files and transported throughout the network using a distributed file system. Other communication methods are possible, such as a web-based approach, but a file system provides a straightforward and well-accepted interface.

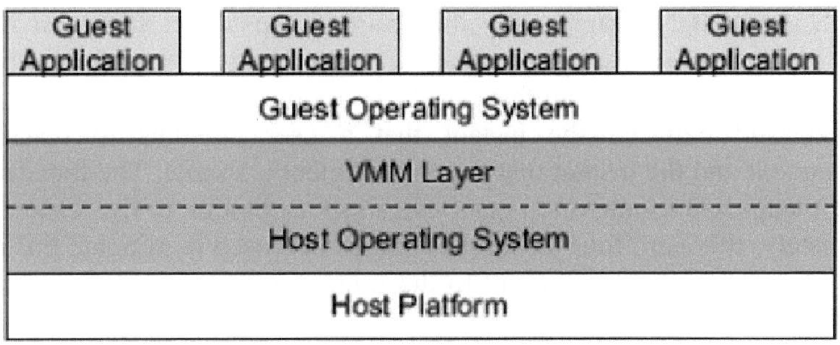

Figure 14-14. Virtual Machine Monitor layer supporting guest OS.

A typical usage model for ISR might be a web-design professional, who must combine information from many independent applications to construct a web page. In order to accomplish this task, the designer is likely to have a highly-configured workstation with all their favorite applications: high-end photo editor, line-based graphics illustrator, web favorites for researching information, a particular "color scheme," and of course the web-design software itself. In order for the professional to effectively move this work environment around, all these applications and their associated state must be moved: simply moving the web-page source around and hoping the new locale has the available applications is not sufficient. Furthermore, if the web-designer is in the middle of an active editing session at home and needs to return to the office, shutting down the execution state and re-starting the applications at their destination would be particularly cumbersome. ISR enables mobility by allowing a user to suspend their entire execution state and move that state through the Internet to resume it at a new location. An alternative to this process would be to use a laptop computer to host all the applications; however, laptops are typically slower than their fixed counterparts and cumbersome to carry from place to place.

As mentioned above, the virtual machine technology provides a level of abstraction such that the suspend and resume machines appear to be similar even if the underlying hardware is quite different. This property is quite important, as the suspend and resume machines will quite frequently differ in terms of processor speed, available memory, graphics devices, or other parameters. Once execution state is restored, the user's environment appears *exactly* the same as the original, including such details as background image, window placement, computation-in-progress, or any number of important factors.

The key challenge for ISR technology is that the encapsulated state of the user's environment can be quite large: tens of gigabytes. Recall that this state includes the user's files, applications, operating system, and dynamic data. Unfortunately, transferring the entire encapsulated state can require quite a long time (tens of minutes), particularly over slow network connections. This time manifests itself as a slowdown in *resume time*, the time elapsed between the instant that a user attempts to resume an environment and the instant that the environment is usable. The transfer time of the encapsulated state often manifests itself as dilation of the resume time. Fortunately, there are four techniques that can be used to mitigate this delay, and make it virtually transparent to the user: proactive transfer, on-demand transfer, caching, and compression.

If the resume location of the user is known prior to his or her arrival, the state can be transferred while the user is in transit to that destination, if not earlier. This *proactive transfer* can reduce the resume time nearly to zero. This approach is particularly practical if the user typically frequents a small number of resume locations, such as home and work. These locations will be kept up to date constantly – providing very low resume times in the common case. In such cases, a further optimization can be made; because the frequented systems are constantly kept synchronized, the systems will only transfer state modified during the most recent session upon each suspend.

The converse of proactive transfer is *on-demand transfer*. In cases where the user attempts to resume at a location that has not been prepared, transferring the entire encapsulated state can require a very long time. Rather than require the user to wait the data is retrieved, in this transfer mode the system fetches blocks of data, as they are needed. This approach enables the user to resume after just a small amount of state has been transferred. The trade-off is that as needed blocks of data are encountered, the system experiences small, occasional delays. These delays result in degradation of the observed performance, referred to as *response time* in this context.

Both approaches employ caching of data on the resume machine. In the proactive case, caching occurs automatically. A similar process occurs with the on-demand transfer mode. As data blocks are retrieved on demand, they are maintained on the resume machine. Only the first access to each block requires a network transfer. Subsequent accesses to the block are serviced from the cache. Recent ISR research has even explored sharing caches between users; portions of users' environments can be common among many users. A large part of each user's environment will remain constant, representing the base OS install and application suite. If several user's with similar software environments visit the same resume site, all but the first user may benefit from blocks left in the cache by previous users.

Another complementary technique is compression. Blocks of data may be compressed prior to transfer. Although compression/decompression adds a small delay at both the suspend and resume sites, the total time is reduced because the size of the resulting data transferred over the network is smaller.

Laptop computers have recently become the platform-of-choice for many mobile professionals: such platforms allow mobile users to travel and still be guaranteed an effective work environment. However, they also require their owners to carry large bags and juggle different power cords and adaptors. Internet Suspend/Resume enables the same attractive work-environment mobility without requiring bulky mobile hardware. The key observation is that full functionality is essential to mobile professionals; migrating anything less than the user's complete environment is unacceptable. Complete migration is made possible by employing virtual machine technology, ISR enables the rapid customization of target hardware to a level of detail that is unmanageable using application-level approaches.

4.3 The Confluence of Architectures

The Personal Server supports the availability of personal data and applications, while Internet Suspend/Resume allows the migration of a full-featured execution environment: two forms of proactive computing that enable situated mobility. Combining the two can solve problems that might be encountered by either one individually. For example, the Personal Server could be used to supply the data necessary to reconstruct an Internet Suspend/Resume execution environment while traveling on an airplane where no Internet connectivity is available. Similarly, Internet Suspend/Resume can provide an environment in which to offload computational agents supporting the Personal Server as it moves around. The larger vision of proactive computing, which aims to mediate the interaction between humans and the physical world, leads us towards situated mobility because it provides a computing system that is not dominated by many small devices each vying for users' attention.

In order to move from place to place, ISR relies on the availability of the user's execution state, nominally through the wired Internet. Although ideal in many situations, there are times when it would be better to provide the necessary data from a local mobile device, such as the Personal Server, to remedy problems with network delays, outages, and security. For example, while visiting a customer's office, ISR users may be unable to obtain Internet access back to a "home" server due to firewalls or other security considerations. In this situation, the availability of data can be very important; by carrying the encapsulated state in a portable device, the user is guaranteed access. The Personal Server may also provide a local repository for storing sensitive data. In some situations, users may not trust the system hosting the ISR technology. By keeping some data, such as encryption keys, on the Personal Server, the user may provide differing levels of security for different portions of their data.

Alternatively, ISR can be used to support the Personal Server model of computing; as users move through the environment, software agents operating on their behalf can occupy virtual machines present in the environment. By executing in such an environment rather than on the user's mobile device, the agents will have better access to environmental resources and reduce the drain on the battery in the mobile device. As the software agents move around, they will expect certain software components and the results of previous computation to be present – functionally provided by the ISR model. When, eventually, a user wishes to interact with their roving agents through a situated display, all the necessary information resulting from the agents computation will be immediately available – i.e., the agents can proactively gather the necessary data rather than supply it to the user on demand. For example, when lunchtime approaches, mobile agents coordinated by a user's Personal Server can start to search for nearby restaurants they might enjoy (again, based on a profile served from the mobile device). When eventually queried to find a place to eat, the system will be able to very quickly respond with a list of pre-computed alternatives, rather than performing the search responsively – all without unnecessarily draining the mobile device's battery. The ability to very quickly access information through situated displays is essential since the Personal Server is intended to be used in highly mobile and dynamic environments.

As hinted in the preceding paragraphs, proactive computing is concerned with managing the interface between humans and the physical world. As computing technology pervades the world around us, the complexity of managing the devices around us will exceed the usefulness of those objects. The most limited resource in these systems is the user's attention, and that resource is consumed rapidly as the user "deals" with computational systems. Even with a small number of limited personal devices, such as a cell-phone, PDA, and digital watch, trying to keep them all functional and properly integrated with a home computing environment can be a daunting task. System designers, therefore, should consider how such systems can invisibly serve the user, rather than attempt to grab the user's attention. Situated displays support this goal by providing a controlled view into a complex system of computing elements; rather than interacting with every device through it's own display, users may be presented with a consolidated view through a nearby, resource-rich, situated display. The use of situated displays is just a single facet of the larger proactive computing vision, but these devices play an especially important role in a mobile context where users are already constantly distracted by the changing environment.

5. Closing

This chapter has described one vision of mobile computing that utilizes situated displays found in the public infrastructure to enable mobility without requiring extensive mobile hardware. This vision is manifested in two emerging research projects, the Personal Server and Internet Suspend/Resume, which extend current handheld and web mobile usage patterns to enhance our mobile experience. Abstracting these concepts, considering the user's perception of situated displays and how they are used to gain access to personal information can be an instructive exercise. This line of reasoning covers the same ground as the previous analysis, but sheds new light on the practice of "remoting" displays and computation: the fundamental concept behind enabling computational mobility. There are two major design approaches to remote execution: complete desktop, where the graphical desktop of a PC is migrated *en masse*, and individual window, where single windows are imported into an already existing desktop. These two techniques seem suited for slightly different uses, especially where collaboration or multi-source operation in involved. This analysis provides a better understanding of the use of situated displays, and specifically how they can be used to support mobility.

In the beginning, display screens were either constructed as monolithic elements, fundamentally attached to the localized computing resources they served, or supported only a highly impoverished sense of remote access. The initial PC, for example, was highly effective at localized applications, such as the spreadsheet and word processor, and was virtually unable to network with other computers. Even in the cases where it was possible to access a computer remotely, the interaction was limited to highly constrained text-only transactions, which were not attractive to the populace at large. The invention of the Graphical User Interface (GUI) incited the modern personal computing revolution, but this enabler was simply not possible over the slow text-only connection. Even TV, which presents a highly popular form of remote viewing is severely limited by its lack of interaction: a one-way medium. Because of these reasons, the popular notion of computing was restricted to complete (and therefore bulky) systems, where a strong connection between display and computing could be maintained.

The first tractable notions of remote interactive displays appeared in the form of "single-window" mechanisms, where one window on a screen would represent a connection to a remote system. Initially, this manifested itself in the form of remote "X-Windows," which individual applications could use to project their windows to a remote display. However, this capability was still severely limited by network latencies, which could become intolerably high for the tight interaction required. With the inception of the Internet and World Wide Web, the web-browser metaphor allowed delay-tolerant access to remote systems. It could (and still does) take many seconds to download a single window – but once a page was localized, it could be interacted with from the local host. This detail ignited a revolution in remote computing, where the emphasis in computing suddenly shifted from the individual computer to the web-based service. However, this delay-tolerant operation still exhibits multi-second delays for remote information access, and can be completely disabled by transient network failures. These delays and disconnections are exacerbated in a mobile context, further compounded by issues of high-cost and increased information needs – concerns that are directly addressed by the Personal Server model, which provides a single-window interface to a low-latency and always-available personal data source.

The ability for "whole-screen" remoting, where users can access their entire desktop environment from a remote display, was eventually enabled by decreased network latencies. Popularized by technologies such as VNC (Virtual Network Computing) and RDP (Remote Desktop Protocol), this capability allows a user to remotely access their complete desktop environment, including desktop icon placement, individual window state, and available applications. For example, if a user is in the middle of pulling together information for a detailed web page, which may include information from many different sources and applications, they can easily stop work at one station and move to a new desktop, possibly in order to discuss their work with a colleague, without having to manually save and restore their working desktop environment. Unfortunately, whole-screen remoting is even more sensitive to increased network latencies than single-window systems, and there is no easy web-browser equivalent. Internet Suspend/Resume steps into this arena by allowing delay-tolerant migration of an entire work environment. By moving the entire execution state of a machine to a new work local, instead of just remoting the display portion, low-latency interaction can still be maintained even though the "original" machine may be very far away.

Independent of latency and availability considerations, there are interesting sharing and cooperative work applications for remote computing systems. As mentioned in the previous paragraph, the ability to walk to another's workstation and easily show them a complete working environment can smooth collaboration. Similarly, the web-browser model allows me to show you personal web content, e.g., my personal photo album, from any internet enabled computer. The situation becomes considerably more complex when two collaborators would like to share information *with each other*, instead of just one person to another. With single-window remoting, the two users could each bring up personal windows and simply drag-and-drop information between them – but this precludes interaction-rich applications, such as for web-editing projects, that may have stringent execution environment requirements. Alternatively, two users could each open a local whole-screen interface, simply sharing the local screen real-estate. Although effective, this technique requires showing two complete desktops on the screen at the same time, which can become very visually cluttering and inefficient; however, this conundrum can be easily mitigated by using single-window interfaces into multiple local execution environments (one for each user), allowing effective collaboration without screen clutter or network delays.

It is key in all these situations that the interactions of these various systems do not draw the user's attention away from the "real world" – the interesting people and things around them. In general, situated mobility helps this by easing the difficulty of accessing data through mobile devices: the Personal Server provides always-available access to personal information, while Internet Suspend/Resume provides a familiar execution environment. By enabling these platforms to better manage the human/computer relationship, either by streamlining connectivity or actively migrating data to a new location, such proactive computing systems can actively reduce the "waiting for download" attention required by the user. Eventually, these systems will merge to provide always-available access to familiar execution environments served by roaming agents anticipating information needs, allowing users to get the information they want without being distracted by the computing resources that they use to access it.

Mobile computing is a powerful tool and is starting to replace "desktop computing" as a hot topic for the future foundation for computing systems research. Network "hot spots," which provide local wireless connectivity, are starting to emerge in many cities and small-town cafés. However, it will be very difficult to displace the advantages afforded by a large screen display and fixed-infrastructure computing resources. The overriding question should not be "what will win: desktop or mobile", but rather, how do we seamlessly blend the advantages and disadvantages of both models: taking the best of both worlds to form a better version of personal mobility. To that end, utilizing situated displays as an ostensibly ironic platform for mobility highlights both the compelling capabilities and design difficulties exposed by such a model. Taking a step back and realizing that "people move around" and "they want access to stuff", *independent* of the technology involved, allows systems that support accurate notions of nobility without unnecessary limitations.

6. Acknowledgements

The authors would like to thank the entire Personal Server and Internet Suspend/Resume teams for their contribution: Mahadev Satyanarayanan, John Light, Roy Want, Murali Sundar, and Alex Nguyen.

7. References

Kozuch M, Satyanarayanan M. Internet suspend/resume. Proceedings Fourth IEEE Workshop on Mobile Computing Systems and Applications; 2002: 40-46.

Perry, M., O'Hara, K., Sellen, A., Brown, B. & Harper, R. Dealing with mobility: understanding access anytime, anywhere. ACM Transactions on Human-Computer Interaction, 2001; 8(4): 1-25.

Tennenhouse D. Comparing Autonomic and Proactive Computing, IBM Systems Journal, 42 (1), Jan. 2003.

Want R., Pering T., Danneels G., Kumar M., Sundar M., Light J. Personal Servers: Changing the Way We Think about Ubiquitous Computing. Proceedings of Ubicomp 2002: 4th International Conference on Ubiquitous Computing; 2002 Sept 30th-Oct 2nd, Goteborg, Sweden, Springer LNCS 2498: 194-209.

Chapter 15

SUPPORTING EXTENSIBLE PUBLIC DISPLAY SYSTEMS WITH SPEAKEASY

Julie A. Black[1], W. Keith Edwards, Mark W. Newman, Jana Z. Sedivy, Trevor F Smith
[1]*Stanford University; PARC*

Abstract: A digital public display system must have the utmost modularity and flexibility. Users must be able to display and interact with any media type on the display, and must also be able to connect to and control a variety of devices from the display. Further, because these systems must be able to adapt to their users over time, public display systems will need to be able to support new media types, devices, and services without additional development work. Speakeasy is a foundational platform that can provide such *ad hoc* communication, and enable interaction among devices with little to no *a priori* knowledge of one another. To explore this platform and the foundation that it provides for a public display system, we developed two digital public displays atop the Speakeasy architecture: a text-based tickertape LED display and a large-format graphical display. In the course of this chapter, we discuss the Speakeasy architecture as well as the development process of these two displays.

Key words: Public display, Speakeasy, extensibility, *ad hoc* interoperability

1. Introduction

Interactive digital public displays provide a means through which members of a community may share different media types easily and effectively. Many researchers have looked at how such public displays might be integrated into our daily lives, both in workplace and non-workplace settings.

K. O'Hara et al. (eds.), Public and Situated Displays: Social and Interactional Aspects of Shared Display Technologies, 359–386.

These displays are typically envisioned as large surfaces situated in a public setting, such as a shared coffee area in a workplace. In most scenarios, a public display will display some "default" content (such as a lab meeting schedule, upcoming events, news headlines, bus schedules, and so forth). But as a user approaches the display, he or she can appropriate it for a more directed interaction, such as to view a personal calendar or check waiting email. To support retrieval of remote data (including both default and personalized content), these displays generally have network connectivity, allowing them to display content from remote sources.

Beyond these obvious characteristics, however, public display systems described in the research literature often share a number of other, somewhat more subtle, characteristics:

- They support **walk-up** functionality. Users can approach and interact with such displays easily without complicated login procedures, having to install software, or explicitly copy their data to the display device.
- They are generally intended to support **collaboration** among multiple users. These users can take advantage of the large screen area (and, possibly, multiple simultaneous input devices) to share information and work together.
- They support **interactions with existing media, information, and devices** that their users bring to the display.
- These devices typically have **no owner**, meaning that often there is no single user who has sole access to the device. However, such displays must **support a range of working styles**. For example, a display in a public setting may be used temporarily by a single user to access private data. Some displays might even inhabit private office, and be used primarily for the display of personal data.

One common thread throughout the criteria described above is that public display systems will necessarily reside in *radically heterogeneous* environments. That is, these displays will not exist in isolation. They will coexist with other devices (PDAs, mobile phones, laptop and desktop computers) and services (web servers, search engines, conferencing software, calendaring systems) that already permeate our environment.

We believe that users will naturally desire—and expect—that the public display systems around them will interact with and complement their existing tools, as well as new tools that may appear. We can easily posit a number of quite mundane such interoperations with existing devices—users may wish to display a calendar stored on a PDA on a larger display for shared viewing; they may wish to "mirror" a laptop's screen to a display already present in a room to give a presentation; they may wish to use an existing video conferencing system with a public display, to have an impromptu conference.

We believe that the ability to interoperate with such a wide range of devices and services (and the respective media types and protocols supported or required by these) can change the character of proposed public display systems. It can extend them beyond being "dedicated" devices, hard-coded for a fixed range of tasks such as shared drawing and calendar viewing, to become truly ubiquitous devices, capable of being used for virtually any *ad hoc* purpose. They would be *appropriable* by users, to be used serendipitously to complement whatever task is at hand, regardless of the other devices or services necessary for that task.

Our explorations into public displays systems are predicated on the belief that, to become truly useful, displays must be applicable to a wide and open-ended range of uses—not some fixed set decided upon by the developers of the display system. In fact, we believe that one of the greatest pragmatic problems in the adoption of robust public displays will be the need for such displays to interoperate with a potentially open-ended set of services, devices, and media types. Without such interoperability, public displays will be used for limited, niche applications, and will not have the arbitrary "walk-up-and-use" property envisioned in the research literature.

Based on our beliefs about the radically heterogeneous environments in which public displays will reside and be used, the system we envision embodies the utmost extensibility: view virtually arbitrary content, on any display system, anywhere. Content can be posted to a "network" of public displays from any device. Likewise, submitted content can be viewed from any display system, including displays in public settings or in a personal office. Further, to allow virtually arbitrary connectivity, we do not wish to limit public displays to compatibility only with devices, services, and media types that have been "hard-coded" into the display at the time it is created. Instead, we want to improve the forward compatibility of our system, to support the media standards and protocols that may appear tomorrow. To date, such an infrastructure has been lacking from most developed display systems.

In this chapter, we describe Speakeasy, an infrastructure developed to support *ad hoc* interactions between different devices with little to no *a priori* knowledge of one another. Speakeasy provides the flexibility needed to achieve the level of interoperability—and future extensibility—required of a public display system that operates in a world of radical heterogeneity.

In general terms, Speakeasy is a mobile code-based architecture that allows users to arbitrarily connect Speakeasy-enabled devices. Leveraging mobile code allows devices (known in Speakeasy as *components*) to dictate how other components should interact with them. This is in contrast to having to agree upon protocols, media formats, and so forth, prior to the production of devices.

One "side effect" of this sort of open-ended extensibility is that an application cannot be expected to understand the semantics of every potential device, service, or media type it may encounter—if we required such semantic understanding to be "built in" to the application in order for it to use a new device, we would be limiting the runtime extensibility that is the very goal of the system. Instead, we presume that *users* will have the semantic knowledge necessary to know when and whether to interconnect two devices, and what such a connection "means." The role of the infrastructure is simply to ensure that connections *can* take place, if the user decides to make them.

As an example, a Speakeasy-enabled public display system may not be specifically coded to interact with a TiVo-style personal video recorder. In other words, it would not necessarily "know" what such a device did, nor when it was appropriate to connect to it. But in our model, a user would be able to display the content from such a device to the public display, if and when he or she deems it appropriate to do so.

1.1 A Scenario

As a motivating example for the style of interaction we foresee for such radically interoperable devices, consider a geographically distributed research group, with most of the group's members in California, but one member, John, in New York. To support their collaboration, this group has two conference rooms set up to facilitate remote interaction. Specifically, these rooms have a large, wall-mounted display under the control of a computerized conferencing system, along with a number of other devices including microphones, speakers, and so on. All of this technology is intended to support information sharing, both within a room, and across rooms.

Even with all of this technology, the "hard coded" nature of most of the software systems in use present a number of hurdles to real interoperation. First, even though the conference rooms are equipped with whiteboard capture systems, these do not interoperate with the video conferencing software. If John wishes to see a drawing on the whiteboard in California, he has to ask others to manually point the camera at the board, or ask a user in California to capture an image of the board and send it to him through a side channel, typically email.

Likewise, the document scanners situated in each room are connected to—and usable by—the PCs in that room only. Again, since the systems are not able to dynamically adapt to new needs, John must request that a user in California scan a document and mail it to him.

Finally, John has found a web page that's relevant to the discussion at hand. In this scenario, he has two options for sharing it with his colleagues in California: mailing the URL (which is, again, an out-of-band mechanism), or pointing the camera at his laptop screen.

These impediments to interoperation have real consequences on the fluidity with which people can collaborate. One can easily imagine that other devices and services containing useful information, which would aid the collaboration, may remain inaccessible without serendipitous interoperability. Our goal, therefore, is to support ubiquitous interoperation of devices and services with display systems.

One can imagine how this scenario might play out using a mechanism for *ad hoc* interactions built atop Speakeasy. Each conference room is equipped with a display system whose functionality grows as more Speakeasy-enabled devices are brought to it. This is fundamentally unlike a video conferencing system, which has a limited set of inputs and outputs; the Speakeasy version of the system is also fundamentally unlike most presently envisioned public displays, which provide a few predetermined modes of interaction, such as displaying web pages or calendars. This new display system can be used in conjunction with any other device or services that is represented as a Speakeasy component, even if the display was not specifically designed to work with these new devices or services.

First, the display can be used for videoconferencing. Any camera that is on the network and has a "Speakeasy presence" (that is, is exposed as a Speakeasy component) can be used with the display, regardless of data format or protocol supported by the camera. We have built a number of such camera components.

Second, our lab has an internally-deployed whiteboard capture system, which is also implemented as a Speakeasy component. While the original intent of this system was to support printing of whiteboard captures, it can easily work with the display, to permit presentation of whiteboard images on either local or remote displays.

Likewise, devices like document scanners, PDAs, etc., can all be used with the display, without software installation or rewriting. Users with laptops can easily mirror their screens to any display using a simple client application, also built using the Speakeasy platform. This allows easy sharing of web pages, and other online content.

In fact, all of these components have been implemented by our group, and all work together to complement the display system—as more components appear, they extend the functionality of the existing components of the system. In addition to the components described in this scenario, we have been building a growing collection of components in other domains, including home audio/visual devices, office services, devices intended to support mobile work, and so on.

To summarize, while an important aspect of public displays is their ability to present and share "community" content, we believe an equally important aspect is their ability to be appropriated for the uses at hand. Supporting this sort of serendipitous appropriation requires the ability to interact with virtually arbitrary devices and services. As we shall see, these same properties of extensibility carry over into the content that is displayed *without* a directed interaction like the ones described above.

In the remainder of this chapter, we explore the extensibility and interoperability requirements of public displays, and discuss the implications of these requirements for an infrastructure designed to support such displays. We then examine the Speakeasy architecture and how it lends itself well to the needs of public displays and environments that require *ad hoc*, many-to-many device connectivity. We have used this infrastructure to develop a basic display system that supports a numerous and extensible set of data types (including still images, streaming video, MPEG movies, and so on), as well as new devices and services, with little engineering overhead. We describe this public display system, as well as explore how it leverages the Speakeasy architecture.

2. Related Work

Many researchers have examined the use of digital public displays to enhance human interactions. Much of this research has focused on the design issues specific to public display systems focusing on the impact and user experience of such systems in workplace settings. Many of the projects, however, do not focus specifically on the requirements and approaches of the backend infrastructure. Specifically, they integrate new media types by special casing each one and hard-coding them into the system.

Many of these projects were discussed in the fall 2003 CSCW workshop entitled "Public, Community, and Situated Displays: Design, use, and interaction around shared information displays," and many are discussed in detail throughout this book. In this section, we look at related work in the area of design and user experience of public displays, as these guide the requirements of our infrastructure. We also look at related systems and architectural approaches to delivering the sorts of extensibility and interoperability that we believe is required for truly flexible public displays.

The Notification Collage (Greenberg and Rounding, 2001) provides an instructive look at the integration of a display system into an office setting.

In this work, researchers have developed a set of useful interactions—such as viewing a slideshow of photographs, a web page, and live streaming video—and have focused on the layout of viewable information upon the public display. The interactions developed by the Notification Collage highlight the need for the ability to easily appropriate new devices and media types. Because of the need to specially integrate each device or media type into the system, supporting new devices and media types requires explicit programming.

Another common backend approach for public display systems has been to rely upon web servers. On such project, currently taking place at the Fuji-Xerox Palo Alto Laboratory questions how to support digital collaboration (Trevor *et al.*, 2002). For this project, researchers ran a web server on each device so that data might be shared across the network, and information about commonly used devices and documents could be reaped from operating system and web server usage logs. This approach is also designed to support the "view anything anywhere" requirements that we have focused on. This system leverages the ubiquity of the web to allow easy viewing of content that is commonly accessible through web browsers. The approach is also, however, limited in some important ways by the restrictions of the web. First, new data types can only be supported through plug-ins. Second, web-based architectures necessarily rely on HTTP as a transport protocol, which may not be appropriate for all media types. Third, user control is limited to web-based forms or simple applets. And finally, this approach requires users to "publish" their data through a web-based interface to the display's web server. Data that resides on devices without web capabilities cannot be easily shipped to the display system.

Since the core focus of the Speakeasy infrastructure is on interoperation among network services, we also present here a brief review of related approaches to interoperation, in both the research and commercial spheres, outside of the focus on public displays.

Remote procedure and method call systems, include Sun's RPC (Sun Microsystems, 1997) and CORBA (Object Management Group, 1995), address a number of "low-level" aspects of interoperability, namely, portability of data and standardization on the mechanisms for invocation of a remote operation on a server. They require agreement on the underlying transport protocols (TCP/IP or IIOP over TCP/IP, for example), and they also require agreement on the *interfaces* that service will implement. For example, a CORBA service will implement some programmatic interface, expressed via the CORBA Interface Definition Language, IDL. Any client of this service must be explicitly written against this interface, and must be restricted to the set of underlying transport protocols that the service is written to use.

More recent Web Services systems, such as Microsoft's .NET (Thai and Lam, 2001), are essentially updated remote procedure call systems that leverage the ubiquity of the Web. These systems generally use Web-friendly specification languages and protocols—for example, WSDL (Christensen *et al.*, 2001) to specify service interfaces, and SOAP (Scribner and Stiver, 2000) as the protocol for invoking operations on services. While these systems hold great promise for interoperation, they essentially embody the same limitations as earlier remote procedure call systems: they require the use of a *specific* transport protocol, no matter the requirements of the application, and—more damaging—they require that clients and services agree on every specific interface in order to communicate.

In both remote procedure call and web service frameworks, these service interfaces are not general—that is, there are large numbers of them, tuned to the particular needs of the service, meaning that no single client can possibly have general interoperability among all of them. Further, we believe that trying to "standardize" on a narrow set of well-agreed service interfaces is fruitless in these systems, because of the limitations that would be inherent in any such interface set. The fact that these systems provide no forms of dynamic extensibility inherently limits the flexibility that could be achieved through a narrow set of "one size fits all" interfaces.

Systems such as Sun Microsystems's Jini (Waldo, 1999), however, *do* provide great flexibility in dynamic extensibility. Jini leverages mobile code to allow clients and services to acquire new behaviour at runtime. In Jini, clients are written against service interfaces as in the case of remote procedure call and web service systems. At runtime, however, services can deliver new *implementations* of these interfaces to their clients. This ability allows clients to dynamically acquire arbitrary new functions and features, provided that they understand the calling interface used to access these new functions and features. For example, a client can be written against a generic "printer" interface. Printing services, then, can deliver service-specific implementations of that interface to their clients, which allow the clients to communicate back to the services using whatever mechanism is most appropriate for the service.

Jini provides a radical degree of extensibility, but does have a number of weaknesses. First, Jini services tend to implement very domain-dependent interfaces (such as for printing, and file serving) that clients must be built to understand. This approach requires that clients have knowledge of the *specific* interfaces provided by a service. Second, Jini dictates a fixed set of discovery protocols used as part of the process to locate new services. The system is not easily extensible to new discovery protocols—such as Bluetooth's SDP (Bluetooth Consortium, 2001) for example—that might be necessary for supporting new devices.

Finally, the iRoom system and related tools from Stanford (Fox *et al.*, 2000; Huang *et al.*, 2001) embody an approach to extensible interoperability that is very different than Speakeasy's. This system uses a shared *tuplespace* (in the style of Linda (Gelenter, 1985)) as a point of rendezvous and communication between clients and services. Entities on the network can *produce* tuples—essentially loosely structured data elements—which can then be *consumed* by other entities. The tuplespace acts as a shared blackboard for data exchange.

Tuplespace systems have a high degree of extensibility: any data that can be represented as a tuple can be posted to the tuplespace, where it can be seen and ready by any other application. If a new type of application comes along, it can create and use its own tuple formats without affecting other elements of the infrastructure. The interfaces to the tuplespace itself are fixed, meaning that clients and services can freely exchange data without worry about incompatibilities in their ability to access the shared blackboard. These approaches do, however, require that clients and services understand the structure of the tuples that they exchange. In some sense, then, these systems shift the problem of interoperation from agreement on service interfaces to agreement on data structures. In practice, however, these difficulties can be overcome through the use of tools that can provide compatibility between old and new services by "rewriting" tuples in the tuplespace (Ponnekanti, 1995).

To summarize, then, the need for public display systems to be able to use a range of media types, devices, and network services has been illustrated by previous work on such displays. We believe that the need for extensibility goes beyond simple viewing of new media types—that public display users will need to be able to appropriate arbitrary resources that they find around them. Current approaches to interoperability impose constraints on this ability. While they allow applications to use *new instances of known types* of services, they do not easily allow applications to use *entirely new types* of services altogether. We believe that entirely new approaches to interoperability are needed that can allow interactions among *ad hoc* and open-ended sets of services.

3. Requirements for Supporting Extensible Public Display Systems

In order to support the sort of extensible "anything, anywhere" public display systems outlined at the start of this chapter, there are a number of technical requirements that must be met.

First, we need to be able to display virtually arbitrary content on a public display. While one could try to "standardize" a preordained set of data types that must be understood by both the display and any devices or services that feed the display, we believe that ultimately this will prove to be an unworkable approach. New content types are appearing all the time, and each typically requires some special accommodation in order to support it—new video formats require new CODECs (compressors-decompressors) for example; new image formats require preinstalled code libraries to parse and display images in these formats. As an example of the continuing explosion of data types, consider the domain of digital audio. Despite the dominance of MP3 as an audio format, new competing formats (including WMA, OggVorbis, and AAC) appear regularly, each with its own virtues and drawbacks, proponents, and so on. A truly extensible public display system—one that can accommodate "walk-up" use without incompatibility, driver installation, software version mismatches, and so on—must be able to support arbitrary new data types as they appear.

To complicate the issue even further, the exchange of certain data types often requires specialized protocols. For example, high-quality streaming video is rarely if ever delivered over a "generic" protocol such as FTP or HTTP. Instead, new protocols are developed that "build in" support for particular media types, and can respond to the particular demands of that media type (ensuring key frame delivery for video, for example). Just as we cannot reasonably dictate a fixed set of data types that the display must support, we can neither dictate one (or even a handful) of data exchange protocols—new devices, services, and media types will appear that (justifiably) require specialized protocols. Again, our public display system must be able to support these, if it is to be able to achieve the ability to interact with arbitrary devices and services.

In order to interact with devices and services that appear on the network, public displays must be able to dynamically *discover* them as they appear. For example, if a user walks up to a display with a PDA, the display should "notice" the PDA and be able to interact with it. Such detection of the comings and goings of entities on a network or in a physical space typically happens through a *discovery protocol*. There are a number of such protocols in use today (SDP, SLP, Salutation, the Jini multicast and unicast discovery protocols, and so on), and different entities on the network will speak different ones. Just as an extensible public display system must support a (perhaps open-ended) range of data exchange protocols, it must also have the ability to use virtually arbitrary discovery protocols.

Of course, discovery protocols (as well as data transfer protocols) may be specialized to work over different physical transports, such as Bluetooth, IRDA, and so forth. Obviously, we cannot download new hardware to a public display device to allow it to use new physical transports. Nonetheless, a flexible solution should allow easy (and transparent) bridging across existing physical transports. For example, a Bluetooth PDA should be able to use and interact with a public display system on an Ethernet, through the addition of a bridge, and without the tedious installation of extra software or configuration.

Public displays may not only be used to view and manipulate media and content, but also control devices and services. For example, if a new web search engine comes online, one may reasonably wish to be able to use this service from a public display. Thus, we need a way to integrate the *controls* for such services into the display's screen management framework. Likewise, we may wish to be able to use the display to control different devices. In a teleconferencing situation, a user in a remote location may view a video stream on the public display, and also use a set of controls to change the camera angle, to track speakers. This camera likely has specialized controls (for zoom, focus, direction, and so on) that are particular to it. While we might be able to create a "camera-enabled" public display with these built in controls, we believe a better solution is to enable the camera to provide its own specific controls to the public display itself.

Because it becomes the device's responsibility to deliver not just its data, but also any needed protocols, media format handlers, and controls needed to use it, our architecture supports connectivity between the central public display and any *arbitrary* device or service controls as it appears on the network. Additionally, such an architecture does not rely upon any "hard coded," predetermined device requirements.

All of the requirements enumerated above represent different dimensions of *dynamic extensibility*: the ability for a display system to acquire new functionality not specifically built in at creation time. Such dynamically extensibility is crucial for supporting *evolution* of the system: the ability to adapt to change—such as the presence of new devices—over time.

One way to achieve such dynamic extensibility would be through a "centralized" approach. The builders of the public display system would provide a means to "drop" new versions of the display software onto the system as it became available. The developers of the display would then devote resources into specifically supporting each new protocol, data type, device type, and so forth, as it became available and accepted in the marketplace. Each new updated version of the software would afford the ability to connect with a few new types of entities on the network.

In contrast, Speakeasy takes a *decentralized* approach that supports a peer-to-peer "marketplace" of services. Rather than relying upon the original developers to establish standards of compatibility, by *dictat*, the Speakeasy architecture allows new functionality to be delivered to the display *only at the time it is needed.* When a new device appears that uses (or requires) a new data type or protocol, the behaviour required to interact with that device is delivered to the display *from the device itself.* In essence, each new device or service carries with it the behaviour that must be integrated into the public display, as well as other devices, in order for it to be used.

Such an arrangement turns the traditional apportionment of effort on its head. In the past, the introduction of a new type of device or service required the reimplementation of *every other* device or service in order to use the new entity; with Speakeasy, only the builder of the new device has to do extra work (to create the behaviour that will be used by clients of the new device); existing clients acquire this behaviour "for free."

In the next section, we present the Speakeasy architecture, and explain how it addresses the requirements established above.

4. The Speakeasy System

The Speakeasy infrastructure we have created allows the construction of applications that can use new devices, services, and networks, without requiring any *a priori* specialized knowledge. While not *specifically* designed with public displays in mind, we have found that our infrastructure supports many of the characteristics of extensible public displays, discussed at the beginning of this chapter.

Namely, it supports the ability of users to display and interact with arbitrary content on a public display. It allows them to control devices and services from the display, without requiring that such controls be "built in" to the display itself. It allows for discovery of new devices that are near it, and can acquire and use new discovery protocols as necessary. A Speakeasy-enabled display system is not limited in the range of media types it can accept, nor in the types of devices or services it can see, use, or control.

Further, Speakeasy indirectly supports the collaborative uses of public display systems. By removing the barriers to fluid display and control, content can be easily accessed by any display in a Speakeasy-enabled display system, permitting collaboration among geographically distributed participants as suggested in the introduction. This same property also indirectly supports the smooth transition between true public displays (non-private content viewed in a public setting), and "private-public" displays (displays used for viewing private content, perhaps even in a private setting such as an individual office). The system supports this by removing the traditional constraints on what information can be displayed where.

In the Speakeasy model, a public display runs a fairly generic application that provides screen management, user authentication, and support for any attached input devices, but has very little other functionality hard-coded into it. This application acts as a client for arbitrary Speakeasy devices and services on the network. As we explain in this section, Speakeasy devices and services have the ability to *extend the behaviour* of their clients, allowing them to acquire new functionality dynamically. In this model, the public display itself merely provides a framework for accessing arbitrary functionality on the network. The function and behaviour of the display change and are augmented as new devices and services appear.

Speakeasy terms any entity that can be accessed over a network a *component*. Components are discrete elements of functionality that can be arbitrarily interconnected with other components, and can be used by applications. They can represent devices (such as cameras, music players, printers, and PDAs), services (such as file servers, and web search engines), and also information (such as files, images, and text). The public display application can be connected to any component on the network in order to receive data from it, send data to it, or control it.

4.1 Speakeasy Basics

Speakeasy takes a radically different approach to interoperation than most existing systems. Rather than attempting to define some large collection of standards for how every foreseeable device or service will interoperate, we instead define a very small, fixed, and generic set of *meta-interfaces*. We call these interfaces meta-interfaces because, rather than defining the mechanisms of communication between two components, they define the *ways in which components acquire new behaviour*. That is, they describe a number of dimensions along which a new component that appears on a network can "teach" its peers how to interact with it.

We believe that this is a tenable approach to extensible interoperability, because there is no requirement for up-front agreement about all possible data exchange protocols, control user interfaces, media formats, and so on. Instead, new devices, when they appear on the network, bring with them the necessary code to allow their clients to interact with them appropriately.

Speakeasy defines four meta-interfaces, which together define the ways in which a component can extend the behaviour of its clients:

- **Data Transfer**: used to extend clients to new data transfer protocols, and new media handling abilities.
- **Aggregation**: used to allow clients to acquire new discovery protocols and operate over new network transports.
- **Metadata**: used to allow clients to query the capabilities and attributes of components on the network.

- **Control**: used to allow components to deliver new, custom user interfaces for controlling them to applications and users.

Since all Speakeasy components use this same set of meta-interfaces, application software can be written against this fixed set, and will work with all Speakeasy components. Most importantly, these interfaces do not need to be able to describe the particular, domain-specific abilities of every possible component. Instead, they only need to be able to describe the ways that new mobile code can be delivered to clients. This code, in turn, is what is responsible for capturing the specifics of interaction with particular components.

In the next sections, we provide a brief overview of how each of these meta-interfaces works. For more technical details, please see (Edwards *et al.*, 2002).

4.2 Data Transfer

The data transfer meta-interface defines, generically, how two components on a network can communicate, without prior agreement on data transfer protocols or data types. In Speakeasy, components that can transfer data exist in one of two roles: data sources, which provide data, and data sinks, which receive data. Sources may represent devices such as cameras, files in a file system, scanners, and so forth. Sinks may represent such items as printers, data repositories, and—especially salient for our purposes in this paper—displays.

When a user initiates a connection between a source and a sink, the data is not transferred directly. Instead, the source provides an *endpoint* object. This is a mobile code-based object that is downloaded into the sink, and provides new functionality to the sink to speak whatever data transfer protocol the source expects to use. For a digital camera source that might provide video over streaming RTP protocol, this endpoint would extend the behaviour of the recipient to speak the streaming protocol appropriate for the content type provided by the source.

Further, a negotiation process is used to allow recipients to acquire new data type handling behaviour at runtime. For example, if a new camera appears that supports MPEG4 video—which the recipient may not understand—the camera can provide code called a *typehandler* that augments the recipient's ability to process this previously unknown format.

Figure 15-1 illustrates this process. Here you see a connection between a network-enabled camera and a display. The display can be very simple, and need not understand any details about video encodings, streaming formats, and so on. Instead, this behaviour is transmitted from the camera to the display at the time the connection is established.

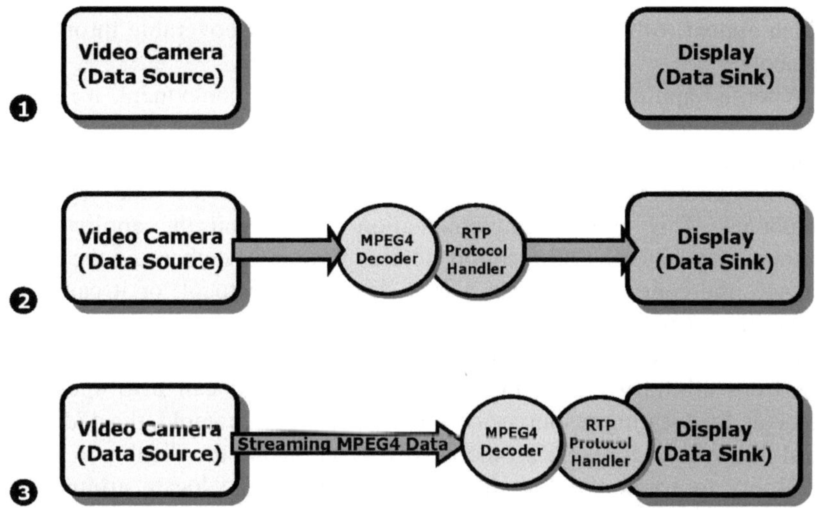

Figure 15-1. In 1, the camera and display have no knowledge of each other's protocols or data formats. In 2, the camera initiates connection by transferring to the display separate bundles of code that allow the display to communicate with the camera and display data received from it. These bundles include a protocol handler for the RTP protocol, and a decoder for the MPEG4 video format. Finally, in 3, data is transferred to the display, using the protocol and encoding appropriate for the media.

Together, these functions of the data transfer interface allow a recipient to be written once, and yet be able to accept an increasing and open-ended set of data types, delivered over new protocols, as new data sources appear on the network. Data sources have the responsibility of providing the recipient-side code needed to allow recipients to talk to them. Note that this arrangement inverts the current paradigm for interoperability, in which all *clients* on a network must be updated before they are able to use a new service. Here, only the provider of the service has to do the work, and clients get the benefit for free.

4.3 Aggregation

The second Speakeasy meta-interface defines the behaviour of *aggregate* components. These are components that logically "contain" other components. We use this interface extensively in Speakeasy: file systems are represented as aggregates (collections of files and folders, each of which is again represented by its own component), as are new discovery protocols (which appear to "contain" all of the components discoverable through that protocol).

When an application interacts with an aggregate component, it retrieves from it a *result set*, which appears to the client to be a simple collection of components. This result set, however, is a mobile code-based object, whose implementation is transmitted to the application by the aggregate component. This custom implementation can extend the application in arbitrary ways—as the application iterates through members of the set, for instance, the code can perform a new discovery protocol, or it can access legacy fileservers on the network.

With this mechanism, a Speakeasy public display can store and retrieve files from arbitrary fileservers on the network, and can also speak new protocols for locating resources on the network. For example, the addition of a Jini discovery aggregate on the network can enable the display to acquire the ability to speak the Jini discovery protocols, and locate arbitrary Jini services on the network.

Further, aggregates can act as "bridges" to new types of networks, including even new physical transports. A Bluetooth aggregate, for example, might discovery Bluetooth devices and provide "proxies" for these devices to a public display application without direct access to Bluetooth hardware itself. This ability happens completely transparently to Speakeasy clients. With the addition of an appropriate bridge on the network, a client can "open" the aggregate representing the bridge, and can see and use any components found on that new physical network. This ability allows the public display to "grow," over time as it can interact with devices appearing around it utilizing new physical transports For example, arbitrary Bluetooth devices, such as PDAs and phones, can be supported through a one-time addition of a Bluetooth aggregate, running on a machine with the ability to communicate both on the Bluetooth network and a wired network; no changes are required to the public display code in order to accommodate this ability. Figure 15-2 illustrates a range of ways in which aggregates can extend the behaviour of their clients.

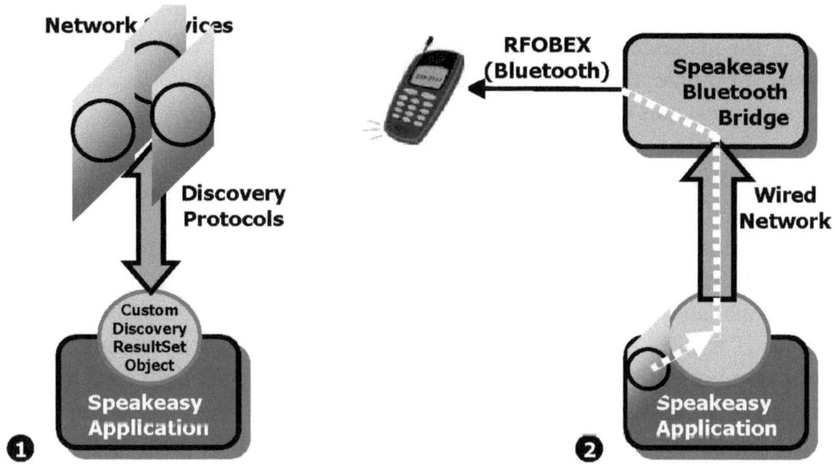

Figure 15-2. These two examples illustrate how aggregate components can be used in Speakeasy. In the first case, a custom result set object has extended the behaviour of the client to allow it to speak a new discovery protocol, and therefore discover devices that may have been previously inaccessible. In the second case, a "bridge" component transmits code to the application that causes the application to use the bridge as a proxy for communication with Bluetooth devices. This allows the application to interact with arbitrary Bluetooth devices within range, even if it does not have access to Bluetooth hardware directly.

4.4 Metadata

The simplest interface provided by Speakeasy is the metadata interface. This interface provides descriptive information about a component—what it is, where it is, who owns it, and so on. The information is organized as simple key-value pairs, with no special organization imposed on either the keys or the values (in other words, component and application writers are free to use this information in any way they see fit).

In keeping with our belief that humans, not systems, will be the ultimate arbiters of the semantics of what a particular component "does," when it is appropriate to use it, and so on, Speakeasy's component metadata framework is primarily intended for human consumption. That is, we do not dictate some overarching ontology for metadata, intended to allow applications to reason about and use the information. Instead, it is intended to allow humans to better browse, and make sense of, the richly networked environments around them.

When a Speakeasy application discovers peer components on the network, it will typically use the metadata of these discovered components to organize them in some way appropriate for display to a user—sorted by location, for instance. These sorts of organizations make it possible for users to easily organize the devices and services on their networks, and find devices and services of interest.

4.5 Control

Finally, the control interface provides a mechanism through which components can deliver custom user interfaces for controlling them. These UI elements can be sent to any Speakeasy client device on the network. For example, if a user at a public display wishes to control a moving video camera component, the controls for that camera can be delivered to the display in order that the user can interact with them.

Most importantly, these user interface elements are themselves implemented as mobile code that is delivered from the component being controlled. This means that recipients don't need to "hard code" user interfaces for controlling every conceivable type of device. Instead, new devices bring along new interfaces for controlling them that can be delivered to arbitrary clients.

Figure 15-3 shows an example of a component user interface being rendered on a handheld PDA. In this case, the PDA is being used as a client device (essentially a fancy remote control) for interacting with other Speakeasy component on the network. Here, the user has used the PDA to connect a Powerpoint file on a fileserver to a networked display. Note the controls that have appeared on the PDA—they provide a miniature representation of the current slide, controls for moving through the slide show, and a display of the slide notes pages. All of this functionality is delivered to the PDA at the time it is needed—the PDA need not be pre-built with it and, in this case, does not even have the Powerpoint application installed.

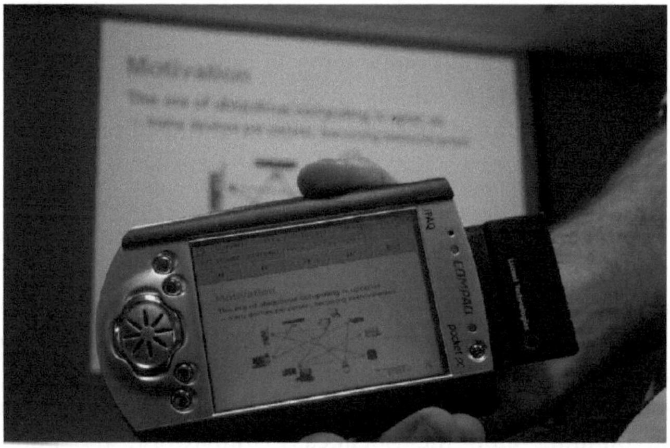

Figure 15-3. A handheld device receives a media-specific control user interface for interacting with a display. In this case, Powerpoint is being displayed on a projector. The interface on the handheld displays slide miniatures, and provides slideshow and projector controls.

4.6 *Caveats and Considerations*

The Speakeasy infrastructure imposes a number of requirements on the devices that host it. Most important is the ability to execute received mobile code. Currently, most of the mobile code that our existing suite of components provides is in the form of Java bytecodes, for portability. We also allow "native" (platform-specific) mobile code to be transferred, but use this only for components that require strong performance guarantees (rendering full-screen MPEG2 video, for instance).

The framework itself is implemented in Java, and thus a Java Virtual Machine (JVM) must exist on any device that *directly* runs Speakeasy. For smaller devices, such as web cams and projectors, we use a "proxy" approach, where a nearby connected machine provides Speakeasy services, and allows the device to participate in the Speakeasy network. We believe there are no reasons that a non-Java implementation of the core framework could not be produced, which would obviate the need for a JVM, although we have not produced such an implementation ourselves.

One obvious downside to mobile code is the potential security risk. Although we see ourselves as consumers of solutions in this area, rather than producers, there are a number of approaches that can be taken to mitigate the potential risk. First, platform independent code such as Java can take advantage of existing mechanisms (the Java Security Manager framework) for protection from malicious code. Second, mobile code can be digitally signed, allowing clients and components to only accept code from known, presumably trusted, parties. Finally, more radical solutions, such as proof-carrying code, could be used for more dynamic forms of protection.

5. Implementing a Public Display System Atop Speakeasy

Speakeasy itself addresses the extensibility requirements outlined earlier in this chapter. There are a number of other requirements, however, and any public display system must "make up the gap" between what the core Speakeasy infrastructure provides and the needs of a real public display. Even when building atop the Speakeasy framework, the public display developer is still responsible for designing the different components of the public display, such as a data storage system, an application that actually displays the data stored, and a user interface to allow community members to add to or examine displayed data. Using Speakeasy, we have begun to develop and deploy two different public display systems, a text-based, tickertape LED display and a more traditional graphical display system.

5.1 A Text-Based Tickertape LED Display

In preparation for our development of the graphical display system, we developed a simple text-based tickertape LED display. The goal was to create a publicly mounted tickertape to which community members could add content from Speakeasy source components that export plain-text data. Building atop previously written Speakeasy infrastructure made the development process simple; in fact, we were only required to write two new modules in order to integrate our LED sign; one to act as an interface between the Speakeasy network and the data to be displayed on the sign and another to actually drive the display, iterating through messages and swapping them when necessary.

As shown in Figure 15-4, the sign hardware was a simple tri-color one line LED display (Alpha 215 by Adaptive Microsystems (http://www.ams-i.com)). The specific sign we chose had a display area of 27 inches (width) by 2.1 inches (height), could display approximately 15 characters at a time, and could store approximately 7,000 characters in memory. By default messages would scroll from right to left and color combinations would be chosen randomly (combinations would be selected from red, orange, green, and yellow).

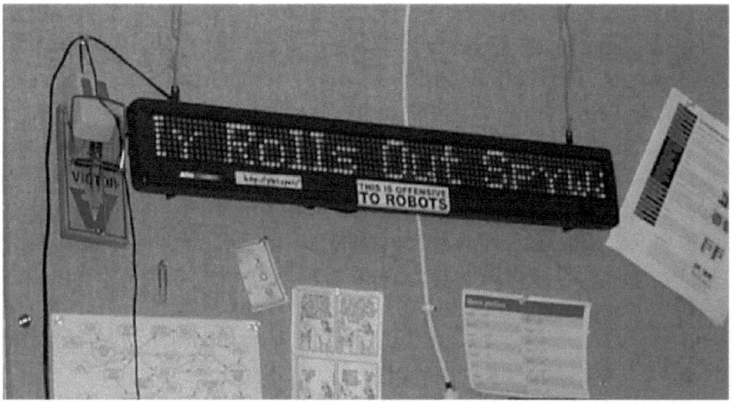

Figure 15-4. The Speakeasy Tickertape LED Scrolling a Slashdot Headline

The tickertape display was first integrated into the Speakeasy network as a sink component that would accept plain-text data. Once integrated, we were immediately able to connect different pre-existing plain-text data sources to the tickertape display and show scrolling versions of any textual data on any Speakeasy-enabled device or service. Because the tickertape display was represented as a sink, it became immediately interoperable with any Speakeasy component that provided textual data, no matter what its protocol, location, and so forth. It became clear, however, that it might also be useful to deploy the tickertape sign as a data source in order that other text-based components might interact with the current contents of the sign. This allowed other clients and devices to "tap into" the sign, without having to know about the specifics of how to interact with it.

Because we intended to deploy this tickertape display as a community display in a common area of our research lab, it was important that non-Speakeasy enabled community members were also able to contribute messages. In order to meet this additional need, we developed an online Java applet so that users could enter a message, the message's origin (perhaps the name of the poster or the author of a quotation), and a duration for which the message would be displayed. Messages contributed using the online applet were converted into the same format as messages contributed through the Speakeasy network and added to the pre-existing display message queue.

Once we had completed development of this text-based tickertape display, we hung it in a common area of our research lab to informally observe interactions with it. We found that the most common types of messages to be submitted were jokes, either poking fun at other researchers or more generally about society and politics. The most common Speakeasy component to be connected to the tickertape was the RSS news feed which parses news headlines (primarily from sources such as Slashdot and NewsForge) into individual lines of plain text. Many of our coworkers mentioned that they liked such information in a public setting.

It was clear once the tickertape had been developed and deployed that there was much excitement and enthusiasm for such a community display. It was not uncommon to see an individual standing in front of the sign, watch something humorous scroll by, run back to her office to post a reply, and return to the sign as quickly as possible to see her message appear on the sign. After lab-wide meetings, the tickertape provided a common conversation: starter, and many individuals would notify the developers if the sign failed to display anything new.

Through this preliminary project, we discovered that community members *would* use a public display and that Speakeasy provided a strong foundation for developing this system. It was Speakeasy that allowed us to easily display interesting streaming content through repeated connections to previously written RSS News feed sources and other text-based components. Integrating the sign into the Speakeasy network required minimal development effort and met all interoperability requirements so that different devices and data could be shared easily and effectively on the tickertape display.

5.2 A Graphical Display System

Although it allowed us to explore the role Speakeasy might play in a public display system, there was one obvious limitation to the simple tickertape display: the system would only accept text messages. Further, because the display provided no input capabilities, users had no way to directly interact with the display (to control the speed at which messages scrolled, or the color in which they were displayed, for instance). Additionally, although the tickertape display did rely heavily upon the flexibility afforded by Speakeasy, it did not take advantage of Speakeasy's ability to support interactions between heterogeneous sources and data types. Thus in order to utilize this functionality we began the development of a graphical display system to be deployed in both public and private areas throughout our research lab. Figure 15-5 shows an early mockup of this new system.

5.2.1 A Revised Architecture

One important additional requirement for the new system was the ability to persistently store content in a repository, from which the display system

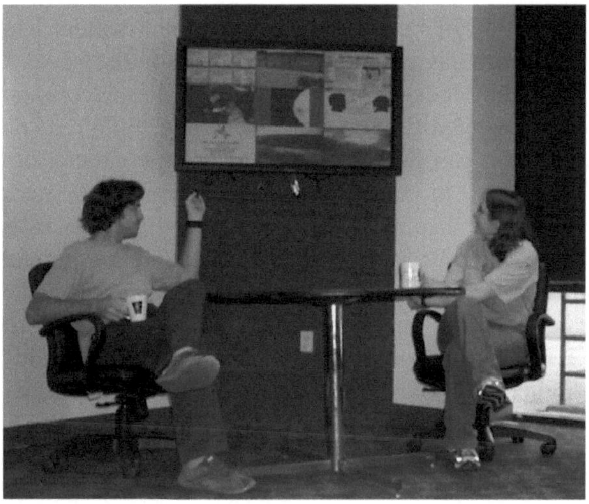

Figure 15-5. Two of the authors interacting with a mockup of the Speakeasy public display

could retrieve it. In the first tickertape version of the system, the display would reconnect to the originally submitted data source whenever it needed to display the source's content. One downside to this is that users may submit a reference to content that was later changed without the user's knowledge. For example, a user might submit a reference to a news website, only to find that a few minutes later the headline displayed on the tickertape had changed because the site had changed.

Because of this obvious limitation in the earlier pilot system, the new system added an additional component to the architecture, a persistent repository of content that "backed" the display. Information could be either pre-loaded and cached in the repository, or stored by reference as in the earlier tickertape system. This arrangement gave us the flexibility to support either "pass-by-reference" pointers to constantly-updating content, or "pass-by-value" content that would be cached directly in the repository. In the case of by-reference content, the display would extract the reference from the repository, and then connect to the data source named by the reference. In the case of by-value content, the display would extract the content directly from the repository, without the need for constant "transient" connections back to the original data sources. The architecture of this new system, then, consisted of the persistent storage component, the public display component itself, and also an applet that would allow non-Speakeasy community members to submit information for display on the public display system.

We have termed this aforementioned data repository the *Media Soup,* and it takes the form of a filesystem-like Speakeasy component that maintains an unstructured collection of both static and dynamic content. Content can be added to the soup from any component anywhere on the Speakeasy network.

Likewise, since the Media Soup is itself a Speakeasy component, multiple displays can be connected to it at any given time. Public displays scattered throughout a location can be configured to draw content from a particular soup when they are in their default "screensaver" mode. When in screensaver mode, the display component periodically transfers data from the Media Soup, presents it for a period of time, and then refreshes with new content from the soup. This "screensaver" is the standard mode in which the displays operate when not under the direct control of a user—content in the Media Soup is presumed to be "public" content, all of which should be displayed periodically. When multiple displays are attached to the same soup, they all cycle through the content stored there for presentation.

In addition to this screensaver mode, the displays can also be used in connections with components other than the Media Soup (to display information from a user's PDA, for example, which might not be "public" content stored in the soup), and can also render controls for arbitrary Speakeasy components. This allows users to walk up and directly interact with the display. (We describe how users interact with and control both the display and the Media Soup below.)

Because of the flexibility afforded us as a result of this architecture, we are able to provide, in addition to a large-format wall mounted display, numerous "private-public" displays that reside in individual offices and act as an individual's portal to the data stored in the soup. Flexible network connectivity allows the display component software to be run in any of these settings—public spaces, or personal offices—and configured to draw content from a particular Media Soup. Additionally, other components (representing printers, laptop computers, PDAs, and so forth) can display content from the soup. Figure 15-6 illustrates the interactions of the display system components.

5.2.2 Interactivity with the New System

Users can interact with the public display system in a number of ways. First, they can add content to the soup directly, via an online applet, which also allows them to specify whether content is to be added by value or by reference. This applet supports the addition of simple content to the soup, such as URLs and files.

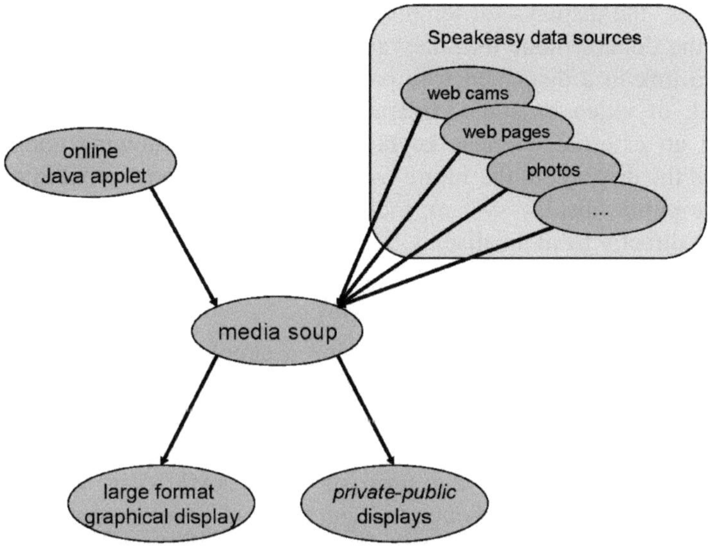

Figure 15-6. Users add content to the soup by connecting Speakeasy sources to it or it via the online Java applet. Data is extracted from the soup for viewing on public or "private-public" display.

Second, users can connect arbitrary Speakeasy components to the soup, using a custom "browser" application. This application is not designed specifically for interaction with the soup, but rather is a generic tool for interacting with and controlling arbitrary Speakeasy components. Using this tool a user can, for example, connect components representing virtually arbitrary devices and services to the soup—for example, web cameras, whiteboard capture systems, and various Speakeasy-enabled audio/video gear. The soup component may then copy data from the source and cache it, or simply store a reference to it, depending on the user's preferences.

Finally, users may interact with a particular display directly, bypassing the soup. Recall that the main purpose of the soup is to provide a set of "default" content that the display will cycle through when it is not being used directly. Since the display is a Speakeasy component, however, it can be appropriated and used for display of arbitrary content, and for interaction with arbitrary components. For example, a user with a laptop can connect a component representing the laptop's screen to the display, to mirror the laptop's display to the (presumably larger) public display. This can be done using any of various Speakeasy client applications we have developed.

Further, interactivity is also provided when the display is in the default screensaver mode of iterating through public content. We allow users to "take over" the displays for temporary interactive use, if something appears during the default mode that they are interested in. For example, users can follow a link in a displayed web page, scroll through a posting, or control playback of video or audio. Interactions such as these are accomplished through an external wireless keyboard and mouse, allowing control over items on the display. In the future we hope to support additional interactions with the public display system, including printing and emailing content in the soup directly from the display.

5.2.3 Scripting Repeated Interactions

The display architecture also supports a simple version of scripting to allow users to programmatically indicate certain indicate certain interactions that should be taken by the display. These scripts are in the form of *templates*, which are descriptions of components, and connections between components, expressed in the form of small XML files. These can be retrieved from the Media Soup, and can be used to recreate common (and perhaps complex) interconnections between the display and other components.

Templates are generated and automatically stored in the Media Soup whenever any direct connection to the soup is made. For example, if a user connects a web camera to the Media Soup (using the browser described above), the soup will create a representation of this action as a template, which identifies the camera and the various parameters of the connection. Once the template has been stored, the user can easily re-execute the template to perform another capture from the web camera, with the same parameters. This automatic generation of templates forms a very simple version of programming by demonstration. Templates can also be hand-crafted to represent more complex connections with various parameters.

5.2.4 Summary of the Public Display Architecture

To summarize, this new architecture, in which the display system is decoupled from the soup that provides its default content, has proved to be extremely flexible. Because both the display and the soup are Speakeasy components, they can accept data from and send data to virtually arbitrary Speakeasy-enabled devices on the network. So, for example, if a member of our research group creates a new service (say, for summarization of web pages, or a new audio CODEC, or to allow a laptop to "throw" its display to another component), the public display system is able to take immediate use of this new functionality.

Further, this decoupling supports the "anything, anywhere" goal laid our earlier in the paper. Since the soup component can be attached to from virtually anywhere, users can run "public-private" displays in their offices that access the same content.

Both the pilot tickertape display and the more advanced soup-based display systems described here have been implemented. To date, our efforts on the graphical system have largely focused on building the Media Soup component, and supporting basic interactivity in the display component. We would like to improve interactivity in the future, through allowing more control over information in the soup that is presented on the public display—for example, to be able to email currently displayed content, and to support better screen real estate management of displayed content.

6. Conclusions

Our experience developing this public display system has shown that the Speakeasy infrastructure provides a strong foundation for the development of public display technology. Leveraging Speakeasy allows us to support numerous data types and allows *ad hoc* interactions between components and devices exporting and receiving viewable data. Additionally, our Speakeasy based system, by supporting flexible interactions between various data sources, the soup, and arbitrary devices, enables a modular public display system in which individuals can view the contents of the public display in numerous locations including large-format wall-mounted graphical displays and "private-public" office displays.

Perhaps most importantly, however, Speakeasy has allowed us to flexibly support media and data types, including new ones created after the display itself. Thus we can develop our public display system to support interactions between devices and services that have yet to be defined and in doing so provide the utmost in flexibility and modularity, not only for the current display system but also for future display systems.

References

Adaptive Micro Systems, http://www.ams-i.com.

Bluetooth Consortium. Specification of the Bluetooth System, Version 1.1 Core. February 22, 2001, http://www.bluetooth.com.

Christensen, E., Curbera, F., Meredith, G. and Weerawarana, S. (2001), http://msdn.microsoft.com/xml/general/wsdl.asp.

Edwards, W.K., Newman, M.W., Sedivy, J.Z., Smith, T.F. and Izadi, S., Challenge: Recombinant Computing and the Speakeasy Approach. In Proceedings of Mobicom '02, 8th ACM International Conference on Mobile Computing and Networking; 2002; Atlanta, GA USA.

Fox, A., Johanson, B., Hanrahan, P. and Winograd, T. Integrating Information Appliances into an Interactive Workspace. IEEE Computer Graphics & Applications, 2000; 20 (3): 54-65.

Gelernter, D. Generative Communication in Linda. ACM Transactions on Programming Languages and Systems, 1985; 7 (1): 80-112.

Greenberg, S. and Rounding, M., The Notification Collage: Posting Information to Public and Personal Displays. In Proceedings of CHI '01 Conference on Human Factors in Computing Systems, 2001; Seattle, WA, USA.

Huang, A.C., Ling, B.C., Barton, J. and Fox, A., Making Computers Disappear: Appliance Data Services. In Proceedings of Mobicom '02, 7th ACM International Conference on Mobile Computing and Networking; 2001; Rome, Italy.

Object Management Group. CORBA: The Common Object Request Broker Architecture, Rev. 2.0. July, 1995.

Ponnekanti, S.R., Lee, B., Fox, A., Hanrahan, P. and Winograd, T., ICrafter: A Service Framework for Ubiquitous Computing Environments. In Proceedings of UbiComp '01; 2001; Atlanta, GA USA: 56-75.

Scribner, K. and Stiver, M.C. Understanding SOAP: The Authoritative Solution. SAMS Press, 2000.

Sun Microsystems. ONC+ Developer's Guide. August, 1997.

Thai, T. and Lam, H. .NET Framework Essentials. O'Reilly and Associates, 2001.

Trevor, J., Hilbert, D.M. and Schilit, B.N., Issues in Personalizing Shared Ubiquitous Devices. In Proceedings of Ubicomp '02; 2002; Gothenburg, Sweden: 56-72.

Waldo, J. The Jini Architecture for Network-centric Computing. Communications of the ACM, 1999; (42)7: 76-82.

Chapter 16

AMBIENT DISPLAYS AND MOBILE DEVICES FOR THE CREATION OF SOCIAL ARCHITECTURAL SPACES

Supporting informal communication and social awareness in organisations

Norbert Streitz, Thorsten Prante, Carsten Röcker, Daniel Van Alphen, Carsten Magerkurth, Richard Stenzel, Daniela Plewe
AMBIENTE research division, Fraunhofer IPSI
Darmstadt, Germany
{streitz, prante, roecker, magerkur, stenzel}@ipsi.fraunhofer.de;

Daniel van Alphen, Product Design, Berlin, Germany. Email: dva@vanalphen.de;

Daniela A. Plewe, Berlin, Germany. Email: plewe@is.in-berlin.de

Abstract: In this paper, we address three major issues, look at their interaction and combination and present our results on how to arrive at solutions for these issues. The issues are: 1) supporting informal communication and atmosphere in organisations, 2) the role and potential of ambient displays in future work environments, and 3) the combination of mostly static artefacts that are integrated in the architectural environment with mobile devices carried by people. Our results can be considered as steps towards the design and realization of what we call "social architectural spaces" in the context of future work environments. These environments will be populated with a range of different smart artefacts that are designed to facilitate awareness and notification as well as informal communication. We address a range of spaces in office buildings including public spaces, e.g., in the hallway, the foyer, and the cafeteria that have not been the focus of research so far. In particular, we present two artefacts: the Hello.Wall, a wall-size large ambient display, and the ViewPort, a mobile handheld device. They are interacting with each other via wireless networks and different types of sensing technology. The artefacts

K. O'Hara et al. (eds.), Public and Situated Displays: Social and Interactional Aspects of Shared Display Technologies, 387–409.

and the software were developed in the EU-funded “Disappearing Computer”-project “Ambient Agoras: Dynamic Information Clouds in a Hybrid Worlds”.

Key words: ambient displays, mobile devices, informal communication, atmosphere, social architectural space, ubiquitous computing

1. Introduction

The role of information and communication technology for the next generation of work environments and office buildings will go beyond its use as mere productivity tools. Information technology will also play a major role as a medium and mediator for supporting informal communication and conveying social awareness and atmospheres in organizations. This is due to new technology developments as well as an increased awareness of and interest in the role of informal communication in work environments. While people have acknowledged the importance of soft skills and social competence for quite some time, the value of informal communication for the performance and the creativity of an organization tends to be underestimated. Against this background, there has been very little work on computer-supported augmentation of informal communication.

Two trends are changing this situation: The trend of putting more emphasis on informal communication and the trend in new technology developments not to restrict computer-based support to the PC workplace anymore, but to support mobile and ubiquitous computing using a wide range of devices. This observation is especially shared by consultants and architects planning new office buildings or restructuring existing ones according to new requirements (Pietzcker, 2002). Informal communication is considered to play an important role for facilitating creativity and innovation as the following statement of the architect G. Henn shows: "80% of innovative ideas created in offices are a result of informal personal communication – despite worldwide data and communication networks. In order to increase the performance, office buildings have to foster and structure the communication between employees. In this way, architecture provides a catalytic function." (Remmers, 1999, translated from German.) In this context, computer-based support for informal communication becomes an important topic when designing the workspaces of the future in terms of what we have called ‘Cooperative Buildings’ (Streitz *et al.*, 1998, 2001).

Informal Communication plays a major role in an organization’s ability to learn. According to Lave and Wenger (1991), shared interests, shared expertise and the passion for joint enterprises are the main attributes that keep a community creative and competitive. Informal communication is also considered to compensate the weaknesses of the formal flow of information, to mediate the organization's culture and values, and to enhance the social relationships within a team (Schütze, 2000). Besides these social functions, informal communication also serves task-related issues: It supports short-term coordination (Fish *et al.*, 1992) and the mediation of specific knowledge (Held & von Bismarck, 1999).

Kraut *et al.* (1990) have introduced the typologies of informal communication as: scheduled, intended, opportunistic or spontaneous exchanges. Ishii *et al.* (1998) show that the majority of interactions are brief, unscheduled, frequent and dependent on physical proximity. 80%-90% of interpersonal interactions in the workplace are not planned meetings; but, according to Schütze (2000), informal communication supported by media does not take place. We argue that this is due to the nature of PC workplaces and propose that employing a broad range of ubiquitous computing devices could help to augment informal communication in organizations.

A prominent augmented computing device supporting informal information-flows within an organization is an ambient display. We interpret ambient displays according to Grasso *et al.* (Chapter 11 this volume) as "large public displays pushing information to trigger synchronous and asynchronous informal interactions in organizations". We also consider the special perceptual conditions described by Wisneski et al (1998) for ambient displays: At the "periphery of our attention" with a kind of "subconscious understanding" and - possibly "engaging all our senses". Furthermore, contemporary architects as, e.g., Gunter Henn (2002) claim that flows of information and knowledge within a building should become a visible component of the building. Ambient displays can help to make these flows accessible.

In this paper, we investigate how ambient displays support informal processes and communication within a corporate building and present an example for the use of an ambient display combined with a mobile device serving this function. We propose that a calm and ambient technology such as our *Hello.Wall* (described below) empowers the user to decide when to focus on and when to ignore provided information. The use of calm technology facilitates the awareness of processes, atmospheres and activities without interruptions or disturbances. The social affiliation in local as well as remote places can be strengthened because of additional awareness of people's activities. Information reaches the attention of team members in a subtle and peripheral way: Users do not pay attention to the stress level, but subconsciously feel the "atmosphere". This is in accordance to the natural ambient displays described by Wisneski et al (1998) as follows: "A sound of a passing neighbour, a shadow at the fringe of our visual field, etc."

In the following sections, we describe our ideas and prototype implementations of what we call a "social architectural space" that facilitates new types of supporting social awareness and communication in organizations. Informal communication and associated social interactions create and involve atmospheres. Our proposal is to develop 'smart artefacts' that are integrated into the architectural environment (here with a focus on ambient displays) as well as mobile devices in combination with appropriate software. Integration can but does not necessarily mean "to bake the artefacts into walls". Even larger artefacts can also be mobile elements and can be positioned at different locations in a building.

In such an environment, parameters derived from the activities of people in the building (or in another location) can be transformed into data representations, displayed and thereby influencing the atmosphere itself. This setup may cause feedback loops, where the display of atmosphere enhances and influences the relevant parameters more or less directly. Communicating atmospheric aspects of an organization includes general and specific feedback mechanisms that allow addressing different target groups via different representation codes. Individuals as well as groups can create public and private codes depending on the purpose of their intervention. The content to be communicated can cover a wide range and will be subject to modification, adjustment, and elaboration based on the experience people have.

An artefact such as the proposed Hello.Wall will allow us to experience formerly invisible, abstract parameters, e.g., activity patterns, now sensually, e.g., by means of light patterns shown on an ambient display. In all cases, it is important to address the information and communication needs of the people involved. One aspect is 'transparency of relationships'; another one is the availability of 'light-weight means for communication'. An important issue is what kind of 'means' can be provided. We are looking at new means that also remedy some of the problems with existing state-of-the-art tools of communication. For example, email has the advantage of communicating explicit information which at the same time is also a disadvantage because of the need to create words and sentences, etc. and its shortcoming to convey information in other ways.

If the type of information to be communicated is more of an atmospheric nature, the way to present and to perceive this information should clearly go beyond standard means as they are currently provided by PCs. This can be achieved by exploiting the human ability to perceive information via many different codes. These can be specific in nature but do not require a level of coding as with words. Furthermore, it is useful to facilitate the "display" and perception of information as a secondary activity in the periphery while being concerned with another primary activity. In this respect, we go beyond contemporary approaches to support informal communication between distributed and co-located team members as e.g. Greenberg & Rounding (2000) suggest. Their Notification Collage is a real-time collaborative surface that allows individuals to attach post-it notes and video streams to a shared surface to foster both formal and informal exchange. While this works appropriately at private desktop machines, the Notification Collage's information cannot peripherally be grasped, because it adheres to the coding of words and sentences. This does not only hamper peripheral perception, but also aggravates the implicit creation of new information due to the explicit nature of words and sentences. Another system called Web Wall (Ferscha & Vogl, 2002) shares most of the characteristics of the Notification Collage. While it lacks the integration of real-time video streams, it leaves the desktop PC metaphor by using mobile devices such as cellular phones to alter the state of the Web Wall. This is a first step towards addressing the integration and fusion of information technology with the architectural space in that creating information is no longer bound to the keyboard on the desk in the office. The architectural dimension is important, because it brings the means of supporting communication back to the location where most of the informal communication takes place, i.e. the hallway, the foyer, the cafeteria, the staircases in contrast to the desktop computer in the office.

Thus, the goal is to create a computer-augmented social architectural space that is inspired by the capability of humans to perceive and to interpret ambient information in order to convey the 'feeling of the place' or 'genius loci'.

2. OUR APPROACH to Ambient Displays

Ambient displays take a broader view of the notion of display usually encountered with conventional graphical user interfaces (GUI) found on PCs, notebooks, PDAs and even on many interactive walls or tables. They are designed to display information without constantly demanding the user's full attention. Usually, this is achieved in a more "implicit" way compared to traditional "explicit" GUI displays.

Ambient displays are envisioned as being all around us and thereby moving information off the more conventional screens into the physical environment. They present information via changes in light, sound, movement of objects, smell, etc. For early examples by Ishii and his Tangible Media Group at MIT Media Lab see Wisneski *et al.* (1998). Other examples have been provided by, Greenberg *et al.* (Univ. of Calgary), Mankoff and Dey (UC Berkeley), Mynatt *et al.* (GeorgiaTech), and Heiner *et al.* (Carnegie Mellon University).

In this paper, we propose and present the *Hello.Wall*. It is a new large ambient display that emits information via light patterns and can also be considered informative art. It has been designed to be both a stimulating illuminated wall element and a distance- and person-dependent information transmitter. The Hello.Wall is combined with the ViewPort in order to extend the general ambient-displays' approach by combining it with mobile devices that act as complementary sources of information. Depending on their access rights (personalization) and the current situation (e.g., distance to the wall; see below), people can use ViewPorts to decode visual codes (here, light patterns), to download ("freeze") or just browse information, to paint signs on the wall, or to access messages announced by a light pattern. This addresses also the issue of avoiding the privacy problem of public displays.

2.1 Hello.Wall

The Hello.Wall is an ambient display transmitting organization-oriented information publicly and information addressed to individuals privately. One can think of it as an organism that radiates the 'breath' of an organization's social body and thereby makes it perceivable towards the inside, i.e. the members of the organization, as well as towards the outside, for example to visitors. Atmospheric aspects are mapped onto visual codes realized as light patterns which influence the atmosphere of a place and the social body around it. While the Hello.Wall serves a dedicated informative role to the initiated members of the organization, visitors might consider it as an atmospheric decorative element and enjoy its aesthetic quality. As an integral part of the physical environment, the Hello.Wall constitutes a seeding element of a social architectural space that provides awareness to the members of the organization.

In this way, the Hello.Wall is a piece of unobtrusive, calm technology exploiting humans' ability to perceive information via codes that do not require the same level of explicit coding as with words. It can stay in the background, only perceived at the periphery of attention, while one is being concerned with another activity, e.g., a face-to-face conversation.

2.2 ViewPort

To complement the Hello.Wall, we propose a mechanism where the Hello.Wall can "borrow" the display of other artefacts, in order to communicate more detailed information. These mobile devices are called ViewPorts. Due to the nature of the ViewPort's display, the information shown can be more explicit and more personal because it is viewed on a personal or temporarily personalized device. Depending on their access rights and the current context, people can use ViewPorts to learn about the purpose of the Hello.Wall system, to decode visual codes on the wall, or to access a message announced by a code.

3. Different Zones of Interaction

In addition to developing a new type of ambient display, our goal was also to make the type of information and the way of its communication context-dependent. The service provided by the artefact should be location- and situation-based depending on the proximity of people passing by. We distinguish between three different "zones of interaction" and their respective modes (see figure 16-1) dependent on the distance from the Hello.Wall:

- - Ambient Zone
- - Notification Zone
- - Cell Interaction Zone

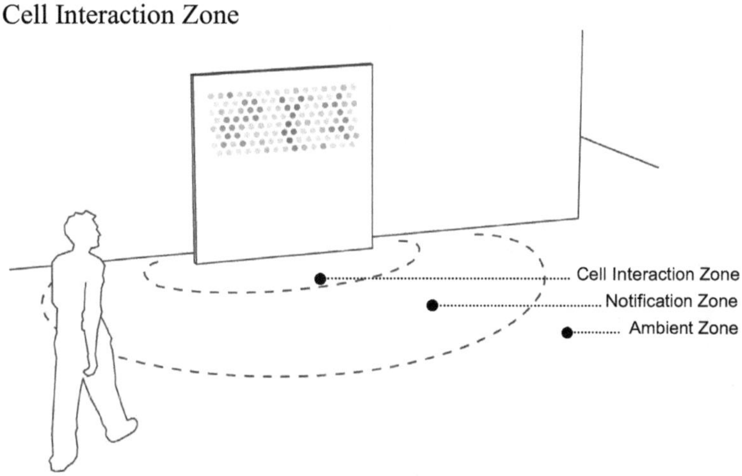

Figure 16-1 Three Zones of Interaction

This is achieved by integrating sensors into the walls that cover two ranges, which may be adapted according to the surrounding spatial conditions. The sensors allow us to introduce "distance-dependent semantics", implying that the distance of an individual from the wall defines the kind of information shown and the interaction offered.

3.1 Ambient Zone

When people are passing by, but are outside the range of the sensors, they experience the "ambient" mode, i.e. the display shows general information that is defined to be shown independent of the presence of a particular person. The parameters chosen to define the atmosphere are represented as light patterns. The pattern shown in the ambient mode could also be called the "stand-by" pattern. Examples are: the number/ percentage of people still in the building, levels of activities, etc.

3.2 Notification Zone

If an individual approaches or passes by close to the wall, the person enters the Notification Zone and the wall will react. The Hello.Wall changes from a stand-by pattern to a notification pattern. This pattern can be a personal pattern relevant only for that particular person or a group pattern that is shown to all members of that group when passing by. These patterns can be "secret" and only known to the people that are notified. While the notification serves already an important purpose, in many cases there is a need to receive more detailed information. This is achieved by combining an ambient, implicit display with another explicit display. We propose a mechanism that we call "the principle of borrowing a display".

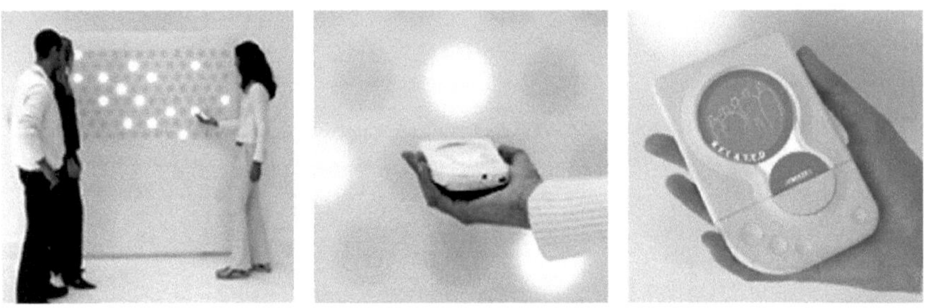

Figure 16-2. Interaction at the Hello.Wall using the ViewPort as a borrowed display.

In our approach and realization, we use a mobile PDA-like device called "ViewPort". The Hello.Wall borrows the display of the ViewPort and the user has all kind of information "at hand".

This includes also a help-function that could explain the meaning of certain patterns. Depending on the actual application, the user can interact and also enter data, download ("freeze") or browse information (See figure 16-2).

3.3 Cell Interaction Zone

The third zone is active, once the person is very close to the Hello.Wall. In this case, the person can approach the Hello.Wall and interact with each single cell (= independent interactive 'pixel'). This is able to store and communicate information in parallel in combination with mobile devices. This feature allows playful and narrative interactions, which other media don't supply. There is also a charming element of surprise that may be discovered via the single cell interaction, because before accessing the cell, there is no hint, what will be revealed.

4. Design considerations for Hello.wall and viewport

With respect to being a stimulating architectural element, the Hello.Wall artefact and also the light pattern language have been designed to have a blurred and rather abstract appearance. As Wolfgang Ulrich (2002) put it: "The more blurred a picture is, the more likely it will serve as a projection surface for the thoughts of its observer." In addition, we work mostly with dynamic light patterns. Although recognizable to users, they are not being predictable and thereby introducing an element of chance or surprise.

The satin-coated Hello.Wall artefact consisting of snow-white acryl as well as the ambient light patterns for the Ambient Zone are pieces of unobtrusive calm technology. The ambient patterns are unobtrusive, because the deltas in movement, in amorphic form changes, and in light intensity are smooth and waving and thereby stay within the periphery of the users' attention. This matches their purpose of mediating qualitative, atmospheric, and rather blurred information. Compared to the ambient patterns, the notification patterns for the Notification Zone, overlaying them and emerging from them, are sharp and more distinct in quality. This again matches their purpose of catching the user's attention when entering the Notification Zone. But still, they can be quite easily ignored.

We take a scenario-based approach to the design of a pattern language as can be seen from the application scenarios presented later. There are some generic feedback and notification elements that are invariant while being complemented by scenario-specific patterns. In addition, for small groups of people, we create personal notification patterns.

The content to be communicated via ambient patterns can cover a wide range and will be subject to modification, adjustment, and elaboration based on the experience people have. The atmospheric aspects of an organization might include general or specific feedback mechanisms that allow addressing different target groups via selected codes that are accessible only for a defined group or individual. Individuals as well as groups can create public as well as private or secret codes depending on the purpose of their intervention. More complex content can be communicated either via the explicit ViewPort display or via more complex light patterns, where combination is achieved either spatially or through sequencing.

Because the newly created pattern language have to be learned by the users, we prefer to keep the patterns simple. We work with simple metaphors in pattern design as can be seen from the examples below. Users can use ViewPorts to decode patterns, but they can also define their own patterns in order to make it is easier to remember them. Some patterns need to become common knowledge within the Hello.Wall's user community, be it people at a certain place or members of a team.

5. Sample Application Scenarios

We defined the general goal of developing new means for the support of informal communication and awareness of social atmospheres and proposed a general approach in terms of the types and artefacts. Now, we describe sample scenarios as examples of social situations. This is to provide an idea on how these means can be used.

5.1 Presentation Scenario at DC Jamboree 2002

The first public presentation of the Hello.Wall occurred in the fall of 2002, at the second Jamboree and public exhibition of the EU-funded proactive research initiative 'The Disappearing Computer' (DC). Visitors of the Jamboree exhibition were asked to take part in an opinion poll regarding the DC Jamboree, the jointly held UbiComp 2002 conference, and their general mood. Two ways of voting were provided. People could either use arbitrary computers and a web interface or the ViewPort in combination with the Hello.Wall.

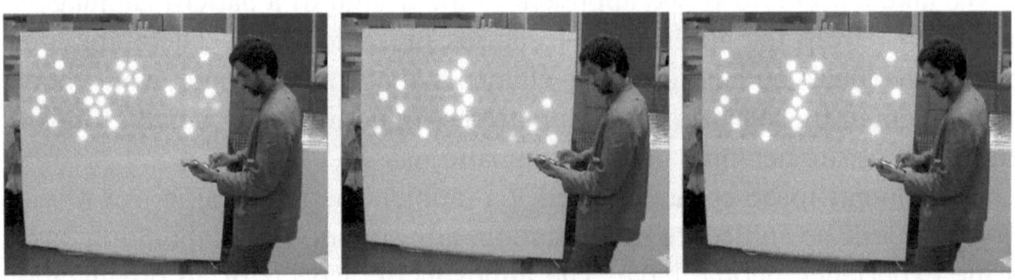

Figure 16-3. Ambient patterns

This example shows awareness and notification patterns on the Hello.Wall related to the opinion poll, users voting for this poll, and users playing a game. In the ambient mode, i.e. from a distance and without interaction, the system displays the present state of the opinion poll. From left to right, the ambient patterns shown in figure 16-3 represent the poll states regarding the DC Jamboree, the UbiComp conference, and the general mood of users. These patterns were looped.

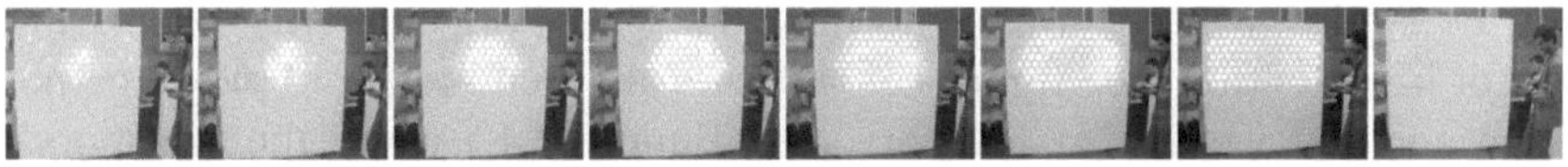

Figure 16-4. "Send" pattern to catch the user's attention

Visitors are equipped with a tag and the ViewPort prototype. When approaching the Hello.Wall, they are sensed and thus enter the Notification Zone. Once inside the Notification Zone, the Hello.Wall displays the "send" pattern (see figure 16-4) asking the approaching user to look at the ViewPort.

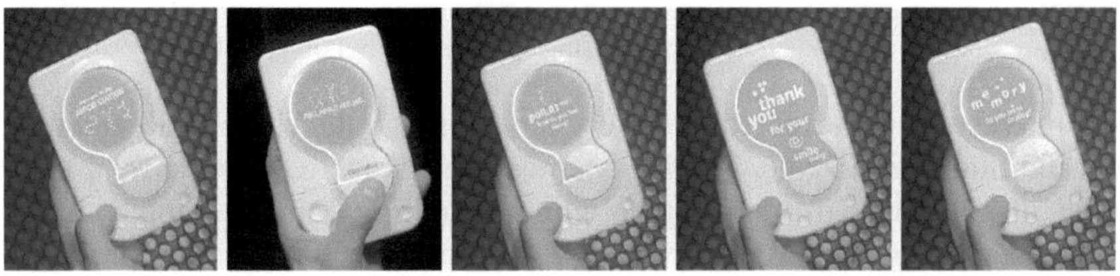

Figure 16-5. Examples for explicit feedback on the ViewPort

Inside the Notification Zone, people are welcomed, given a short introduction about the displayed patterns and then asked to take part in the poll. The first three pictures in figure 16-5 are sample ViewPort screens from this interaction sequence

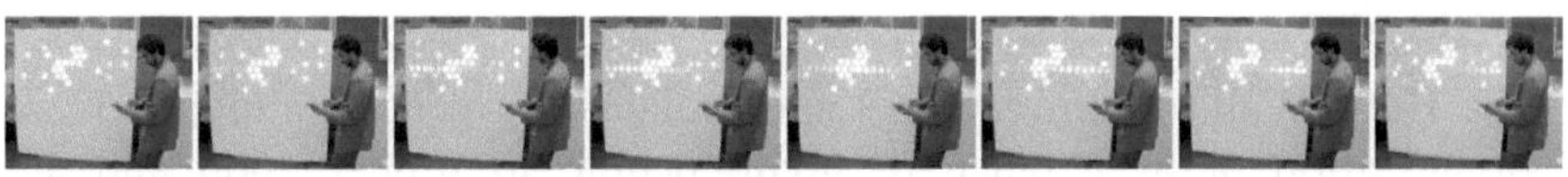

Figure 16-6. Interaction feedback on the Hello.Wall

Each time users answer a question, the Hello.Wall immediately changes to the corresponding ambient pattern and shows an illuminated light stroke crossing the Hello.Wall from left to right in order to acknowledge the input (see figure 16-6).

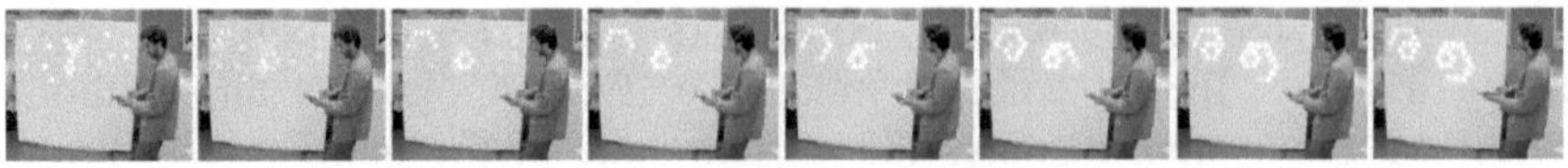

Figure 16-7. "Smile" pattern ('thank you')

When users submit the last question of the poll, the Hello.Wall gives them a "smile" while at the same time the ViewPort explicitly thanks the user for his attention (see figure 16-7). Users are then invited to play a game, i.e. an adapted version of Memory (see figure 16-8) while the "memory" pattern is displayed on the Hello.Wall, which consists of randomly distributed static light points.

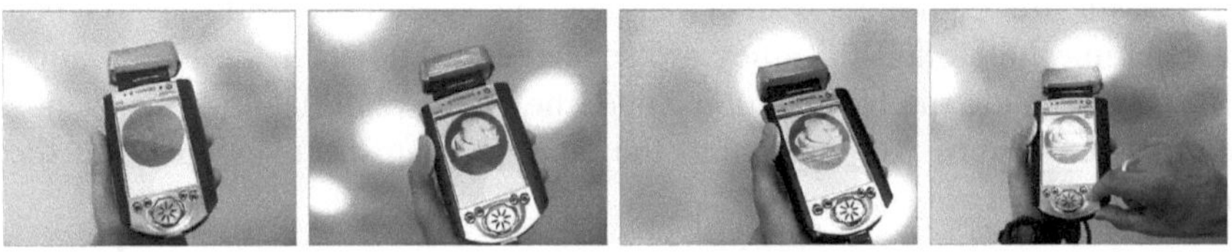

Figure 16-8. Playing Memory using an earlier ViewPort prototype

If interested and attracted, the users can approach the Hello.Wall and thus enter the Interaction Zone. Playing Memory, users uncover single light-cells of the display one after the other while searching for matching pictures which are displayed on the ViewPort. It has to be noted that multiple users can play this game in parallel, since the cells are independently interactive.

5.2 Further Sample Scenarios

In this section, we present four application scenarios that are taken from a video produced for the UbiComp 2003 conference (Prante *et al.*, 2003).

ActivityCapture

The Hello.Wall system captures and radiates the general atmosphere in an organization or at a place to invite people to reflect upon and act accordingly - reflection in action. It is based on monitoring and sampling sources of atmospheric aspects: Deadlines, todo-lists, physical activities, nature of movements and sounds, physiological parameters, the way people interact with digital data, etc. Atmospheric aspects to be mapped onto light patterns could also be extracted from conversations (Basu *et al.*, 2001).

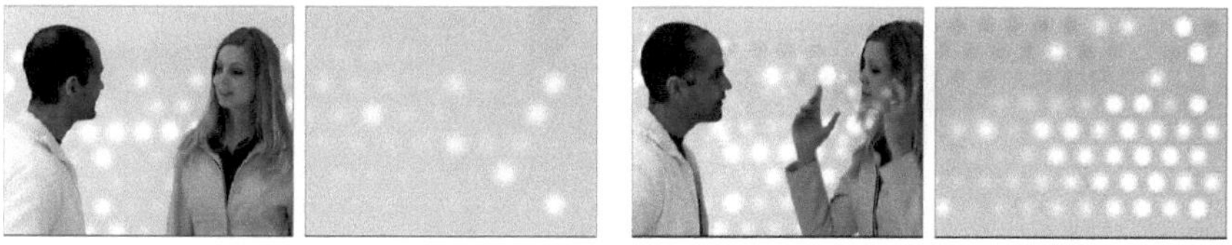

Figure 16-9. A calm pattern (left) and a more pulsating pattern (right)

An overall relaxed atmosphere in an organization is captured and reflected by the system displaying a calm visual code. Increasingly nervous and vibrant activities lead to more dynamic and pulsating reflections on the wall (see figure 16-9).

HaloCapture

Beyond reflecting the general atmosphere, the ambient display can also distribute more specific and directed information through luminous codes. As an example of a code that is known to the whole organization, we propose the halo-pattern that mediates commendatory comments.

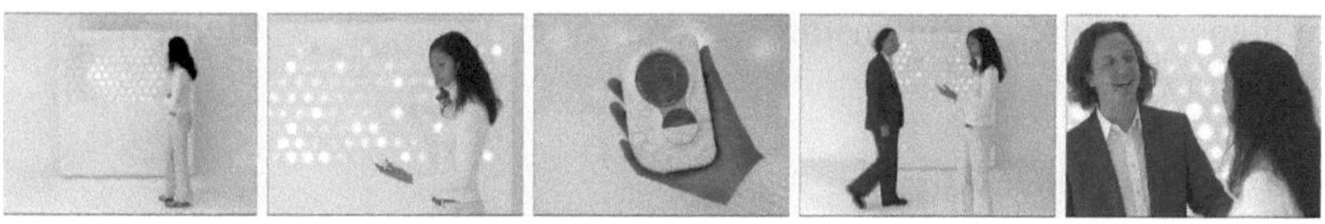

Figure 16-10. Mediating commendatory comments

Outstanding performances are publicly rewarded by this pattern, when the particular individual is sensed by the Hello.Wall (see figure 16-10). Depending on access rights, people can view more detailed information using ViewPorts. Other people passing by and noticing the halo-code can take this opportunity to say something nice to the awarded person (see figure 16-10.).

InitCapture

To form a team, it has proven useful to gather the potential members face-to-face. The communication flow is rich, direct, and can create an atmospheric and powerful experience. Team-building processes are initiated and trust can grow. To define and show membership of groups, people have always used codes, sometimes visual. We emphasize a sense of belonging to the same team by having a "secret" code that is known only to the group.

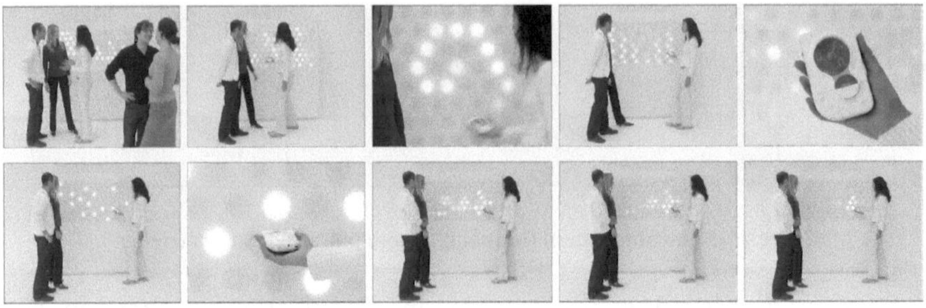

Figure 16-11. Team initiation at the Hello.Wall

For the following, please refer to figure 16-11. Members of a team to be initiated gather at the Hello.Wall. As a sign of identification and belonging, they define their "secret" visual code. The system senses the team members, registers their code, and sends an affirmative feedback - explicitly, which can be viewed using a ViewPort and a visual code radiated by the wall. As the system now knows the team, it loads up the mebers' prepared work folders related to this meeting. The results are immediately shown and can be accessed by the team members cell by cell or all at once. Please note that simultaneous interaction using several ViewPorts at a Hello.Wall is supported as well.

Team-specific ActivityCapture

When people work together, they maintain awareness of each other helping them to coordinate activities and find opportunities for collaboration. This group awareness involves several types of knowledge about what is happening in one's collaborative environment. One example of group awareness is knowledge about the activity level of one or more group members.

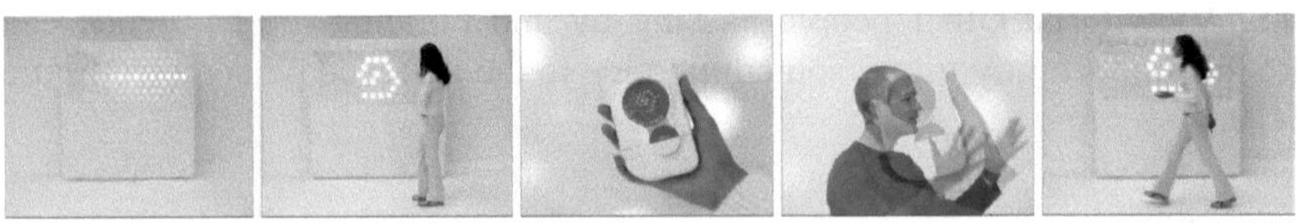

Figure 16-12. Mediating activity levels among team members

Publicly known atmosphere-emitting visual codes in combination with visual codes defined by a team are used to mediate activity levels among the team's members (see figure 16-12). In addition to helping with coordination and pointing to collaboration opportunities, this provides an ambient medium for keeping yourself aware of the vibes within a team.

5.3 Installation for User Testing at EDF-LDC

As part of our user testing efforts in the Ambient Agoras project, the Hello.Wall has been installed at the site of our cooperation partner Électricité de France (EDF) at the Laboratory for the Design of Cognition (LDC). We have created a second version of the activity-pattern.It reflects both the atmosphere and the activity level at a place or within a team.

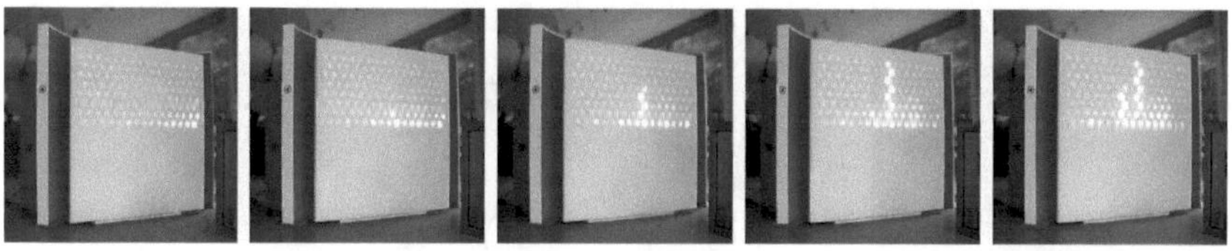

Figure 16-13. Second version of activity-pattern (very low)

First, the better the atmosphere, the bigger the amount of light in the waving patterns. Second, a low activity level is represented as only a few light "tails" ascending, whereas a higher level of activity results in more light "tails" ascending.

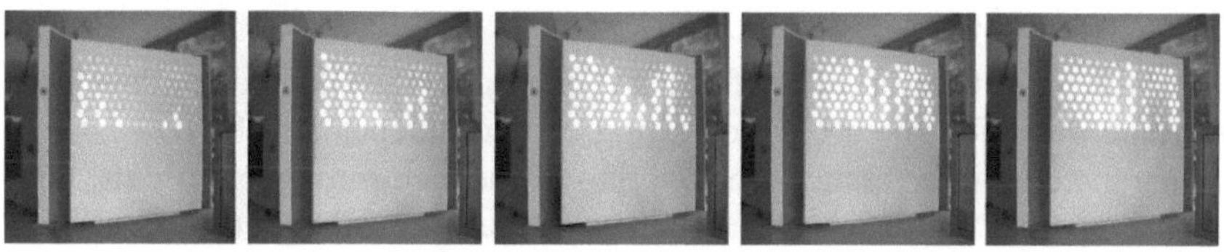

Figure 16-14. Second version of activity-pattern (very high)

Figures 16-13 and 16-14 present the two extremes of the activity-pattern.

6. Realization of Hello.Wall and ViewPort

For the prototypical realization of our ideas, we decided for a combination of stationary and mobile artefacts. In this section, we describe the technical realization of the Hello.Wall artefact as an element of the architectural space and the ViewPort artefact as a mobile device that can be sensed and interact with the Hello.Wall in various ways.

6.1 Hello.Wall – Artefact and Technology

The Hello.Wall is a stationary artefact with integrated sensing technology. It does not have a standard type of display but is able to "display" or communicate ambient information.

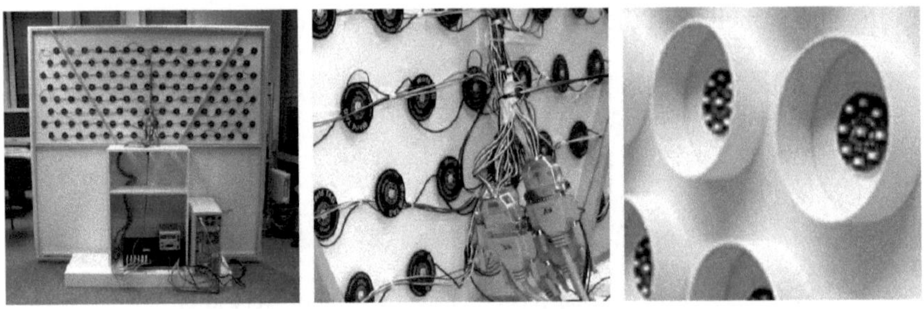

Figure 16-15. From left to right: rear view of the Hello.Wall; wiring and transponders for each InformationCell; InformationCell with LED cluster.

Sensing Technology

For the identification of artefacts and individuals we decided to develop a two-stage detection hierarchy consisting of two independent RFID systems. To guarantee an interference-free overlap of the electromagnetic fields, both systems operate in different frequency ranges. For the detection of by-passing individuals or mobile devices we use a passive long-range-system with two large-scale antennas, which are integrated in the lower part of the Hello.Wall. This enables us to detect up to 50 tagged objects per second within the Notification Zone.

In addition, each of the 124 cells at the Hello.Wall contains an LED cluster and a short-range transponder (see figure 16-15). Hence each InformationCell is unambiguously identifiable by mobile devices equipped with short-range readers. For clear identification of each cell it is essential that the electromagnetic fields of the adjacent transponders do not overlap. To ensure interference-free reading the transponder's antennas are tuned to cover the whole cell without affecting the transponder fields in neighbouring cells.

Driver Interface

The Hello.Wall artefact is controlled by a standard PC using a special driver interface. To adjust the brightness of the LED clusters we developed a control unit using pulse width modulation. Figure 16-16 shows the schematic layout of the developed circuit board. The complete driver interface consists of 16 Circuit boards and an additional board for the generation of a reference signal.

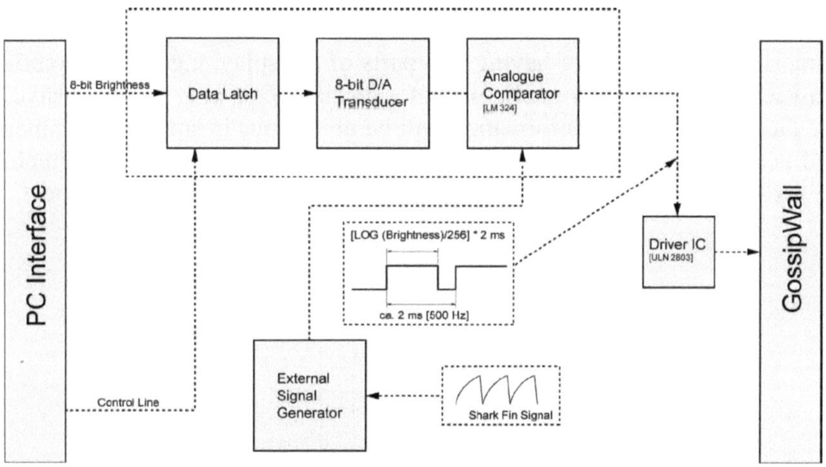

Figure 16-16. Schematic layout of the driver interface for one LED cluster.

The brightness value for each LED cluster is stored in a data latch. A D/A converter transforms this value into a direct voltage U_D. The resulting output voltage is then stabilized by an operational amplifier (op-amp). To receive smooth transitions between sequencing brightness levels, a capacitor is connected to the positive input of the op-amp. Hence the luminescence of the LED clusters can be determined by the size of the capacitor.

As a reference signal for the comparator we use a 500 Hz signal, which is provided by an external signal generator. Minimum and maximum values of the light intensity can be tuned with two trim potentiometers by adjusting the zero-point and the amplitude of the reference signal. A second op-amp is used to amplify this signal, before it serves as a reference input for the analogue comparators. The output of the comparator is "high" as long as the voltage U_D is higher than the reference signal. This results in a pulse width modulated signal with a cyclic duration factor that is exponentially dependent on the voltage U_D and hence the brightness.

6.2 ViewPort – Artefact and Technology

The ViewPort is a portable artefact with a pen-based interactive display and integrated sensing technology. It can be used as a personal, temporarily personal or public device for creating and visualizing information. It also provides the functionality of visualizing information "transmitted" from other artefacts that do not have displays of their own and are "borrowing" this display as, e.g., the Hello.Wall. The current version of the ViewPort comprises the concept of having two parts of a display, e.g., to differentiate between a private and a public part of a display. This is to be responsive to the fact that sharing of information will be ubiquitous in smart environments and keeping personal data private will be a major challenge. Active mobile devices such as the ViewPort are key components of a smart environment.

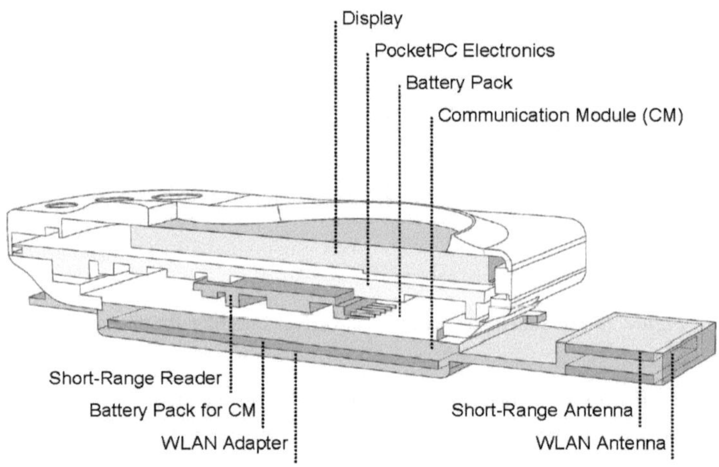

Figure 16-17. Cross-section of the ViewPort

The ViewPort is developed on the basis of a PocketPC (Compaq IPAQ series) with a 200 MHz processor and a touch-sensitive color display. Its functionality is extended through a passive short-range reader unit and a wireless LAN adapter (see figure 16-17).

The integrated RFID reader operates with a frequency of 125 kHz and allows reading ranges up to 100mm. In addition, the ViewPort is equipped with a long-range RFID transponder. Thus the ViewPort can be detected by stationary artefacts in the environment, e.g. the Hello.Wall, while at the same time identify nearby artefacts through its own reading unit. The software developed for the ViewPort is able to establish a connection to the Hello.Wall via a WaveLAN link and to utilize the short-range sensors of the ViewPort hardware. This combination enables the device to offer services that are aware of the context in terms of the spatial information of the ViewPort device and the state of the Hello.Wall.

6.3 Interaction between Hello.Wall and ViewPort

Since by-passing individuals can be recognized, there is a range of interaction opportunities including individual information through mobile artefacts as well as anonymous and public communication.

To support the interaction between the different components we use two independent RFID systems and a wireless LAN network. People within the Notification Zone are detected via two RFID long-range readers installed in the lower part of the Hello.Wall. Once a person is detected the identification information is send to the controlling PC for further processing. Depending on the kind of application, data can be transmitted to the ViewPort via WaveLAN or distinctive light patterns can be displayed for notification. Within the Interaction Zone, people can access the information "stored" in each cell by reading the cell's ID with the integrated short-range reader of the ViewPort. With the received data the ViewPort can access the corresponding information stored on the controlling PC. The following figure (figure 16-18) shows a schematic sketch of the ViewPort and the Hello.Wall coupled via RFID technology and wireless LAN to enable a coherent, engaging, and even immersive interaction experience.

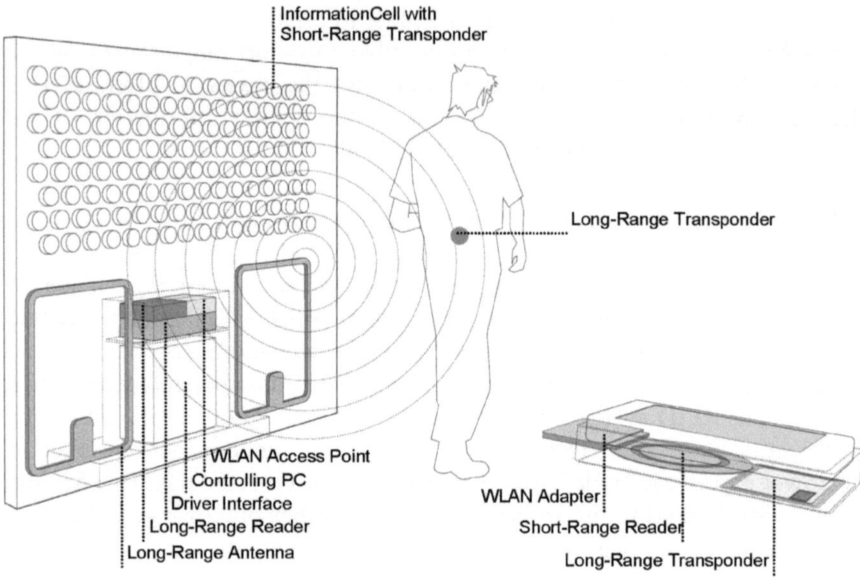

Figure 16-18. Communication and Sensing infrastructure of Hello.Wall and ViewPort

7. Conclusions

In this paper, we presented the concept, design, and implementation of a new combination of ambient displays with mobile devices in order to facilitate and convey informal communication and atmospheres in organizations. Our overall goal is to augment the architectural envelope in order to create a social architectural space using means beyond traditional architectural elements, furniture, or standard information technology. The approach is an example of changing and expanding the role of information and communication technology for the next generation of work environments and office buildings. It will go beyond its mere use as productivity tools by playing also a major role as a medium and mediator for supporting informal communication and conveying social awareness and atmospheres in organizations. In the EU-funded project "Ambient Agoras", where these artefacts were developed, we also use the metaphor of transforming places and spaces in office buildings into marketplaces (= "agora" in Greek) of ideas and information in order to indicate this change of purpose.

Our own previous work on computer-based support of activities and work processes that went beyond the single-user desktop PC scenario was very often concerned with support for team work in electronic meeting rooms (Streitz et al, 1994). The work presented here extends not only this direction but also our subsequent development of the i-LAND environment (Streitz et al, 1999) and the second generation of Roomware® components (Streitz et al, 2001).

There are three major differences. First, we extended the content to be dealt with from productivity-oriented information to information about states of people and the organization, e.g., presence, activity levels, attitude, atmospheric information, etc. Second, and partly as a consequence of this change in content, we are exploring new means for communication that are different from the standard explicit displays resulting in implicit and ambient displays, in our case the Hello.Wall. Third, we introduced a mobile handheld device with a new form factor, the ViewPort, a device that can be "borrowed by other artifacts" as, e.g., the Hello.Wall. This type of interaction and interchange seems to us a new promising concept we will explore more in the future. Of course, the work presented needs to be evaluated and put to use in real work contexts. We started this in the "Ambient Agoras" project together with our partners by setting up a pilot installation at EDF in Paris. Based on the empirical results we expect from the evaluation, further work on the conceptual framework, and additional design iterations, we will test and improve our approach of designing a social architectural space using ambient information displays and mobile devices.

8. Acknowledgements

This work is supported by the European Commission (contract IST–2000-25134) as part of the proactive initiative "The Disappearing Computer" of "Future and Emerging Technology" (FET). We thank our partners EDF, DALT, Wilkhahn, and wiege for contributing in the project "Ambient Agoras: Dynamic Information Clouds in a Hybrid Worlds" (www. ambient-agoras.org). Thanks are also due to the members of the AMBIENTE research division (www.ipsi.fraunhofer.de/ambiente) and our students for their various contributions and the implementation of hardware and software.

9. References

Basu, S. *et al.* Towards measuring human interactions in conversational settings. *Proceedings of IEEE CUES*, 2001

Ferscha, A., Vogl, S. Pervasive Web Access via Public Communication Walls. In *Proceedings of the Pervasive Computing Conference*; 2002; Zurich, Switzerland,: 84-97.

Fish, R.S., Kraut, R.E., Root, R.W. and Rice, R.E. Evaluating Video as a Technology for Informal Communication. In *Proceedings of the CHI'92 conference on Human Factors in Computing Systems*; 1992; Monterey, California, USA: 37-48

Grasso, A., Muehlenbrock, M., Roulland, F., Snowdon, D. Supporting Communities of Practice With Large Screen Displays. In K. O'Hara, M. Perry, E. Churchill, D. Russell (eds.) *Public and Situated Displays: Social and Interactional aspects of Shared Display Technologies*. Kluwer, 2003: chapter 11 of this book.

Greenberg, S. and Rounding, M. The Notification Collage: Posting Information to Public and Personal Displays. In *Proceedings of the CHI 2000 Conference on Human Factors in Computing Systems*, The Hague, The Netherlands: 515-521.

Held, M., von Bismarck, W.-B. The acceptance and support of informal communications in organizations. In *Proceedings of the 9th European Congress on Work and Organizational Psychology: Innovations for Work, Organization and Well-being*; 1999; Helsinki, Finland.

Henn, G. Architecture of Knowledge, Karin Krontaler, in: *industriebau* 06/2002, www.henn.com.

Ishii, H., Wisneski, C., Brave, S., Dahley, A., Gorbet, M., Ullmer, B., Yarin., P. AmbientROOM: Integrating Ambient Media with Architectural Space. In *Extended Abstracts/ Summary of Videos at CHI'98 Conference on Human Factors in Computing Systems*, Los Angeles, CA, USA: 173-174.

Kraut, R. E., Fish, R., Root, R., & Chalfonte, B.. "Informal communication in organizations: Form, function, and technology". In *Human reactions to technology: Claremont symposium on applied social psychology*, Oskamp, S. &. Spacapan, S. eds. Beverly Hills, CA: Sage Publications, 1990

Lave, J., Wenger, E. *Situated Learning. Legitimate Peripheral Participation* Cambridge: Cambridge University Press, 1991

Pietzcker, M. Was sind wesentliche Einflussfaktoren auf zukünftige Bürokonzepte? (What are the relevant factors for future office concepts?) Presentation at *"Future Office: Fachkonferenz für zukunftsorientierte Raum- und Flächenkonzepte für neue Arbeitswelten"*. (Conference on future-oriented concepts for new work environments); 2002; Wiesbaden, Germany.

Prante, T., Röcker, C., Streitz, N., Stenzel, R., Magerkurth, C., van Alphen, D., Plewe, D. Hello.Wall – Beyond Ambient Displays. In: *Proceedings of UbiComp'03, 5th International Conference on Ubiquitous Computing*; 2003; Seattle, WA, USA, to appear.

Remmers, B. Vom steinzeitlichen Palaver zur modernen Kommunikationsförderung. In: N. Streitz, B. Remmers, M. Pietzcker, R. Grundmann (Eds.), *Arbeitswelten im Wandel - Fit für die Zukunft?" Menschen, Organisationen, Technologien und Architektur an der Schwelle zum 21. Jahrhundert*, Stuttgart, Deutsche Verlags-Anstalt, 1999: 36-59

Schütze, H.-J. Informelle Kommunikation unter Medienvermittlung. *Workshop at D-CSCW 2000: "Verteiltes Arbeiten - Arbeit der Zukunft"*, München., 2000; München, Germany; http://iundg.informatik.uni-dortmund.de/projekte/workshops/moka/1

Streitz, N., Geissler, J., Haake, J., Hol, J. DOLPHIN: Integrated meeting support across LiveBoards, local and desktop environments. In: *Proceedings of CSCW '94 Conference on Computer Supported Cooperative Work*; 1994; Chapel Hill, NC, USA : 345-358.

Streitz, N., Geißler, J., Holmer, T. „Roomware for Cooperative Buildings: Integrated Design of Architectural Spaces and Information Spaces". In N. Streitz, S. Konomi, H. Burkhardt, (eds.) *Cooperative Buildings - Integrating Information, Organization, and Architecture. Proceedings of CoBuild '98*, Darmstadt, Germany, LNCS 1370, Springer, 1998: 4-21

Streitz, N., Geißler, J., Holmer, T., Konomi, S., Müller-Tomfelde, C., Reischl, P., Rexroth, P., Seitz, P., Steinmetz, R. i-LAND: An interactive Landscape for Creativity and Innovation. In *Proceedings of CHI'99 Conference on Human Factors in Computing Systems*; 1999; Pittsburgh, Pennsylvania, USA: 120-127.

Streitz, N., Tandler, P., Müller-Tomfelde, C., Konomi, S. "Roomware: Towards the Next Generation of Human-Computer Interaction based on an Integrated Design of Real and Virtual Worlds". In: J. Carroll (ed.) *Human-Computer Interaction in the New Millennium,*. Addison-Wesley, 2001: 553-578

Ullrich,W. *Die Geschichte der Unschärfe*. Kleine kulturwissenschaftliche Bibliothek, Band 69, Berlin: Klaus Wagenbach Verlag, 2002

Wisneski, C., Ishii, H., Dahley, A., Gorbet, M., Brave, S., Ullmer, B., Yarin, P. Ambient Displays "Turning Architectural Space into an Interface betweenpeople and Digital Information". In N. Streitz, S. Konomi, H. Burkhardt (eds.) *Cooperative Buildings - Integrating Information, Organization, and Architecture. Proceedings of CoBuild '98*, Darmstadt, Germany, LNCS 1370, Springer, 1998: 22-32.

Index

FSC
www.fsc.org
MIX
Papier aus verantwortungsvollen Quellen
Paper from responsible sources
FSC® C105338

If you have any concerns about our products, you can contact us on
ProductSafety@springernature.com

In case Publisher is established outside the EU, the EU authorized representative is:
Springer Nature Customer Service Center GmbH
Europaplatz 3, 69115 Heidelberg, Germany

Printed by Libri Plureos GmbH
in Hamburg, Germany